In memory of Jim and Kathleen

CONTENTS

Preface

My father, Norman Safarik, born in Vancouver in 1918, is a remarkable man. Now in his ninety-fourth year, he still lives alone in his house in North Burnaby where he keeps busy reading, gardening and puttering around. With the exception of basic training and going overseas with the Seaforth Highlanders in World War II, he spent his whole adult life working at the Campbell Avenue fish dock on the Vancouver waterfront.

He started working full-time in the fishing industry when he left high school and didn't retire until he was in his late eighties. For more than sixty years, he worked at or ran Vancouver Shellfish and Fish Company. Along the way he built a crab-fishing operation on the Nicomekl River in South Surrey and a fish plant in Tofino.

More than anyone I have ever known, my father is a man who loved his work. For him, paradise was the fish dock with its attachment to everything about the sea and the fascinating world of fish.

Every morning just before the sun came up and the seagulls arrived to perch on the fish shed rooftops, hatch covers came off draggers and the hum of the unloading cranes signalled the beginning of another day. Sharp eyes watched out for the trollers who were coming into the basin to tie up and sell their catch. Within a short time hundreds of people of every nationality were at work in the adjoining companies. The wharf would spring to life with trucks, fork lifts and fish buggies coming and going along with fishermen, deck hands, shore workers, office workers, peddlers, fish store operators, restaurateurs, postmen, mechanics, salesmen, boiler inspectors, fish buyers, fisheries officers, harbour board cops, ice house men, firemen, lawyers, hustlers, touts and gamblers and the fishing boats that came and went after unloading their catches. While all around the basin, inside and outside of enormous sheds, fish was being unloaded, carted, piled, bought, sold, processed, packed and shipped to the fresh-fish markets, to cold storages, or to customers in Canada and other locations around the world.

To say the least, my father knows a lot about fish. He grew up in and worked in the prime years of the fisheries on the Pacific coast. He has seen the cycles of fish for nearly a century, and he has lived through the best of times and the worst of times of the industry. He bought and sold millions of pounds of fish, and he lived his life large in the annals of an industry that was notable for its share of outrageous characters.

My father is a storyteller. He has always been a storyteller. As he moved into old age, his health has stayed with him and his mental faculties have remained sharp. He can still remember the details of fish prices from fifty years ago and the names of boats and their owners, skippers and crewmen. He can look at a salmon and give you a complete rundown on it, even telling you what river system it likely came from. He is a living repository of practical knowledge about fish, as well as stories about the waterfront and world of buying and selling fish in Canada and elsewhere. During the years he spent on the waterfront, Father always knew what was going on. He had a wide circle of friends among fishermen and fish companies as well as among his employees, customers and business connections. I would categorize my father as an astute businessman who happened to work in an environment that he loved.

My father is a man of energy; he never really retired. At the end of his working life, he started writing down his memoirs by hand onto lined paper and then stapling the pages into bundles and sending them to me by mail. I am the son who missed out on the experience of working everyday beside my father. I grew up on the fish dock with my brothers Jimmy and Howard, but while they stayed in fish their whole working lives I escaped to another place.

When my father started writing his memoirs down, I made a deal with him. After a period of five years, I had accumulated two good-sized cardboard boxes of his foolscap handwriting. I agreed to rewrite his stories and help him put them down on paper in format that might make them publishable. We had a lot of discussions on the phone and in person about extending them and adding details to them, until we finally had a draft. We began this project over a decade ago.

All of my life, I have thought of myself as being much different than my father. Working on this project with him, I have discovered that I am very much my father's son. We have argued a lot in our lives, and now I realize it is because we have always had something important to argue about. He attacked this writing job with his usual wealth of energy. I put a similar amount of energy into cajoling him to remember the details and to illuminate the scenarios, while I gerrymandered and massaged his prose trying to keep the story in his voice. Sometimes he hated the version that I hacked out from what I thought was purple prose, and I was humbled into starting over again. I got bored when he told the same story twice or more, and he got fed up with me when he thought I was misinterpreting his stories or making him sound too literary.

My father is an astonishing man who despite his longevity remains lively with a mind like a shiny steel trap. He is a straight-ahead type who freely gives his opinion. All of his life he has taken a keen interest in the environment. As this project developed, it became obvious that he intended not only to tell anecdotal stories about the fisheries but about a bountiful resource that was plundered and treated irresponsibly until it was but a shadow of its former glory. My father admits his part in contributing to this disastrous scenario. During these final years of his life, he has spent a great deal of time thinking about how the fisheries might be revived if only people in all sectors would come together to improve and preserve the environment, work toward restoring the food chain in the ocean, reject damaging fish farming and cease the senseless slaughter of scarce and threatened fish stocks.

Allan Safarik
March 27, 2012

AFTER THE CATCH

The salmon as we knew them sixty years ago in British Columbia are virtually gone. I doubt the salmon runs will ever return to anything close to their original strength. Too many streams have been destroyed by urban encroachment or by the clear-cutting practices of the logging industry. Fifteen years ago, the Department of Fisheries and Oceans issued a bulletin claiming five hundred streams were destroyed and hundreds more had five or six hen fish — as they put it — returning to spawn. Each stream has its own subspecies of salmon that have adapted to the strength of the flow in that particular stream over thousands of years.

When a salmon run is extinguished, it is almost impossible to replace this run with fish from another waterway. People are under the illusion that salmon hatcheries can repair the damage, but there is no such simple solution. Hatchery fry are not as elusive as wild salmon fry, so they become easy prey for predators almost as soon as they are released. The damage to creeks and rivers could be repaired over time, but the cost of such an undertaking would take an enormous financial commitment, one that our society would undoubtedly reject. Clear-cut logging and salmonoid enhancement — reversing the decline — are not compatible and never will be, because streams go dry without an adequate tree canopy to hold back the snowmelt.

We cannot sustain a fishing industry with one run of salmon that allows a commercial fishery only one or two days fishing per week over five weeks of the year. The coho and spring salmon runs that were the backbone of the trolling industry are on the endangered list, and the pinks show in numbers only every three or four years. In the past, the season for coho opened the first of April and was closed at the end of February. The springs and chums were open twelve months of the year. Now the season opens in July or later and ends about the middle of September except for a few days of gillnetting in the Fraser River to clean up stragglers not strong enough to reach the spawning grounds.

Ten years ago, contractors would not deliver logs under twenty inches in diameter because they could not recover the cost of delivering them to a mill, so they buried, burned or dumped them into the ocean when nobody was looking. Is it possible that the forestry department was unaware of this practice? Now it is common to see trucks coming out of the bush loaded with broken ends and timber that is only five or six inches in diameter. Once logging was an honourable, romantic way of life that made British Columbia prosperous. Today, because of modern logging techniques, many loggers have become displaced people removed from the industry that sustained them and their families. Suddenly the public has become appalled at forestry practices, and so individual loggers and their families have paid the price.

We killed fifty million bison for their hides and tongues in a period of fifty years. In the past seventy-five years, logging has removed more than half the timber from British Columbia and the salmon resource has almost been killed off. Trees and salmon are invaluable resources that should be harvested for the benefit of everybody in the province. However, one valuable resource should not be destroyed for the sake of exploiting another resource. We should guard our assets and demand responsible behaviour in all of our primary industries. Progress should not be allowed to diminish our ability to naturally recover from exploiting our renewable resources. Where habitat is destroyed through careless or illegal use by ruthless individuals, the punishment should fit the crime. Too often in the past, huge companies have been given only token fines for despicable activities. Wherever habitat is destroyed, the damage should be repaired promptly by those responsible for the destruction.

Most people cannot comprehend the vast runs of salmon that once inhabited all the waters on our Pacific coast. Millions of salmon were taken with primitive equipment that would be laughed at now. Each year millions of fish were caught, and every stream that was even a couple of feet wide had salmon spawning in it. Salmon entered streams like the Seymour, Lynn, Capilano, Indian, Coquitlam, Stave, Nanaimo and thousands of other similar creeks and rivers on the Lower Mainland, Vancouver Island and other places in the province. Spawning salmon were so thick at times in the late fall that schoolboys played games catching them by hand and releasing them back into the teeming masses.

Today, hundreds of streams in British Columbia are barren. Hundreds of other streams have disappeared because of industrial, mining, urban or agricultural development that has filled them in. The salmon resources were abused by a number of factions. At times salmon was treated as a pest because it interfered with industry. Sand and gravel were indiscriminately removed from creek beds to use in cement for construction projects. Spawning grounds were debased and devalued for future generations. The cyclical nature of a resource-based economy in the decades following the war set the clock ticking on the destruction of salmon habitat. The forest industry has damaged almost every watershed in our coastal areas. Many creeks are still suffering from the legacy of logging camps. These camps often blocked up creeks to provide water for camp purposes. Scores of these dams remain, no longer in use, fouling streams so salmon cannot reach spawning grounds.

Pulp mills, slow, methodical poisoners of water resources, were located near and depended on large quantities of fresh running water for their processing. This was another secretive industry that operated with few controls, with the blessing of the government and without adequate assessment of damage done to fisheries resources. Who knows what lurks in the history of that industry. Hydro dams have also contributed to the demise of our salmon stocks, as have irrigation demands, and road and railway construction. Streams that once sustained enormous runs are now considered a success if six or eight hen salmon are found in their waters.

Throughout Canadian history, fisheries bureaucrats and politicians have consistently managed to bungle every aspect of fisheries conservation on both the East and West Coasts. Their astounding legacy of mismanagement continues unabated to this day. The major issues on the West Coast — habitat destruction, pollution, overfishing, over-large fleets, herring roe fisheries, fish farming and lack of faith between nations in negotiating treaties and regulations — remain unsettled.

Science has given us much information about the ocean and the creatures that inhabit the depths. However, when applied to solving the problems of various fisheries, this knowledge has never added up to much. Canadian federal fisheries predictions and policies generated by the experts have resulted in a series of sad failures that have haunted the West Coast fisheries for decades. After several years of catastrophically low sockeye salmon numbers, the 2010 Fraser River run of over twenty-five million fish, the biggest run in history, caught the experts by surprise. The cycles of salmon returning to spawn in the river systems on the Pacific coast are an age-old process of harmony and balance. This sudden unexpected return of millions of fish during one strange year produces more questions than it answers about what has happened to the fisheries over the long haul.

Caught between lobbyists from sectors in the industry and environmental groups, the federal government had become less transparent as time passes, gagging government biologists and stonewalling the public. In August 2011, Kristi Miller, a fisheries scientist, told a federal inquiry that government officials close to the prime minister of Canada prevented her from addressing the media about the research she conducted into the 2009 sockeye failure. (Ten million sockeye were expected to return to the Fraser River, but only one and a half million showed up.) A Canadian Press report, posted on

August 25, 2011, quoted Miller as saying: "I learned only through the inquiry process that the decision of not allowing me to speak to the press after the Science paper came out of the Privy Council Office and not from DFO."

The tragic story of the wild salmon in British Columbia is the result of a legacy of abuse and mismanagement. Its final chapter may be written in the annals of history in a science-fiction scenario. Growing farmed fish on our coast is akin to growing wheat in flowerpots in Saskatchewan. The reduction of the trolling fleet has meant the demise of quality hook-and-line-caught fish for fresh fish markets. Free-ranging wild fish that swim for their lives are being replaced on restaurant menus and at fresh fish markets by cheaper farmed fish that are raised on pellets and antibiotics. Hundreds of thousands of farmed salmon, afflicted by diseases that are unknown in wild fish, are raised in confined net pens. Thousands escape each year and swim in the same waters as the wild stocks. In August 1998, fisheries biologists indicated that DNA testing had found evidence, for the first time, of naturally spawned Atlantic salmon in the Tsitika River on Vancouver Island. A year later, juvenile Atlantic salmon were discovered in Amor de Cosmos Creek about thirty miles north of the Tsitika River. These were shocking developments for the many scientists and experts who said it couldn't happen.

What does this mean to the wild stocks? Only time can answer that question fully. Is it possible that after all the hard lessons learned, we will risk the future of the wild stocks of salmon by creating an industrial incubator that will increasingly nurture and release genetic weaklings and freaks at a frightening rate into an already complex environment? Science is too important to be left with the scientists. As one writer has put it, "What we're seeing is the beginning of a biological invasion." Thoughts of disease, predation and disharmony come to mind. The greatest watersheds in the universe stripped of their biological material and memory. Wild fish being replaced by aliens from another ocean, bringing disease, or massive colonization and generations of new competitors for food and space in an already declining environment. How can we risk taking a chance when the blueprints for disaster are already on the table?

I have seen the salmon so thick in the Seymour River that they were crowded to the edges of the stream, moving slowly up current with their backs sticking out of the water. By the middle of September even a blind man could have caught fish with his hands. The salmon were a solid mass like a dark cloud at the mercy of every predator. In my years around the river, I never saw anyone molest the fish at this stage of the season. Now the fish are gone and so is the river as a salmon stream and recreational resource. Nobody wants to swim in or even visit a slime-and-junk-filled creek that has only four or five inches of water in it. In British Columbia the salmon are gone from creeks and rivers because their habitat has been destroyed by land speculators, builders, logging, pulp mills, mines, industries and overfishing. Poor resource management policies and lack of regional and international co-operation have exacerbated the problem. No resource should be abused or harvested to the point of extermination.

The smell of progress is bound to reduce our quality of life in an aesthetic sense if we are to keep up with consumer demands. It would be ideal to have plenty of hydro power, full employment in the woods and a strong industrial and manufacturing base. However, you can't eat a kilowatt, an ingot of aluminum or a two-by-four. Even a bucket of herring would look pretty good to a person who has not eaten for a few days.

TERMINAL CITY

I began working full-time for my father's company, Vancouver Shellfish and Fish Company, in 1936, after attending high school in the depth of the Great Depression. My parents, John Safarik and Emilie Safarik, née Petrak, had come to Canada at different times early in the century from landlocked Czechoslovakia. Ironically, my father, a butcher by trade from a country with no access to the ocean, had by the mid-thirties firmly established himself in the fish business.

Father was a Slovak born in 1888 in the village of Keof near Bohuslava about ten miles from Brno in Moravia. His parents were small landowners who raised livestock and eventually had a family of thirteen children. At that time Czechoslovakia was a part of Austria, which was allied with Hungary, Germany and Turkey. War clouds were threatening and young men were facing the prospect of being drafted into the army. On a whim, John decided to join some of his friends who were headed to the New World. In 1906, at the age of eighteen, John arrived at Ellis Island in New York City with hundreds of other immigrants. From there, he went to work in a steel mill in Pittsburgh. His passage was to be paid out of a work contract; passage overseas and room and board were provided in addition to one dollar per day for a six-day work week of twelve hours per day on a one-year contract. When his contract was up, Father moved to Chicago where he worked in the Armour meat plant. Eventually, he travelled by rail into Canada. He worked for a short time on a farm in Saskatchewan before he moved on to Seattle and then to Vancouver. The day he arrived in Vancouver he obtained employment at the Burns slaughterhouse.

My mother, Emilie Petrak, was born in 1900 near Prague. She came to Canada with her family when she was nine years old on the steamship *Montrose* sailing from Antwerp. After a stormy early spring crossing that took two weeks, they arrived in St. John, New Brunswick, and boarded a train for the long journey to New Westminster, British Columbia. Emilie's father had purchased a parcel of land in Newton from the CPR through a Czech bank. Unfortunately the land was covered with timber and proved to be unsuitable for his purpose of starting a small farm.

My parents met at a Czech picnic in Stanley Park. On December 18, 1916, Mother and Father were married in a simple ceremony in Christ Cathedral in Vancouver with only a few family and friends in attendance. She was sixteen and he was twenty-eight. It was a lasting union that endured for almost sixty years.

They moved onto an acreage on Eton Street at New Brighton on Burrard Inlet where they kept milk cows, calves, chickens, ducks, geese and horses, which my father doctored and resold, and a dozen suckling pigs that he bought at the farmers' market near Main and Hastings. The milk cows were kept mostly for our own use. Skim milk and buttermilk were fed to the hogs and chickens. Mother sold the butter. At the East End acreage Father built a killing room with a cement floor and running water. He sold veal, pork and lard to butcher shops, restaurants and to Woodward's Department Store. Mother grew a large garden, took care of the fowl and raised me and my two brothers, Edward and John. As my father gradually got more involved in the fish business, the land became useful as a grazing pasture for the horses he used to pull his fish wagon.

In 1917, John Safarik and his partner, William Steiner, opened the Vancouver Shellfish and Fish Company on the Gore Avenue fish dock. It was a long, successful partnership that saw them relocate to a new location in 1926. They became charter tenants at the Vancouver Harbour Commission Wharf on the waterfront at the foot of Campbell

Avenue. This wharf with its enormous fish sheds, which eventually housed many fish companies, was an unloading facility with an ice house and berthing slips for fishing boats. The Vancouver Harbour Commission Wharf became commonly known as the Campbell Avenue fish dock. By 1936, my father had replaced his horse-drawn fish wagon with a truck and our family had moved to a new location.

Long before dawn each morning we travelled west from our house on North Penticton Street in the oldest area of Vancouver, Hastings-Sunrise, on our way to Campbell Avenue fish dock on the harbour. We followed Powell Street beside ribbons of railway tracks that passed along the waterfront. The fish dock was located beyond the tracks and behind the massive brick expanse of the British Columbia Sugar Refinery.

At that time every freight train entering the city had transients on board, sometimes on top of almost every boxcar. In winter these poor souls were sitting in half a foot or more of snow that covered the cars. It was a cruel time for these unfortunate people who were travelling the country back and forth desperately searching for work. I wondered how many were killed in attempts to board boxcars or fell off when they lapsed into sleep or froze to death on the long hauls through the mountains.

Nearly every morning I observed the same sorry spectacle and heard the screams at the Campbell Avenue crossing that fronted our dock as the freights slowed down entering Vancouver city proper. The railway dicks and both city and provincial police would greet each load of transients by liberally swinging their long clubs. As soon as the travellers saw the welcoming committee they leapt from the boxcars and dispersed at a run in every direction. Most of them managed to escape but the ones who didn't received beatings. Hungry men, stiff from their long ordeal in cramped circumstances, seemed to get a sudden shot of adrenalin when they saw the well-fed bully boys and they sprinted across the tracks onto city streets and down back alleys. Sometimes temporary shelter was provided by soft-hearted citizens until the police attempting to round up the vagrants moved on. Many of these men worked their way through the city and disappeared into the scrub brush on the False Creek flats.

The unlucky ones who were roughed up and sometimes badly beaten were escorted to the eastern edge of the city limits and told to get out of town. Bed and breakfast were not provided, and these poor men walked the railway tracks away from the city with hunger pangs gnawing at their guts. Others were rounded up when they broke cover to beg citizens for food. If they were a distance from the waterfront, they were put in holding cell for a few hours and fed a baloney sandwich before also being escorted out to the city limits and warned not to return. Very little sympathy or food was offered to these unemployed citizens because the hardhearted politicians in power were almost completely without compassion. Decent law-abiding men who were willing to work were treated like vermin. Some of the men who were chased out of town waited on the outskirts for a day or two before they jumped another freight and attempted another perilous passage onto the waterfront. Aware of the vicious greeting party, many chose to jump from the freight as it approached the Rogers Sugar refinery about a mile from Ballantyne Pier where the police were housed.

Ballantyne Pier and Campbell Avenue fish dock were both built as political plums by the government of the day, eager to curry favour with friends. Ballantyne Pier remained a sleeping giant for many years, with only a boatload of Japanese oranges being unloaded once or twice a year just before Christmas. It saw increased activity during the war years but then fell asleep again. Campbell Avenue fish dock was another matter. At first it remained largely unoccupied until the Harbour Commission Board came to its senses and reduced the rent. The result was that many of the tenants from the city-owned Gore Avenue fish dock moved to Campbell Avenue. My father was an original tenant, having moved in in 1926. Campbell Avenue quickly became the centre of Vancouver's fish buying and processing industry and remained so for decades. Billingsgate, Lions Gate and Seaport Crown were also among the original tenants. It was the only installation in Vancouver Harbour that paid for its keep and made a profit during the Depression. In later decades, more than twenty-five million pounds of fish passed through this facility each year.

On Saturday mornings, transients and unemployed people appeared at Campbell Avenue because we gave away all the ground fish that was left over from the week before. This offering was usually less than five hundred pounds, but on some Saturdays over one thousand pounds of whole fish were handed out to grateful citizens.

Our house on Eton Street had a closed-in back porch where Mother fed many hungry transients. We got up at four a.m. to get ready to go to work, and often there was knocking at the back door as soon as the kitchen light came on. They came before daylight to avoid detection because there were residents in the city who reported them to the police. If two or three men appeared, they were invited to eat with us at the table in the kitchen. A larger group were fed at a table on the enclosed porch. Many of these people were young boys in their teens from the prairies. Sometimes a fourteen- or fifteen-year-old would show up with older men. Mother invited these boys in to sit at our table while the rest ate on the porch. "Look at these boys!" she'd exclaim to Father with tears in her eyes, "This is a shameful thing to happen to our youth." She not only fed people, but if their clothing was lacking or worn-out she gave them socks, sweaters, coats, trousers and even a pair of shoes if they happened to fit the prospective wearer. My parents were immigrants who had come to Canada to find a better life. They were disturbed by the sight of so many hungry, homeless people also on the move looking for a better life. My parents' house, like others in the community, became known in the hobo jungle as a place where a hungry person could get something to eat. Not everybody shared my parents' social concern. These were dark times and a disgraceful interlude in our country's history.

Some of these unemployed were saved from perishing from the damp during the winter months by the many sawmills with beehive burners that burned sawdust and waste wood continuously night and day. At night many people slept beside the burners, covering themselves with sawdust and waste wood to keep warm. Their clothing became saturated with woodsmoke, so you could always identify them by the smell. It was not uncommon in winter to come across a man sleeping under a pile of newspapers that was covered in frost. False Creek flats were covered with small shelters made from wooden packing crates or any other lumber that could be salvaged for that purpose. Hundreds of people bivouacked there for survival, squatting in improvised shelters, cooking what food they could find on open fires in various types of tin cans or pails. Most of them were good honest folks down on their luck who didn't bother anyone except to solicit for work or food. There were few disturbances, so the police kept out of the area. Many long-term residents in the city had no idea there was an underground jungle of transients and unemployed living outdoors in the heart of the city.

Times were really tough in the Depression, so tough that the fish being unloaded was pulled up the dock to our plant in rickshaw-type wagons. It was cheaper to use manpower than to burn twenty-cents-a-gallon gasoline in the company truck. We were the lucky ones able to survive by selling substantial quantities of cheap seafood in our Western Canadian market. We also sold to Americans along the Pacific seaboard and took a stab at selling in the New York and Chicago markets. A bonus was that we had the best fish and shellfish in the world to eat for free or for, at most, two or three pennies per pound.

THE TRAWLERS

By the 1920s, there were three or four vessels bottom trawling with nets for ground fish — sole, flounders, skate, ling cod, rock cod, crabs and a few other incidental fish — to supply the Vancouver market. They fished in English Bay and up to about one mile south of the bell buoy situated at Point Grey. They went out at four a.m. and came in by four p.m. to unload their fresh fish, which was in demand. These were small vessels, under forty feet in length. They fished five days a week and delivered a mixed catch weighing under two thousand pounds. The soles they brought in were all good sized, between fifteen and twenty inches. All the fish had a fresh, sandy-water smell that most newly landed fish doesn't have today.

By the mid-1930s, seven or eight vessels, forty to forty-eight footers, were catching ground fish for the Vancouver market. These larger vessels had more power and had extended the range by fishing in the Gulf of Georgia. They worked in a triangle that stretched from the Light Ship (a weather ship with a blinking light and fog horn anchored a half mile out from the mouth of the Fraser River), south to the U.S. border where it separated Point Roberts from Canada, then northwest out to the middle of the Gulf and back towards the Light Ship. Over the years, both Canadian and American fishing boats were arrested for fishing in foreign waters. Usually, the fish was confiscated and other penalties were levied. There were incidents where each crew member was fined five thousand dollars or more.

During high school, I worked most of the summers in Father's fish plant, Vancouver Shellfish and Fish Company, commonly known as Van Shell. One of the ground fish skippers, Jimmy Martin, had a crewman with the habit of getting liquored up and missing the four a.m. departure. When this happened, Jimmy would approach Father and say, "John, I'm taking Norman out with me today." Father always let me go. He knew I wanted to go, because while he paid me eight dollars per week, Jimmy paid me ten dollars each day.

Long before light we untied and slipped out of the basin into the main harbour. Jimmy's nephew, George, was the other crew member and he made breakfast as we passed under the Lions Gate Bridge. By the time we rounded the bell buoy at the end of Point Grey and set course towards the Light Ship, breakfast was finished and I was washing the dishes. Old Jimmy was out on deck checking the gear and net for tangles.

Jimmy Martin was a Scot who had immigrated to Canada with his family before the First World War. He was married with one daughter. For many years he delivered his entire catch each day to Van Shell. Most bottom trawlers sold their catch to one company and zealously guarded their market. It was difficult to sell fish in the thirties, so each fisherman made sure he supplied his company with all the fish he caught to reduce the chance that they might buy from another boat.

Jimmy was a gentleman to everyone who knew him. A gentle soul might be a better way of putting it. With a perpetual smile on his face, he explained the reason for every order he gave to me so I understood why and how it was done. Lines were properly coiled from underfoot so as to be in good order when they were required. Fish pews and knives were touched up, and then we had coffee while we waited to arrive at the spot he chose to begin fishing, about a mile and a half out from the Light Ship.

I remember one trip in particular. George and I put the net over the side, then George let out the steel cable on the net doors so they were about sixty feet back of the boat. Then old Jimmy increased the speed to bring the net to the surface. He came out on deck to eyeball the net to make sure it was open and not tangled or turned over. By this time, George was in the wheelhouse waiting for Jimmy's signal. He slowed the engine and dropped to about a quarter of our speed while Jimmy slackened the winch and slowly played out the steel cable until the net reached the bottom. The way the boat handled and the drag on the equipment told him the net was on the bottom a hundred yards behind the vessel and working properly. He then tightened the bead on the winch as hard as he could and drove a wedge under it for good measure before he went inside to take over from George.

The funnel-shaped net was dragged along the sandy bottom for two hours and then it was winched up into the boat. A strap was put around the neck of the net and it was winched up to the top of the boom through a block that was attached there. Each time the net was lifted, the fish in it were shaken down towards the bag end of the net. The net was about one hundred feet long and it took three or four lifts to shake all the fish down into the bag end. A strap was put around the net for the final time as the whole bag of fish weighing five thousand pounds or more was lifted over the stern deck. A release on the bottom of the bag was pulled and the fish spilled out onto the deck.

Then the snap on the bottom of the bag was locked and the net was let out for another two hours to drag along the seabed. George and I went to work sorting the fish on the deck while old Jimmy sat behind the wheel keeping us on course. After a while he came on deck and dressed the three large spring salmon and the five twenty-pound halibut that we caught in the first set. He worked quickly and in ten minutes he was back in the wheelhouse. George and I sorted the soles by size into fifty-pound baskets and then took turns icing them down in Gregory boxes. All the soles were laid in belly-up by hand and carefully iced. We shovelled small soles and other species, which were mostly still alive, over the side.

We kept the flounders that were under eight pounds but threw larger ones overboard since there was no market for them. We cut the wings from large skates and kept the silver perch, rock cod, red squid, octopi and the few red snappers. About a thousand pounds of grey cod was pitched over the side to float away on the surface. Soon a few hundred seagulls were in our wake swooping over the carnage, picking eyes and meat from the carcasses. The bladders on the grey cod had blown up and were protruding from their mouths when they reached the surface in the net. Though most of them were alive, they had lost the ability to swim back down into the depths and floated belly-up, so the gulls had no problem piercing their bladders with their beaks.

We opened the scuppers and washed small sole and the array of other, non-commercial or undersized sea creatures into the waves. Finally, there were twenty-five ling cod (six- to fifteen-pounders), resplendent in their mottled rattlesnake skins with razor teeth and sharp spines. Jimmy came out to give George a hand. They killed and dressed the cod while I watched the lesson. A heavy knife was used to cut the spine at the back of the ugly wide head. The cod shuddered for a moment and then lay still. The head was cut off behind the gills in such a manner so that when it was twisted and pulled, the guts came out with the head. Bellies were slit, blood was scraped out, carcasses were washed with buckets of sea water and the fish were iced in the hold.

We made three drags that day, leaving the gear out for about two hours each time. In the third drag we caught five or six sockeyes along with the usual tally of ground fish. For a time sockeyes began jumping all around the boat, falling back into the green water splashing like raindrops from the low grey clouds.

When we were in shallower water, closer to shore, we made a short, half-hour drag for crabs. The result of this endeavour was a haul of two tons of Dungeness crabs dropped onto the deck. We hand-picked one hundred and fifty dozen good crabs and iced them in boxes to quiet them down and prevent them from crawling about the hold. Ice puts them in a stupor and they stop moving immediately and become completely docile. The rest of the crabs were shovelled overboard.

Our total catch for the day included one hundred fifty dozen prime crabs, three large red springs (about twenty pounds each), twenty-five hundred pounds of sole, eight hundred pounds of flounders, five hundred pounds of skate wings, one hundred pounds of rock cod, fifty pounds of red snapper, one hundred pounds of silver perch, forty pounds of red squid, one hundred fifty pounds of ling cod, three octopi (each weighing about twenty pounds) and one hundred and twenty pounds of halibut. When we unloaded at Campbell Avenue and the fish was weighed, the *Curlew M*'s catch was worth four hundred and fifty dollars gross. From this Jimmy paid George fifteen dollars, I got ten dollars, sixty dollars went for ice, five dollars for groceries, ten dollars for fuel and whatever Jimmy figured for wear and tear on his net, steel cables, boat maintenance and insurance. Still, Jimmy Martin and the *Curlew M* were making eight thousand dollars per year when schoolteachers were taking home less than two thousand.

In the winter of 1936, on December 22, when Jimmy was coming home from his last trip of the season, tragedy struck. On the way back from fishing at Nanoose Bay on the inside of Vancouver Island, Jimmy decided to stop in the mouth of the Fraser River to wash out the net. This procedure included dropping the net over the side and letting out the cable so the doors would spread the net and the boat was run ahead at full speed to work the seaweed, small fish and slime from the webbing.

While the steel cable was playing out, a line attached to the net caught Jimmy by the leg and dragged him overboard. He grabbed on to the head rope in the mouth of the net in order to prevent himself from entering the net. As long as the boat went full speed ahead, the net remained on the surface with Jimmy hanging on for dear life. He was dressed for cold weather with a heavy jacket, rubber pants and gumboots, so he probably wouldn't have survived even if he had missed the net because it is pretty hard to stay afloat dressed in that kind of outfit. For some reason, only his brother was with him on that trip. Marty threw three or four Gregory boxes overboard for Jimmy to grab, but they wouldn't have kept him afloat even if he had managed to catch one of them. He would have gone down in the mouth of the net with the box. The water was ice cold and it was just a matter of time before Jimmy, numbed to the bone, let go of the rope and entered the net.

Marty decided to slow the boat and winch in the cable that was attached to the doors that held the net open. He was hoping to get the net in close enough to throw a strap around it and lift the net quickly out of the water with the boom. At the best of times, with an additional deckhand, it took seven to eight minutes to accomplish this procedure. As soon as he slowed the boat, the net went down below the surface with Jimmy still hanging on. Now the race was on to winch Jimmy aboard the vessel. He got the net in as quickly as he could, but precious minutes ticked by. The wait was too long for Jimmy. This gentle man was beyond help when his brother got him free from the net and laid him out on the hatch. He worked on Jimmy for about an hour trying to bring him around, but by then he could see it was useless, so he covered him with a tarp, secured the net and proceeded towards Vancouver Harbour and the slip at Campbell Avenue.

We saw the boat arriving, so as usual we stood on the dock to welcome the fishermen home. Marty tied the boat up with only one line and came up the steel ladder to the dock still dressed in his rubber pants and gumboots. We knew something was wrong. He went into shock when he repeated over and over again that Jimmy had drowned. We helped him into the office and Father poured him a whisky in an attempt to calm him down. He sat in a chair with his head down repeating that phrase, "Jimmy fell overboard and drowned in the net." Finally, he looked up and told my father that Jimmy was under a tarp on the hatch. He asked my father to take charge of the situation.

Father had Jimmy taken away to the hospital so that a death certificate could be made out. A fisherman's drowning is a terrible event at any time of year, but it seemed even more tragic when it happened just before Christmas. The nearest of kin were contacted and relatives arrived at the wharf to take Marty home.

Jimmy was a good friend to everyone on the wharf and his passing left us dumbfounded. I went to Jimmy's funeral to say goodbye. He lay there with one gnarled hand across his chest and a peaceful look on his face. To this day, when I think of our dear friend Jimmy Martin, I remember the slight smile on his face, in life and in death.

THE MAN FROM NEW YORK

A customer we desperately depended on in the 1930s named Ianstasse travelled annually from New York to Vancouver to buy frozen white springs from us and from one or two other companies. Each year he arrived in the last week of August. The white springs he bought were hot smoked (kippered) and sold to the Jewish markets in large eastern U.S. cities. Some years that gentleman bought more than two hundred thousand pounds of large frozen salmon from us, and he paid cash when the fish were delivered into his account at Vancouver Ice and Cold Storage.

J. Martin, who was the chief shareholder of the cold storage, also eagerly depended on the freezer order. We all waited for this buyer each year like children wait for Santa Claus. When the short stocky man arrived, a box of expensive cigars and a bottle of the best Father could buy were waiting on the table before him. All of his teeth were crowned with gold so that they literally gleamed in the sunlight. The man with the golden smile always seemed to be in a hurry. He smoked a cigar, had a couple of belts, quickly made his business deal and then departed in the waiting taxi. Ianstasse was either a large player in the smoked fish business or he was acting as an agent for a number of smokers in large American cities. We suspected the latter, but his money was good and he was a congenial fellow so nobody bothered to inquire about his business. During the friendly meeting Ianstasse laid down his purchase order without any discussion about price. He was the big buyer we were waiting for and he knew exactly what he was willing to pay. There were no other buyers in the wings, so he knew he could write his own ticket. I'm sure that even Canadian Fishing Company, one of the largest fish companies on this continent, was anxiously waiting for his arrival as well. B.C. Packers were in bankruptcy at the time, so they were not in the picture.

Takahashi represented the Fraser River Japanese Co-op, and he hauled these springs to our plant in ten- to fifteen-thousand-pound loads with two dump trucks. Each load was backed into our plant and released, without being weighed, onto a pad of ice laid over our cement floor. The dressed, head-off loss was twenty-five percent and we paid the co-op on weight delivered to the cold storage. There was trust on both sides because we depended on each other, and to my knowledge there was never a dispute. The Japanese Co-op also depended on the order from Ianstasse. Otherwise they had only a cannery market for this fish, which paid only a cent and a half per pound, which was less than half the price they received from us — and the canning market did not want the white springs to begin with. I believe Takahashi also delivered large quantities of these fish to Canadian Fishing Company and to Canadian Fish and Cold Storage as well. We all sold our white springs to the same customer, Ianstasse.

The Jewish markets, wherever they were located, ate kippered salmon made only from white springs. For some reason the meat of the fish had to be white without even a trace of red or pink in it. Some lots of white springs bought for the Jewish trade from dealers not familiar with that situation were rejected because the flesh had pink streaks or a tinge of colour. This same market ate plenty of cold smoked red spring salmon (lox) with gusto, but for some reason barbecued fish had to be made from springs that were pure white in colour.

About three or four percent of the springs we received from the Japanese Co-op still had a silver skin and good red meat. These bright salmon were fish that had just entered the river and had not discoloured or faded out yet. These fish were graded out when the salmon were being dressed and they were sold for a higher price. The whites were all sold to Ianstasse for three and three-quarter cents per pound and the good red-meated fish were sold for six to eight cents per pound. The bonus from the sale of the red meated fish was split between us and Takahashi. It was a hard way to make a buck.

We also bought a lot of prime winter-run steelhead from the Japanese Co-op. Most of these fish were shipped, iced in the round, via Canadian Pacific Railway Express to various buyers in Manitoba, Ontario and Quebec. Waldman in Montreal was the big buyer and most of the time he wanted all of them. However, to protect ourselves, we shared them out in case Waldman should cancel. The best prices paid for these fish were from Jewish buyers in New York, after the New Year each season. Most large steelhead runs were in winter or early spring. We were kept pretty busy selling them. Summer steelhead runs were never up to much. Each week only three or four hundred pounds of incidentally caught fish were delivered, so there was never a problem in selling them.

One Boxing Day found me icing six tons of round steelhead and wondering what we were going to do with them. We always iced this fish in the round (without dressing them) because they kept far better that way. Fresh-caught steelhead, still stiff when well iced, would hold up to twenty or more days if kept very cold and sealed from air under ice. I wondered at the time what we were going to do with these Christmas steelheads because after the holidays people are full of turkey and are also broke. For a week or two business was very slow. The New York market was a gamble, but calls were made to buyers in that city to gauge the prospects. Word came back that the demand for steelhead was good and a buyer asked us to ship them rail express. We immediately got our act together and made an arrangement to ship the steelhead. I believe we paid ten cents per pound for the fish, and express freight charges were twenty cents per pound. We would have approximately thirty-six hundred dollars tied up the cost of the fish and freight. The cost of sixty two-hundred-pound fish boxes, worth eighty-five cents a piece, plus half a day's labour charges for four men at thirty cents per hour rounded out our total investment to about four thousand dollars.

We decided to go for it. Soon empty two-hundred-pound fish boxes were coming down the chute. We filled them as quickly as possible with iced fish, and the lids were nailed on and two wire straps were put around the boxes to keep them from bulging. The boxes were hauled to the railway station and loaded to stand on end in what they then called iced cars. At that time refrigeration was provided by chunks of ice that were spilled between a double wall that surrounded the inside of the boxcar. It was a primitive setup but it seemed to do the job well enough. The express train always pulled out of Vancouver at eight p.m. for Eastern Canada. This journey would take about six days because the train made short stops in Winnipeg and Toronto and Montreal to unload fresh fish. We had to wait it out with our fingers crossed to see if our gamble paid off. We hoped for the best, but you could never completely depend on those damn Yankee traders, so anything could happen.

A week later when I arrived at the plant I noticed that Bill Steiner was smoking a House of Lords cigar, worth twenty-five cents, rather than his usual five-cent White Owl. Father had a smile on his face and also sported a two-bit cigar. It was obvious that we had scored on the lot of steelhead we had shipped to the Big Apple. I was stunned when Steiner turned in his chair and informed me with a chuckle that we had grossed a dollar a pound for our fish. It was almost like a dream. We made an eight-thousand-dollar profit on just over a four-thousand-dollar investment. It was almost too good to be true. We immediately made arrangements to make another shipment to take advantage of a favourable market. Two days later another shipment was on its way. Again we waited for the results of our gamble. We knew that the New York market was a fickle boom-or-bust affair and it was possible not to recover the freight charges and the cost of the fish. It was a dangerous proposition and not to be undertaken without investigating it thoroughly. A week later we again got good news. Our fish sold for seventy-five cents per pound so we netted about forty cents a pound. Once again, this was a fabulous profit. Bear in mind that we only made three or four cents a pound on fish we sold in Western Canada or along the American Pacific seaboard.

By this time we were walking on air but keeping our mouths shut so as not to give away any information that might put competitors onto our game. We did not want the competition to flood the market and cause the price to crash. We knew that we had been very lucky with our first two shipments to the most volatile market in the world. Now we pondered the chances of making a third shipment. We sat in the office weighing our chances for another shot at the big market. We had experienced disaster there in the past and we knew every shipment was a pure gamble. The information we received from our contact in the big city was still favourable. However, since our contact received a commission on the sale of our fish, we thought his judgement to be suspect.

Finally, we decided to make another shipment and hope for the best despite the fact that we felt we were going to the well too often. The fish was packed and shipped and there was nothing to do but wait a week and take our chances. We made a call or two and discovered that while the market had declined, it was still generally favourable. Seven days later when I arrived at the plant I could hardly stand the suspense. I rushed up to see Bill Steiner. All the years he worked with Father he was the first one in the office each morning. He turned and looked and me and I noticed the cheap White Owl cigar clamped in his jaw and my heart sank in my chest. Steiner looked at me and said, "Don't worry, Norman, we did all right." We lost the cost of the boxes and the labour charges for packing the fish but we just about broke even. However, in the larger picture we were way ahead of the game.

I heaved a sigh of relief and any thought of shipping additional steelhead shipments to New York City went out the window. In fact, we were very lucky. We scored twice in a row and broke about even on the last shipment, so we had no complaints. Some of our competitors who made shipments after we packed it in not only lost the cost of their investment but ended up paying the freight charges. At the best of times it was a dangerous business for experienced dealers, and not a market for greenhorns to dabble in.

THE CALIFORNIA CON MAN

The Los Angeles market was touted as a profitable area, so we made a trial shipment of steelhead to a new broker who advised us he could sell our fish. We cleared about twenty cents a pound on the lot so we were riding high. The gods were still smiling. We increased the next shipment and again came out of it with a fair profit. The broker advised us that the market was still good and urged us to increase the weight of the next shipment.

We should have been wary and checked out the situation with some of our other contacts, but for some reason we got careless and completely trusted our new broker's advice. We increased the third shipment to fifteen thousand pounds unaware that we were being set up. Then came the bad news that the broker couldn't sell the fish and wanted to know what he should do with it. Immediately we got on the phone and called every dealer, large and small, that we could find in Los Angeles. Finally, after sweating it out for a day, we managed to sell all of our fish at cost. We were able to pay our freight and make about one hundred dollars.

The broker should have advised us that the market was plugged and to only ship what he could sell. In reality, he couldn't sell any of the fish and he was merely speculating at our expense. By his attitude, we suspected that he had set us up in an attempt to dump our fish to his friends and split the profit. But through our perseverance we managed to find a buyer. When the cheque from the sale of the fish arrived we discovered that the broker who misled us had insisted on a five-percent commission before he would release the fish to our buyer. Even though he got us in trouble and had no part in the sale of the fish, he was still greedy enough to take a commission, which meant we took a complete bath on the deal. There was nothing we could do about it except scratch him off our list of business contacts. It wasn't long before this same sleazy broker was back on the phone trying to talk us into shipping him fish, but we resisted.

Imagine our surprise when the California con artist walked into our office at Campbell Avenue, wearing a pie-plate straw hat and smoking a cigar that was three times too big for his face. His handshake was like holding onto a wet dishtowel and he made a glib attempt at asking us to make him our exclusive broker in California. After listening to his baloney, Father told him that he was not dealing with a bunch of Mexicans like the ones he was screwing all the time down south. The gent's smile vanished when Father fixed him with his killer stare, the one that he used on us at home during a squabble when we were kids. Soon after the California dude left the office in a hurry, with Father directly after him suggesting that a boot in the ass might cure whatever was ailing his business practices. The man jumped into the taxi waiting on the wharf and departed the scene, never to be heard from again.

For years after we shipped most of our steelhead to Morris Waldman in Montreal and we never had a problem. We made less than we could in a riskier marker, but at least we could sleep at night because we knew that Morris was completely honest and reliable and he always paid. We knew that Morris reshipped most of the fish to New York and Chicago and probably made more on the fish than we did — but so what, he had has own expertise in the marketplace.

LIVE COD

In the 1930s at least six million pounds of dressed live cod was produced each year by approximately eight hundred fishermen. They sold their fish through their own fishermen's association that rented an office in Father's fish plant. The Cod Association was a Japanese organization, with a few non-Japanese members, that controlled more than a dozen packers that delivered live ling cod and also spring salmon they caught while fishing for ling cod. (Live cod is fish slaughtered less than eight hours after it is caught.) A usual load for a packer was twelve thousand pounds of live cod, two thousand pounds of salmon, plus one thousand pounds of rock cod and snappers. There were days when a packer unloaded twenty thousand pounds of cod and more than five thousand pounds of salmon. The fish was only a few hours old, except for the salmon, which was probably no older than two days. The fish was caught on hooks using handlines and kept in live boxes until the packer appeared, one or two times a week, depending on the weather.

When the packer came into view, the fishermen prepared to slaughter the live fish to send it to market. Some fishermen, especially the Finns, delivered their own fish to Campbell Avenue and slaughtered it at the wharf. We dumped freshly killed fish onto the clean cement floor and pitched on shovel after shovel full of crushed ice until it was well covered. Each time a shovel full of ice hit the fish, all the headless fish slapped their tails like tap dancers slowing the beat until another shovel full fell over them, until they were completely buried under a white blanket of ice. Rigor mortis did not set in for at least another twelve hours and then this fish became so hard it was difficult to cut with a knife.

Every weekday morning at five a.m. there would be two to five cod packers tied up at Campbell Avenue Fisherman's Wharf with ten to fifteen thousand pounds of what was then called live cod in each vessel. A price was set for the day and the fish were sold in three sizes. Small, four to six pounds, were sold for four cents per pound. Medium, plus six to twelve pounds, brought the highest price, selling for seven cents per pound. Large, plus twelve up to forty pounds, sold for four cents per pound. The price was lowered on unsold fish after ten in the morning, and the cod was divided among the buyers in proportion to the volume of number-one price fish each company had paid earlier in the day.

A live cod fisherman jigged for fish with a couple of handlines that were baited with small fish (herring, perch, sole, rock cod, flounder) that were seined or beach-seined for that purpose. The live cod were segregated by size and each size kept separately in partitioned live wells in the hold of the vessel. If they were mixed up, the big cod would swallow the smaller cod whole. A twenty-pound cod had no trouble swallowing and digesting a ten- or twelve-pounder. Fish could be kept for a couple of weeks without a problem in these live wells, which had a continuous flow of fresh sea water through holes drilled in the hull of the vessel.

The cod was starved for two or three days before the day when the packer pulled alongside the fishing boat in some quiet cove and the fish was slaughtered and iced for shipment to Campbell Avenue fish dock.

All the fish was caught in the Gulf of Georgia between Campbell River and Ladysmith on Vancouver Island, so it only took six to twelve hours from the time it was slaughtered until it arrived in Vancouver. Nobody would eat a fish that had the guts in it. If by accident a round fish came in with the dressed cod, which happened on occasion when the fish was killed at night, the crew on the packer threw it overboard into the harbour.

The Japanese fish companies always got the cream from the Cod Association. Things were pretty equal if we were at the dock when hatches were lifted, but if we were late we got the short end of the stick. When bad weather conditions caused cod to be in short supply, we got less than the Japanese companies.

"Step on it," Father would order when were late for work because company had stayed too late the night before or because we were late getting away from the house. We flew over the wooden block paving on Powell Street with the back end of the truck rattling as it vibrated over the uneven wooden blocks that were left over from the turn of the century. Every morning we passed a big flatfoot on his way to the police station. He had to walk about eight blocks to get on the electric streetcar and had only himself to blame for being passed by us. One Sunday, just at dusk, he took the trouble to walk over to our driveway and give Father a ticket because one of his headlights was flickering off and on. Mother and Father had been out to Newton to check on my great aunt, who was more than eighty years old. Scott Road and Newton Road were full of potholes and a wire had come loose. Father was really ticked off. When the policeman stuck out his thumb imploring us to pick him up, Father would go apoplectic. "Norman, don't stop for that bugger. Imagine giving me a ticket for a blinking headlight when I was nearly in my driveway. What kind of a neighbour is that?" The five-dollar fine was unimportant. Father considered it an insult from an neighbour. The old man especially enjoyed passing him by when it was raining heavily.

The routine was the same each morning. If cod was scarce, Father would implore me to get as much as I could. If there was a large surplus he cautioned me to take as little as possible. When there was a surplus of cod the price dropped half a cent every couple of hours until it was all sold. Father had a point there. It was a game played every day by buyers and sellers without any hard feelings.

The Cod Association had a couple of wagons, like rickshaws, that had a large box between two high steel wheels. There were two long shafts for pulling them along. Off I would go down to the floating part of the dock for our share of cod. I put the wagon alongside and the Japanese fishermen would pitch the quivering fish into the box. If there were lots of fish they would not stop until it was overflowing. Then I would have to pull it away to stop them loading it to the top. The box held about eight hundred pounds when it was level and probably nine hundred pounds when cod tails were drooping down over its sides. So the battle went on. Sometimes when cod was plentiful, hands would pitch additional cod into the buggy before I could get away.

When I pulled the buggy down the floating dock, two Japanese fishermen pushed for all they were worth from behind. There was a span of the dock that went up and down with the tide. At high tide it was almost level, but at low tide the span had a twenty-five percent grade to the top of the dock. Well, we would get the wagon going at full speed and hit the bottom of the span at full tilt. At a half tide it was a breeze, but at an extremely low tide the span was quite steep so we had to pull and push our guts out to make it to the top. When the span had a very steep grade I would zigzag up to ease the strain from a straight uphill pull. On one occasion the box was overloaded at an extreme low tide, so three-quarters of the way up I ran out of gas. The two pushers were also bagged. Suddenly we were in trouble when the wagon came to a halt and slowly began to roll backwards, picking up momentum as it went downhill. The Japanese pushers ducked out of the way and I had to let it go. The wagon with almost a thousand pounds of ling cod on board went flying down the ramp while the three of us gasped for breath. When the wagon hit bottom it flipped over backwards, luckily depositing its load on the floating dock. Two six-by-six timbers on each side of the dock kept any fish from dropping into the water. We turned the cart right side up and reloaded it and, with the aid of two additional pushers, we managed to get it to the top without any more trouble.

That was it for me. From then on I drove the truck down and, after loading it, backed it up the span to the top of the dock. I never pulled that wagon again. Gas was two bits a gallon and probably less than a cup was used to pick up the cod. I'm sure my Japanese friends on the packers also enjoyed the change as much as I did. I told Father, "If God wanted a man to pull a wagon, he would have provided him with four legs." That seemed to be a good enough argument, since he never said a word about the new procedure.

Live cod was gourmet quality eating, not like the net-caught fish that are delivered to the docks today. Fish that are ten to fifteen days old with the guts still in them have only three or four days' shelf life by the time they are filleted. Once we unloaded hook-and-line-caught ling cod that was twenty-three days old. It was better than cod taken by trawl, ungutted and iced for three days. The fisherman who delivered the ling cod had become stormbound. Each time after he had gone fishing a storm blew up for a couple of days. Some of his fish were ten days old, some were twenty and some were twenty-three days on board. He was fishing the North Coast in January at a time of bitterly cold weather. At night he went ashore in his skiff for snow, which he took back to his vessel and packed around his fish. At port he got top price for his fish. We respected a fisherman who would go out fishing at that time of year. Today a lot of fish goes on the market that is only really fit for the bin. It certainly wouldn't have been acceptable in the era before the war.

Millions of pounds of live cod were taken each year from Gulf of Georgia waters without a shortage of fish. During the war, sunken gillnets were used to catch dogfish sharks and soup fin sharks in the Gulf, and millions of additional pounds of ling cod were taken at the same time. Today the Gulf of Georgia is a barren sea, closed twelve months of the year for cod fishing, even for sportsmen. What happened to the fish stocks in the Gulf of Georgia? Overfishing certainly contributed to the problem. The demise of ground fish and salmon in the Gulf is largely because of overfishing the forage fish that cod and salmon feed on. After working in the fishing industry every day for over sixty years, I believe the loss of our great resource can be attributed to a lack of feed for the major food fish species. Frankly, there are not enough herring to go around. This fish, so critical to the food chain, has been seriously affected by the herring roe industry that supplies the Japanese market. The herring has been so badly reduced in scope, size and quality it is almost impossible to find Pacific herring that are large enough for human consumption. Cod and salmon are facing the same situation and their stocks have seriously declined.

SPANISH PETE

One morning after I finished hauling fish brought in by the Cod Association fishermen I noticed a couple of trucks and several Chinese peddlers sitting around on the floating dock waiting for somebody. I looked down the harbour and saw Spanish Pete Ambrose coming in with the *Belarus*. She was low down on the waterline, so I knew she had a load of fish on, and that is what they were all waiting for. Pete's boat was about forty-two-feet long and he fished strictly for black or copper rock cod, silver perch and for starry flounders for the Japanese and Chinese markets. It was all cash and carry, and Spanish Pete was becoming a very wealthy man. He was a specialist who became very good at catching boatloads of this type of fish. It was rumoured that Pete had money in every bank in Vancouver under aliases to avoid the tax department. In the end they got him anyway and he damn near died from shock before the government was finished with him.

Pete was noted for his bad temper. Many times I saw him so mad he threw his hat on the dock and jumped up and down on it. Muttering curses and talking to himself were daily occurrences. He was seldom in a good mood. It was only between trips when he came down to check on his boat that he seemed relaxed and content. This was because there was a lady about to arrive to join him on his day off.

Pete was an excellent fisherman, easily one of the best on the whole coast. He drove his crew without mercy and changed crews often but he was a highliner and the shares he paid his employees were higher than they could earn working on other vessels. It always amazed me that Pete could take out a greenhorn and return to port with a deckhand who seemed more like a veteran than a green man.

On this day I noticed one crewman sitting in the bow of the boat as far as he could get away from Pete in the wheelhouse. I noticed the other deckhand sitting in the stern of the vessel as far away as he could get from Pete. Pete was rough with his mouth and he had a way of alienating people. Body language said it all as they tied up to the dock. I wondered if Pete would chew out his crewmen before the unloading. I could see that nobody on board was saying a word.

When they got closer to the wharf, I discovered that the man in the bow was Scotty Neish. He sat there with a sour expression as he caught my eye. The other man, who I did not know, was staring at Spanish Pete through the wheelhouse window with a grim look on his face. When they jumped off, Scotty tied up the bowline but the stern man was not quick enough so the vessel swung out a bit. A loaded vessel and an ebb tide made it very difficult to pull the stern into the dock, so Pete had to jump and help the man on the stern pull the back of the boat into the dock. When Pete tied up the stern line, I could already see that he was talking to himself.

Pete stalked over to the cab of my truck and all he could keep repeating was "You see what kind of crews I've got," while he flapped his arms up and down like he was going to take off. One of the Chinese buyers made the mistake of climbing aboard and starting to take the hatch cover off. Pete jumped aboard and kicked the man in the rear end so he flew halfway across the hatch, and then he ordered him off the boat.

The buyers stood in silence as Pete dictated the prices and got his beam scale out onto the deck. He ordered the crew to take off the hatch covers so they could begin unloading. I thought it was time to leave, so as soon as Pete removed his hand from the truck window frame I said so long to Scotty and drove off. When Pete got arrogant to people, he became a thoroughly unpleasant man. I had witnessed so many of Pete's tantrums, I seldom hung around long.

Pete had good fish and his customers made money selling his catch so they took his abuse in absolute silence. Later, Scotty told me that Pete shut up when he and the other crewman threatened to leave and let him unload the fish by himself. He was all shook up so he muttered loudly to himself to vent his anger. Scotty said that Pete was so crabby that none of the buyers bothered daring to dispute or even check his weights. Pete would never have cheated anyone. In fact, he gave good weight to his customers, but on bad days he ignored standard business conventions. Pete divided his catch according to the quotas he assigned each customer. The peddlers were excited by the quality of his fish and they fought and argued over the supply. But when they heard Pete muttering and observed his menacing posture, the peddlers remained calm. They accepted his abuse as a cost of doing business.

Bill Faulkner was an old standby for Spanish Pete. He worked with Pete for three years before the Second World War. He was the only crewman who seemed able to stand the strain of working with Pete. Spanish Pete had no family and he was a glutton for work. Bill Faulkner, quick to catch on to Pete's fishing methods, became his right-hand man. When Bill went off to war it was rumoured that Spanish Pete banked a deckhand's share with an accountant for Bill. I'm sure that was the case. Spanish Pete treated Bill like a son. After I came back from the war, old timers told me that Pete talked about Bill constantly and missed him terribly. He could hardly wait for him to come back.

Spanish Pete had a new vessel built to his specifications for bottom trawling. It was launched shortly before the Pearl Harbor debacle and the federal government conscripted Pete's new boat, *Tordo,* for use by the gumboot navy to service our Pacific coast with supplies to the military situated in various areas. There was worry that the Japanese were going to attack on our coast.

Pete was horrified but he had no choice but to go along with the war effort. He rigged up another older vessel that he was able to charter for his fishery. This leaking old tub, unsuitable for government work, delivered a lot of fish for Pete. When the war ended, Bill Faulkner came back and went back on the ocean in the older vessel while Spanish Pete fished on his *Tordo*, which was released from government service. Pete was rejuvenated when he got Bill back. Bill was the son Pete never had and he looked out for the old man's interests. Most people were touched that an irascible old bachelor like Pete would adopt a young man like Bill and pretty well give him all the attention and privileges one might grant a natural child.

Pete was making fantastic catches with his new vessel. Dogfish livers brought anywhere from forty cents per pound to six dollars per pound. Pete was making one trip a week that brought him twelve to twenty thousand dollars gross. His boat share was whatever he took and there was still a big payday for each of his crewmen. If the crew took in one thousand to fifteen hundred dollars per week they were not going to question the wild man about the split. Bill remained with Pete regardless of the changes Pete made to his three- or four-men crews. Pete drove both the crews on either vessel. They made a lot of money but they knew Pete. There were many unpleasant voyages, especially on the *Tordo*. This created a cloud that hovered over the vessel, making it obvious to outsiders that weird things went on.

One of Pete's crew was from Newfoundland. He was a quiet fellow who hardly spoke and kept aloof from the other crew. It was said that he had been in a coal mine explosion a few years earlier. His face showed the ravages and he carried the dark blue tattoo marks of coal dust. He rarely joined the conversation but acknowledged comments with a nod of the head or a smile. His fellow crew said he was a nice fellow who worked hard and jumped at doing any extra tasks that might come up during a trip. He lived with a woman who had two teenaged girls whom he adored and considered as his own. He couldn't wait to get off the *Tordo* at the end of a trip and head home to his house with a bag of fresh fish fillets he cut while travelling home from the fishing grounds. It was the same each trip. He took home all his pay, the fish and his laundry.

On one trip they had good fishing and quickly filled the *Tordo* with dressed ling cod, rocky sole, brill sole and red rock fish, so they left the fishing grounds ahead of schedule to arrive in Vancouver on a Thursday instead of Friday. When the Newfie arrived at his home he found a man in bed with his beloved. There were harsh words spoken and the woman ordered him out of the house. He departed from his own house without any of his possessions. Not even a change of clothes. He returned to the *Tordo* to get over the shock and weigh his options. He decided to go back to reason with his girlfriend. Unfortunately, he took a hammer and a heavy sharp knife used for butchering ling cod. The affair ended with him almost beating the new boyfriend to death with the hammer and cutting the unfaithful woman's throat. He returned to the *Tordo* to wait for the police.

They sent a squad of policemen to the waterfront in the early morning hours to apprehend the despondent killer. Spanish Pete, asleep in his bunk, had no knowledge of the events of the day until eight policeman crowded into his cabin with their flashlights. The Newfie went peaceably without resisting to the police station. Spanish Pete came to talk with Father. He told him that he knew the Newfie was not to be trifled with. He felt lucky that he had kept his peace with the gent or he might have had his own throat cut. However, he was devastated at the loss of such an excellent crewman.

The Newfie was sentenced to hang, but after an appeal and the whole sad story came to light, his sentence was commuted to life in prison. Boyd Shannon got him out of jail ten years later, on religious grounds, and gave him a job in his cannery. He worked six weeks for Boyd and then he vanished from our scene for good.

Finally, Spanish Pete decided that he would retire and allow Bill Faulkner to fish on the *Tordo*. This new business arrangement allowed Pete to stay ashore and relax a little, and Bill, the chosen one, would eventually take over. Pete put a lot of thought into his affairs and now he was going to reward Bill for all his years of service by setting him up to be his successor.

However, unlike Pete, Bill was not a driver who worked the crew twelve to fifteen hours a day on the fishing grounds. Compared to Spanish Pete, Bill Faulkner's catches were just average. This burned the old Spaniard because he was a highliner who was used to bringing home the *Tordo* filled to the hatch cover with five- or ten-thousand-pound deck-loads from the last drag. Sometimes these fish were less than twelve hours old.

Pete walked around the wharf muttering that Bill was in again with only three quarters of a load, while the highliners showed up with full loads. Pete was a millionaire who didn't need the money but he couldn't stand it when the *Tordo* made trip after trip with less than a full load. As the owner of the *Tordo,* Pete received the owner's share. Bill knew that Pete was rich and he mistakenly thought he could work at his own pace with a more relaxed crew. Bill had inherited Pete's old crew. They didn't exactly belong to the Spanish Pete fan club. They were making less money than when Pete was in charge, but everyone got along in a far less strenuous working atmosphere. They found it difficult to forget the abuse and ridicule that Pete had heaped on them. They saw him as an old timer who had already had his day in the sun. They did not encourage him to come down to work on the gear and break bread with them. In fact, they wouldn't even have a coffee with him. This did not stop Spanish Pete from coming to work on the net and gear after every trip regardless of how cool the reception. It was Pete's vessel and his gear.

Bill refused to spend any of his own money on the upkeep of the *Tordo*, and Pete did not want to take the money out of his share. They still fished with the old-style beam that stuck out from the side of the vessel when the net was fishing, while all the highliners had converted to fishing with a drum fastened to the deck at the stern. With a drum, fishing was more efficient. The net could be hauled in quicker and the fish dumped more easily. Everybody had converted to fishing with a spool fastened at the stern of the boat to reel in the lines and net, except for old Pete and his *Tordo.*

It wasn't Bill's boat so he was wasn't going to spend the fifteen to twenty thousand dollars it would cost to convert the vessel to fish with modern gear. So it came to pass, with Bill bringing in much less fish, that Pete decided in a moment of pique to fire Bill and two of the crewman. He hired two new green crewmen and took the *Tordo* fishing with himself back in the wheelhouse. Ten days later the old man returned with less than a quarter of a load. He had lost the net, broken the beam and damaged the rigging. When the *Tordo* touched the dock, the new crewmen were gone.

This was about the end of any further dialogue between Bill Faulkner and the old Spaniard. Bill had no trouble getting a job as a crew member on one of the highliners. It wasn't long before people were offering Bill the chance to be a skipper again. When I saw Bill, I told him it was foolish to completely ignore Spanish Pete. It was obvious Pete's days on the water were over. I said, "Jeezuz, Bill, you fished with him for twenty-five years and I know damn well that old Pete has a soft spot in his heart for you. He has barrels of money and no living relatives. If you make peace with him, I'm sure you could talk him into the refit for modern gear. Besides, he owes you for all the years you put up with his crap." In my mind I figured that old Spanish Pete would probably leave the *Tordo* to Bill in his will. I mean, what else would he do? Bill Faulkner was like a son to Pete.

I did not know at that time that Spanish Pete had a daughter with one of his old Spanish girlfriends. When he died, he left her the *Tordo*, one of his houses and two hundred thousand dollars cash. He left two hundred thousand dollars to a couple who always came to pick him up when the *Tordo* came into port. He left another few hundred thousand to others from his past. He also left two houses to two old girlfriends.

He did not leave one single dollar to Bill Faulkner. Even though they were not on good terms, everyone figured Bill would at least get the *Tordo*. Nobody could really understand what the problem was between the two of them. Bill was like the son who didn't always get along with his father but managed to work for him for most of his life.

People who knew Spanish Pete well were completely surprised

when Bill was left out of the will. Spanish Pete never said a word about it nor did he speak harshly of Bill. Bill in return never spoke harshly of Pete. When asked about the breakup, all that Bill would do was smile. He didn't want to talk about it. Bill was really a quiet person who abhorred conflict. During the years he was with Spanish Pete, Bill had a calming effect on Pete. He surely worked hard enough in Pete's employ, and he should have been treated better by Pete.

Eventually, Bill took on one of B.C. Packers' large trawlers and he never looked back. He made a good living, and when I passed the time with him when he came down to Campbell Avenue to see old friends he always spoke well of Spanish Pete. Once in a candid moment he told me that he never expected Pete to leave him anything. His friendship with Pete was about something else. Personally, I thought Bill Faulkner was more of a man than Pete. I've never understood how Spanish Pete, with all his money and property available to be left to his daughter and friends, could have failed to do the right thing and leave the *Tordo* to the man he treated and mistreated like a son.

THE LUTAFISH EATERS

The "Wild Bunch" were a group of young men of Icelandic extraction who came to the West Coast to seek employment in the fishing industry and ended up working for years on Campbell Avenue fish dock. They earned the moniker Wild Bunch from their peers on the waterfront because of their penchant for hard work and hard partying.

They were descendants of Icelandic emigrants who settled in Manitoba before and after the beginning of the last century. Historically, many Icelanders settled around Lake Winnipegosis. They fished that huge lake for a variety of freshwater fish that included whitefish, lake trout, pickerel, northern pike and goldeye. They fished from small boats in the summer and through thick sheets of ice in the winter. Low fish prices and the extremes of weather drove some of the younger men westward where they continued working in the fishing industry.

Dory Strumphert came west after the stock market crash in 1929. Soon after arriving he brought out a fellow Manitoban called Minty who had a peg leg. Somebody thought his leg probably froze in one of those bad Manitoba winters. Together, Dory and Minty started up the Reliance Fish Company. They imported a labour force of Icelanders from the buffalo province to work in their fish plant. Forty below temperatures in winter, blackflies and mosquitoes in summer combined with a deepening Depression aided their recruitment. One of the new arrivals told me he slept with his horse to keep warm in winter when he was commercial net fishing through the ice on Lake Winnipegosis. Sun-dried fish in summer and freeze-dried fish in winter along with wild game and root crops were the staples of the diet of the times. Fishing for freshwater fish was a tough way to make a living under primitive social conditions. Nobody had heard of welfare, relief, let alone old-age pensions. When "Bennett Buggies" were in style, mere survival was a difficult proposition. It is a credit to their character that a community of hardy Icelandic stock remains to this day deeply rooted in Manitoba. The boys who came west and entered the fish business were as tough a group of men as could be assembled in one place.

Dory and his company of compatriots flourished in the West Coast climate, processing fish six days a week on Campbell Avenue. The help hit the filleting tables at seven a.m. They threw their fish up onto tables from what must have seemed like an endless pile on the cement floor. That was the only time they put down their knives for a change of pace until the whistle blew at twelve noon. Coffee breaks were unheard of. These came into vogue later, a perk unions brought in during the war years when a new workforce was taking over. At one p.m. the Wild Bunch went at it again and did not put down their tools again until four p.m. so that they could begin cleaning up the plant. By five p.m., they were either upstairs cooking their own food, which largely consisted of fish, or they ate at one of the local cafés, buying their evening meal for twenty-five cents. These men worked for seven or eight dollars per week and they were in no mood to throw around what little money they had in their pockets. In the evenings they sat around playing cards or planning how they were going to escape the poverty that was making slaves out of them. By nine p.m., they were bedded down or resting in suitable areas available in the fish plant. In winter, a number of them, anxious to stay warm, slept in the sawdust bin adjacent to the smokehouse. The terrible times produced a superior, hardy man who endured awful conditions in order to try and get ahead.

Saturday night was whoop-it-up time in the Reliance plant. A few cases of beer and a half-dozen bottles of cheap hard liquor were purchased, and a bevy of local girls arrived to provide the entertainment. Then the boys were on their own until they ran out of gas. The partying was usually pretty wild and the boys often got out of control. However, they kept it among themselves. Nobody ever got seriously hurt and the police were never in attendance.

On Monday morning, for better or worse, all of them were back at the tables cutting codfish. By this time, most of them had recovered from their partying ordeal. The odd character who opted for a two-day bender was looking frazzled but none of them ever missed a day of work. They couldn't afford to. Minty and Dory kept production at a high level. Slackers need not apply. Any grudges left over from Saturday night's debacle would be iced until next time.

Lutafish is a national dish for many Scandinavian peoples. This delicacy consists of a product made from codfish. The whole fish is gutted and split open butterfly style with the backbone removed so it can be dry-salted. It remains in the salt until it is cured and then it is placed in a liquid lye solution for further curing. Finally, it is repeatedly soaked and washed in fresh water to remove all the lye and salt. This causes the flesh of the cod to puff up and swell like a sponge. Lutafish is to Nordic people what haggis is to Scotsmen. The Icelanders working for Reliance put the stuff up each year for various Christmas celebrations.

From my observations, it went well with good rye bread and plenty of any kind of whisky. One winter the boys got careless and when they broke out the lutafish all the lye had not been soaked out of the salt cod. Well, the whoop-up commenced and they began feasting on their favorite delicacy while washing it down liberally with firewater. Soon stomach cramps were putting a damper on the festivities. The lye left in the lutafish was trying to burn holes in their stomachs. Before long someone had the good sense to call for an ambulance. One by one as they were stricken with pain they were hauled off to hospital to have their stomachs pumped out. None of them suffered any serious side effects and after the holiday season they were all able to resume cutting fish. They were a tough, happy young bunch who will never be duplicated.

When the Depression began to ease towards the end of the thirties, conditions improved for all of us, including the Wild Bunch working in the Reliance plant. Wages increased to the point where they were able to afford their own places so they no longer lived in the fish plant. However, working conditions still remained primitive on the waterfront. Dory's younger brother Julie, who was a giant of a man, set the pace in the fish plant. A slacker or a weakling had no chance to survive even a day in his company. Julie also acted to suppress any unrest or union activities that might get a toehold in their plant. The Wild Bunch worked like a well-conditioned machine. Most of them stayed with the company during the war years, but things began to change when it ended. Two of the Wild Bunch came to work for our company, which had the union, and with it better working conditions and benefits. Others gradually left as they found better opportunities elsewhere.

Gunnar Stevenson, who chewed a clove of garlic each day directly after lunch, was a master of his craft, and he came over to Van Shell and became foreman of our filleting operation for several decades. Standing at the metal table on his wooden pallet wearing a long black rubber apron, Gunnar set the pace, while managing to keep the peace among our multicultural filleting crew of Icelanders, Japanese, Yugoslavians and aboriginals. In the fish plants the filleters were specialists who made top dollar. Our filleting room was governed by provisions negotiated between management and the United Fishermen and Shoreworkers Union. There were strict rules concerning shifts and working conditions. Filleters called into work were guaranteed at least four hours' pay, even if they were sent home early. They received high hourly wage rates with generous provisions for overtime. Usually, the non-union companies employed a system of piecework and avoided paying benefits to their workforce. In our plant, the filleters were generally a high-strung group of free thinkers with a pecking order that rivalled opera. Gunnar was the fastest knife in the west, taking on all comers. He had strong opinions and the standards were set by his example.

By the mid-sixties the original Wild Bunch had dispersed and Minty had retired. Near the end of the decade, Dory Strumphert sold the business and also retired. Reliance continued in business for some years after that under two regimes of new ownership. Poor management and indifferent workers eventually put the company into bankruptcy.

Vancouver Shellfish and Reliance were spirited competitors, but we got along well with the Wild Bunch. Julie was a bit sullen at times but Dory never failed to offer a cheerful greeting when a chance meeting occurred. He was about the same age as my father, so I always remained respectful when dealing with him. I had a chance meeting with Dory about fifteen years after he had retired. I hailed him in a friendly manner but he seemed not to know me. I was astonished since we had rubbed shoulders for thirty years. I will never know if a burning resentment produced an obvious snub or if his mental faculties had deteriorated. In any case, he merely walked away, ignoring my presence. Throughout the years I kept in touch with many of the Wild Bunch. We reminisced and they kept me abreast of all their news. They were rock-solid men who were peaceful and industrious in all their endeavours.

THE BACKMAN BOYS

The Backman bunch, as I knew them in 1935, were three strapping brothers and a sister, Lena, who were commanded by a little man with one eye. They were a Finnish family who fished for salmon and ling cod in the Gulf of Georgia. Probably one thousand fishermen worked at catching live cod in the Gulf of Georgia. Another fifteen hundred fishermen trolled for salmon. About a third of the salmon trollers hand-trolled from salmon skiffs that were especially built for that purpose. They were double ended to make them easier to row. About four million pounds of live cod was landed each year at Campbell Avenue. More was landed in Victoria and other towns. The Backmans from the Pender Harbour area, if not the best, were certainly in the top five percent of the live cod fishermen on the coast.

The old man was a quiet man but even when he was calm he had the look of an eagle about him. When angered he was as savage as any grizzly bear. The boys never argued or talked back to their old man when he was setting down the law. Old Backman had trouble controlling the boys when they came to town to sell their fish and had money in their pockets. Each son had his thirty-five-foot fishing boat fitted with live wells to hold their catch. The family pooled their resources, travelling and fishing together. Their sister Lena, a sweet girl, had learned to be a survivor in order to keep up with the wild antics of her brothers. They came to town twice a month to deliver their fish. When they came in, the four boats swept through the First Narrows like a navel squadron. The old man's boat was always out front like a flagship leading the way. There were no radios on small vessels in those days, so the Backman tribe communicated by screaming loudly at one another and by hand signals.

They all tied up one behind the other at the slip at Campbell Avenue, and the old man departed up the dock to negotiate prices for the fish in all four boats. When he returned they clustered around him for a few minutes discussing business and getting their orders. Hatches were uncovered and live ling cod were brailed from live wells onto the dock for slaughter. Live cod were quickly decapitated and dressed, the livers and heads saved and the innards thrown overboard into the harbour. They worked together like one machine so that in less than two hours each man's catch, weighing in at approximately fifteen hundred pounds, was ready to be carted up the dock and weighed. They received seven cents per pound for fish in the six- to twelve-pound range, six cents per pound for fish over twelve pounds and four cents per pound for four- to six-pound fish. Cod livers, averaging about three pounds per hundred pounds of cod, were worth about one dollar per pound, which came to a tidy sum, considering the amount of fish they brought in. Ling cod heads were given away to other fishermen who cut out the cheeks or used them for fish chowder.

During this era, all codfish delivered for sale in Vancouver had to be killed on the grounds and iced immediately or held in flooded live wells to be slaughtered on delivery at the packer or on arrival at the wharf in town. Nobody would buy or even think about eating a fish that was delivered dead in the round. If a round fish was overlooked and turned up in a load of dressed fish, it was pitched into the garbage bin.

There is a huge difference in quality between fish that is cleaned on the grounds, washed in sea water and properly iced and fish that is dumped by the ton in the round into chilled sea water or iced in the round. Some vessels remained on the grounds for ten days or longer, so the stomach contents dissolved with the intestines before the catch could be processed. Loads of round fish that came in were routinely dispatched to reduction plants to become meal or food for animals.

They were not considered fit for human consumption.

Once the ling cod was sold, the Backman boys washed down their vessels and spruced themselves up in a hurry for the trip downtown. The old man counted out the boys' cash while giving them a stern lecture about staying out of trouble. When he finished his speech they bolted up the dock and headed for the bright lights. The old man stayed behind to guard their boats while the boys were gone. He could be observed wandering around on the float, checking tie-up lines and making repairs. Other fishermen stopped by to swap stories, but generally the old man stayed by himself waiting for their return.

The next morning the old man was up at daybreak, as was the habit of his life. He had ordered the boys to be back at their vessels before first light but often he was still alone waiting their return. By evening his mood had turned sour and he was pacing up and down the wharf glaring from his one good eye. The other uncovered eyeless socket gave him a fierce wild appearance that became positively frightening when he glowered and fretted about their whereabouts. By the second morning, usually at least one of the boys had come back to the dock. The old man's ravings could be heard echoing from the water. Soon the offender was sent off to find his brothers. This was not an exact science, and sometimes the one dispatched to find the others would go back on a bender and complicate the issue. When Lena arrived to visit her father, it often became her job to go downtown and round up the boys. Woe be it to them if the old man had to go and bail them out of the slammer. When the boys saw Lena, they knew it was time to give it up and head back to their vessels before the old man showed up in person.

By the end of the third day, the brothers, rounded up one at a time, were assembled before him in the various states of their hangovers. The old man paced in front of them raging like a mad bear, shaking and stammering, spit flying from his lips as he cursed and raved, waving his arms and poking his bony finger into their faces. It finally ceased when he ran out of breath and his energy had been all used up. Occasionally, one of the boys would be AWOL for a week or more and then the old man went on the rampage. When the offender arrived sheepishly at the wharf he received a barrage of profanity. The boys took their tongue lashing in silence. When it was over, all was forgotten, and they returned to being a loving family.

Once assembled they departed from Campbell Avenue wharf at first light. The old man as usual led the way and the boys travelled along behind in a kind of flotilla. They vanished in the distance and the dock seemed empty and dull without the sound of his voice barking out orders like an admiral ruling the fleet. The Backmans were good people: they worked hard, made money and tried like hell to spend it, despite the old man's protecting ways.

One of the Backman boys, who tended to party harder than the rest, if that was possible, discovered a cod reef just outside the First Narrows of Vancouver Harbour. At that particular spot he hauled out one hundred and fifty to two hundred and fifty pounds of cod per day. This son decided to break with family tradition. He saw no need to journey further out to the Gulf of Georgia when he could catch all he needed at this spot. The old eagle could do nothing with him, so he and the other brothers left him and proceeded out into the Gulf. For more than two weeks this son landed each afternoon to sell his fish and head downtown to spend the money. He rolled back in just before daybreak and set out for another day's work.

During the bottom of the thirties, a butcher made about ten dollars a week, so ten or fifteen dollars per day was a lot of money. A twenty-six-ounce bottle of whisky cost about two dollars and fifty cents, rooms were cheap, ladies of the night were relatively inexpensive, and this son was maximizing his partying. Everyone at Campbell Avenue wondered how long he could keep up the pace. Fortunately for him, the cod on those small isolated reefs played out in about twenty days. The weary young man, all out of money, departed to join his kin on richer grounds. He was welcomed back into the fold with open arms and everything in the family returned to normal.

LITTLENECKS

In the 1930s, Vancouver Shellfish and Fish Company and the B.C. Clam Company, owned by the Hynek family, were competing fiercely in exporting littleneck clams from British Columbia to the U.S. market. There was a huge market for clams in the United States during the months of June, July, August and September. Clams spawned in the summer months, and the U.S. regulations closed down domestic clam digging during those months. Canadians were allowed to dig clams in the summer but were forbidden to dig them in January and February when the clams were in their best condition. It all made no sense. Undoubtedly palms were greased considerably and constantly to keep this arrangement in place. We also had an open crab season in May, June, July and August, when the crabs were in their worst condition, moulting from their shells. The American season was closed at this time of the year. Canadian companies shipped cooked crabs to the United States on a daily basis during these months. The product was not very good, but anything sells when there is a shortage, and the U.S. customers wanted them badly.

American buyers played one company against the next in order to try to keep the prices down. The Haines Oyster Company was the largest buyer in Seattle. Waterfront and Whiz Fish were smaller buyers, as were two or three other companies. There were also buyers in Portland and in Los Angeles. The most gentlemanly buyer was Mr. Brenner from the Olympia Oyster Company in Olympia, Washington. He was a square shooter who never demanded credit or made deductions from any shipment.

Haines Oyster Company took about one hundred and fifty eighty-pound boxes of clams a couple of times each week and sometimes smaller shipments in between. The clams were all washed and packed in eighty-pound wooden boxes with the lids nailed down. The principals in Haines Oyster Company were hard nuts who negotiated a tough price for the season and made deductions on a weekly basis with a large deduction each year coming from the last shipment of the season. Buyers in Portland and Los Angeles took no deductions from their shipments. The smaller buyers in Washington State also made deductions, but they were insignificant compared to the Haines Oyster Company, which had muscles in the marketplace. Haines ripped us off as often as they could get away with, which was most of the time because we needed their business.

When Mr. Brenner, a blocky man with a ruddy face who wore a white Panama straw hat, appeared on the scene, buying for the Olympia Oyster Company, things improved. Suddenly Olympia was buying more clams from us than Haines who we were still supplying. Best of all, Brenner made no deductions. In fact, Brenner complimented us on the quality of our clams and never complained when we shipped him more boxes of clams than he ordered. When Haines Oyster Company tried to make deductions, we cut off the supply and told them they would only resume in the future without deductions. The Olympia Oyster Company were interested in increasing their allotment and this lever gave us the opportunity to put it to Haines and the other con artists. Within a short time, deductions were unheard of and the trade became lucrative.

Many clams came from the Gulf Islands. Our clam camp was situated in False Narrows about fifteen miles from Nanaimo. The clams were all shipped in eighty-pound wooden boxes via CPR ferry to Vancouver. From Vancouver the clams travelled via Great Northern Railway each day to various locations in the United States. Leaving at nine p.m., the clams were in Seattle by midnight and unloaded by eight o'clock in the morning. Clams arrived in Olympia and Portland later the same day, and in Los Angeles the following morning. Our camp in the False Narrows consisted of a cookhouse, a bunkhouse, and a large float for measuring and boxing clams with a shed on it that held pre-cut box lumber to make several thousand boxes. The shed also stored nails, hammers, spare clam forks, thousands of jute bags and rain gear.

Clams were dug on the beaches into wire baskets that held forty-five pounds. Each filled basket was dipped and shaken in sea water to remove sand and then dumped into jute bags so they were clean with no foreign objects included. The average digger could fill ten to twelve baskets with littleneck clams each day during a tide. Nobody could beat Frank Latta when it came to digging littleneck clams. He always topped the next best digger by three or four baskets.

When I went to the camp with the payroll and shipping instructions for the next two weeks, I always stayed for a couple of days to join in the clam digging. I wanted to make a decent impression, so I dug like hell trying to at least be within a basket of the best diggers. So I decided my only hope was to dig like a machine if I hoped to keep up. As soon as we hit the beach I quickly scouted a good location that was not previously dug and went to work. For four hours I turned over the sand pebble and broken shell beach, picking up six to twelve clams every time the fork turned over in the mixed gravel ground. I sweltered in the burning sun. I rushed to the water's edge to wash each basket of clams, and my racks of littlenecks mounted as I toiled at the task. I never chanced a look to see how Frank was doing. In fact, I couldn't seen him anywhere around. This was not unusual, as the best diggers always kept to themselves, away from other diggers. At last the tide was rising quickly to cover the clam flats and it was time to load our goods and transport our sacks of clams to the packer boat. It took several trips with fourteen-foot boats to get all the clams onto the packer before making the trip to our clam camp. Each digger's sacks were kept in a separate pile so they could be identified at the camp where payment was made.

I waited for Frank to mention how many sacks he had dug but he remained silent on the issue. Finally I couldn't stand it so I asked him. Twenty-three baskets, he answered. I stood with my mouth open when he told me, because that meant he had dug more than a thousand pounds of clams in just over four hours. "How many did you dig?" he asked with a sly grin.

I was deflated like a balloon when I blurted out, "Seventeen."

He knew that I was trying to be a big shot when really I was an upstart. "Never mind," he said, "you'll do better next time."

I knew I was certainly not destined to be in his class. I resigned myself to trying to be better than the average for the day. Frank, lean and tough with huge hands, was truly a digging machine of a man.

A top digger at our camp in the Depression days could earn twelve to fifteen dollars a day, but he had to work without letup to do it. This was more than the best fallers were making in the big logging camps and a lot less hazardous. A good average digger could earn seven to ten dollars a day. Some men and a few Japanese women treated clam digging as part-time work and made five dollars a day. The Japanese diggers were not paid cash but were issued weight slips. The payment to them for the clams they dug was made by the Japanese agent at their settlement. Every day he arrived when the packer brought the workers in from the grounds. He wore jodhpurs, carried a cane and was accompanied by his brace of large German shepherds. He collected the weight slips and an envelope with the cash and then paid each Japanese digger for the day's work. He raked off twenty percent of each digger's total for his services. When the diggers were standing around waiting for their settlement, he occasionally stopped to berate one of them for low productivity.

Twenty-five diggers would produce at least fifteen thousand pounds of clams in a shift. One hundred to one hundred and fifty shipping boxes would be filled immediately. Any surplus was dumped into rafts so a supply could be built up for shipments when there was no tide. These rafts held about twenty tons of clams. The rafts were constructed upside down. Planks were fastened to ends of each float with long drift bolts. Two-by-fours were nailed across the logs to form the bottom. The logs in the bottom of a raft were sixteen to eighteen inches in diameter. The rafts were well nailed and were bolted together to prevent them from coming apart. As the clams were dumped into the raft, they sank down in the water so that they were always covered with sea water. This kept seabirds from having a feast. To trim the raft over, many stones were piled on one side of the raft to weigh it down below water level. A line was fastened to the other side and a packer pulling hard on this line flipped the raft right side up.

Clams would keep up to twenty days in the rafts in good condition. Longer than that, some would die and have to be culled out so they didn't contaminate the others. Clams need to be kept out of sea water for six or eight hours and kept in sea water eight to twelve hours to duplicate the tidal conditions on the beach. If clams are kept submerged they die in about three weeks. Clams in jute bags, if they are kept submerged too long, will contaminate themselves with their own waste. After about seven days they begin to die off. If clams in jute sacks are refreshed each day with salt water they will keep longer but never as long as they could be kept in the rafts. Clams kept in modern nylon bags, refreshed in sea water, keep longer than they could have been kept in rafts in the old days. Oddly enough, clams dug high up on the beach and longer out of water on low tides kept longer than clams dug lower on the beach near zero tide. Clams that were exposed for little more than one hour at low tide died more quickly when out of water, lasting five or six days.

Everyone but the cook helped box the clams. They had to be aboard the CPR vessel by five p.m. for the trip to Vancouver and U.S. points south. Frequently the boat sailed late to accommodate the shipments of clams. The clam business was a big deal for the CPR during the Depression. The ferry crew were there, blasting the whistle at us as our truck approached at a mad clip, waiting to help get the clams aboard when we were running behind schedule. Loading the boxes by hand onto the ferry took fifteen minutes, then the ferry left, impatient to make up for lost time.

If one of the packers had clams on board for our company, I would run the truck down on the floating driveway at Campbell Avenue to load them and truck them back up to the plant. The five to fifteen thousand pounds of clams were carefully stashed in one corner and a few shovels of ice were pitched over them to keep them cool. Two to three thousand pounds of clams would be left on the truck for delivery in town to the various establishments we sold clams to on a daily basis. The Only Fish and Oyster Café on Hastings took up to eight hundred pounds on a holiday weekend, especially when the loggers were all in town for the fire season in summer or if the snow drove them from the woods in winter. The Only took at least three hundred pounds per day in slack periods. The Fish and Oyster Bar on Granville Street also used a lot of clams each day and at least six gallons of shucked oyster meat to go with them, plus five hundred to one thousand pounds of large ling cod (fish twelve pounds up to forty pounds each). The Fish and Oyster Bar used three to four thousand pounds of large cod on holiday weekends. The Fish and Oyster Bar was a gold mine — it certainly sold more fish than any other restaurant in Vancouver to this day. The only exception might have been the Devonshire Hotel restaurant. No establishment today even comes close to using fifteen percent of what each of these two customers took.

My usual job was delivering fifteen hundred pounds of clams every day to various restaurants and hotels in Vancouver. George Hynek had the same job working for his family's B.C. Clam Company. We raced through the city in the morning when it was still dark attempting to reach the best customers, who generally took one hundred and fifty to two hundred pounds of clams every day. George sold about the same amount of clams as I did each day. In fact, we were fierce friendly competitors who had breakfast each morning together at one of the places that bought clams from us. At breakfast we took turns laughing at one another, depending on who got waxed that day. This friendly competition carried on until the war brought it to an end. Most of the good customers bought half their clams from each of us.

George and I had a gentleman's agreement, more or less, when we sold clams in Vancouver. There were three Chinese peddlers who sold clams out of a rickshaw-type wagon to customers who bought less than fifty pounds of clams. George and I never sold to any place that took less than fifty pounds. We left that business to the three peddlers. I can't swear that neither of us bull-fudged now and then, but we were both smart enough not to begin a turf war or a price war that would, to our detriment, benefit the customers.

One peddler, Jung Kee, who favoured George, always bought a few pounds more from him than he did from me. I was determined to keep my share of the business, so whatever George left in this man's shack, I duplicated. Well the poor guy was getting more clams than he could sell. One day I arrived at the shack and a padlock was on the gate with a note pinned to it that read, "No clams today." I wondered if George had delivered clams to him that day, so I decided to take a look. I climbed the six-foot fence around the shack and discovered George had delivered three hundred pounds of clams that day and left his bill on the top sack of clams.

Being a super salesman I hoisted three hundred pounds of clams over the fence, one sack at a time and gently dropped them so as not to break any shells. I then climbed over and stacked them alongside George's pile and left my bill on the top bag. A week later I showed up there and again a note greeted me with "No clams today."

This time there was one strand of barbed wire stretched across the top of the fence. One strand of barbed wire never stopped a super salesman, so I climbed over the fence to take a look to see if George had delivered clams. Sure enough, two hundred and fifty pounds of clams were stacked there with George's bill on top of them. Again, I hoisted two hundred and fifty pounds of clams over that fence and deposited them alongside George's goods with my bill on them. Well, when Jung Kee saw that, he put three strands of barbed wire up, and I still delivered my share of clams into his shack.

Finally, he gave up. He was waiting for me when I arrived with a sly grin on his face. He asked me to show him how I got the clams over the fences, so I did. I pulled the pickup as close as possible to the fence, stacked the sacks of clams right up and then got my hook and rope out. I stood on the cab as I hooked each sack in turn and dropped them gently over the fence. Then I shook the hook free of the sack and proceeded to repeat the manoeuvre. Climbing the fence was a breeze for me. I had had plenty of experience climbing the barbed wire fence at the PNE.

Jung Kee laughed out loud and looked me over with twinkling eyes. He pulled his hand out of his pocket and held out a key to me. "No clams next week," he said. "One week you and one week George. Okay? I let you know how much." I nodded that I understood. He was giving me half the business.

George asked me out for breakfast. He asked me how I managed to win Jung Kee over. "Easy, George," I said, "I just charmed the old guy into giving me half of his business." I know George never believed me, but then I never found out what he did in his attempt to get all the Jung Kee's business, so we were even.

When George beat me to a good customer, he gave me a big laugh. I repaid the horse laugh when I got ahead of him. We called a truce now and then and devoured pancakes, bacon and eggs with toast for twenty cents. Pancakes with coffee was fifteen cents or less. Every restaurant had clam chowder and clam nectar on the menu. No matter what the soup offerings were, clam chowder was a constant. It was in demand and restaurants served it by the gallon. The loggers who moved into the city during the fire season or during the idle winter months were big business. When they had five month's wages in their pockets they had a burning thirst, a desire for female companions and a yen for good chowder. Clam nectar was the remedy for a good hangover and those gents drank it by the barrel.

Father and old Hynek finally decided to join forces. From then on, for a number of years, our company financed the venture and took care of the paperwork. My brother Ed spent a summer or two at the False Narrows camp taking care of our business while he was a university student. For the most part the Hynek family took care of the operation on the grounds and it all worked out. This joint venture put the advantage completely in our court regarding deductions by American buyers, and they could no longer play games trying to start a price war. Another advantage of our merger was that mills competed for the contract to produce box lumber. In the Depression, fifteen to twenty thousand boxes at forty-five cents each was a good order. The lumber had to be free of knots, cracks and warpage. Most years a mill in Vernon, B.C., got the business because they supplied the cleanest boards.

However, conditions were starting to change. The Japanese were removed and sent to camps in the interior of the country. Diggers quit to join the army or to take up employment in shipyards or government departments. Digging clams was hard labour in all kinds of weather conditions and it was piecework, paying one and a half cents per pound. Unemployed people took to it as a lifeline, but eventually for lack of diggers the joint venture fell apart. Both companies still dabbled in the clam business, but there were more lucrative opportunities in the fish business that took a lot less effort. So the clam business went into decline.

George Hynek and I remained friends until he died of cancer in 1965. He worked for years for Edward Lippset, the largest supplier of fishing nets, trolling gear, rope, hardware and other supplies to the fishing industry. George's brother Jerry passed away a couple of years before George. Ed and I are among the last veterans left over from the clam wars in the thirties. Alice, Elsie and Walter Hynek are still living. Walter, like my brother John, was too young to participate in that business. The two Hynek girls might have worked for a time in the cookhouse. The Hyneks were hard-working people. Jerry Hynek could match Frank Latta on the clam beach and even managed to beat him fifty percent of the time. That was a feat, because he was the only man on the coast I knew who could make that claim.

In the heyday of the clam business, nobody would buy a manila clam, also known as Japanese littlenecks. These clams came into British Columbia with the Japanese oyster seed that was imported to seed our oyster farms. Manila clams were considered a parasite because the shell was dark, the meat was dark and orange-coloured, and they had much weaker nectar. The trade in Canada and the United States wanted our native littleneck clam, with its white or light brown shell, white meat and a strong clam nectar. Native littlenecks take twice as long to open their shells when they are steamed. Today chefs in the high-speed restaurants favour the manila clam, which opens almost instantly in boiling water. The meat in manila clams is easier to free from the shell. Nobody will ever convince me that the manila clam is even close to the native littleneck for taste and quality and strength of nectar. Unfortunately, the manila clams are interbred with our native clams and in the end will completely replace our own native species to our sorrow, just as the Japanese oyster displaced our super little native Olympian oyster.

PEDDLERS

In the early thirties, more than one hundred and fifty Chinese men peddled fish, purchased at Campbell Avenue fish dock, around the Greater Vancouver area. About thirty of these men were waiting, each morning before daylight, in front of our plant. They were dressed identically: black cotton padded jacket with tight fitting sleeves, black cotton trousers with stove pipe legs, and felt boots. Each outfit was topped with a large woven bamboo hat and they carried a rolled-up rain cape for protection from inclement weather.

When the doors opened they rushed into the plant and started pitching fish as fast as they could into piles. Sometimes trouble occurred when one of them took fish from another man's pile because he did not get enough to supply his customers. Then all hell broke loose until Father waded in to settle the dispute. During the years I witnessed a few no holds barred fights between excited peddlers. On one occasion when Father attempted to break up the combatants, a third man who spoke English urged Father to let them fight it out. When Father tried to settle the dispute this man who was quite fat made the mistake of giving Father a sharp jab in the ribs. I can still see his hat fly off as Father thumped him a good one. That ended the fracas immediately and the thumpee did not come back for his fish until Father went into the office. The next morning all was forgotten and peace reigned again. The thumpee was noticeably contrite, keeping himself busy trimming, washing and stacking the fish into his carrying containers.

Once in a while Father would catch one of the peddlers stealing from the company or from one of his fellow peddlers. This caused Father to remain vigilant on the floor like a commander inspecting his troops. He took the weights of each lot of fish purchased and recorded each man's tally on a long sheet of brown wrapping paper with the price beside the pounds.

These men bought fish six days of the week. On Saturday mornings they arrived early because that day, in addition to buying more fish, each man settled his accounts. A number of them gave me fifteen cents to check Father's figures. Mr. Lee always gave me twenty-five cents but insisted that I add up the sums twice. Several of the peddlers had the same name. How Father kept track of them was a mystery to me, but most days he seemed to have it pretty well in hand. Infrequently one of the peddlers would balk at his total and insist that the bill belonged to another. This would cause a heated argument between peddlers that might get out of hand. Father had his own system and he was a shrewd arbitrator. Whenever he caught a cheat he escorted the offender to the door by his collar and seat of the pants and flung him out onto the dock. Usually he managed to stare down the combatants until the man who owed the total paid the bill. When the peddlers were busy trimming and washing fish in a flurry of activity, Father stood eying the moving mass intently as they went about their business. From time to time he would walk out among them and move one fish from one pile to another man's pile with his long-handled fish pew or throw the fish back onto the company pile. For a long time I was in the dark as to how he kept everything straight. No one said a word or challenged his decisions. The culprit who was padding his pile would completely ignore Father's actions. The man who received the extra fish back onto his pile acknowledged it with a sharp look at Father and a string of curses at his fellow peddler.

"How did you know that fellow stole a couple of fish from us?" I asked.

"Come here and I'll show you how I know. When I weigh their fish, I count each lot and mark the count and weight against each name.

When I see one of them has an extra fish or two, I look to see if the piles on each side of him have the correct count. If one of their fish are missing, I return it from the thief's pile. If they each have the correct amount I return the fish to our company pile."

I can't remember them ever disputing Father's activities in keeping the record straight. Father stayed neutral and never said a word one way or the other except for a smile at the culprits, who knew what it was all about. None of these peddlers had any ill will towards Father even when he caught them red-handed. It was a game played by some of them, and I have no doubt that from time to time when Father was distracted for some reason that some of them won the game. When the goods were all packed away in their carrying containers, the peddlers paused long enough to make a roll-your-own cigarette before they departed with a wave of the arm.

My first job consisted of delivering a ton of clams to several restaurants and a few fish stores every morning just as the sun was peering over the horizon. In winter it remained dark for a couple of hours as I made the deliveries. I always waited for Mr. Lee to give him a ride down to the West Vancouver ferry wharf. He sold his fish in the hills of West Vancouver. I was astonished by how well he coped with the terrain. Most people would have expired after a couple of days of his normal routine. He was a fine gentleman. I still picture him in my mind, sitting up straight as a ramrod puffing on his rollie while he waited in the truck for me to make my deliveries between the fish dock and the ferry terminal. He always managed to get his containers from the back of the truck before I could help out, then waved and trotted off with that jerky gait towards the ferry slip.

With thirty-plus peddlers coming in early on Saturday mornings to pay their weekly bills in cash, a considerable amount of money crossed the table in the plant where they settled up with father. I estimate each Chinese peddler brought in approximately forty-five dollars to clean up his tab. This combined with money paid by the MacFarlane boys and Ciccone and some of the other peddlers added up to a surprisingly large sum. It was not unusual to have two thousand dollars in the cash box. Considering the average tradesman earned ten dollars per week and nine hundred dollars bought a new Dodge car, it was a tempting amount for thugs to go after.

One Saturday morning I noticed three toughs standing by the sliding door watching the procedure as the Chinese gents squared their accounts. I also noticed Father glance at them now and then. When the last peddlers had departed, these thugs made their move. They split up and came at Father from two sides. I grabbed a hickory-handled fish pew and was about to go to Father's assistance. However the action was too fast for me and it was all over in twenty seconds. Father hit the first one coming in so hard, he dropped on a pile of fish and never moved. The second man attempted to kick Father, but Father, quick as a flash, grabbed him by his foot and swung him around, knocking the third man onto the fish pile. Father swung the thug around over the top of boxes of fish so many times, I thought he was going to kill the poor guy. When the second thug was getting up from the pile of fish, Father kicked him below the belt so hard that if he had been a football at centre field he would have gone over the goal posts. By now the three ruffians had received more than enough punishment and were desperately trying to get away. The first man had recovered sufficiently to take off out the doorway with Father in hot pursuit. When Father gave him a parting shot to the back of his head, his woollen cap flew off his head. He did not bother to stop to retrieve it. The other two managed to limp out the door while Father was busy with their friend. The last I saw of them they were moving with some difficulty past the ice house. It all happened so quickly I stood with my mouth open, fish pew in hand without being able to help at all.

Father came back to take the cash into the office. He had a faint smile on his face. "I guess I gave those guys a lesson they'll never forget, eh, Norm," he chuckled while I stood holding the fish pew in the ready position. He figured those guys would never come back but decided it would be prudent to put the money in the safe before the peddlers left the building in order to avoid being isolated with thugs in the future. I had retrieved the woollen cap by then and was brushing it down to remove a few fish scales that clung to it. To my joy I found the woollen cap was brand new with a bright shiny lining. The guy must have had that cap for a brief time. I wore that cap for only a couple of years in the freezer, and with its warm ear flaps it served me well. Father was easy to get along with, but everyone just knew by his bearing that he was not a man to trifle with. Years of hard physical work and his straightforward personality made Father a dangerous opponent in a bad situation.

During the thirties, three Chinese merchants dominated the fish business in Chinatown. All three operated retail-wholesale businesses and they conducted all their affairs with cash. Man Chong, the largest dealer of the three, was an unscrupulous man who had to be kept under surveillance whenever he came into the plant. He haggled intensely over every purchase and attempted to short his bill at every opportunity. There was no doubt that Man Chong was a clever businessman and he used every manoeuvre possible to reduce the cost of his bill or increase the amount of product that he took from the building.

Hong Chong, on the other hand, was a quiet, intelligent man who never raised his voice. In fact, he hardly spoke at all. Our prices were fair and the same to each of them no matter what measures Man Chong devised to try to get a better deal. Hong Chong was always cheerful and courteous. After he did his business he climbed the stairs into the office to smoke his pipe with Bill Steiner. Willy, as we called him, smoked a variety of pipe tobaccos when he wasn't smoking a cigar. When Hong Chong arrived in his office, Willy offered him a choice of tobacco. After he made his choice, the two of them sat together in private contemplation smoking their pipes. Hong Chong had lost half of his thumb years before in an accident in a cannery. I was intrigued by the way he tamped down on the red coals in his blackened pipe with the stub of his thumb without showing any sign of pain. By the time he finished his pipe and was knocking the ashes from the bowl, his truck would have arrived and been loaded and he would get up without a word and depart. He was a man who was well informed about the fish business. He always paid his bill in full on time. Orders from Father to his workers were to treat Hong Chong with respect at all times since he was a loyal customer and a gentleman to boot.

Old Hong Chong was so quiet that he regularly sat in the darkest corner of the office without us remembering he was there. Sometimes he arrived in the afternoon to inspect freshwater fish that we had imported from Alberta or Saskatchewan. He often fell asleep, if Willy was busy and could not attend to his business immediately. One day Steiner arrived in the morning and said, "You'll never guess what happened last night!" It seems he received a call from Hong Chong at ten p.m. and for a moment he could not imagine what he wanted. Hong Chong had fallen asleep in the old high-backed chair, and everybody went home without noticing he was still there. He was calling from our office for Willy to come down and unlock the door to let him out from the plant.

Sing Lee, the third Chinatown fish merchant, also sold fish across the counter in Chinatown and supplied many Chinese restaurants in Chinatown and in different parts of the city. Sing Lee was high strung, as was his girlfriend Ruthy, who helped him with his business. Man Chong and Hong Chong were much bigger buyers, so their ration of fish was larger when fish was scarce in winter. This drove Sing Lee into paroxysms of fits. When fish were plentiful he attempted to buy fish for cash directly from the fishermen. Man Chong also bought fish directly from the fishermen but he was careful to continue buying from the company as well because he knew that sooner or later we would have fish delivered to us by packer when there were no fisherman available at the dock to sell for cash.

Sing Lee was devious and greedy at the same time. When fish were available in summer, we sometimes went days without seeing him because he was buying fish for cash on our dock in the depths of night to avoid detection. However the wholesalers at Campbell Avenue had ways of finding out about these clandestine activities. When fish was scarce, Sing Lee would appear three times a day looking to make purchases. This amused my father, who used these opportunities to tell him he wasn't a good enough customer to get product during shortages. When Father turned his back, Sing Lee would scream at him and hiss like a snake. On one occasion when Father refused him, Sing Lee began to yell at him while his girlfriend wailed in the background. After conferring with Man Chong and Hong Chong, Father decided to allow Sing Lee three or four hundred pounds of fish to sell over his retail counter.

Retailers buying directly for cash from fishermen was a no-no as far as the dealers on the dock were concerned. In those days none of the dealers on the dock made retail sales. This was the rule and there were no exceptions but one, Woodward's stores. For many years Woodward's bought live cod from one particular fishing family. The dealers figured there was a long-term relationship there, and nobody rocked the boat except when there was a shortage of fish in winter.

After the war there were a couple of additional Chinese retail-wholesalers in Chinatown who always attempted to get their fish directly from the fishermen. I remember a vessel with sixteen thousand pounds of black cod (sable fish), some ling cod and snappers that was unloading in front of our place. We had taken off about seven thousand pounds when the fisherman came running into the office and wanted his fish back. After agreeing to prices for his load, he had received a cash offer from one of the new Chinese merchants. We put the fish back onto his boat and he moved over to the B.C. Fishermen's Independent Association unloading facility and unloaded his fish. The buyer counted out thirteen thousand dollars in cash; a one-hundred-dollar bill fell on the dock, and the gent put his foot on top of it while he continued counting.

All the fish companies had to make out purchase slips in triplicate for the Department of Fisheries and Oceans, which were picked up every Monday morning. The Chinese merchants made out no slips and reported nothing about these transactions. This caused the Campbell Avenue dealers a lot of distress, but when they complained to Department of Fisheries and Oceans, their gripes were ignored.

In winter when fish landings dwindled we always had a problem dividing up the fish between our customers. It seemed nobody was satisfied. Each customer received a share in relation to the amount of fish that was purchased when fish was plentiful. Many customers showed up who never bought fish from us in the other seasons. We forced them to wait until the regulars were satisfied. Sometimes this created an impossible situation as the strangers attempted to rush in and claim a share for themselves. This problem had to be handled delicately when we took the fish away from them to hand out to our regulars. Father delegated me the job of standing by our closed door and only allowing regular customers into the plant until they were satisfied. Then I let the others in five at a time. In the end most of the customers were able to get fish but not the sizes that they desired.

On one of these days when we had a rush of customers and a scarcity of fish, Man Chong decided to disagree about full payment for some fish he bought the previous week. He stood there in his long overcoat with pockets sagging with money, waving his arms and haranguing Father. He wore a blue skullcap and danced around like a strange skinny bird with his overcoat flapping around his legs. First he pleaded, then argued, then cursed both in English and Chinese. I waited for the explosion as Father stood there with his tally sheet, refusing the money that Man Chong was pressing on him, insisting that he pay his full bill. Suddenly, Father had Man Chong upside down by his ankles with his coattails down around his head. As he shook him up and down, silver coins poured out of his pockets and landed in all directions on the cement floor. A horde of peddlers stood silently in astonishment watching the action. Then Father set Man Chong on his feet and picked up enough quarters and fifty-cent pieces to settle his account.

Father went back to his other customers while I helped Man Chong recover the rest of his money. Over and over again he pronounced Father a son of a gun before he stormed away. An hour later he was back again with a smile on his face patting Father on the back calling him a son of a gun. Father invited him into the office and poured him three ounces of Scotch, which he slowly sipped as he declared that Father was still a son of a gun. Eventually he departed in a good mood and the incident was forgotten. For about two weeks after that exhibition, peace reigned in our plant, as all the peddlers were on their best behaviour.

One morning Man Chong quietly slipped by us into the office to confer with Bill Steiner. Willy leaned back in his chair as Man Chong engaged him in earnest conversation. Finally Steiner made a phone call and then seemed to give him some sort of instructions. Man Chong, looking worried, slipped silently out the door and quickly departed. I wondered what that was all about, and Father muttered as he watched Man Chong walk out onto the dock. Father thought maybe the fish inspectors had pinched him for handling poached fish. In any case, he seemed pretty worried about something. After a lull in sales we went in the office and Father asked, "Bill, what was that all about?"

Willy turned and remarked, with a chuckle that shook his portly frame, that Man Chong had contracted a dose of clap from one of the girls who worked in Chinatown. "He asked me to recommend a doctor who could cure him of his malady. I phoned my doctor for his advice and passed it on to the old guy."

Man Chong disappeared from the scene for several days without anyone knowing his whereabouts. None of the peddlers knew where he had gone. Sleepy, his driver, showed up each morning in his place to claim Man Chong's share of fish but he wasn't talking. Ten days later Man Chong appeared on the dock and headed straight towards my old man. He patted him on the shoulder and thanked him for making sure Sleepy got a fair share of fish.

"Goddamn those girls in Chinatown, no good Johnny!" he declared.

"Goddamn those white girls no good," he repeated for emphasis.

"Why don't you try one of the black ones next time," Father advised with a loud guffaw.

"Oh no, I like the white girls more better," he remarked to everyone in general. "Goddamn those white girls!" he declared again as he went about his business.

Sing Lee and his girlfriend continued in their usual manner. They were either buying directly from fishermen for cash or loudly proclaiming that they were not getting their share. All through the winter months they performed their comic tragedy before the assembled throng of peddlers. Sing Lee ran the gamut of emotions from pleading to venomous, while his girlfriend, with a diamond ring on every finger, wailed buckets of tears. Hong Chong, who never raised his voice or complained about anything, stood by smoking his pipe. Watching the act unfold he said it best in a calm voice, "Sing Lee is crazy."

Mornings at Campbell Avenue were always the same routine. Boats were waiting to unload their catches and the peddlers and merchants were waiting to elbow their way into the plant to be among the first to pick from the piles of fresh fish spread out over the cement floor. Their mood depended on the weather. If it was stormy and there was a shortage of fish, the situation could get nasty with people pushing and cursing at one another. If fish was plentiful, the crowd would be joking and laughing as they carefully examined each purchase.

The peddlers were not allowed access to the quantities of graded salmon, halibut and other fish that were iced up in totes that held eight hundred pounds of each species of fish. These totes had lids on them. This fish was reserved for our restaurant trade and for shipping orders elsewhere in Canada or for sale into the United States. We didn't allow anybody to handle or dig through these totes because the more fish is handled, the quicker it deteriorates. We got top dollar for fish we shipped into the United States, but it had to be in perfect condition with little loss of scales. It was out of the question to let someone rummage in eight hundred pounds of fish in a tote to chose six fish. It would meaning weighing the fish again and the labour of re-icing and packing the tote. We also received preferred prices from the top restaurant trade in Vancouver and we endeavoured to supply these customers with a superior product.

We brought in a great variety of fish that was in demand for the Asian trade. This included silver perch, red perch, yellow eye snappers, black rock cod, quillback rock cod, kinky fish, shad, live carp and several species of freshwater fish. They also brought great quantities of spot prawns and live Dungeness crabs. Chinatown easily went through ten thousand pounds of large spot prawns per week. The Chinese merchants each purchased several hundred pounds of prawns each day they were available. The fish that the Chinese and Japanese merchants bought had to be absolutely fresh, and they were fanatics on this issue. Sometimes the fish was so fresh, rigor mortis had not set in yet. If a large shipment came in, they would refuse to take the same fish the next day, so we had a problem selling this fish. In order to deal with this problem we divided our shipments and spirited half the fish into an adjoining part of our plant and buried it in crushed ice and covered it with tarps. The following day or even two days later, we advised them that a new shipment had just arrived and they all rushed down to buy the same fish from the lot that had arrived a couple of days earlier. When we had several large shipments during parts of one day, we suddenly had a big problem. Then we were forced to hide the bulk of the fish and deal it out on a daily basis until it was all sold. Very seldom did we ever have to dump any fish. Whenever they determined a lot was yesterday's fish, they walked around it and would never buy any of it.

One cold winter morning there was the usual hassle in front of our door. Frost glittered on the snow and the cold would have made anyone shudder at the prospect of leaving the heated cab of the truck. Sing Lee and Ruthy were at the head of the line waiting for us to open the large sliding door. Ruthy had her arms out like the wings of a bird of prey guarding a dead victim. As soon as the door opened a crack, she slithered in through the opening and rushed over to a pile of five thousand pounds of fish, spread out her arms and jumped on top of it. "I want it all, John," she screamed, in a voice loud enough to awaken the dead. "I will pay the price. I want it all."

Father was still at the door with the peddlers crowding in behind him. Man Chong stood to the side in long brown coat and usual blue skullcap muttering, "She big mouth," over and over again in bewilderment. Hong Chong watched in amazement, forgetting to puff on his perpetual black pipe. Father ordered Ruthy's removal from atop the pile, which was done with much wailing and crying on her part as she kept repeating the words, "I want it all." Father became quite stern and his loud voice soon dominated Ruthy's feeble wails. When Ruthy was composed, Father shared out the fish while Ruthy lamented that Father was unfair in not recognizing her right to buy it all.

Peace was restored a short time later when the other merchants realized Ruthy's latest melodrama was not playing well. Everybody went back to the normal routine of putting their fish in piles. It wasn't long until Ruthy was up to her old trick of trying to add to her pile by taking fish from Man Chong and Hong Chong. When Hong Chong attempted to recover his fish, Ruthy struck him in the arm with her fish pick. The fish pick was a lethal weapon. It was the same sturdy tool used for grading lumber in mills. The end of the pick penetrated Hong Chong's clothing and made a nasty wound in his arm. Sing Lee stood frozen in silence while Father grabbed Ruthy by her collar and marched her out the door. She dropped the fish pick, which I retrieved. That was about fifty years ago and I still have it hanging on my wall above my tool table.

There was a great clamour from the peddlers and merchants about Ruthy's bad behaviour, but fifteen minutes later she was back in the plant. It was useless to do more about it. Hong Chong went up the stairs to the office where he peeled out of his coat, sweater and three shirts while old Bill Steiner got the first-aid kit out and sprinkled a liberal quantity of iodine on the wound and put a bandage on it. Father treated Hong Chong with about four ounces of internal medicine from a Black Label bottle of Scotch whisky and all was well. Hong Chong accepted the experience in silence. He left with a fish under his good arm on his way to see his Chinese doctor about treating his other limb. Even Sing Lee was shocked by Ruthy's attack on old Hong Chong and admonished her for having gone too far. This nasty incident caused Sing Lee and Ruthy to quiet down their campaign, but after a few months they were back into their old habits. They seemed to have no shame in inciting any crude form of drama to try to get their own way.

One morning in the sixties, I arrived at the plant in a truck with five tons of live crabs. As usual the Chinese merchants were already there waiting for me. While I was turning the large truck around so I could back into the plant, Sing Lee climbed onto the back and was pulling on a rope handle on one of the boxes to move it so he could open the lid to examine the crabs. As I backed to the edge of the dock so I could negotiate the confined turn, the rope handle pulled out from the end of the box. I heard his terrified scream as his momentum carried him in a back dive off the end of the truck overboard into the chuck. The truck deck was four feet high, the dock was ten feet from the water at high tide, and the trouble was there was a zero low tide, which added another fourteen feet into the drop. Sing Lee back flipped twenty-eight feet before he hit the sea.

I jumped out of the truck, rushed to the edge of the dock and looked over at large bubbles that were breaking the surface. Ruthy, who had been standing beside the truck, was also looking over the edge wailing at the top of her lungs. I scrambled down the steel ladder to the fender log below to see if I could rescue him. I was worried that he might have hit the log at the bottom before he slid into the water. At that time *Brown Bear* and *White Bear*, two packers, were tied to the dock unloading Alaska sockeye salmon. Two crew members on the *Brown Bear* witnessed Sing Lee's fall and they were astounded that he hadn't landed on their deck or on the large fender log at the bottom. By an astonishing bit of luck, Sing Lee had landed in the three-foot space between the enormous metal-decked packer and the fender log, and that saved his life.

One of the crewmen joined me on the log and the other stood by with a coil of rope while we waited for something to happen. It seemed a long time before Sing Lee broke the surface. He reared up out of the water about two feet and went down again so fast we failed to grab hold of him. We knelt down to get ready if he came up a second time. He did with a loud howl and we grabbed hold of him. I don't know if anyone has tried to pull a hundred and twenty pounds of soaking wet, screaming maniac, whose rubber boots and overcoat were full of water onto a three-and-a-half-foot slippery log. It's pretty hard to do without falling into the water. We held him in place while the other deckhand passed the line around Sing Lee's armpits. A crowd had gathered on the dock overlooking the action and someone operating the crane lowered the bucket down to the water level and we loaded him into the bucket for the ride up onto the wharf. There was plenty of life in Sing Lee — up he went with his arms pumping and legs thrashing — so we figured he'd be all right. When they got him out of the bucket and laid him out on the wharf, he stopped yelling and went into convulsions, flopping around on the dock like a fish out of water. Ruthy was running about picking up the coins that had fallen out of his pockets onto the planks.

In the meantime a paddy wagon arrived with a couple of Vancouver's finest boys in blue who inspected Sing Lee for ID. When the ambulance arrived they loaded him onto a stretcher and whisked him away. By then we knew he would recover, and all that seemed missing was his wool cap and some loose change that had fallen through the planks into the water below. Ruthy tried to get into the ambulance with him for the ride to the hospital, but for some reason they would not let her join him. We thought that strange because Sing Lee's English was not very good and, since he was hysterical, it was reasoned Ruthy should have gone along to comfort him. In the end, she got into her car and followed the ambulance to the hospital. A few hours later she returned with the news that Sing Lee was okay but that he would have to remain in the hospital for a few days to recover from his ordeal. She also confided to us that Sing Lee's fish-buying money had disappeared. About fifteen hundred dollars was missing and she wondered if anybody knew where it had gone and what she should do about it.

We knew where the money went. That's why Sing Lee went solo to the hospital. Everyone was outraged to realize that Sing Lee had been relieved of his bankroll on the trip uptown. For a while Ruthy raged on about the injustice of it all, but her inquiries went nowhere. After a few days Sing Lee was back in his store in Chinatown and Ruthy was happy he was alive so she stopped pursuing the matter.

Sing Lee only came back to Campbell Avenue twice after that unfortunate incident. The Buddhist priests advised him that the gods did not favour his presence on the fish dock. Eventually he returned with some friends and a priest in a saffron-coloured robe for religious ceremonies to give thanks for being spared. The ceremonies involved a couple of roasted chickens, a dozen potatoes and some vegetables and fruit. Each item had a lit candle inserted in it and they were left on the edge of the wharf. The items remained for several days until the wharf man washed them off the dock into the harbour and they floated away on the tide.

From that day on we dealt, for better or worse, only with Ruthy. She continued her habit of flopping down on a pile of fish declaring she wanted it all while the other buyers stood by with concerned frowns on their faces. To emphasize her claim, she sometimes managed to slip a fish into each pocket of her coat. We never argued with her about it but simply added the fish to her total bill. She seemed to manage quite well without Sing Lee directing her activities, and his store was always full of fish and bustling with customers. Ruthy's habit of diving onto piles of fish and putting them into her pockets did not improve the quality of the atmosphere that clung to her figure. While she was well dressed and boldly made up, with rosy cheeks and blood-red lipstick, for nearly all the forty years she came to the wharf she continued to wear the same olive green coat with oversized pockets. On a warm day the stench was strong enough to make your eyes water. She always snuggled up to me when she came in for coffee and confided how much the diamonds in her rings cost. She claimed one of them was worth fifty thousand dollars. I had no doubt of it.

FISHMONGERS

Old Man MacFarlane was in our shed every morning. He arrived as the Chinese peddlers and merchants rushed in to battle one another for position on the floor. He slowly puffed on his curved pipe as he surveyed the mob and viewed our piles of fresh fish. Father would give him the eye and old Mac followed him into the upstairs office where he received a three-ounce shot of Scotch whisky.

We knew what fish he required for his store in Kerrisdale and it was already put away for him. The old man picked out additional lots of fish that took his fancy. After his truck was loaded for him, he departed with a wave of his arm. Old Mac, a shrewd businessman, was a fixture until one of his legs was amputated and he was forced to retire. Then his son Doug took over the store and carried on where his father left off until he passed away. The store is still there, seventy years later, in its original location, owned now by Johnny, MacFarlane's grandson.

Old MacFarlane's two sons, Doug and Alex, peddled fish door to door out of covered trucks. They arrived within minutes of their father each morning to pick out their daily requirements. They each sold more than two hundred and fifty pounds of fish per day and made a very good living. Doug ran a streetcar for the B.C. Electric for a year or two but quit that job because he could make twice as much money peddling fish.

Old Man Parker, the English fishmonger, was also on the scene a moment after the padlock was removed from the door. His store was on 4th Avenue just a block north of Granville. He quickly picked out his quota of top-grade fish and hurriedly departed with a reminder to Father to get the fish up to his store as quickly as possible. He was a kindly man who paid in cash each day. In the mid-thirties, Parker, in his seventies, seemed a very old man. He never left our plant without informing us in a very courteous manner about the list of varieties and the qualities of fish he used to sell in the store he ran in good old England.

Parker sold his store to a Mr. Brown. I never knew his given name. He was always called Mr. Brown. He and Mrs. Brown were two of the finest people I have ever known. They remodelled Parker's store and sold fish and chips on one side. Mr. Brown ran the fish counter and Mrs. Brown made and sold the fish and chips. Mr. and Mrs. Brown were inspired to get into the fish business by a personal miracle.

Mr. Brown was a coal miner from Nanaimo. He told me that one day while eating his lunch there was a rumble in the mine. The space where he had been hacking coal out of a seam in the ceiling collapsed. By moving over to have his lunch, Mr. Brown was saved from being buried alive with his pick and shovel, and Mrs. Brown escaped becoming a widow. Mr. Brown said that was his last shift in the coal mine.

As he was a friend of my father, Mr. Brown came to visit him at the fish dock. Father listened to his plight and asked him if he had five hundred dollars to invest. He also asked him if he knew anything about fish. Mr. Brown said, yes, he had that much money and he advised he could do any job. Old Man Parker was not well and was looking for someone to buy out his business. Father advised Mr. Brown to buy him out. Father knew that Parker had a real good business.

After the sale, Father made arrangements with Old Man Parker to stay on for a couple of months. He thought it important that Mr. Brown learn how much fish to buy, how to cut it, and how to best serve his customers. It turned out to be a very wise investment for Mr. and Mrs. Brown. They expanded the business and ran it successfully until they retired. Twenty years later the store was torn down for a new complex.

Ciccone was another fish peddler who had sold fish in East Vancouver for more than forty years. I remember him when I was in grade two at Franklin School. Ciccone served his customers by always arriving on the same day each week at exactly the same time. One day our school principal called us to the window and, pointing to Mr. Ciccone's old blue truck, he said, "There is a successful businessman, always exactly on time. If you pattern your life after him you will also succeed in life." I wondered about that many times.

Doug MacFarlane took over his father's first-class store in Kerrisdale, and Alex MacFarlane was operating five stores while driving around in a Cadillac. Forty years later Ciccone, who sold nothing but the top-grade fish, was still peddling fish in the same way from his ancient blue truck.

Teddy Burnett, a tubby Irishman about fifteen years older than me, was an incorrigible practical joker. The Burnetts had an old-fashioned brick smokehouse on Alexander Street in Gastown that turned out far better products than can be bought anywhere today. They smoked mostly kippers, Alaska black cod and salmon. Old Man Burnett would give me a dozen kippered herring made from Point Grey morning fish that were dripping with oil. The herring were still warm from the smokehouse. They were absolutely out of this world. Fresh kippered fat Pacific summer morning herring were about one pound in weight.

For days when I was making my early morning deliveries of clams I noticed a foul smell in the cab of the truck. I looked everywhere but I couldn't locate the source of the smell. I removed the seat and washed out the cab with disinfectant, but the smell only got worse. I lifted the hood and inspected the engine but saw nothing that could cause such an odour. Finally, one day when Father was using the truck, he stopped to look for the source of the smell and he found it. At the back of the engine where it was difficult to see, Teddy had jammed a grey cod in such a way that it could not drop out. The maggots had disposed of most of the fish by then but a few fried maggots and the juice still remained on the fire wall separating the cab from the engine.

Father guessed the culprit immediately. "That Teddy Burnett is sure a comic," he said. "Wait a while and we'll get even with that smart alec." Father was a great believer in the theory that if anyone cheated in some way or played a lousy joke that caused some discomfort, to double the ante when the opportunity came to return the compliment. About a month later Father said to me, "I got Jimmy Martin to bring in two large round grey cod and I have them iced in the back bin, and now it's time to get even with Teddy. I'll take Ted to lunch and you fasten one grey cod on the firewall between the cab and engine of his truck. Then take the second cod, wrap it in parchment, and jam it between the springs under his truck seat. Punch the paper with several holes so the blowflies can enter, and then lie it flat and put the seat carefully back in place."

Father had a leisurely liquid lunch with Teddy to give me time to do the job. Five days later Teddy showed up and complained about the grey cod that was fried to the back of his engine. "Hold my hood up, you twit," he said, "while I fork out that rotten cod with a fish pew. I should have known why your old man took me out to lunch and bought me drinks. Hold the water hose while I scrub the firewall and back of the engine. Jeezuz, that smell is enough to turn my stomach."

"Well, you started it, Teddy," I replied with laughter.

All the while he grumbled and cursed as Father smiled and winked at me. Poor old Teddy had got rid of some of the problem, but there was still an horrible odour emanating from his truck. Ted was quite heavy, and as he drove his old Ford truck along the cobblestones along Alexander Street to his smokehouse the smell and putrefaction from the rotting cod wafted out through the holes in the package below his seat. The next day he showed up again and ordered me to hold the hood up while he scrubbed the back of the engine and firewall again. He was not in a good mood, but I reminded him that he had started it.

Teddy was a ladies' man but he couldn't haul his girlfriends around in a truck that turned their stomachs. Basically he was a red-blooded stud champing at the bit who had become housebound because his truck smelled worse than the city dump. One day when he was inspecting his truck for the twentieth time he noticed a maggot on the rubber floor mat. That was when it finally dawned on him that the stink was coming from under his seat. In a frenzy he pulled the seat out of the truck and threw it upside down on the ground, and there was the lethal package fastened between the springs. Some of Teddy's workers told me that the package moved with about two pounds of wriggling maggots and that a cloud of blowflies flew into Teddy's face when he attempted to remove it. The whole episode put Teddy in a wild rage, but there was nothing he could do. He was merely a victim of Father's policy that one good screwing deserved a double screwing. I never forgot the motto and adopted it as a policy.

Teddy Burnett got himself in bad trouble when he enclosed a bottle of rye whisky in Chris Johnson's fish order to the Blackburn Market. The Blackburn Market, which was right downtown, was either the best or second-best fish store in Vancouver. Chris Johnson's son was an alcoholic. His drinking problem was so bad he couldn't keep a job, so he worked in the store. His old man kept his eye on his fish counter and his son all day. When I arrived with fish, the son begged me to bring him a bottle. When Chris began buying fish from us again, after I patched up a feud he had with father, he warned me never to give his son a bottle or even a drink. "Kid," he said, "if I catch you giving my boy liquor I will never buy a fish from you again. Take care because you'll never get another chance at my business if you let me down."

One day I arrived at the store with a load of fresh fish to find Chris Johnson standing in the alley with his hand on his hips while Teddy was loading his fresh smoked fish back onto his truck. "I told you what would happen if I caught you hiding whisky in the fish when you delivered my order. Now you get to hell out of here with your fish and don't ever come back."

When I unloaded my goods and was leaving, Teddy was waiting for me down the alley. He begged me to deliver his fish for him. I told him I had to go back and check it out with Chris because I didn't want to lose his business. I went back to talk with Mr. Johnson about the situation and asked him if he would take Teddy Burnett's fish from me.

"Yes, I will, kid, but make sure that Irish rascal pays you a good commission for doing it. Your company will bill me from now on for his smoked fish because I don't want him around this place." This situation continued until I left the company for the army. I never found out if they patched up their relationship. I kind of doubted it, because Chris bought a lot of smoked fish from the London Fish Company owned by Sid Humphreys.

BLUEBACKS

In the thirties, a thousand or more hand-trollers in rowboats fished for salmon in the Gulf of Georgia. These fisherman caught up to three hundred cohos per day and spring salmon as well.

The season on bluebacks (Gulf cohos) opened on the first day of April. No fish could be kept that were under two and one half pounds round weight, although a quarter of the fish taken were marginal in weight (between two and a quarter and two and a half pounds). Some of the coho salmon exceeded three pounds and there were some four-pounders throughout a load. Colonial Cannery packers would start arriving at Campbell Avenue by nine o'clock in the morning. To give some idea of the vast quantities of coho, or bluebacks as they were called in my time, I looked back to the landings at Campbell Avenue fish dock on the first day of the new open season in 1936.

The *Chief Skidegate* (formerly a rum runner), a ninety-footer, was the first to arrive with sixty thousand plus pounds of bluebacks. *Emma K* and *Roy Roberts* (converted rum runners), both seventy-footers, each with forty thousand pounds, arrived an hour later. *The Resort* and *Rage Reef*, in the forty-five-foot class, docked at noon with twenty-thousand-pound loads. Greek brothers were in with the *La Paloma* and the *Tsuru*, both loaded with dressed bluebacks. Brother John was in with the *Seven Seas* and the *Gigilo* each with twenty-five thousand pounds of dressed bluebacks from our Polier Pass camp. Several Japanese packers were in with full loads of both dressed and round bluebacks.

A few spring salmon were mixed in with the bluebacks, but

they were seldom more than four or five percent in volume of the deliveries. Undressed bluebacks sold for six cents per pound, and dressed fish were worth ten cents per pound. Dressed red springs were five cents per pound, while dressed white springs sold for a lowly one cent per pound, and steelhead sold for one cent per pound. Pink salmon (humpbacks) sold for eight cents per fish. Only about thirty percent of the springs were a true red colour when the fish averaged under six pounds. These fish were not fancied by the canneries. Large spring salmon stay in deeper water in the daytime, while coho salmon are near the surface. Immature springs from one to five pounds were probably shagged off the hooks.

It was rumoured that one fisherman caught twelve hundred bluebacks in one day. It would be impossible to work the gear and also dress that many fish in one day, so they had to be sold in the round to a buyer. It was common to hear that fishermen on the West Coast of Vancouver Island claimed they had dressed and iced five or six hundred fish in one day.

Sockeye salmon were all net-caught in seines or gillnets because trollers did not discover how to catch them on hooks until the late sixties and seventies. Even in recent times, fishermen have not learned how to catch a number of subspecies of sockeye salmon on hook and line. In areas like Kennedy Lake, Nit Nat and in the Somas River that empties into the Alberni Canal and various other runs, they catch the odd sockeye on hooks but not enough to make it pay.

When the season began, Colonial would can salmon in two twelve-hour shifts. They contracted Chinese and native Indian labour through a contractor who collected the money from the cannery owner and paid the workers. The other twenty-five or thirty canneries that operated in our coastal areas also operated in this manner. Other than shutting down for a day or two to service machinery, or when runs of salmon slackened as new runs moved in and earlier runs petered out, the canneries in most areas continued to operate from April into the middle of February, when they were putting up late-run chums.

In the thirties I made a trip to Polier Pass, where our company kept a fish-buying scow for live cod and salmon, especially for bluebacks in season. The packer made two trips per week to pick up full loads. Dressed salmon was taken day or night and iced into two-hundred-and-fifty-pound boxes. These were called Gregory boxes because they were introduced in the 1920s by Old Man Gregory of Port Alberni. The boxes were about two and a half feet wide, four feet long and ten inches deep. They were built of sturdy lumber (full one-inch sides and bottoms with one-and-a-half-inch ends) and they were used again and again. They were used by the industry for more than fifty years and were far better than the heavy plastic bins in use today. These boxes could easily be washed and bleached. The wood was a good insulating material and they were cheap to build. Today, these boxes are still called Gregory boxes, although there are not many of them around. They have been replaced by plastic totes.

The Gregory family were an independent, family-owned and -run fishing company. British Columbia Packers eventually bought the old man out, and millions of pounds of fish were shipped from Port Alberni to be sold in Canada or shipped to export markets. One member of the Gregory clan was still associated with B.C. Packers more than sixty years later.

Some cod were killed at the camps and iced in these large heavy boxes when fishermen had filled their live wells and had no room for additional fish. The cod fishermen arrived at the camp on packer days to deliver live fish, which was killed on the spot, dressed, iced and boxed. First the packer unloaded groceries and other supplies for the camp store, and then unloaded four or five tons of ice, which was dumped into the ice house through a hatch. This ice was used to ice down salmon, cod and other fish that was delivered while the packer was away. When the packer returned, the boxes of fish in the ice house were stowed in the hold.

Several boats with live fish in wells would tie up beside the packer and the slaughter would begin. The cod were first on the list because they were bigger fish and harder to handle than the four-pound bluebacks that followed. Removing the gills and dressing ten to twelve thousand pounds of coho salmon was backbreaking work. It was done this way in order to get top dollar on the fresh fish market. Fish that was destined to the canneries remained in the round for the short trip to port. In slow periods even fish that were deemed canners were dressed at the camp.

Workers stopped for coffee and a sandwich a couple of times during their shifts, but the work basically went on day and night. When the workers took a break during a slow period, they baited hooks with slivers of white skin from salmon throats and fished for two- or three-pound rock cod. If the tide was right, it was possible to catch three or four hundred pounds of rock cod in a very short time. Rock cod, highly valued by Asians in Vancouver, were worth more to them than bluebacks. Camp crews made extra money fishing rock cod on the side and shipping it to market on the packer.

At night, the camp lights pit-lamped the herring and other bait fish, which came to the glow like moths. Rock cod, ling cod and salmon churned through the masses of bait fish, gulping them down in a mad feeding frenzy. Fish skittered across the surface, chasing herring that were jumping in the air trying to escape the massacre. The bite lasted until the change of the tide.

On slow afternoons at Campbell Avenue, when work in the plant had ground to a halt, we sometimes went sports fishing in the harbour. One afternoon we took our fishing gear aboard a forty-eight-foot packer and headed out to Bowen Island. When we got midway to the island we hove to and drifted on a glassy sea. With a one-ounce sinker on the main line and a strip of fresh herring on a double hook set on a three-foot leader we proceeded to cast. We had no spinning gear but stripped off a hundred feet of line and flung it out until the bait lit with a splash when it reached the end of the slack line. We had to be careful not to stand on any of the coils or the line would snap back and the herring strips would go sailing into the air.

My friends on deck near the waterline noticed three or four salmon following the herring strips as the line was wound in. Even when a fish was caught, other salmon followed attempting to tear off a piece of the herring strip from the mouth of the unfortunate fish. Standing on top of the wheelhouse twelve feet above the water, I could see scores of small salmon. A hundred or more were attempting to catch each herring strip. They were like a blue cloud moving after the bait. These small salmon were all spring salmon, in the one-and-a-half- to three-pound size. We had a fish on every time we made a cast. Since we did not want these small fish, we patiently released them after every cast.

It was the last week of August and we were in search of large-sized bluebacks. We kept on casting out as far as we could and speeded up pulling in the line to avoid catching these small fish. For a time we had no luck since our herring strips were being torn to pieces by the clouds of immature fish. After casting this way for an hour or more, suddenly I got a solid jolt on my rod and the reel screamed out line. Fifty yards away a large coho leaped six feet out of the water and proceeded to run for another thirty yards. He made three spectacular jumps in rapid succession. On the third jump, the sinker and strip flew out of his mouth and he was gone.

It was impossible to keep the small salmon from our hooks, so we fired up the Cat in the engine room and pointed the bow towards the Lions Gate Bridge. Just as dusk was beginning to arrive, we passed under the bridge at the First Narrows and entered the harbour while city lights blinked on. It was full darkness by the time we tied up at Campbell Avenue under the dull yellow dock lights that looked down from old-fashioned fish sheds. Though we had caught no fish, it was a good day on the water. I have never gotten over the thrill of hooking that fish. I wondered if it made it to the spawning grounds or if it was taken by a gillnet fisherman or by a predator. It was a beautiful fish with power to spare. I wished it well.

I have always believed that the bluebacks in the Gulf of Georgia came from spawning grounds in the thousands of smaller streams, like the ones that entered Vancouver Harbour and Burrard Inlet from the North Shore Mountains. And from the even smaller creeks, now mostly in culverts, that flowed into the inlet from the south shore. Bluebacks had very red meat, even redder than sockeye salmon. When canned they were highly prized in the British Isles and brought a higher price there than canned sockeye salmon. These fish were voracious feeders that thrived on the once-immense herring and shrimp stocks that existed in the Gulf of Georgia. Gulf shrimp were of a good red colour, so perhaps this factor accounted for the bright red flesh of Gulf bluebacks. The coho caught on the West Coast and in northern areas are not as red as Gulf fish. Shrimp from here are also of a paler hue.

Bluebacks migrated from streams right after the new year. This migration increased with the freshets that arrive in spring. The fish in their millions, probably already two years old, were four to eight ounces in size when they entered the sea. When they reached the ocean they fed voraciously on jack herring and shrimp. A fish that was eight ounces on the first of January would increase its weight to two to four pounds by the beginning of April. These eight-ounce feeders' average growth was four ounces per week. By the late fall or early spring of the following year, when they are ready to return to the spawning grounds, if feed is available, they can grow to ten or twelve pounds or more.

In my years at Campbell Avenue fish dock I have observed large red-skinned cohos with hooked noses and black heads in Vancouver Harbour in January and February. I have seen bright silvery bluebacks entering North Shore streams in July. There may be some overlap of runs, or perhaps some fish do not remain in the ocean as long as others. I leave it to the experts to ponder this subject in their scientific treatises. My experience is all practical. I am convinced that blueback coho spent their entire three- or four-year life cycles in small streams and in the Gulf of Georgia. I question the theory that they travelled around either end of Vancouver Island to the open Pacific or journeyed to the Gulf of Alaska. There may have been other cohos from the Fraser River system, Knight Inlet or Butte Inlet that left the Gulf and migrated up north into Alaskan waters.

THE CARRIAGE TRADE

Our company took pride in specializing in importing items for fancy private clubs and high-class eating establishments in Western Canada. Father's partner, Bill Steiner, spent a great deal of his time on these projects. We imported fresh frog saddles from Louisiana in twenty-pound wooden pails. Live turtles that weighed up to one hundred pounds came in on the fenced decks of freighters from the Caribbean. Live lobsters packed in ice and seaweed in wooden barrels came from the Atlantic provinces. We imported frozen pheasants from China. In addition, our company, in a joint venture with a botanist who had immigrated to Canada from Czechoslovakia in 1929, introduced the white Champion mushroom to the American continent.

We kept the live turtles in pens and fed them with lettuce and cabbage leaves and green seaweed. It was my job to douse them with sea water three or four times a day. The chefs killed them by placing a hot iron on their backs and chopping off their heads when the heat forced them to stick their heads out from their shells. I never had the time to remain and watch the rest of the butchering process, but I imagine it was quite a complicated business.

A couple of guys from the West Kootenays arrived at our place in 1934 and propositioned us to finance them for an eighteen-foot clinker-built boat with netting so they could catch Kokanee trout for the specialty trade. These red-meated trout are actually a landlocked sockeye salmon usually in the ten-to-twelve-ounce sizes but they can grow to three pounds in large lakes. They claimed they had a permit from the government to take Kokanee trout from Christina Lake for commercial purposes. This kind of deal was right up Steiner's alley. It would be another unique product that would enhance our repertoire of specialties that set us apart from other companies. We were already driving the competition mad, so here was another item to give them another case of heartburn. It was surprising how much business we gained by having some novelty items in our inventory of seafood products. However, the fifteen-hundred-dollar investment they required was something to seriously think about. During the Depression in Vancouver one could buy a good house for that kind of money.

The deal was that we were to finance the operation and recover our costs and expenses from the fishermen's share of the fish. Father was skeptical because all sorts of characters showed up from time to time who turned out to be con men or were impractical dreamers with crazy ideas. After a lengthy parley with Willy and these gentlemen, Father judged the men to be honest. Since he was good at assessing deals and was not often wrong about a man's character, Father joined with Steiner in approving of the arrangement. He agreed to finance the project and it became a money-making deal that lasted for over a decade.

The boat and netting were bought and shipped via the Kettle Valley rail line to Grand Forks. There were no lawyers or paperwork to sign but just a handshake to seal the bargain that assured us that we would get all of the fish at an agreed-upon price. The cost of our investment was to be recovered over a certain period of time from the payments for trout that were delivered to our plant at seventy-five cents per pound.

The men began fishing for these trout in the fall, from about the first of October to about the end of November, before the real cold weather set in. The Kokanee trout were shipped to us by CPR railway via the Kettle Valley Coquihalla route. The red-fleshed fish, packed in ten-pound wooden boxes, arrived at our plant in excellent condition with no scale loss or blemishes of any kind. It was a far superior eating fish compared to the yellowish-pink-meated farm-raised trout on the market today. These trout, almost all in the ten-ounce category, became extremely popular with the carriage trade. We enjoyed a profitable association with these fishermen from about 1935 until 1947. Then sportsmen petitioned the provincial government to shut down the commercial fisheries on Christina Lake, and the government agreed to terminate the arrangement.

I doubt that this commercial fishery had a negative effect on the stocks of Kokanee trout in this lake. The same amount of fish was shipped each year for nearly twelve years without fail. The yearly catch of between six and seven thousand pounds never seemed to have an adverse effect on the lake's fish stocks. However, that was as much fish as we could sell to the luxury restaurants and fancy clubs that paid a dollar and a half per pound. We purposely kept the volume small rather than sell a larger volume at a lower price. It was far more lucrative and a more sensible proposition to sell this exotic specialty item in small quantities. It was another item that allowed chefs to acquire something special that other companies couldn't get unless they ordered from Van Shell.

Our monopoly in the trout business did not exactly end on that note. A short time after the Christina Lake fishery was shut down, a Japanese gentleman showed up and offered us a five-thousand-pound-per-month quota of Japanese farm-raised trout in eight-ounce sizes packed in five-pound boxes — thirty pounds per case. These Japanese farm fish were white flesh and bland compared to the Christina Lake Kokanee trout, but they had appeal because they were the only thing available for the market. We readily accepted his offer and enjoyed another five years with a good item to market. By this time, the demand for trout was so great that we had to ration the fish to our customers. Again we sold at fixed prices to our customers without any complaint.

There is an old adage that sooner or later all good business deals come to an end. This happened to us in a sudden way when the trout we were selling for two dollars per pound appeared in Woodward's stores for ninety-five cents per pound. We were promptly put out of the trout business. A few months later trout were selling in every chain store at the low same price. Now that trout was no longer an exotic high-priced specialty, it lost its cachet in fancy establishments. For a while sales hung on, but after the public got used to the product, sales dipped and trout once again became less readily available. The trade can be a very fickle and unpredictable master.

THE INDUSTRY FLOUNDERS

Fur ranching on the lower mainland and in the Fraser Valley began in the dirty thirties. Two of these ranches were located in Burnaby. Walter Mead's large operation, with at least a couple of thousand mink, was located on Mead Avenue, and Hoppy's place, with about six hundred mink, was at Sperling Avenue and Broadway. Hoppy's five-acre ranch was situated on the corner where the hydro substation now sits, on land that was expropriated from him for a pittance by the old British Columbia Electric Company. Hoppy cursed B.C. Electric for years and refused to sign his property away. He took solace in running off B.C. Electric representatives who constantly hounded him to sign and he refused to take the money.

Eventually, mink ranching moved into the Fraser Valley because land was cheap at the time, feed was available and the climate seemed perfect for mink.

Horsemeat, available for five cents per pound, was the standard feed. This ready market for horsemeat greatly reduced the population of wild horses in the interior of the province. When horsemeat reached the unheard of price of ten cents per pound, the mink ranchers began looking around for cheaper fare.

I entered the picture in 1938, when Pete Ambrose, fishing on his new boat, the *Tordo*, came in late on a Friday night with twenty-five thousand pounds of flounders. Nobody would buy his fish. At the time, I was twenty years old, working for my father and looking for an opportunity. Pete, getting pretty excited about his predicament, walked up to me and said, "Norman, unload the boat, wash it out, give me ten bucks and the whole load is yours." Impulsively I accepted his offer, gave two men three dollars each to unload the boat, and for the sum of sixteen dollars was the proud owner of more flounders than I could ever imagine.

Father was a bit perplexed at my impulsive purchase. "Do you know how many flounders that is!"

By then I had a pretty good idea, since there was a pyramid of them on the fish plant floor. After we sold two thousand pounds to the Blackburn Market on the corner of Robson and Seymour Streets, for four cents per pound, I was relieved to have recovered the money I put out. But it hardly touched the pile.

After giving the problem some thought I decided to load a thousand pounds on the back of our truck and drove out to see Hoppy. I offered him the flounders for three cents per pound. Hoppy was skeptical but I argued that fish was a great part of a wild mink's diet, so after hearing me out he relented and took five hundred pounds to get rid of me.

Early the next morning, Hoppy phoned me. "By jiminy," he said, "the mink are crazy about your flounders! Can you bring me another five thousand pounds for my freezer?" At three cents per pound, the flounders were less than half the price of horsemeat. Hoppy announced that for the time being he intended to alternate feeding his mink horsemeat one day and flounders the next. He figured that diet might be better for the mink and certainly suited his bottom line.

By Sunday midnight I sold the balance of those flounders to a score of mink ranchers for three cents per pound. Three or four refused to buy the fish but took twenty- or thirty-pound samples to try it out. It took a lot of talking before I sold the last of the flounders. I believe that was the first time fish was used for mink feed in British Columbia. On Monday morning Father looked around the plant and asked me where the flounders had gone.

"I sold the whole works for three cents per pound and here's the money." I handed him a brown paper bag.

He counted out half the money. "This is for the company. You get the rest," he said, handing me a wad that contained three hundred and fifty dollars. On that Sunday I made more money than Bob Hope made in one day and now I was in the mink feed business.

In those days we were paying the Burns reduction plant to haul our offal away. I asked Father if I could have the offal for nothing. With a smile on his face he told me to go ahead and take it but cautioned me I would have to take it all, because Burns would not pick up small lots. I went through the same process with scrap fish as I did with the flounders. At first the ranchers were unsure it would be suitable feed for their mink, but in a short time it became quite acceptable.

In the years that followed about forty small draggers worked the mouth of the Fraser River as well three or four larger vessels that were unfit to work on the West Coast in winter months. They dragged the mouth of the river and on the Sand Heads continuously every day of the year. The larger fish went to the fish markets as food fish for processing while the undersized fish became mink feed for four or five cents per pound. The mink ranching industry in the Fraser Valley steadily escalated until it was using eight to ten million pounds of fish per year.

This situation continued until the Fraser River bank was completely vacuumed of almost every pound of fish regardless of size. Finally, it became uneconomical for even the small boats to continue fishing when they could only catch three or four hundred pounds of fish or less in a twelve-hour day. Scores of draggers were fishing in the same way all over the Gulf of Georgia, without Department of Fisheries and Oceans interference to prevent them from taking illegal, undersized fish, until the Gulf was practically barren of ground fish.

During these years, the herring were cleaned up and sold to reduction plants for fish meal and, in later years, for the roe, which was desired by the Japanese. Consequently there was greatly reduced feed fish left to sustain commercial stocks of ling cod, grey cod and other species of flat fish, including soles, halibut and flounders. Without an abundance of smaller prey fish, the larger fish began feeding on juvenile fish of their own species. The rape of the Gulf of Georgia began more than fifty years ago. Now I doubt this area contains even five percent of the fish that once swam in its waters. The lack of herring has also drastically affected the salmon stocks.

The mink farmers were receiving up to forty dollars or more for their best pelts and twenty to twenty-five dollars for run-of-the-mill goods. It cost about eight dollars to feed the mink to maturity. The mink ranchers began selling breeding stock to the Russians, Japanese and Scandinavian countries for three hundred and fifty to five hundred dollars or more per breeding pair. Within a short time, the Japanese, Poles, Russians and other European producers were raising and selling forty million mink pelts every year. This unfortunate business decision brought enormous repercussions for British Columbia producers. The price of pelts fell until the local ranchers were reduced to receiving five to nine dollars for their pelts. The British Columbia mink ranching industry collapsed because of the ranchers' greed and their lack of foresight in protecting their industry. Later the same mistake occurred when we exported salmon eggs to foreign fish farms to the detriment of our own commercial fishing industry.

The fur industry in the Fraser Valley was never able to fully recover because of the increased worldwide overproduction of farmed furs. Poles and Russians had enormous North Pacific fishing fleets working twelve miles off our coast. Large steel draggers delivering to mother ships depleted fish stocks in order to supply foreign fur ranches with cheap feed that enabled them to glut the market with cheap furs. This action not only further reduced fish stocks in the North Pacific but ruined the market for Canadian farmed fur.

By the time Canada had a three-hundred-mile fishing limit in place, various foreign fishing fleets had denuded our fishing grounds. In addition, after the three-hundred-mile limit was in force, foreign fleets were allowed quotas because they pleaded hardships and lobbied successfully to continue fishing in our waters.

The Department of Fisheries and Oceans gave the Japanese a large quota of our prized black cod (sable fish) for a number of years because the Japanese offered to provide statistics on our squid resources. The Japanese overfished our black cod and we received statistics that were well known to everybody but the Department of Fisheries and Oceans. The Russians saved the North Pacific grounds adjacent to Alaska for their own future use while fishing worldwide in every territory. Foreign fleets received a free ride while screws were continually tightened on regulations governing Canadian nationals, making it difficult for them to compete with foreigners. Canada put observers on foreign fishing boats to monitor fishing quotas, but the heavily mechanized fleets handling vast quantities of fish, at speed, made it impossible to keep track of the amount of fish caught and processed. Finally, Canada closed the barn door after the proverbial horse (in this case, fish) was long gone.

Sometimes I think of that load of Pete Ambrose's flounders that I flogged to the mink ranchers. Ground fish that were once plentiful on the Fraser River bank are but a memory, like wild horses in the Chilcotin. Sure they exist, but in numbers that place them among the mostly vanished. What started as a local industry escalated into reckless, international exploitation of resources that have threatened a whole range of species and destroyed others. We seem to have learned nothing from the well-documented lessons of natural history. The more we know, it seems, the greater our chances of confusing the issues and bungling the solutions to monumental problems.

THE FISHERMEN'S BALL

In the thirties, when Jim Pope was about thirty years old, he and his wife and black cocker spaniel made two round trips a week to Campbell Avenue fish dock with his forty-foot double ender loaded with small early sockeye for Sid Humphreys at Colonial Cannery. These were fish that were attempting to get into Powell Lake in the Pender Harbour area. They were a small species of sockeye that averaged about three and three-quarter pounds each. These wonderful small early sockeye also entered into the Nit Nat and a few other areas on the coast. Most of these runs are ancient history today, decimated by industry and creek-robbing seine boats. A number of families, mostly of Scottish and Finnish origin, depended on this run for most of their income. Jim's father owned the store in Egmont, which was up the channel about twelve miles from Pender Harbour. The Scots sold their fish to B.C. Packers. Jim fished, and because he had good connections, he was able to buy enough fish to make the trips to Colonial worth while.

Jim Pope was a very good fisherman. He had several vessels, including *Welcome Pass* and *Willow Point*. Jim was also a good promoter and that helped out some. The result was he did quite well in the fishing industry. He taught Bill Kitsel how to bottom trawl on the *Welcome Pass*. Bill took over the *Welcome Pass* and fished it for a couple of years before he built his own boat, named the *Sharlene K*. Bill Kitsel was also an expert fisherman, a hard worker, a good businessman and lucky, to boot. He became very wealthy and has been retired for a number of years.

Tommy Wilson, who owned the *Cape Norman*, also delivered his dragged fish into the Campbell Avenue fish dock. Tommy was on par with Bill Faulkner, a quiet, good-natured man who was one of the best fishermen. Kitsel, Pope, Wilson, Jack Eagland, Spanish Pete Ambrose, Tom Scoretz, Louis Summers and Faulkner were always the highliners. Faulkner caught enormous quantities of fish when he took out one of B.C. Packer's large vessels. He handled more than two hundred thousand pounds of fish per trip at the peak of the season.

Tommy Wilson's *Cape Norman* was loaded when it held sixty-five thousand pounds of iced fish, so he compensated for that by making twice as many trips as the others to still remain a top producer. When they fished for grey cod in Nanoose Bay each year, right after Christmas, Tommy delivered two full loads a week right on into the spring. More than ten vessels worked that ground each season. They took turns sweeping up Nanoose Inlet, loading their vessels in less than two days. I estimate that more than two million pounds of prime large grey cod was taken out of the Nanoose Bay area each spring.

Whenever the *Cape Norman* was tied up at Campbell Avenue and the crew was uptown, you could bet they'd be all together bending their elbows in some drinking establishment. Tommy was quite a character and his crew were particularly devoted to him. Tommy would be sitting with his wife and friends at an adjoining table, but the boys were never too far away. One evening when my wife, Kathleen, and I went out for a beer, we no sooner entered the bar than we spotted Tommy. He caught my eye and headed directly over to join us. His crew followed in single file. I stood up to move my chair to make more room for the crew, who all looked to be in fine form.

Tommy turned to his crew and said, "Not here, boys. Can't you see there's a lady present." Pointing to a nearby table, he directed, "Sit there. And keep it respectful." From time to time, Tommy would turn with a smile to speak to his boys and then he would continue with our conversation. "The boys are in their cups," he said. "When they're like they are tonight with their despicable language, they're unfit company for any lady."

Bill Faulkner's young brother Dave was there as part of Tommy's crew that evening along with Bob Sherburne. That was the last time I saw young Faulkner and Sherburne and the last time I sat down to enjoy a draft or two with Tommy Wilson, as good a man as there was on the coast. A few months later, the *Cape Norman* left Comox with a load of herring and travelled down to Nanaimo and then attempted to cross the Gulf of Georgia in stormy weather. She was lost with all hands. No trace of her was ever found.

The beam trawlers fishing from Campbell Avenue had a co-op set up that benefitted them for tax purposes. They were a co-op when it suited them, but a private business when that was more advantageous. These kinds of organizations are often formed to fix prices and keep everybody onside. However, it seemed that in most issues the four directors dominated the organization. Some of the other members accused them of arranging to always have their own vessels in port at opportune times to receive the top fresh-fish market prices. Most of the fishermen received top prices for thirty percent of their loads and freezer prices for the balance. Freezer prices were two cents per pound less than the fresh market prices. These settlements caused a lot of hard feelings between boat crews, so that every once in a while trouble would flare up, resulting in punch-ups. Most of the fishermen were an independent lot to begin with, and all sold to their own markets. In any case, politics were rampant and the directors became very powerful within the organization.

At the end of each year a big party was held in one of the ballrooms of a major Vancouver hotel. There was plenty of good food, and liquor flowed like a tide over the throng. It was at these big events that matters that had been festering for a long time were finally settled, after quite a bit of alcohol had been consumed. After one of these affairs, a director came away with two black eyes and another left with lumps as big as chicken eggs all over his head. Of course, these were fishermen, and during the year there also were some sessions of settling of scores in the organization's office. I was told, by someone in the know, that the year-end windup of black eyes and lumps was courtesy of Tommy Wilson, a short time before the *Cape Norman* was lost.

There were some independent trawlers who did not join the Beam Trawlers Co-operative. One of them was Julius Barth, with his *Dorbarth* (his wife's name was Dorothy). Another was Sandy Peterson, with the *Miss Jean*. Sandy was a good fisherman, a highliner, who delivered all of his fish to our company. This caused some hard feelings with the co-op, but we made it a policy to buy from everybody. When the independents were unloading, some of the directors came over to harangue them to sell through the co-op. Sometimes arguments ensued and old scores were settled all over again.

Sandy had Portuguese immigrant fishermen in his crew. They were good men and they handled the eighty-five-foot vessel well, except for one careless night. Fishermen for some reason nearly always leave port just after midnight. It was Sandy's habit to leave at that time for the West Coast fishing grounds. No doubt Sandy took the *Miss Jean* out of the basin into the harbour and out into the Gulf and set her on a course to clear Victoria. Then he turned over the wheel to one of his crewmen and turned in. Most likely he left orders to wake him if there was a problem. His crew were used to this arrangement and they took over until they reached Victoria. Then Sandy would get up and take over until they cleared the south end of Vancouver Island and then set a course for the fishing grounds.

The *Miss Jean* never made it. Somewhere between Vancouver and Victoria, carelessness or an oversight cost all these men their lives. A large steel tugboat towing heavily loaded barges caused the *Miss Jean* to flip over as she crossed over the three-inch steel towing cable between the tug and the barges. These steel cables are very heavy and the two thousand feet of line they let out is eight to twelve feet below the surface, midway between the tug and its tow. The weight of the heavy cable allows it to spring up or down to compensate for waves or swell so it does not cause a jerk at either end of the cable. Many a vessel has passed over a towline without knowing it because the cable had sagged to a depth where it could be crossed. Nobody except the man on watch on the tug would have known that the *Miss Jean* had turned over.

There is a light on one side of the front end of each barge and a light on the back end of the last tow. These lights are not very large or bright, so in a haze or a faint mist they can easily be missed. Experienced fishermen and mariners are extremely vigilant when they see a towboat. They immediately search for the object the towboat is pulling to avoid crossing between tug and tow. However, in spite of the care taken to avoid such an accident, through the years there have been a number of such incidents, and in most of them the crews perished. Sandy and his men on the *Miss Jean* remained alive in the overturned vessel. Rescuers could hear them hammering inside the hull. Obviously they were in an air pocket.

How to get them out was the problem. I believe it could be accomplished today, but thirty-five years ago they did not have the equipment or the knowledge of how to go about it. In this case, they snubbed up the *Miss Jean* between the towboat and another large vessel. When they cut a hole into the hull, enough air blew out so the *Miss Jean* sank down lower in the water and the air bubble the men were in filled with water and they drowned. It was a sad occasion for all of us. We knew in our hearts that an innocent man at the wheel probably made a mistake, unknowingly crossing the towline, and it cost them all their lives. When the *Miss Jean* was salvaged the marks where the cable rubbed the hull were there to prove what had happened.

On some mornings there were three or four vessels in to unload assorted sole, ling cod, true cod, black cod and other fish. We would take fifty thousand pounds of fish for the fresh fish market at a price of around twelve cents per pound, and the balance, up to fifty thousand pounds of fish, to freeze at ten cents per pound. Crews would unload with a will, because the first fish off brought premium prices. Slow unloading meant those vessels received freezing prices for most of their fish. Fishermen like Scoretz, Spanish Pete and Kitsel ruled their crews with an iron fist, like ancient British naval captains. They urged the crew to unload more quickly to take advantage of the fresh-fish market prices. Sometimes freezer prices dropped three or four cents per pound if business was bad or there was too much fish for sale.

Scoretz had lost one eye, and on a hot day the glass eyeball in his head would itch, so Scoretz would take it out of the socket and put it in his pocket. Now when Scoretz got mad at the crew for some infraction, or anybody he disagreed with, he was a sight to behold as he stood crouched like he was ready to spring at any moment with one glaring eye and a red eye socket with an eyelid flapping up and down over it. He had a colourful vocabulary too. It seemed at times that Scoretz was going to blow up and disintegrate. I cannot remember when he did not have at least one blowup while he unloaded his *Haste* or later the *Mr. Wind*.

One morning Scoretz was in with the *Mr. Wind* loaded right down to the scuppers. There were three other vessels in, and the fish was slowly going out for freezing prices. Scoretz, in a foul mood, was down on the deck washing pen boards and cursing everything in general. He had removed his eye and his intimidating stare scared away any of the hangers-on who were attempting to bum a fish from him. He had about eighty thousand pounds of fish, and sales were so slow it looked as if Scoretz might have to finish unloading the next morning. He and his crew were anxious to unload and wash out the boat so they could go home for a couple of days. A fisheries inspector from the Department of Fisheries and Oceans arrived and decided to climb down the ladder and inspect the *Mr. Wind*'s hold to see if Scoretz had any illegal halibut on board. The officer had the law on his side and the right to inspect the *Mr. Wind* for contraband. Scoretz kept his peace but his flapping eyelid over the bare eye socket kept time with his muttered curses as he continued working.

The officer came up and informed all present that there were no illegal halibut in the hold. Scoretz already knew that and he was not amused with the holdup in the unloading procedure. The officer then demanded to inspect the galley and captain's quarters for illegal fish.

Scoretz was working himself up to an explosion and he was having difficulty containing his anger. After a few minutes the officer came out of the galley with about five pounds of fresh halibut fillets that he had removed from the refrigerator. He informed Scoretz that he was laying a charge against him for having illegal halibut on board. In his excitement at making the bust, the inspector went on to tell Scoretz that the *Mr. Wind* and the load of fish were liable for arrest and seizure by the crown.

This was all Scoretz could stand. He screamed out a piercing curse and thrust the high-pressure stream of water, which a moment before was stripping slime from pen boards, into the officer's face and blew the hat off his head. The hat with the Queen's emblem on the badge flew high in the air and sailed under the dock to light upside down under the public toilets that directed their flow directly into the basin. In addition to losing his hat, the officer received an instant bath from the stream of water Scoretz had directed at him. Scoretz continued to give the officer the high-pressure water treatment as he climbed the steel ladder back up to the wharf. His screams and curses turned the air blue and attracted every one's attention.

Spanish Pete stood with a foolish grin on his face, asking, "What happened?"

Julian Gordon, the Beam Trawlers Co-op business manager, and a number of startled fishermen stood in groups waiting for the police to arrive and take Scoretz away. Within ten minutes, a dozen Department of Fisheries and Oceans officers had arrived to gather around their drenched comrade. A few of the higher ups also showed but they were wary of the situation and kept their distance from the *Mr. Wind*. The Department of Fisheries and Oceans had been running quite a campaign against illegal halibut, but this was the first time an officer had actually looked to see what a crew had been eating. Some of the fishermen were grumbling about how petty the Department of Fisheries and Oceans was becoming. In any case, it soon became obvious that the police had not been called.

For months, a section of Department of Fisheries and Oceans officers patrolled the fish dock in a show of strength. Wild rumours changed the story at least two or three times each day. Some were predicting that Scoretz would spend a least a month in the cooler and that he would be assessed a ten- or fifteen-thousand-dollar fine. Others figured that because of the time that had passed, Scoretz would beat the rap. He had thrown the evidence overboard after the officer had left the *Mr. Wind*. Without evidence, the only possible charge would be assault. Time has a way of healing a wound, and after six months had passed, all was forgotten, only to be remembered occasionally for a laugh.

Scoretz, a talented fellow, built the *Haste* and then followed that by building the steel-hulled *Mr. Wind*. He retired to the Sunshine coast and built a sailboat to sail around the world. However, it burned to the waterline shortly after it was launched. Today, Scoretz is taking it easy. I doubt he removes his glass eye very often now because he doesn't have to sweat out a living the way he did in the old days. It was a good thing the Department of Fisheries and Oceans decided to back off. Scoretz was a good man who contributed greatly to our country with the people he employed and the taxes he paid. Four or five pounds of halibut fillets in *Mr. Wind*'s galley was no big deal when some big companies were bringing in boatloads of net-caught halibut, out of season, for test purposes.

VON ARNIM

In the thirties, the Japanese fishermen dominated the Fraser River salmon fishery. They also dominated the West Coast trolled salmon industry. Their association there was ruled with an iron fist. The organization had large ice packers that gathered day-caught fish from the Japanese trollers and from the few white fishermen.

At that time, no other companies had buying stations on the West Coast. There were no roads, except from Port Alberni, at that time, so fish could not be transported by truck from the West Coast to markets in Vancouver. Consequently the Japanese organization, with their large East Coast style packers, dominated the trolled salmon industry in that area. Salmon caught by the substantial Japanese population in Tofino, Ucluelet and Port Alberni was sold to the highest bidder in Canada or the United States.

The Gregory family had a fish-buying station in Port Alberni and probably were the dominant buyers there. B.C. Packers was in bankruptcy, so they had no trolled salmon buying stations anywhere on the coast. The Canadian Fishing Company had a large seine salmon fleet in the Depression and they controlled the halibut fishery as well. Most of the other companies concentrated on net salmon — gillnet and seined fish — for their canned production.

The white fishermen dominated the trolled salmon fishery in the Gulf of Georgia, in almost all the areas between Vancouver Island and the mainland. They caught millions of pounds of bluebacks each season. In my opinion, bluebacks were creek cohos that spent their entire life cycle in the Gulf of Georgia. These fish, eight to ten ounces in size, exited creeks by the millions during the spring freshets. They were voracious feeders, gaining almost a pound per month, so by the end of the year some of them weighed up to twelve pounds. By then they were three years old, having spent the first two years of their lives in the creeks.

The day after the coho season opened in the Gulf of Georgia, at daybreak more than three hundred thousand pounds of bluebacks sat in packers in front of Sid Humphreys' Colonial Cannery, at the Campbell Avenue fish dock. Some quantities of fish were also delivered dressed, packed in crushed ice for the fresh-fish markets. Any sports fisherman of that era could catch fifty of these fish in half a day. You could see a cloud of salmon attempting to grab the herring strip. It was common knowledge that some commercial fishermen caught more than a thousand bluebacks per day.

Most of our fish buyers and fishermen had keys to our plant, so on many mornings a variety of fish had been unloaded in the night and was iced on the floor. Father had good connections with many fish buyers all over the coast, so we had plenty of fish arriving, even in the winter. Some packers unloaded at Campbell Avenue in the mornings, and fish came in by the Union Steam Ships to various points where we picked it up by truck. We received a steady supply of fish from the Gregory family in Port Alberni (before they were bought out by B.C. Packers), from Winter Harbour on the West Coast of northern Vancouver Island, from the Live Cod Fishermen's Co-op, the Koyamas and a score of other buyers working in the Gulf of Georgia from Ladysmith to Campbell River, and from Von Arnim in the Pender Harbour, Egmont area.

Von Arnim packed trolled salmon, making one or two trips per week. When the war broke out, Von Arnim vanished and we never saw him again. It seems he sold his packer for whatever he could get for it and crossed the border into the United States before he made his way back to Germany. Bill Steiner, Father's partner, was a Czech Jew, and Von Arnim was German, but they got along famously. Steiner was educated in Austria and spoke German fluently, as did most Czechs. Czechoslovakia was part of the Austro-Hungarian Empire, and did not officially exist as an entity until the breakup after the First World War.

About a year into the war, we received a letter from Von Arnim that had been sent from somewhere in Africa. The letter contained an informal photo of German military offers gathered around a solemn General Rommel. Van Arnim was in the centre of the photo with his arm draped around the general's shoulder. The text in the letter said, "Hello, Willy, how are you keeping? How is John and the rest of the crew? We are having a ball over here. I hope to see you all again some time in the future. Until we meet again. Von Arnim."

Strange things happen in one's lifetime, and this was one of the most bizarre incidents I can remember. Nobody answered his letter and we never saw or heard from him again.

THE GAMBLER

How Julius Barth became a fisherman is a wonder. Originally from Hungary, Julius talked about his short life in the military in Europe. Once while we were in our cups, he got up and pulled a picture of himself out from behind another larger picture on the wall in his wheelhouse. It was a photo of Julius in uniform holding a rifle with a fixed bayonet.

Julius saw action against Czechoslovakia when Hungary attempted to recover some of its territory that was awarded to it by U.S. President Wilson when the victorious allies broke up the Austro-Hungarian Empire. The war over the border between Slovakia and Hungary lasted only a few months. I was interested in hearing about that border war, which I figured must have been pretty hot, because I knew two Czech immigrants who had been wounded in that conflict, one shot in the leg, the other in the forearm.

I was fascinated by how Julius became a fisherman in British Columbia, and a pretty good fisherman at that, when he never saw ocean until he was more than thirty years old. What he had going for him was that he was a hard worker and he had a lot of good ideas, some ahead of his time. It seemed he could solve any problem and catch fish too. But Julius had one strike against him that would always keep him down. He was a gambling addict. He was a dedicated poker player who could not quit when he was ahead of the game. He also played with some unsavoury characters who knew how to keep him on the hook. Obviously, from time to time, Julius was allowed to win some money.

This made him totally overconfident and only made his mania worse. The slickers who made a living playing poker got a good hold on his obsession. On average he was losing eight hundred to twelve hundred dollars a week. This constant drain on his resources meant that Julius became a hell of a fisherman in order to finance his obsession.

Julius lived with his wife, Dorothy, on a small farm in Surrey. They had chickens, hogs and two or three milk cows. Dorothy ran that end of their business. No matter how bad his gambling affliction, he always managed to find his way home.

It was a mystery how Julius acquired the all-steel sixty-five-foot vessel he named the *Dorbarth*. We know that after the Second World War shipyards were attempting to diversify and two steel-hull vessels of identical size and shape, fitted out with three-hundred-and-fifty-horse Caterpillar engines were built for the fishing industry. Fishing boats were always built with nice lines, not only to be practical but also to be beautiful. These steel-hulled vessels were seaworthy and well powered but they were ugly ducklings that nobody wanted to own. Nobody had ever seen such ugly contraptions, so they sat ignored in the shipyards. When the lucrative business that had been provided by the war years came to an end, most of the shipyards were having trouble surviving. These two experimental vessels were sold below cost on a trial basis with a small down payment. Somehow, Julius acquired one of these vessels. Perhaps he got lucky at the poker table. I was never able to find out how the vessel got into his possession.

Julius went out with the *Dorbarth* at four a.m. each morning to the Sand Heads, five miles off the mouth of the Fraser River and beam trawled, that is, bottom trawled. On the average day, he came in with two thousand pounds of mink feed for three cents per pound — about sixty dollars worth. Two hundred pounds of skate wings at three cents per pound — about twelve dollars. Two hundred pounds of flounders at three cents per pound — about six dollars. Five hundred pounds of legal sole at ten cents per pound — about fifty dollars. Odds and ends brought him another twenty-five dollars. A couple of cans of dogfish livers could net him another eighty dollars. The whole trip would add up to about two hundred and thirty dollars. He fished by himself. God only knows how he was able to do that, but it meant that there was no crew to split with. His fuel bill, at nineteen cents per gallon, could not have amounted to more than nine dollars per day. He knitted in most of the holes in the net by himself with treated twine, and ice was about twenty bucks per day. He was not hard on his gear, and expenses were cheap, so he was making money.

He came back in at about five thirty p.m. He unloaded his *Dorbarth* by himself and in less than half an hour he had on his suit, shiny shoes and a brown Stetson and was ready for the poker game. He drew the two hundred–plus dollars for his catch and hurried down the dock to go downtown to meet the boys who were waiting for him. Julius lived on fish, fish soup with bread and coffee and very little else to supplement his weekly diet. On weekends he went home to Dorothy. Sometimes he took a drag on future earnings before he went home. We had no objections to advancing him fifty or one hundred dollars or more. During those times, shipyard workers made five bucks a day and the average worker made fifty cents per hour.

Sometimes Julius left Vancouver with the *Dorbarth* for a month or two. We speculated that he was on charter packing fish for some company up coast, or he was beam trawling and hauling his fish into Klemtu or Rupert. Maybe he was trying to escape from the gambling routine. Like a homing pigeon, Julius always returned to Campbell Avenue and he often had twenty or thirty thousand pounds of good fish on board.

The fish was unloaded, the *Dorbarth* was washed out ready for the next trip and then Julius would receive three to five thousand dollars for his catch and depart for town where the vultures were awaiting his return. Four days later, Julius would return to the fish dock, borrow a thousand dollars on his next trip, buy ice, fuel and groceries and depart for the fishing grounds. He might return in two weeks or a month. How he managed to deliver a good load of fish by himself was a mystery to everyone.

The steamboat inspectors would inspect every vessel over ten tons capacity to see that there was a life raft or lifeboat aboard, life jackets, fire extinguishers and a good compass and to make sure that the vessel was in seaworthy condition. This inspection was done every three years. Some time after one inspection, someone had borrowed Julius's lifeboat and failed to return it. Without the inspector's permit he could not clear the harbour to make a fishing trip, and without a lifeboat he could not get that permit.

On this occasion he had a charter to pack salmon for the National Cannery operated by Boyd Shannon. As usual Julius was broke and now he couldn't leave this port without a lifeboat or life raft. We had a skiff in our loft that was a spare, so I loaned him the skiff and two hundred bucks. He was elated and he promised to square up with me after his trip for Boyd. As usual he was running the *Dorbarth* by himself. He had to sleep sometime, so he would set the boat on a course and turn on the automatic pilot. He set his alarm clock for the estimated time it took him to reach the point where a new course would have to be set. Again the automatic pilot took over when he cooked his meals or fiddled with the engine. Automatic pilots were a handy way of steering a vessel, but a crewman had to stand watch at all times to avoid deadheads and other vessels. Setting the automatic pilot without a man on watch was like playing Russian roulette. It was unsafe and completely against the law.

However, as usual, Julius reached his destination and loaded seventy thousand pounds of salmon before his return trip to Vancouver. Once again he put on the automatic pilot at various points on the return trip while he slept, cooked meals and attended to other chores. Somewhere along the return journey, the alarm clock failed to wake him up. No doubt he was extremely tired so he slept on until the *Dorbarth* ran aground and the rumble woke him up as she slid over the uneven bottom.

The vessel was hard aground and no matter how hard he revved up the engine he could not back the *Dorbarth* off the bar. Fortunately for him, the hull was not damaged but the tide was going out and soon the *Dorbarth* would fall over on her side. Once that happened she would never rise with seventy thousand pounds of salmon in her hold. She would fill up with water and then the ball game was over. The tide went out, the *Dorbarth* fell over and the incoming tide filled her up. It seemed like Julius had no option but to get to shore with my skiff and report the accident to Boyd Shannon and the insurance company. At that time, seventy thousand pounds of sockeye salmon was worth more than one hundred thousand dollars, so the insurance company would not be thrilled with the news. But Julius had other ideas. He stayed on board and pitched the seventy thousand pounds of sockeye over the side. I believe it took him two tides to accomplish this task.

Once the *Dorbarth* was relieved of her load and the water was pumped out she righted herself. Julius flushed out the engine with three oil changes after he ran the engine for five minutes each time, and he took her in to Port Hardy to clean up the engine room, wheelhouse and to repair electrical equipment. Whether he did the work himself or got the work done on the cuff is anyone's guess. The insurance company was choked, but Boyd Shannon was quite elated. The canned salmon market was in a slump, so he would have lost money on that load. Fifteen days later when Julius showed up at our plant with a load of ground fish, we noticed Boyd was laughing instead of crying about the sinking. Because he was an extremely religious man, obviously he thought God was looking after him and Julius. I'm sure the payment from the insurance company did much to ease Boyd's spirit.

Another time, young Jack Shannon arrived on his *Shannon M* with a load of drag fish. He stopped to talk to me on his way home to tell me about the strange encounter he had with Julius and his *Dorbarth* when he was crossing the Gulf to Vancouver. "I thought I saw a long log with a seagull sitting on it, as often happens on those waters. The closer I got the stranger it appeared. Finally, I looked through my binoculars and I could make out a man sitting on some object. When I got closer I realized it was a capsized vessel with a man on it, and a short time later

I recognized Julius Barth sitting on the bottom of his *Dorbarth*. I took him aboard and continued on my way to Vancouver while radioing in for a salvage crew to come out and save the *Dorbarth* from sinking."

Julius explained that his net had snagged the bottom on some solid object. No matter how hard he tried pulling from different directions he could not free the six-thousand-dollar net from the snag. As a last resort he decided to pull up on it until he tore it off to salvage what he could. He still had the old-style beam trawl that pulled the net in from the side of the vessel. He winched in the cable until the boat keeled over to a point of almost no return. In the last try to free his net, he tipped over the *Dorbarth* a fraction too far and she slid down on an oily swell. His *Dorbarth* slowly turned over and Julius scrambled around onto the bottom and sat there like a seagull on a log.

If Jack had not been passing by on his way home with a load of fish, and if the wind had come up, that would have ended the story without anyone knowing what had happened to Julius. Once the air bubble that was preventing the vessel from sinking escaped in a rough sea, the *Dorbarth* would have gone to the bottom like a stone without a trace to let anyone know what happened. I doubt Julius would have survived if the *Dorbarth* had sunk. His body would have been found floating in some backwash, and then it would have been a guess as to what had happened.

The salvage boat righted the *Dorbarth*, pumped her dry and towed her into Vancouver. They even salvaged the net without tearing it up too badly. By the next afternoon, Julius had flushed her out again with several oil changes and it seemed to be in good running order. Normally there is a lot of damage to the engine when sea water drowns it, but Julius seemed to escape any serious consequences with his Cat engine. Three or four oil changes and a lot of elbow grease to clean it up inside seemed to do the job. Some of the electrical equipment had to be replaced, but in four days he was nearly ready to go fishing again. He had the net spread out on the dock as he furiously mended the torn areas and replaced the twisted bridles that were so damaged they would not pull out evenly.

There is a bond that holds fishermen together. Old timers marvelled at Julius for his ability to work the *Dorbarth* by himself. They stood around shaking their heads at his adventures. With time on their hands, they gathered to help Julius mend his net, free of charge. A few days of repair, a five-hundred-dollar drag from our office, and with fuel, ice and groceries aboard, Julius was ready to go by himself on another fishing trip.

Finally, the day came when the Cat engine in the *Dorbarth* required a proper overhaul. Sleeves had to be replaced in the cylinders. Rings had to be replaced on pistons, bearing shells had to be replaced in the connecting rods and the crankshaft had to be inspected. This was a major job that included all new gaskets, spacers and many other items. The engine had taken a beating with two sinkings and now proper repairs had to be made.

This major overhaul would cost at least twelve thousand dollars in a proper shipyard, and obviously Julius did not have the money nor could he get credit in the shipyards. He decided to do the work himself. Julius was a pretty good jack-of-all-trades but this was more than he could handle. Joe Mills, who was an ex-navy man and a retired heavy-duty diesel mechanic, took pity on Julius and began advising and supervising the work. Pretty soon Joe had his coveralls on and all his tools aboard the *Dorbarth* and he did the work with Julius helping.

One day I encountered Joe in his grease-saturated coveralls taking a breather. "How is it coming along?" I asked.

He answered, "I couldn't stand by to see that old fool work on that engine. When monkey mechanics get finished with a job like that, either the crankshaft will snap or a piston or two will come out the side of the cylinders. I agreed to do the work for five hundred bucks up front and a couple of thousand dollars on the cuff. I know where I can get a lot of parts at a way better price than Julius will ever manage. I felt sorry for the poor bastard, so I've allowed myself to get sucked into the job. I'm doing it because he's a nice old guy and I'm a damn fool." Joe, an Englishman from an industrial part of that country, was a fine mechanic and a character who worked on a lot of different vessels.

Each day Joe arrived at Campbell Avenue in clean coveralls and he went home like chimney sweep. "My old woman is getting pretty mad at me for coming home late and so dirty. Jeezus, she's threatening to leave home if I keep this up." Every day Julius escorted Joe to lunch at the cafe on the fish dock for a sumptuous lunch. He knew that Joe was working cheap and his heart wasn't completely in it. Julius figured that if he trumpeted Joe's skills he'd help him get other jobs but Joe remained unimpressed.

About a month later came the big day when Joe was going to push the button on the starter engine that turned the big engine over. Everybody had their fingers crossed, including Joe because he had improvised a lot of the work.

Julius had a couple of good bottles of Scotch whisky on hand for the event and a crowd went down to observe the performance. Julius opened a bottle and both he and Joe took a pull out of it. Joe took his coat off, rolled up his sleeves and descended into the engine room. There was a whir as the gasoline starting motor barked into life without hesitation. Joe let it warm up a little, then poured the coal to it as he threw in the clutch that would turn over the big Caterpillar engine. It sprang to life as diesel fuel sprayed onto its cylinder heads. That old Cat was turning over evenly without hesitation and no black smoke was puffing out of the stack. Everybody was smiling at the sound of the power turning over in that engine. Joe and Julius came out of the engine room and each took another liberal pull on the opened bottle. Then two additional bottles were uncorked and it was drinks all around. They ran the engine all afternoon while they congratulated one another on a job well done. Julius tossed the empty bottles into the basin and opened more bottles of Scotch. Soon he and Joe were staggering around slapping each other on the back. I wondered what Joe's wife had to say to him when he arrived home in that condition.

Right after the overhaul, Julius, with another drag to cover fuel, ice and groceries, departed by himself for a trip of fish. He owed money so he had to get moving to bring in cash to pay his obligations. Twelve days later he was back with about forty thousand pounds of top-grade fish worth about twelve thousand dollars. I looked down at the boat and saw two First Nations women pitching fish into the unloading bucket. A third one holding a cup of coffee and a sandwich peered out from the galley. Julius was full of energy. "How do you like my fish, Norman?" he asked. "How do you like my new crew?" The fish was unloaded in jig time. Julius got paid, and a day later he departed to the fishing grounds. He decided the only way to keep his crew was by providing lots of good food and booze and to spend very little time in port so he wouldn't have to go looking for them. He managed to get out of port without anyone going AWOL and ten days later he was back with another load.

On the third trip he arrived back without his female crew. Instead he hired a couple of itinerants to go in the hold and fill up the unloading bucket. Dempsey Neuman was there to pick up a couple of tons of mink feed and he asked Julius if he had any halibut on board. Julius said he did and he would get one for him shortly. "Norman," he said, "I have a few halibut aboard but you always tell me you won't take them. You can have them if you want because you take all my fish."

"No, thanks, Julius," I replied. "I have enough trouble now without looking for more grief." Fresh halibut, out of season, was a serious offence with a heavy fine and even some possible jail time. I didn't want any part of that trouble for a lousy few dollars. I wouldn't even risk taking one gift fish home. With my luck, a zealous inspector would stumble on it and I would be crucified. If Father saw an illegal halibut he would have gone nuts because we were in the fish business as a profession and we couldn't afford to take stupid risks. No, I didn't want any part of even taking one illegal fish home to eat. It was one thing for the large fishing companies to have their trawlers deliver fifty to one hundred thousand pounds of dragged halibut (illegal for anyone else) and another for some poor guy to get caught with one fish. Major companies always had permission to take a substantial quantity of illegal net-caught halibut on the pretext given by the Department of Fisheries and Oceans that it was for scientific reasons. However, these big companies had directors who all wore the right school tie and they all belonged to the same club, so they operated under special dispensations, as one of them put it to me.

Julius descended the ladder to his boat and climbed down into the hold. There he pulled out a twenty-pound halibut and threw it into the bottom of the unloading bucket. When Dempsey dumped the bucket into his truck the halibut landed on top. One of the inspectors from Department of Fisheries and Oceans who happened along spotted the fish. Instead of confiscating the fish, he informed Julius that he was going to come down to inspect the hold of the *Dorbarth* for illegal halibut.

Julius popped out of the hold and ran to the wheelhouse. The engine had been idling to keep the pumps working. Julius put the boat in reverse and pushed the throttle wide open. The overhauled engine responded beautifully so that the bowline snapped, pulling out two pilings from under the dock. Then Julius put it full speed ahead and the back tie-up line snapped. He backed up again and turned the *Dorbarth* to depart from the dock but he forgot about the two guys in the hold and the unloading bucket that was fastened to a steel cable. It's one thing to break a three-quarter-inch manila rope line and other to snap a nine-sixteenth of an inch steel-wire rope. Julius had the engine wide open and the brake on the crane could not hold the wire, so it began to run out. When it got to where it was spliced on to the winch drum, it snubbed up the *Dorbarth*. The *Dorbarth* was caught like a fish on a line: a one-hundred-and-fifty-pound steel unloading bucket with about six hundred pounds of fish in it was hooked to one end of the steel cable in the hold, while the other end was fastened to a steel crane that was bending back and forth like a fishing rod. The bucket with the load of fish came up out of the hold but got caught under the edge of the open hatch.

Finally, after surging ahead under full power for three or four minutes, the unloading bucket came free and fell into the basin. The crane sprang back straight. We wound in the steel bucket, which came up still half full of fish. We all watched as Julius departed under full power and we saw the last of the *Dorbarth* as it rounded a high dock and went out of sight. The two fellows in the hold might not have figured out what had happened, but they had had enough sense to get out of the way of the flying bucket and that probably saved them from injury. In the meantime, Dempsey had had enough moxie to realize he was probably going to be pinched for the halibut in his truck. He quietly slipped behind the wheel and left the dock while everybody was occupied watching the action.

Where they came from nobody knew, but they appeared like mushrooms after a rain. Suddenly there were three or four additional inspectors on the prowl. The original man on the scene said, "I'm going to lay a charge against Julius and the *Dorbarth* for having caught halibut illegally with a net out of season."

"How are you going to do that without evidence?" somebody asked.

"There is evidence," he replied, "in the truck."

Somebody else piped up with "What truck?" Dempsey was long gone and the fish inspector was running up and down the dock looking for his truck. Now it was time for the rest of us to leave before they began trying to sign us up as witnesses to substantiate their charges.

About four hours later the *Dorbarth* arrived back at Campbell Avenue. By now Julius had disposed of the rest of the evidence. Inspectors descended on the *Dorbarth* like a swarm of angry bees. They searched in every nook and cranny, but there was not one halibut left aboard. Julius had given the two itinerants twenty-five bucks each and dumped them off at another dock. Now he denied that he had any halibut aboard and that was that. He claimed the fish the inspector saw was a white skate. The inspectors were fuming. They repeatedly tried to question Julius and informed him they were going to charge him. After a few days, with no witnesses or evidence, they had no choice but to give up.

I told Julius that he was lucky. I warned him that the next time they would land a seaplane beside him and catch him with the goods and put him right out of the industry. I believe that Julius normally followed the rules, but in an attempt to pay his debts off in a hurry he decided to sell fresh halibut out of season. Before that we had never heard of the old Hungarian being in trouble with the fisheries authorities.

Julius made three more trips that late summer and then he vanished. Fishermen wondered what happened to him. Rumours said that he went down with his boat. Others said that he died, and so it went on. Two year later I received a phone call on New Year's Eve just before we were leaving the house. I recognized the voice. "Is that you, Julius? Where are you calling from," I asked. "Heaven?"

"Hell no," he replied, "I'm tied up in front of your plant with the nicest load of fish I have ever delivered to you. My girls are busy unloading it into your plant now. Don't worry, we'll ice up the fish properly and not let anybody into your plant. And don't fret, I haven't got any halibut!"

The next day I slept in after a raucous New Year's celebration, and it took a substantial amount of strong coffee to bring me around. I decided to go to the dock to see if Julius had delivered a load of fish or if he had been talking with me on a direct line from the pearly gates. Sure enough, there was Julius bouncing around full of vim and vigour, proud of himself as he always was when fortune was in his favour. His three crewman had finished unloading the *Dorbarth* and were washing out the hold and scrubbing down the pen boards.

Julius had about a seven-thousand-dollar trip, so I believe a hot time in town was in order. Seven thousand dollars was a lot of cash in 1958. Soon a celebration was engulfing the *Dorbarth* with deliveries of groceries and booze to spice up the evening. Julius insisted I join the party, but I was still badly hung over from the night before so I went back to my home in North Burnaby. After a few days of partying, Julius's crew had disappeared for unknown destinations. For the next few days his boat was quiet, and then he finally showed up in my office and said he wanted to tell me a story,

He started off by declaring he had to get rid of the all-women crew for a while or they would do him in. Then he told me his strange tale. He had been fishing by himself and was on his way down with twenty-five thousand pounds of mixed bottom fish. He was very tired after a week of hard work so he put on the automatic pilot and decided to catch a bit of sleep. Again the damn clock failed to rouse him, and the *Dorbarth* ran aground on a winter evening on a deserted area of the northern coast. The shock of the grounding woke him up but he was caught fast with no way of escaping. It was freezing hard and he knew he had to get off the *Dorbarth* before she heeled over and filled with water. He was lucky to have the skiff that I gave him aboard, but somebody had borrowed the oars. Stowing matches, an axe and a heavy coat, he launched that skiff and paddled about two hundred yards to shore with a pen board. There he made a fire to keep himself warm and then he cut down two trees large enough to hack out a couple of oars. The skiff had dried out, so some of the seams were leaking. He cut enough material from his shirt to stuff in the leaky seams with a knife blade to keep her from taking water on too quickly. Then he launched the skiff and departed his warm fire in a snowstorm for Ocean Falls, which was about one hundred miles away.

Luckily a tug proceeding up the strait in the morning stopped to pick him up. They asked him where in the hell he thought he was going in a leaky skiff in a snowstorm. It must have been a sight when they eyeballed his hand-carved oars. Luck was with him again they pulled into Bella Bella and Julius was able to recruit a native crew who helped him to once again salvage the *Dorbarth*. They took him to his vessel, which was half-submerged with half a load of fish in the hold. At low tide they pitched the fish out and the *Dorbarth* righted herself on the incoming tide. Again after drying her out and changing oil three or four times after the engine had run for three or four minutes, he was ready to go fishing again. It was right after this adventure that he arrived outside our plant on New Year's Eve with another load of fish.

After that trip, I never saw Julius Barth or the *Dorbarth* again. To this day nobody has been able to clear up the mystery. Perhaps he went to Rupert to fish for the co-op and remained there. Who knows where he dropped his anchor? I suspect he turned on the automatic pilot and went to sleep once too often, and a freighter or a tug with barges in tow ran over him. But that's mere conjecture. The fact was, Julius Barth was a unique specimen who lived a charmed life for a long time. For years and years I questioned old timers and fishermen about Julius and the *Dorbarth*, but nobody ever came up with an answer.

STRADIOTTI BROTHERS

In the Depression, the Stradiotti brothers bought spring salmon, steelhead and sturgeon for us in the Fraser River. Father had cut his connection to a cannery on the Fraser River, so we required a steady source of good fresh salmon on a daily basis, and the Stradiottis knew how to handle fish for the fresh market.

The Stradiotti brothers bought net salmon for us and for the Queen Charlotte Cannery, which was operated by Jim MacDonald. Sockeyes were not sold on the fresh-fish market and by law could not be exported in a fresh or frozen state. We sold any sockeyes we bought incidentally for very little over what they cost us. The market for canned spring salmon and coho was poor because the colour of these salmon varied a lot. Springs can come very red, medium red, pink or white, and net-caught river cohos canned out a pale colour, so these fish were a cannery nightmare. We didn't want the net-caught sockeyes and Jim's cannery didn't want the springs or cohos, so the Stradiotti company bought fish for each of us. The cannery also took the net-caught river pink salmon (humpbacks) and chums because they were cheap. They paid about eight cents for chums and three to five cents for humpies because the quality and colour were not good enough for the fresh-fish markets.

The river chums and humpbacks that were canned in those days were sold to the poor southerners in the United States, to the Caribbean market and to poor populations in various parts of the globe. I believe some of this canned fish was also consumed by British armed forces because it was cheap — five to six dollars or even less for forty-eight one-pound cans packed in a wooden case. The protein level was high enough in this fish, but the taste just wasn't there.

The Stradiotti brothers also operated a small fleet of tugs on the Fraser River and one or two larger vessels in the Gulf of Georgia and on the West Coast of Vancouver Island. They also salvaged logs when that kind of work was available. Buying fish was probably only twenty-five percent of their business. There were four boys in the family who ran the various businesses. The patriarch in the family was retired and took no part in the businesses other than the money he had invested with his boys. He was the chef in the Hotel Vancouver for many years and he bought substantial quantities of fish and shellfish from Van Shell, so we had a long connection to this family that lasted for nearly fifty years.

Aldo, the oldest of four brothers, supervised the business from an office on the north bank of the North Arm of the Fraser River where the family towboats were berthed. Rex, Henry and Napoleon were the field men looking after the towboat, fishing and salvage businesses. Henry also fished on the *Carolina Maria*, the family seine boat, named after their mother. I never got to know Henry very well because he passed away in a tragic accident before we could get well acquainted. The *Carolina Maria* foundered off Savary Island one winter evening when it was engaged in fishing herring for a reduction plant. Henry managed to swim to shore on Savary Island but died from exposure before he was found. It was one of the many tragic accidents and sinkings that occurred in the fishing industry off the coast of British Columbia.

Napoleon delivered most of the fish to our plant daily for decades, so we knew him well. Sometimes his brother Rex made deliveries as well, but he was mostly occupied working on the river. Spring salmon (king salmon, chinooks, blackmouths) are the first salmon to enter the river in the springtime, which is why they are named spring salmon. Nap would show up about the middle of January with one or two large white springs that weighed thirty to forty pounds. These would be the first spring salmon of the season and they were cut into steaks that were eleven or twelve inches in diameter. These spring salmon would shame a farm-raised salmon for quality; there is no comparison between the wild fish that fattened up in the ocean on herring, needle fish, anchovies and pilchards and the soybean-fed farm fish that dominate the market today. These springs were so fat, they made their own oil when the steaks were broiled or fried. The flesh was fat and firm, not sloppy and mushy like the soybean-fed farm fish that are all antibiotics and grease with no shelf life in the flesh.

Each morning Nap would arrive with a precious load of beautiful salmon. He had been up most of the night buying these fish, but he always had a smile on his face and gave us the latest news from the river. Nap was an easygoing fellow about five foot seven inches in height and about three and a half feet across the shoulders. He was a weightlifter and wrestled for sport. Nap was the strongest small man I have ever met, a gentle man but not a fellow to be trifled with. Once one of our employees got into a playful shoving match with Nap when he was in an agitated mood. Quick as a flash, Nap grabbed him by the neck and seat of his pants and held him up over a tank of water and muttered, "If you don't lay off, I'll chuck you in the brine." This was a guy who weighed about one hundred and eighty-five pounds and Nap lifted him like a feather.

In addition to buying fish from salmon fishermen, Napoleon was taking ground fish from about fifteen small vessels thirty-five to forty feet in length. These small vessels were catching sole, flounder, grey cod, skate, pollock and dogfish off the mouth of the Fraser River. At one time this area extending out to the American border (fifteen to twenty miles south of the mouth of the Fraser River and then west halfway across the Gulf of Georgia to Vancouver Island) was one of the finest fishing grounds for all species of ground fish, salmon and crabs on our Pacific coast. These vessels each caught up to two to three thousand pounds of mixed fish per day, most being lemon sole. The legal limit for a sole was thirteen inches, but these fishermen took everything that came up in the nets. The illegal undersized fish went to the mink farming industry for feed, and twenty percent of the legal fish came to our plant via Nap's truck. Nap also had a contract to haul the undersized illegal fish to the fur breeders co-op mink feed plant.

The grounds at the mouth of the Fraser River had been overfished by the larger vessels such as the *Shannon M*, *Phyllis Carlyle*, *Curlew M*, *Tordo*, *Sea Angel*, *Willow Point* and *Welcome Pass,* to the point where it was no longer economical for these larger vessels to work the area. These larger vessels moved to the east and west coasts of Vancouver Island, where virgin grounds lay to be exploited. The small vessels that were strip-mining the Fraser River shoals were reduced to scratching for seven to eight hundred pounds of fish per day at three cents per pound for undersized fish and seven to eight cents per pound for legal-sized fish. The average wage then was fifty cents per hour, so the smallest two-man boats, making fifty to one hundred and fifty dollars per day, were still making a good return. However, the larger fishing boats that had moved to the West Coast could load their vessels with three or four drags per day with a bottom-trawl net and catch fifty to ninety thousand pounds of prime legal-sized fish per day.

Why the Department of Fisheries and Oceans allowed the smaller vessels to take all sizes of bottom fish off the mouth of the Fraser River to the point of no return is a mystery I'm sure will never be answered. That was more than sixty years ago, and to this day this area has not recovered. The largest fur-breeding area in the world, the Fraser Valley, is also ancient history.

Nap hauled this marginal, legal-sized ground fish into our plant for several years at the rate of five to ten thousand pounds per week. We didn't really want the fish because labour costs of processing it were too high. It was a marginal situation only viable in the wintertime when bad weather caused shortages of ground fish. Then you could sell any sized fish. However, to keep the peace and retain a supply of the best salmon in the world (Fraser River spring salmon from January to mid-August) we kept quiet. After the middle of August, the trolled red springs from the West Coast were better to eat than the Fraser River fish.

Every morning Nap showed up with fresh iced gillnet-caught salmon only two to ten hours old. It was hard to find a spring salmon under twenty pounds, the fall coho were eight to twenty-five pounds and the steelhead were eight to twelve pounds. In September and October, the steelhead were fifteen to thirty pounds each. Some mornings when we opened our big sliding door there were two- to ten-thousand-pound loads of sturgeon laying on the cement floor. Sometimes Nap showed up with eight thousand pounds of sturgeon and then came back with ten thousand pounds of salmon.

One morning Nap arrived with his truck loaded with salmon and jumped out with his usual wide grin and banter. "I darn near didn't make it this morning," he said and he held a misshapen lead slug in the palm of his hand. "This morning I dug that out of the wall of our fish camp with my jackknife. A guy came into the ice house after midnight as I was icing a delivery of salmon. He was packing a revolver and he demanded the buying money. To hell with him. I grabbed a fish pew and threw it like a spear at him with all my might. Damned if I didn't miss him by a few inches. He fired a shot at me, and here's the slug to prove it. I took after him with another fish pew, but I gave up the chase after another bullet whizzed by my head. He was a bad shot, but he sure meant business. I figured drawing a third shot might be tempting fate."

The Stradiotti brothers were quiet, efficient businessmen who handled millions of dollars in cash over the years without being robbed. Napoleon was built like a brick, with a pugilist's nose and cauliflower ears from all his amateur wrestling bouts. I think any robber that Nap got his hands on would have ended up in a very sorry condition. He handled two- to three-hundred-pound boxes of sole from his truck as if they were minor weights.

We did a huge business with the Stradiotti brothers for decades without any arguments. Outside of negotiating weekly salmon prices, there weren't even minor disagreements. In 1947, the Crescent Beach Oyster Company had rebuilt their forty-two tender they used to jockey scow-loads of oysters to their shucking house. The manager of the company was a drunk who sometimes failed to stay on top of his company's affairs. There had been a bad winter with lots of ice built up in the Nicomekl River. Some of that ice was more than six inches thick and it was in big heavy chunks as it flowed out of the river at a speed of about five miles per hour. The rebuilt boat was damaged around the rudder, so a slow leak gradually filled the vessel. It did not sink completely, but there was quite a lot of damage done inside to the electrical system. Another shipyard bill would not make the shareholders of the Crescent Beach Oyster Company happy, and rumours were out that the boat was for sale. They had a smaller boat that could do the job, so the larger vessel was really unnecessary to their business. I dropped into their office and asked if the vessel was for sale. They said I should come back at the end of the month after their next board meeting and they'd let me know.

I didn't have much money in the bank, so I asked Napoleon if he wanted to buy the vessel with me on a fifty-fifty basis.

"Okay," he said. "If it's any good. When can I look it over?"

"How about right now," I said. We jumped into his truck and departed for Crescent Beach. I got Aldershaw's permission and we went over every part of the vessel. The motor ran evenly and idled smoothly.

"How much do you think we can buy it for?" Nap asked.

"I have only about two thousand bucks in the bank, so four thousand bucks is my limit if you take half of her."

"This vessel is worth a lot more than that," he said. "I doubt we'll get her for that low a price."

I answered, "Nap, that's all I can raise, so that has got to be the limit of our offer."

"Okay," he agreed.

A couple of days later we arrived at Crescent Beach Oyster Company's office in Vancouver and we were ushered in to meet the head man. "Is your boat the *Cracker* for sale?" I asked.

"It is," he advised.

"How much are you asking for the vessel?" I inquired.

He looked us over carefully and then said, "Forty-five hundred dollars."

I responded, "That's a little steep for us, so I guess we'll have to pass."

He said, "You guys just out of the army?" I nodded. It was the truth — both Napoleon and I had gone overseas. He rattled his pencil on the table for a few seconds and then asked, "How much money do you have?"

"Twenty-two hundred," I answered with my best hounddog expression.

He paused for a moment, then said, "She's sold to you for twenty-two hundred dollars. You can take her away as soon as your certified cheque is on my desk."

A few hours later we were back with the cheque. The next morning I drove Nap out to Crescent Beach and he departed with the *Cracker* headed for the North Arm of the Fraser River. We operated that vessel jointly for five years, and then in 1953 Nap offered to buy my share for the eleven-hundred-dollar investment plus an additional two thousand dollars profit. I agreed, so after that the *Cracker* belonged to the Stradiotti brothers. The transaction took place on good terms and it was business as usual with Nap.

MONSTERS AND MONEY

There were a great many large sturgeon caught in the Fraser River by gillnet fishermen who were fishing for salmon. On some mornings we had five or six thousand pounds of live sturgeon on the floor. These fish would remain alive for several days, as long as some water was running across the floor and they could suck it in through their gills.

Most of these fish were fifteen to sixty pounds in weight, but there were always ten or twelve fish that weighed from two to five hundred pounds and the odd fish that weighed closer to one thousand pounds. These were dispatched by hitting them on the head with a three-pound hammer, the larger ones with a ten-pound hammer. Jack Reynolds, one of our employees, hooked a six-hundred-pound sturgeon with a long-handled hook, behind the gills, to pull it onto our platform scale to weigh it before it was sold. The fish lashed out with its tail and broke Jack's leg, and this was after my brother Ed had hit it on the head with the ten-pound sledgehammer.

I don't know how large the white sturgeon grows, but we had one that weighed in at fourteen hundred pounds plus. Once, Canadian Fishing Company phoned us to ask if we wanted to buy a sixteen-hundred-pound sturgeon and we agreed to take it. However, when it arrived we discovered that it had already been dressed. They had removed all the caviar. From the look of the few prime black eggs that clung to the body cavity, Father figured the fish had contained more than one hundred and fifty pounds of caviar. At that time the eggs were worth more than one dollar per pound, while the fish itself was worth about twelve cents per pound. Because the fish was dressed out with roe removed, we declined to take the fish and sent it back to Can Fish. A sixteen-hundred-pound dressed fish with one hundred and fifty pounds of roe and fifty pounds of guts and twenty pounds of blood would be close to two thousand pounds.

We paid fifteen cents per pound for the sturgeon and sold the fish for twenty-five cents to the Chinese merchants. We also shipped sturgeon and other fish to all the major cities in Canada and to some cities in the United States. Some of the larger fish had eggs in them, which was worth one dollar per pound. If any of the sturgeon had caviar in them, we bought it back from the Chinese merchants for two bucks a pound. A one-hundred-and-fifty-pound fish could have forty pounds of caviar; a five-hundred-pound fish could have more than seventy-five pounds; a thousand-pound fish might contain as much as one hundred and fifty pounds.

The Chinese bought the large white sturgeon, which they butchered into chunks for sale to their customers. It was always a guessing game as the crafty buyers surveyed the large fish and prodded their bellies. If one of them bought a four-hundred-pound fish and it contained sixty pounds of roe, he had a winner. He paid one hundred dollars for the fish and he received one hundred and twenty dollars for the caviar. This meant he got the fish for nothing and made twenty dollars profit. Most of the Chinese merchants were avid gamblers and they took great delight in examining the live fish in hopes of buying one that was full of roe. Out of twelve large fish, two might have good black caviar, two might have grey roe (worth fifty cents per pound) and two might have cream-coloured roe that was worthless. Of course, the males had no roe. The merchants who hit the jackpot were all smiles as they carefully removed the caviar from the fish. The others would curse their luck to the high heavens.

Father urged them on, pointing out the fat fish that was sure to be full of caviar. Sometimes the fish was full of oolichans (small smelt) and everybody had a good laugh about it except the buyer, who was loudly lamenting his rotten luck. Every morning the same game was played with all the merchants circling the fish trying to make up their minds. When one buyer made his move, the others all jumped in and bought up the fish, and then the laughter and curses would begin as the bellies were opened. The lucky ones laughed with glee and thanked Father profusely for picking out their lucky fish, while the unlucky buyers swore that they had been cheated, claiming Father knew which ones were the good ones and so it went until they departed with smiles or curses. The Chinese passed on fish that weighed more than five hundred pounds. These larger fish were beheaded, gutted, butchered and shipped to Waldman in Montreal, or Eaton's in Toronto or to some buyer in the United States.

The fourteen-hundred-pound fish we had was a problem because it was a female with a large belly. It had more than one hundred pounds of good caviar in it, but because of its enormous size it was going to be difficult to sell. Father sent a telegram to the buyer at Eaton's in Toronto asking if he wanted to purchase a large sturgeon. The buyer promptly replied to ship the fish. Father neglected to inform him exactly how large the sturgeon was. After receiving the order, we bought lumber to build a box suitable for shipping the whole fish, which was about eighteen feet in length. We built a coffin to hold this giant sturgeon and packed eight hundred pounds of crushed ice around it and into its belly. We then nailed on the lid and put wire straps around the box at two-foot intervals to keep the box from bulging. Now we pondered how we would get the two-thousand-pound box onto the truck that was taking it to the CPR express station. We managed to lift the coffin with the co-operation of our crew and the Chinese crew who worked next door in the cannery. The shipping papers were in order, the box was on its way east and we crossed our fingers hoping the buyer at Eaton's would not have a heart attack when he saw the fish.

About a week later the phone call came from the Eaton's buyer in Toronto. Bill Steiner was reluctant to take the call, so Father picked up the receiver, wincing. It was good news. The buyer said they were thrilled to have received the magnificent fish, it was all sold, and he wanted another shipped immediately. They had to remove a window in the store to accommodate the fish on a specially built counter. The fish was displayed for two days before it was butchered and sold. He claimed people were lined up for more than a block waiting their turn to view the monster. We shipped many other large sturgeon to Eaton's in Toronto but none of them ever approached the size and weight of the fourteen-hundred-pounder.

FISH COPS

One day Napoleon Stradiotti showed up with ten thousand pounds of sturgeon and we began selling them as fast as they were weighed in. Presently a couple of DFO inspectors showed up and said, "You sold some undersized sturgeon." At that time the fish had to be at least thirty-six inches long. There were always one or two fish in every load that might be quarter of an inch short, but if you stretched them, you could make them thirty-six inches.

The Fish Cops had caught one of the Chinese merchants with a dozen fish that were four to six inches too short, and he told them he bought the fish from us. He did buy some fish from us, but not the small ones. The fishermen on the river often sold their undersized fish to the Chinese merchants for less money and for cash because the commercial buyers, including Nap, would not willingly take undersized fish. Why bother — who wanted to get pinched? To take the heat off himself, this merchant told the Fish Cops he got the fish from us and produced bills to back up his argument. He had three hundred pounds of sturgeon in his truck but he only bought one hundred and seventy pounds from us.

I pointed this out to the Fish Cops. I suggested he bought the small fish elsewhere so we were not responsible.

They picked out about twenty marginal fish from the load and began to measure them. After an hour or so they located two fish that were just short of the thirty-six-inch limit. I went over and stretched the fish out to the legal length but they said they would have to ticket me because stretching the fish was a no-no.

I was fed up with the greenhorn Fish Cops. I could not convince them the Chinese merchant had told them a big story. So I grabbed a huge knife that we used for butchering large halibut and I cut each of the fish in question into four pieces. "Now," I said, "I'll be happy to tell this story to a judge rather than listen to your crap, so why don't you pinch me and then get the hell out of here." With the evidence destroyed, they were up a creek without a paddle. They stood around speechless and then turned on the unfortunate merchant and seized his three hundred pounds of sturgeon as evidence and left.

None of the markets on Campbell Avenue knowingly handled illegal fish, certainly not to profit by handling it deliberately. However, fish was delivered by buyers at night who had keys to the plants. In the morning when the fish was graded and weighed by the company, it was not unusual to discover one or two fish that were illegal if they were not stretched out a bit. When an unreasonable inspector with little common sense showed up, there could be a problem. The last time I was in court over a situation like that was when two enthusiastic inspectors managed to find two undersized crabs (about a thirtieth of an inch undersized) in a load of fifteen thousand pounds of crabs.

They seized our crabs and attempted to sell them back to us. We advised them that we would not buy them back from the Crown and that they should sell them elsewhere. They attempted to sell the crabs to other buyers but could find no takers because there was a glut of crabs on the market and because our friends who competed with us would have none of it. This left them with no option but to come back hat in hand and ask us to take back the crabs. Crabs at that time were worth about one dollar per dozen, so we offered them twenty-five cents per dozen for the one thousand dozen just to get them off our backs. There was nothing they could do but accept our terms.

I appeared in front of Magistrate Orr. He asked how many crabs were in the total load. Then he asked how many crabs were found to be undersized. When the inspectors pulled two crabs out of a brown paper bag, he asked how much too small they were. One inspector held a crab up to the light and his measuring stick across its back to show the magistrate that it was in fact a width of a little over a hair undersized. The good old magistrate blew up like a bullfrog and he exploded, "What is the meaning of laying a charge in such a frivolous case?" He fumed. "I don't ever want to see either of you inspectors in front of me again on this kind of matter." He turned to me and explained that the law did not allow even one undersized crab, so he would have to levy a fine. "You are fined two dollars and fifty cents, and the costs are two dollars and fifty cents so that will be five dollars; pay the clerk on your way out."

The inspectors spoke up, pressing for confiscation of the crabs.

"Who paid for the crabs?" the magistrate asked.

"Our company did," I answered.

"Then the crabs belong to the Vancouver Shellfish Company," he ruled and ended the session with a verbal attack on the inspection department.

When I spoke up to clarify the matter, he ordered the department to return our two hundred and fifty dollars it got for selling us back our own crabs.

Over the years we managed to survive the aggressive attitude of each new inspector who came to work for the department. It was like getting a cold or athlete's foot. Sooner or later the situations were solved and peace reigned until another zealot arrived. The worst scenario was when a conspiracy was hatched by the department to lay a charge or when their inspectors lied blatantly. I suspect the large fishing companies were encouraging the department to lean on the small companies. It was like siccing a dog after a bunny. As the years went by, inspectors with common sense remained in limbo while fanatics got the promotions. I say that with dismay, because some good men never got a promotion. I will say it again, no company on Campbell Avenue made money selling illegal fish.

Inspector Haines was a dedicated guardian of our fishery resources. He was a good man but inclined to kill a fly with a stick of dynamite.

He was a regular visitor at our crab-loading dock near the mouth of the Nicomekl River in Crescent Beach. He was always in an officious mood, very businesslike. If there were five hundred pounds of crabs or five thousand pounds of crabs, he had to go through every box and measure every marginal crab. He did not know how to handle crabs properly. It is always the crab that is underneath the one you are picking up that will grab you.

On hot summer afternoons, it did not do the crabs any good to be handled and transferred from one box to another, especially when they were in a biting mood. When they hung on to his gloves he shook them off on the dock as he sorted through them. The fishermen would have to remain there to pick up the restless crabs, tie up the boxes and stack them in the shade. If the truck was already there, they would help to load them. A burning thirst would torment the fishermen as they patiently stood by, watching the exercise in futility. The pubs in those days closed for an hour by law around five p.m. There would be Haines fussing with the crabs as the fishermen cursed under their breath and repeatedly glanced at their watches to see if they could make it to the pub before it closed.

This ordeal took place at least once a month on the last day of the fishing week, Friday afternoon. Mr. Haines seemed oblivious to the torment and distress he caused to these thirsty men, and to my knowledge, with all his measuring, he was never successful in finding even one undersized crab. However, there was no point in antagonizing him because it only made him more diligent in his duties. Late one Friday afternoon I was forced to pull my truck off into the brush to avoid a collision with Haines, who came tearing up our gravel road in his old car. I was curious what had brought on his hasty departure.

Hank was looking a bit sheepish when he explained he accidentally ran over Haines's foot as he wheeled a three-hundred-pound box of crabs up the dock on a dolly. Hank said, "I didn't do it deliberately, but he sure took offence; I must admit it did put a dent in his polished shoe. He said he was going to get the police and have me charged with assault."

This was an idle threat that was never followed up. During that year there was a huge glut of crabs, and no fishermen had any need of taking small crabs. For the rest of the summer, Haines avoided our crab-loading dock, but when I saw him in the city, he informed me he was going to check us out every time — whatever that meant. It was puzzling because he had stopped his Friday-afternoon measuring sessions. Perhaps it was because he had turned his attention elsewhere.

Napoleon Stradiotti started complaining about Haines's activities on the Fraser River. It seemed that Mr. Haines was in the habit of tying up his patrol boat each evening at the Stradiotti fish-buying camp on the river. As soon as the sun began to set, Haines pulled in with his *Swallow Tail*. This drove Nap crazy, because when the fishermen who were coming alongside to sell fish saw the *Swallow Tail* they buggered off. The fishermen avoided fish inspectors whenever they could but they avoided Haines like he had the plague. Nap was subjected to the spectacle of watching his customers wave as they passed by on their way to the next buyer down the river. The ones who owed Nap money found it easy to explain why they were avoiding him by pointing to Haines's patrol boat, always glued to Nap's camp. Nap was a polite man who did not want to disturb Haines, but something had to be done because most of the fish were caught at night and he wasn't getting his share.

Early one morning Nap arrived at Campbell Avenue with a huge load of fish. This was a sudden change. I quizzed him about it and asked him where he got the new pair of oars that were also in the back of his truck.

"Oh, those belong to Haines," he said. "He owes me that much for the fish I lost while he kept tying up to my fish camp." After a time Nap said, "I'll tell you about it, Norman, if you promise to keep your mouth shut."

I swore not to breathe a word of it to anyone and waited for his story.

"I waited for the fusspot to get into his bunk and then I removed the oars from his skiff and chopped off his tie-up lines. I watched his mast lights as the *Swallow Tail* drifted down the river. Eventually I noticed the lights hadn't moved for some time so I assumed he had run aground. I took his oars because I wanted the old fart to remain on the boat until the incoming tide in the afternoon floated him off the sandbar. In the morning his *Swallow Tail* was sitting high and dry with water all around it. He was marooned until the next high tide took him off in the afternoon. I don't think the old fart will want head office to know what happened. All day, the fishermen were giving him a silent wave and thumbs-up as they drifted by with gillnets strung out in the deep water."

For a week we waited to see what would happen. Each day Nap showed up with his truck loaded with salmon. "I haven't seen the old fart in our area at all," he confided in a low voice. "I guess he got the message that we don't want him tying up to our camp." After that, Haines maintained a low profile and was seldom seen on the river. He stopped coming to our camp in Crescent Beach. About a year later we heard that he had retired and that was the last we saw of him.

THE KING OF FISHMONGERS

Morris Waldman was one of a kind. We sold fish to him from the 1930s until he retired more than fifty years later. Often, we shipped more fish than he ordered, but it did not seem to faze him; we never had a complaint. He must have had some wonderful connections to keep all that fish moving. For one thing, he had the best retail fish store in the world. He sold millions of pounds of fresh fish across the counter in his Montreal establishment. His connections in the United States were unparalleled.

Morris brought in fish to his big store by the truckload, from all over the map. His store opened at six a.m. and the lineup to get in was almost a block long. I know because I went to Montreal, and when I tried to enter the store I was told by one of employees to go to the end of the line. I had to explain that I was not there to buy fish but to see Morris before I was allowed into the store.

We also shipped steelhead to other people like Booth in Winnipeg, Hamilton Finley in Hamilton, Eaton's in Toronto and Booth in Toronto. However, most of the fish went to Waldman, and when he wanted all of it, he got all of it. We could not afford to trifle with such a fabulous customer and we never did. This relationship remained in place for decades, until Morris became ill and sold his store.

To give some insight into the volume of salmon Waldman handled, here is an example of what we did with him on one business day, and we shipped to him for years on almost a daily basis. One day Morris ordered four three-thousand-pound air-freight containers of fresh trolled coho salmon. I took the liberty of shipping him seven containers. That was on a day when we unloaded five West Coast trollers at our plant in Vancouver and three reefer truckloads had arrived from our plant in Tofino. The bank manager was always pressing us for money regardless of the fact that we were making the largest profits in the company's fifty-year history. I was sweating it out as usual and had to move fish, so move it I did.

Morris had phoned a couple of times that afternoon, but my son Howard was afraid to talk with him. Finally, Howard came to me and said, "Morris is on the line and insists he must talk to you or me, and it's going to be you because I advised against shipping him so much fish."

I answered the phone with a sinking feeling in my stomach, and when Morris asked how many containers we shipped, I broke into a sweat. I sparred around with Morris and told him we had shipped a few more fish than he ordered but we would fix it up if he got stuck. There was a silence on the end of the line for about a quarter of a minute while I waited for the inquisition to continue. I had been on the receiving end of a couple of tirades from Benny, Morris's brother, when I took the liberty of overshipping product and I feared that Morris was going to skin me alive.

Morris was smoother than Benny. There was a chuckle on the end of the line and then in a quiet voice, Morris asked again, "How many containers did you ship me, Norman?"

"Well, Morris, I have to move fish and I know you can sell it, so I sent you seven containers. We will guarantee that you don't have a loss, but please do the best you can for us, Morris." There it was, out in the open now, and I cringed waiting for a tirade.

Again there was silence for ten seconds followed again by that chuckling sound on the other end of the line. Then in a quiet voice Morris asked if I could ship him two or three additional containers as well as the seven that had already left. I was speechless. Morris went on admonishing me not to send more than four additional containers.

"Norman," he said, "that'll be enough for today. I'll order more fish as soon as my customers need some, perhaps even tomorrow." He was still laughing when he hung up.

That was Morris Waldman for you. I don't ever remember him making a deduction or speaking to me in a rude or harsh way. He also advised me who not to ship fish to and provided information and contacts that were invaluable to us. Once I shipped fish to a character who Morris thought I should avoid and got properly stung. "I told you so," Morris said, in his usual calm voice.

There will never be another person in the fish business like Morris Waldman. I believe his retail and export sales at that time exceeded sixty million dollars and it was all in seafood. It just amazed us, the variety of seafood he imported from various countries, and the vast store of knowledge he had acquired about the fish business and his fellow man. Morris Waldman was the king in his domain, a wonderful man who was simply one of a kind. His like will never be seen again.

THE TRADE

No fish companies filleted fish in the thirties. Filleting was done by kitchen help in restaurants and hotels. Stores sold whole fish or steaks, which were cut with an extremely sharp knife with the aid of a wooden hammer. Very little fish was filleted in plants until after the Second World War. Before then some custom work was done when large catches of fish were delivered. This was accomplished with a good deal of bitching. Father especially frowned on filleting fish. "The next thing you know they'll want us to cook it for them!" he'd declare with sarcasm.

My brother Ed and I filleted the first grey cod delivered to Campbell Avenue by S. Koyama via his vessel the *Kathleen S* in 1937, out of Nanaimo, B.C. This grey cod was caught in Nanoose Bay, which has been taken over by the U.S. Navy for a weapons-testing ground and is off limits to fishermen. Nanoose Bay once produced two million pounds of large grey cod on a yearly basis. The fish was caught by draggers in December, January and February.

All four thousand pounds of fillets recovered from Koyama's grey cod was sold in a day at Woodward's store, located between Hasting and Cordova Streets, during one of their popular five-cent sales days. Woodward's store sold half a million pounds of fish each year.

Blackburn Market, at Robson and Seymour and operated by Chris Johnston, sold almost as much. Spencer's main store, west of Woodward's, sold one hundred thousand pounds annually, as did the Bay, at Georgia and Granville, Jackson's Meat Market, and the Grand

Union Market, east of Woodward's. Model Market on Fourth Avenue sold about one hundred and fifty thousand pounds per annum.

Old Man MacFarlane owned a marvellous store in Kerrisdale. His son Alex, in a prime location on Granville and Fourteenth, sold a substantial amount of top grade fish on a daily basis. In the Depression, sons Douglas and Alex MacFarlane peddled fish from trucks. Alex MacFarlane's store on Granville was the jewel of his four fish stores. Douglas stopped peddling and took over his father's store in Kerrisdale when the old boy retired. His son Douglas still runs the business sixty-five years later.

Ciccone, Ross and the Chinese peddlers provided Greater Vancouver with the best fish that was available, not very long out of water. Fish stores and peddlers sold all hand-picked top-quality fish. They were particular about the shellfish and were always on the lookout for something special for their customers. They didn't just sell fish, they did it in style. Their customers were discerning clients who expected a variety of fresh seafood handled in a certain way.

Chris Johnson appeared promptly at seven every morning to buy the fish for Blackburn Market. "How much do you want for the pinks?" he'd ask after fixing on me with his eyes.

I paid eight cents a piece for the pinks, so I'd quote him twelve cents.

"Send me fifteen hundred fish at eleven cents each." That sounded all right to me. "How many flounders in that pile?"

"Five thousand pounds," I informed him.

"How much, kid?" We paid two and a half cents so I quoted him four and a half cents.

"Send them over for four cents, okay?" And so it went for years in a daily routine that moved an incredible amount of fish.

Five or six hundred pieces of pink salmon and a thousand pounds of lemon sole or flounders was a normal day's order for that store. He also ordered hundreds of pounds of kippered salmon and hundreds of pounds of fresh shellfish on a daily basis. Sometimes Chris ordered three or four thousand pounds of fresh halibut. Woodward's was the only outlet that could come near matching the Blackburn Market.

Two of the biggest breaks our company got were when David Love opened the Fish and Oyster Bar on Granville Street and when a Mr. Parker (the pie man) showed up from Edmonton and made a deal with us to broker our fish to a number of customers in Alberta.

David Love had already taken over and was operating his family's restaurant, Love's Café, also on Granville Street, in the 1930s, when he opened the Fish and Oyster Bar. Love's was the only establishment in town that still employed only male waiters, each with an apron fastened around his midriff in the old style that was left over from the turn of the century. The Fish and Oyster Bar, at that time was simply the best restaurant account in the city. It paid COD each day for every delivery. More seafood by dollar value was sold in the Fish and Oyster Bar each day than was sold in a score of other restaurants around town. Eight to ten gallons of oysters, gallons of canned clams, thirty pounds each of crab meat and shrimp meat, four to six hundred pounds of large line-caught head-off ling cod, a case of scallops and twenty-five pounds of sole fillets were the norm every day of the week. They didn't sell halibut, salmon, chicken or meat. It was a real oyster bar with fish and chips as a specialty of the house. They stocked five thousand pounds of ling cod for the Christmas and New Year's holidays. A Chinese man named George cut all that cod into fillets and portions with one helper whose name I have forgotten. The Fish and Oyster Bar was a godsend to us, and during the hungry thirties it became almost our bread-and-butter customer until things opened up when the war began.

Father had done business with David Love's father in Love's Café for many years. When David and his sister were children, my father was very close to their dad, so when David took over Love's and started the Fish and Oyster Bar he gave my father one hundred percent of the business. This was a windfall and gave us a huge shot in the arm during hard times. The Fish and Oyster Bar on Granville Street remained open until about 1975 and we retained that business through three or four owners

Only Fish and Oyster Café at the corner of Carrall and Hastings Street, founded in 1914, was one of the oldest restaurants in Vancouver. They also used fabulous quantities of littleneck native clams in their small establishment. They had only one entrance and lacked restrooms, and for years they got a special discount for being our oldest account. Their specialty was steamed littleneck clams and clam nectar twenty-four hours a day. This small restaurant that had no back entrance used three to four hundred pounds of fresh clams daily and four to six hundred pounds on good days. When the loggers hit town because of snow or the fire season shut down the woods, business in this small establishment went wild. During the Christmas and New Year's period, they used five to six hundred pounds of clams a day and sometimes needed more. Nobody heard of Red Tide or the faecal count in those days, and nobody got sick even though clams were on the menu daily for years.

Eventually, the restaurant in the Devonshire Hotel, also a valuable customer, became the biggest seafood restaurant in the city. They remained a huge customer until sadly the hotel was demolished. They would order one hundred thirty-pound cases of shrimp meat, one hundred thirty-pound cases of crab meat, one hundred cases of king crab legs and one hundred forty-pound cases of lobster tails as well as a huge variety of other seafood items. I doubt there will ever be another customer like the Devonshire. Establishments like that come only once in a century.

Mr. Parker sold a variety of pies in Alberta, and he was well liked so it worked out really well for us. For many years, until he retired, Mr. Parker sold our fish to about twenty accounts on a weekly basis. The accounts that we sold to in Alberta because of Mr. Parker were extremely important to our bottom line. We shipped thirty or forty boxes of fish to Parker's customers in Alberta every Friday. These were one-hundred, one-hundred-and-fifty and two-hundred-pound boxes, so quite a large volume of fish was moved each week. Formerly, Canadian

Fishing Company had all the business in Alberta. What we shipped went to their estranged customers, and this made them very unhappy.

Suddenly we were stepping on the toes of one of the largest fishing companies in North America. They didn't like it and let us know that they weren't going to take it lying down. Right off the bat they refused to buy shellfish from us, except for what was going to Al Hager's table. Hager was majority shareholder in this subsidiary company of the New England Fish Company (and CEO and president of Can Fish), and he liked his gourmet quality shellfish, which we readily supplied to him. They also refused to sell to us when we were short of some products. No company, large or small, has every item all the time so there is always a certain amount of trade that goes on between fishing companies.

Fortunately for us, Canadian Fish and Cold Storage, a French-owned company, had opened a plant on Campbell Avenue fish dock and they were quite willing to deal with us. Jack Evans, a long-time employee of the Canadian Fishing Company, used to stop by once in a while to inform us that we were in for it, for daring to stand up the almighty Can Fish. For years, we had purchased frozen fish from his company. This frozen fish had ten- to twelve-percent glaze on it, and when we requested a glaze allowance, Jack would reply with a smirk, "Take it or leave it." This attitude increased our incentive to buy directly from fishermen and store our own fish. We stopped buying frozen salmon from Can Fish when Canadian Fish and Cold Storage gave us a generous glaze allowance. The result was that we became competitors on the fishing grounds as well as in the trade. In our case, Canadian Fishing Company severed diplomatic relations and they remain severed to this day, more than fifty years later.

The CNR provided a pool car freight service to the prairies every Friday afternoon. Pool car rates were subsidized by the federal government at two cents per pound less than the regular freight and this service was supposedly available to all shippers of fish. However, Canadian Fishing Company managed to get control of all the space in the pool car and we were out of luck. We were forced by the manoeuvre to ship our goods at the higher, regular freight rate. It was tough for us to take, but we put up with it for more than a year. When we investigated we discovered that Can Fish was only shipping seven or eight boxes of fish that were occupying about fifteen percent of the pool car space. Our twenty-five or thirty boxes on the same train were being shipped to the same destinations at the higher rate. We took this matter to court and won our case against Canadian Fishing Company and CNR. The court ruled that it was against the law to monopolize the space in the pool car because this was a federal government subsidy that must be available to all shippers of fish. No doubt somewhere in the hierarchy of directors, Can Fish and CNR had some kind of connection that provided for this cozy relationship. Perhaps it was by being by far the largest overall shipper of bulk loads of fish to the eastern seaboard that Canadian Fishing Company was able to throw its weight around to get an advantage.

After the rebuke by the court, it was no holds barred in Alberta as we competed fiercely for the business in Edmonton and Calgary. The hatred towards us increased until it became a vendetta. Jack Evans, poor soul, was in a terribly agitated state, continually coming around to warn me of dire consequences. He was a dedicated company man who acted as if his company was being run directly by God. He never forgave us for defying his corporate saviour.

THE HAGERS

While this battle raged we remained on cordial terms with Al Hager and his family, who had controlling interest in the Canadian Fishing Company. Al would phone and ask me to put up a special order of crab meat or shrimp meat for some event he was hosting. He knew we had top-of-the-line goods. I always made sure he got the best crab with a lot of leg meat in his parcels.

"Norman, I'm sending Bill down to get the crab meat. When Bill arrives at your plant, please phone me." Bill, one of Al's sons, had a tendency to stop for a drink whenever he had the chance, so Al attempted to keep track of him. In an hour or two Bill would arrive in a chauffeur-driven car. Since the trip took only ten minutes, it was obvious that Bill had stopped for libations along the way. Invariably I would get another call from Al about half an hour after the first one. "Is Bill there yet?" he'd ask. "Now Norman, remember to call me when he picks up the crab meat." Bill was always in good spirits.

I often wondered how he managed to talk his old man's chauffeur into stopping at a bar. I would drag a protesting Bill to the phone to call his father and then listen as he promised his father that he would come right back to their plant without any stops along the way. When Bill climbed back in the limousine, I would phone Al and let him know that Bill was coming back. Al would phone back again in an hour or two, wondering if Bill had really left. I imagine the chauffeur must have lived a charmed life, since he always seemed caught between the wants of father and son.

Al Hager was a very wealthy man. He employed a uniformed chauffeur with leather leggings to drive the family limousine. They had a cook and a serving staff. I believe there were four boys and three girls in the family. They lived in Shaughnessy with all the other wealthy people. There was a large family summer home in Crescent Beach on Millionaire's Row and the private Silver Valley Gun Club on the north side of the Pitt River just before it entered Pitt Lake. Although I was invited to some of the siblings' homes, I was never really accepted by their crowd or ever invited to the Gun Club.

Al Hager went to his grave without reforming Bill. It was a sad business that deeply troubled the old man to the end of his days. Bob, the oldest son, who also had the booze problem, eventually saw the light and gave it up, but in the end it killed Bill. I imagine that brood of kids being brought up in such a rich family were a tough bunch to control, but I believe Bill was the only one who didn't really make out well in life.

Once at a private party with several of the Hager siblings during the course of the evening, there were some wild remarks made about me and our fish company. Knowing that I was a privileged guest, I was determined to ignore the insults, especially since my wife, Kathleen, was present, constantly kicking me in the shins. And because I respected the Hager family and the agitation was coming from only one drunken family member. As more liquid lightning flowed, the dialogue became more vicious as the person was determined to continue belittling me throughout the evening. These insults were ridiculous since Canadian Fishing Company was a huge corporation while our company, Van Shell, was a very small player.

I managed to hold my tongue for the longest time but got a little upset when I noticed that some of the hangers-on present were amused by my discomfort. Finally, I couldn't stand it any longer when a particularly degrading barb was thrust in my direction. I rose to the bait and blurted out, "I may be associated with a small company, but at least I'm making a respectable living for myself and not depending on handouts, like you are." My statement dropped on the room like a bombshell as every conversation halted and all eyes in the room turned to stare at me and my antagonist.

I realized at once that I had committed an unpardonable sin by tarring them all with the same brush when it was only one out-of-control drunk who was picking on me. The complete silence was broken when the bigmouth stood up and challenged me to step outside and settle the matter. Getting into a brawl was the last thing I had in mind, but I was in no mood to back down. I also recognized that my opponent was a softy who had done very little physical work in his life and that if he stepped outside with me he was doomed.

As we walked outside I kept my eyes on the fellow, watching to make sure he wasn't about to sucker me into anything before I was prepared. I took off my new suit jacket and rolled up my shirt sleeves.

Suddenly he got a big smile on his face and began to laugh loudly before he began his apology. "Jeez," he gushed. "I was only kidding. Let's go in and have a drink and forget about it." I was astounded by his sudden change of heart. I was also relieved because I didn't believe beating on one of his sons would have gone down well with Old Man Hager.

I followed the son back to the party in silence. There were big smiles all around the room and suddenly a festive atmosphere took over. Soon his sister came over and informed me confidentially that her brother was big bluffer who always acted like a jerk when he was under the influence. "He tried to bluff you, but when you refused to throw in the towel he took the coward's way out. Don't pay any attention to him, we all know what he's like." I didn't know what he was like, and the situation wasn't that amusing to me. We remained at the party for a short while longer and then departed.

Subsequently I attended several social events at various family member's homes. They really were a fine family. Once or twice I suffered the same problem with the son whenever he got supremely under the influence, but I learned to deal with him pretty well by ignoring his bad mouth.

CHICKENS AND WHALES

The halibut fishery was completely dominated by fishermen of Scandinavian descent — Norwegians, Danes and Finns. A few Germans and one or two other nationalities competed with this fleet of fishermen who took three-quarters of the eighty-five-million-pound quota until the American government put U.S. waters out of bounds to Canadian fishermen.

Since then our quota has been a paltry amount, under ten million pounds. At its peak, the halibut fishery was an immense Canadian fishery dominated by Canadian fishermen up into the Gulf of Alaska. The halibut exchange at Campbell Avenue put through immense quantities of fish. I once counted thirty-three vessels on the board. Three or four of the larger boats had more than one hundred thousand pounds of exchange halibut. One vessel had one hundred and forty thousand pounds of fish but the average boat was between twenty-five to sixty-five thousand pounds of halibut. Canadian vessels also delivered the best quality halibut, which was in great demand in American markets. Thousands of people were employed by this fishery and it paid very decent wages.

There were only three halibut and salmon exchanges on the whole Pacific coast. One was in Prince Rupert, the second was in Vancouver and the third one was in Seattle, Washington. Probably half the halibut sold in Prince Rupert and Vancouver was bought for American companies. Almost every Canadian fishing company that was a member of these exchanges bought halibut for themselves and on a commission basis for American companies. The halibut exchange was a truly democratic organization with spirited bidding being the rule of the day in spite of what some fishermen maintained. I have seen a B.C. Packers buyer and a Canadian Fishing Company buyer almost come to blows and threatening each other as they left the exchange. There was no quarter given in the Vancouver exchange, and bidding both in Rupert and Seattle were governed by prices paid on the Vancouver exchange.

The rules of the fish exchanges were as follows. A fisherman could refuse the bid, then go back on the board in the afternoon or on the next day, or refuse the bid and go to Seattle to sell his fish on the exchange there. However, if he sold to some company that was not a member of the exchange, he could not sell his fish on any of the exchanges for the rest of that year. Most of the halibut ended up in American markets. Our company bought up to one million pounds of halibut to speculate with, and the rest was bought for American companies.

No Japanese fishermen penetrated the halibut fishery because the Scandinavians controlled it and in one way or another kept their claim undisturbed. Only one Japanese-owned vessel fished for halibut for one season. One night someone fired a high-powered rifle at the Japanese crew, almost killing one of the crew members. He was severely wounded but recovered from his injuries. After that no more trips were made by that vessel and the fishery remained in the hands of the Nordics.

After the Second World War ended, the fishing industry suffered from overproduction. A great deal of effort had gone into increasing production to provide food for the Allied effort and hungry liberated people in Europe. Cold storages and cannery warehouses were bulging with fish that could not be sold because liberated areas were beginning to produce enough food to sustain their own populations. New companies that jumped into the business to take advantage of the wartime boom were slow in realizing that economic conditions were changing. Prices to fishermen were escalating while markets were shrinking. It was only a matter of months before these new independent companies began reducing prices to try to gain customers from the older established companies. In the end, these tactics meant that many companies were on the road to bankruptcy.

It was a sad chapter in the fish business. Large old-line companies attempting to retain their market share were forced to mimic the policies of unrealistic buyers in a shrinking market. The industry in general was slow to pick up on what was going on. Prices to fishermen remained high. Some companies bought fish at any price to insure that they retained their market share regardless of the consequences. Perhaps they felt that if they continued this way, eventually the opposition would go under. Substantial profits that had been realized by large and small operators alike, during the heady wartime period, were quickly disappearing in this wild, wired period of market adjustment.

When I returned from overseas I went back to work for my father and William Steiner at Vancouver Shellfish and Fish Company. One day Father sent me to the halibut exchange on Campbell Avenue fish dock to buy a boatload of fresh halibut. The fish came in four grades — chickens were six to ten pounds, mediums were ten to sixty pounds, large were sixty to one hundred pounds and whales were one hundred pounds plus. That morning prices were chickens for six cents, mediums for eight, and large and whales for eight-and-a-half cents per pound. There were ten boatloads for sale that morning. The smallest vessel held fifteen thousand pounds of fish, while the larger ones would unload up to eighty thousand pounds of halibut. I bought two boatloads, one with twenty thousand pounds and the other with twenty-five thousand pounds.

After the sale at the exchange I returned to our fish plant. Father, raising an eyebrow, asked me why I had bought so much fish when he instructed me to buy only one small boatload.

I replied, "How can we lose money buying halibut so cheaply at six to eight cents per pound?"

He looked hard at me, shook his head, and said nothing more. That afternoon we easily sold most of the fish for a fair profit. The next morning I went back to the exchange and repeated the exercise, buying two larger lots of fish and again selling the bulk of it the same afternoon at a decent profit. The rest of the week I continued buying boatloads of fish at the exchange, which I moved quickly at a fair markup. Father and Steiner were becoming a little distressed at the escalating prices. Within ten days, chickens had risen to ten cents, mediums to fifteen cents and large and whales were sixteen cents.

We carried on buying fish and freezing the unsold portion of each day's purchase until we had seven hundred thousand pounds of halibut in cold storage. When the price on the exchange reached fourteen cents for chickens, twenty-three cents for mediums and twenty-four cents for large and whales, I stopped buying and merely became an observer. Each morning for several weeks, from seven a.m. until ten a.m., I sat in at the exchange at Campbell Avenue and watched as prices to fishermen increased at a fierce rate. Prices passed thirty cents, then thirty-five, then forty, and finally ground to a halt at forty-two cents per pound for chickens, forty-three and a half for mediums, and forty-five cents a pound for large and whales.

On one memorable morning I counted thirty-two vessels with loads of halibut on board for sale at the exchange. This included three or four vessels with loads in excess of one hundred thousand pounds. In those days, the quota was eighty million pounds and it was exceeded by eight to ten million pounds before the fishery could be shut down. During those years the fish exchange at Campbell Avenue fish dock in Vancouver Harbour was the premiere fish exchange on the Pacific Coast. Landings at Campbell Avenue surpassed landings in both Prince Rupert and Seattle. For a number of years, more fresh halibut was landed in Prince Rupert, but eventually Vancouver became the number-one port for unloading halibut and black cod (sable fish). The exchange also handled salmon, although most salmon fishermen sold privately off the exchange.

The day after halibut reached the forty-two cents per pound mark, I arrived at the exchange to find that I was the only buyer present. The skipper from the one vessel available for sale that day asked me, "Where are all the buyers? Are you going to bid on my fish?" I shrugged as I walked up to the board and marked down ten cents for chickens and twenty-five cents for mediums, large and whales. I expected the skipper to refuse my bid. He looked around and said, "I guess you're the only bidder, so where do you want to unload the fish?"

"Take it to our plant," I directed as we walked out from the exchange.

By this time, July, the net salmon season had opened and many vessels that were combination fishing vessels, both long liners and seine boats, had changed over and were now fishing for salmon. Only the genuine long liners remained on the grounds to fish for halibut for the balance of the season. This meant a huge reduction, to about half the usual number of vessels fishing for halibut. Still, one or two long-line vessels appeared on the Vancouver exchange at regular intervals. Each time halibut was placed on the exchange I was the only buyer present. Time after time I walked up to the board and placed my bid, ten cents for chickens and twenty-five cents a pound for the balance available, and without any competition purchased the fish. Obviously the buyers who had loaded up with halibut at forty to forty-three cents a pound had a belly full and could not sell their overpriced fish. There is no doubt that in some cases their banks had stepped in to halt the wild increases in prices for that fish. However, most likely the companies realized by then that they were going to be hung out to dry with overpriced fish and backed away from the exchange to lick their wounds.

It was a strange feeling to be the only buyer day after day and take the fish for sale with one lone bid. Normally fifteen to twenty buyers were present to vie for the fish, and a hired exchange employee chalked up each bid as they were placed. Both Father and Steiner began to fret as our halibut inventory increased. They thought I had taken leave of my senses. They couldn't argue with the fact we were buying halibut for half the average price, so they went along with me.

On a summer morning as usual I was the only buyer present when one load of thirty thousand pounds was put up for sale. I put my lone bid on the board and talked with the skipper to pass the time while waiting to see if another buyer would show up. Suddenly Jack McMillan entered the exchange and glanced at the board. "Norman," he said, "you're buying a lot of cheap fish. In fact you're getting it way too cheap and this has to stop." In those days, Jack was known as the fishermen's friend. He made a living providing bait to the long line vessels that used hooks to catch fish. He also made it his business to interfere in the sale of a great many loads of fish that entered Vancouver harbour. His attempts to be the fishermen's advocate did not go down so well with the companies when he implied that buyers were cheating the fishermen. The fishermen finally got wise to his act when he went into the fish business for himself.

On this particular morning, Jack was full of himself as usual. With a smirk cast in my direction he quickly strode up to the board and increased the bid by five cents per pound in each category. Then he came back and sat down with a patronizing attitude that was intended to impress the skipper. He loudly informed me that my price was too low and a higher bid by me would be in order. However, I stood my ground and informed MacMillan that he had just bought himself thirty thousand pounds of halibut.

He turned to me and said, "Surely you're not going to let me take that cheap fish away from you, are you?" Again I informed him that he was the proud owner of a boatload of halibut as I walked away. He ran around the room and confronted me before I got to the door. In a desperate tone he said, "Look, Norman, you can have the fish cheap. Just bump my bid up five dollars and it's yours." At that time five dollars was the lowest bid that could be put on a load sold at the Vancouver exchange.

I declined the offer and walked back to my office with Jack at my elbow begging me to take the fish off his hands. I refused to do so. "Jack, you wanted the fish, and now it's yours. I don't want the fish at the price you bid." I could see that Jack was extremely agitated, but it was a lesson he deserved and he would have to live up to his actions.

It was a sticky situation with McMillan but really no concern of mine. I don't know if his bid was something he did at the spur of the moment or if B.C. Packers put him up to it. In any case, the halibut ended up being unloaded at B.C. Packers. Perhaps someone there had put Jack up to his stunt and then had to bail him out. Ten or twelve thousand dollars was a substantial sum of money at a time when the average worker was making about forty dollars a week. Since he became so upset, it's possible that Jack had trouble raising the money to pay for the halibut. I do know that he learned a painful and embarrassing lesson that kept his nose out of our business for a while. The skipper who owned the fish that Jack purchased was somewhat unimpressed by Jack's bravado. I believe Jack still ran us down to the fishermen as the wicked buyers but he definitely toned down the rhetoric to the point where neither the companies nor the fishermen paid him much attention.

In some ways, Jack was a slow learner. Some time later he managed to infuriate Father when he showed up in front of our grading tables with tubs in place for unloading and threw a monkey wrench in the works by telling the fisherman that he had sold to Father at way too cheap a price. Everything ground to a halt as the red-faced skipper climbed the steel ladder to the dock and attempted to renegotiate the prices offered, and agreed upon, for his fish. In the meantime McMillan climbed down the ladder onto the vessel and sat in the galley drinking coffee, egging on the crew while the argument above continued. When McMillan appeared on the wharf again, I had to hold Father back in order to give the nuisance a chance to get away. McMillan had a healthy respect for the old man and always managed to keep his distance when the old man had him in his sights. The skipper was unsuccessful in his attempts to renegotiate the prices. However, the ensuing conflict caused hard feelings and delayed unloading. With our union crew that meant increased costs. This scenario began to be repeated on an ongoing basis. Jack McMillan was becoming an annoying pain that seemed to appear at the most inopportune moments. Father got serious and told me that what goes around, comes around, and that when the time came we would pay McMillan back with considerable interest.

Eventually, McMillan went into the fish business on a larger scale and his relationship with fishermen faded. One of the Sigmund brothers delivered his catch to Jack on a regular basis. This relationship soured soon enough, and the Sigmund brothers decided to take action against Jack. One afternoon as I walked by McMillan's fish shed I was startled by what I saw taking place. Two Sigmund brothers were holding Jack up by each arm while a third brother, an amateur boxer who never quite made the big time, but was nevertheless pretty handy with his dukes, was knocking the stuffing out of Jack McMillan.

I could see that Jack's lights were already out as the stalwart brother struck with measured blows to cause the greatest amount of damage. I rushed in and told the boys that enough was enough. I shouted, "He's out of it now, you better stop before you kill him." They eased off and turned their attention to me. "Listen, boys," I said. "This town has a hanging judge and if you proceed to kill him you'll all swing on the same day. I'm doing you a favour, so lay off before you're sorry as hell." They looked at each other and dropped Jack to the wet cement floor and marched out of his plant, but not before telling me that he had cheated them on the weights on their fish deliveries.

I wasn't kidding when I warned them about the consequences. In those days Judge Manson hanged all the killers for better or worse. I helped Jack to a chair and cleaned him up as well as was possible under the circumstances and sent him home in a cab. Jack had taken a terrible beating, so it took him a long time to recover. It was almost a month before he showed up again. To my way of thinking, he never really ever regained his usual sparkle. No doubt he discovered the hard way that not all the fishermen were his friends. The following spring one of the

Sigmund brothers, the tall one, Bob, I believe, was drowned while fishing for herring.

After that halibut season, when prices escalated to four times the norm, closed, I decided to unload our inventory as quickly as possible. Old timers in the business warned me that in a short time the weak sisters in the business would be dumping halibut in an attempt to recover their costs without worrying about making a profit. In view of these forecasts, I decided there wasn't a moment to lose. At the same time, Eric Turnel of B.C. Packers assured me that we were going to make a lot of money with our cheaper inventories of halibut. He told me the consortium had set prices at sixty cents per pound for the sale of halibut in carload shipments. On that same day I rushed back to our office and spent the rest of the day unloading our fish for fifty-eight cents per pound. By quitting time that day, we had only sixty thousand pounds of halibut left, and we were keeping that for local sales. I breathed a sigh of relief. Father and Steiner, who had remained uptight over the large inventory, were both relaxing smoking House of Lord cigars.

I met Malcolm McCallum a day later when he arrived at our plant to ask our intent regarding our inventory of halibut because he had also been approached to hold his price at sixty cents per pound. At that time McCallum Sales (Malcolm's company) was owned by Nelson Brothers. Malcolm had sold out to Nelson Brothers at Ritchie Nelson's insistence when he was overloaded with West Coast trolled salmon and had the bank breathing down his neck. What Malcolm did not know was that Nelson Brothers was owned by B.C. Packers, who were his arch enemies in the trolled salmon fisheries. When I told Malcolm that I had moved most of our halibut for fifty-eight cents per pound, his brow clouded over and he sighed softly under his breath, "You beat me to it, you bastard." He jumped from his chair and departed in a rush declaring that he was going to sell his fish right then.

The next evening he arrived with a forty-ouncer of vodka, still cursing me because he could only get fifty-five cents for his halibut because I beat him to it, so he had to take less. He slowly shook his head as he continually refilled his beer glass with vodka. "I wonder what the consortium are going to say to us when they find out that we have both sold our halibut."

We quietly speculated it would take them three or four months to wake up to the fact that they would probably be taking a bath on their halibut. Malcolm was the only man I ever encountered who could drink what seemed like endless beer glasses of vodka for days and come back to his office with a razor-sharp mind. Nobody ever took advantage of Malcolm, be he drunk or sober.

True to Malcolm's prediction, it was not until the first of March that I received a call from B.C. Packers that they wished to see me. They were still holding the price at sixty cents per pound, but sales were small and by now it was obvious that they were stuck with a couple of million pounds of large halibut. They were fortunate to have large fish, because the steaking market in California was hot. However, they were unable to get more than forty cents per pound for the fish, which ensured that they were about to take a financial bath on halibut. They were looking for someone once removed to sell their fish. Someone they could trust and rely on to get them the best returns as quickly as possible before the new season rolled around with even lower-priced fish. They ended up averaging forty-three cents a pound for halibut to the fishermen. If in the new season prices dropped to fifteen to sixteen cents per pound, they would be in for terrible losses. This was likely to happen, since high prices slowed sales and buyers who were hung with high-priced inventories were not going to repeat the process. The companies that were all licking their wounds would be looking to get dirt-cheap fish to make up losses from the previous season.

Two and a half million pounds of halibut that cost up to forty-eight cents per pound made even a company like B.C. Packers, with more than three hundred million dollars in sales, nervous. At a loss of twenty cents per pound, it would cost them a half a million dollars. The department responsible would hear about it in no uncertain terms and there was the possibility of heads rolling. Those responsible were in a panic, looking for someone they could deny even knowing to sell their fish. Otherwise, if they dumped their own fish on the market at a loss, they might have to pay old reliable customers a rebate to cover the losses they would suffer as a result of having to sell fish B.C. Packers sold to them below B.C. Packer's own dumping prices. So B.C. Packers had a problem that was keeping several employees awake at night. The sooner their fish was sold, the better the returns from these sales because, as time passed, prices could only go lower.

They wanted me to sell their fish for not less than fifty cents per pound. I would be paid three-quarters of a cent a pound commission. My advice to them was that it was not possible to sell at that level. "You are not in the ballpark," I told them, "but I'll give it a try." As I left I remarked, "Don't hold your breath."

Driving home, I pondered where I could sell their halibut. It seemed obvious that it could only be sold to B.C. Packers' biggest competitors and their worst enemies. Only the largest of companies would be able to purchase so much fish in such a short time frame. I decided to phone Frosty Frank Metalgin in the United States. Frank had the halibut steaking order for the chain stores in California in his pocket. Frank hated B.C. Packers with a passion, and they returned the hatred in equal measure. I knew that Frank could move this fish on a large scale, and with a little espionage I found out that Frank was short of fish to steak. Frosty Frank would be the best candidate, but I knew I might be dealing with a hot potato because of the bad blood between the two companies.

Frosty Frank was of Slavic origin and my father was a Slav who came from Moravia so we had similar ethnic backgrounds. Frank and I had a good relationship and he gave me the first chance to provide him with any fish he could use from Canada. I phoned and made an appointment to have lunch with Frank and then departed for Bellingham, Washington, to pick him up at the largest cold storage on the Pacific Coast, where he processed his fish. He had ten large

Butcher Boy saws cutting up halibut and salmon, two shifts a day six days a week, for the California market. After a fine lunch and a couple of doubles of the best the bar had to offer, I broached the subject of large halibut for his steaking operation. Only halibut over sixty pounds is steaked and halibut over eighty pounds is preferred. Actually, the larger the halibut the better the recovery. Fish up to several hundred pounds in weight are even better. I knew that Frank was down to steaking forty-pound fish and the waste from these smaller fish was very high. Not only is the recovery from smaller fish lower, but small fish slow the steaking process, making the operation more costly.

I mentioned to Frank that I had a good source of large fish including whales (the one-hundred-pounds-plus fish). Just what the doctor ordered to give Frank the optimum results in his steaking business.

"Who has the fish?" he asked, staring intently into my face.

"What difference does it make who owns the fish?" I replied, "as long as the price is right."

"It must be B.C. Packers," Frank rightly guessed, with a wicked look in his eyes. "Simple," he said, "they're the only company that would have that amount of fish on hand."

"Frank," I argued, "what difference who owns the fish, provided you get a good deal?"

Frank smiled. "Offer them thirty cents per pound or let them choke on it."

"Frank," I continued, "you can't buy large halibut for even forty cents, so why not take advantage of the situation?"

"All right," he sniffed. "Forty cents per pound it is and not another penny more. Do you hear me, Norman? And you get the commission out of them. Am I making myself clear?"

"Yes, Frank, perfectly clear," I replied. "Leave it to me and I'll get back to you in a few days." I knew that Frosty Frank would never deal directly with B.C. Packers, and now I would have to pull together a deal that would satisfy true enemies.

Frank had his heels dug in at the forty cents while B.C. Packers continued to cling to their fifty cents figure. It seemed there was no solution to the impasse no matter how hard I sweet-talked and cajoled each party into finding a compromise. It soon became evident that Frank was in desperate need of the fish just as B.C. Packers were desperate to sell. I reasoned that the logjam had to give sooner or later. After numerous phone calls to both parties and a couple of trips to Bellingham I began to realize that both sides were beginning to give a little. I reasoned with Frank that if he raised his bid to forty-six cents there was a good chance to make a deal and at that price he could make a lot of money. After three more days of tough negotiations, I finally got both parties to the forty-six-cent level. I was relieved that the ordeal was coming to a conclusion. If there were no last-minute hitches in the deal, Van Shell stood to make twenty-five thousand dollars commission. I was careful not to let B.C. Packers know who was about to purchase their large fish. My good friend Brad Hall, head man at Booth Fisheries Seattle plant, had agreed to purchase a substantial quantity of the medium-sized fish.

The day after the deal was made Eric Turnel sent word via Dick Lamb that he wanted to see me at once. I thought to myself, something must have happened to the deal. I entered Eric's office fearing the worst. "We want to know who you are selling the fish to," he demanded.

"I can't tell you that, Eric, and it's unethical of you even to ask," I replied.

"Well Norman, it's out of my hands," he replied. "It's up to you if you want to sell our fish."

"Eric, why the hell didn't you tell me that in the beginning? You said you were desperate to move the fish and now you're getting particular. I have no time to deal with your crap. Thanks for nothing but a big waste of time," I sputtered as I left his office.

Two hours later Dick Lamb was back on the phone, and soon after I was back in Eric's office having another heated argument about the halibut. He promised that they would not go around me if I told him who was buying the fish.

"I'll think about it," I said. "I'll let you know in the morning. But to tell you the truth I'm fed up with the whole situation and I find your attitude intolerable. What does it matter who the hell buys your halibut as long as you get rid of it at the best price?"

I phoned Frosty Frank to inform him about the turn of events and he reassured me that he would not buy anything directly "from those whores" were his exact words. He followed that statement with a few more choice curses before he hung up. Brad Hall also promised to protect my interest, so I felt reassured that there wouldn't be a double cross at the end of the transactions. I still felt that B.C. Packers were being unreasonable and I was pretty sure that the deal would collapse before being consummated. I was so upset by the wasted time and added expenses that I had burned up, that I didn't bother to contact Eric on the following morning.

At eleven a.m. Dick Lamb turned up at my office and said that Eric had sent him over to get me. Dick was a good friend of mine, and on occasions when B.C. Packers were short of trolled salmon for their export market I sold them frozen salmon from our inventory. I also bought fish occasionally for B.C. Packers from their chief competitors so nobody would find out about it. Dick repaid me by keeping me informed about up-to-date export prices and a number of other delicate matters that afforded our company an opportunity to make a profit.

I entered Eric's office with Dick, who stood back to listen in on the conversation. Eric swore to me on a stack of bibles that the fish could be shipped as soon as I told them who my customers were. He also swore on his word of honour that he would not go around me.

"Eric," I said, "it's against my principles to divulge that information and if I did, I know that you would not let me sell your fish."

Once again Eric assured me if was merely a technical matter and that if I told him the name of the customer, he would not interfere with the deal no matter who the customer was.

"Surely you must have an inkling," I replied. "The only customer capable of processing that volume of large halibut is your biggest competitor in the California market. He hates you with passion just as you hate him with equal intensity. Now do you know where I am selling all of your large halibut?"

Eric started to rise from his chair. Before he reached his full height he exclaimed, "Not Frosty Frank!"

"For Christ's sake, who else?" I replied. "Who but Frank could steak that volume of fish in three months and pay for it? Do you know anyone else? Obviously not or you'd be selling the fish yourself."

Eric, turning white before my eyes, opened his office door and indicated I should leave immediately. The last words that I heard from his mouth before the door slammed shut were "None of our fish will ever be sold to that unsavoury character."

By the time I got back to my office I had cooled down somewhat, but I was still in a foul mood. I was angry at being pushed around by Eric, whom I considered to be nothing but an incompetent flunky. I decided that it was best to let it go for now and that in the future there would be plenty of opportunities to stick it to B.C. Packers. I figured at the rate he was going with his deficient business acumen, it was only a matter of time before Eric lost his head on the corporate chopping block.

About an hour later Dick Lamb dropped in and told me to relax. "Norman," he said, "we both know that Frosty Frank will never buy from us, and Brad Hall has already told Eric to go and fly his kite elsewhere. Any money says before the end of the day, Eric will be back trying to resurrect the deal. Just make sure you have everything nailed down so Eric can't weasel out of your commission after you've sold the fish. The facts are that Eric is under enormous pressure to get rid of that fish."

Sure enough, before the business day was over I received a call from Eric, who summoned me to his office. I entered his office where he sat with a sour look on his face, flanked by a couple of B.C. Packer executives. Now he was all business without a trace of a smile or an apology for his previous rudeness. "You can go ahead and sell our fish, Norman, but we do not want to know who you are dealing with. You are not to divulge that information to anybody, period. We will provide you with the weights and you will be responsible for bills of lading and custom documents, and you must pay for every delivery on a seven-day basis. We are selling the fish to you, so you are responsible for payment, and we don't give a damn who you sell it to." Eric was doing a complete about-turn from his previous position. I'm fairly certain he must have been getting orders from someone higher up to get on with the show.

I arranged immediately to move the halibut out on a two-truck-per-day delivery basis until the supply was exhausted. Their fish was number-one quality, and from then on everything went as planned. I collected the money from Frank on a weekly basis, and we paid it out four days later in order to give the cheques time to clear so our money would not be used in any of the transactions. From time to time I drove down to Bellingham to have lunch with Frosty. It was his turn to buy now, which he did with a smile as he speculated repeatedly how it must burn B.C. Packers' ass to unload their frozen halibut stocks to him at less than their cost.

The day arrived when Eric Turnel informed us that the last of their halibut was going out, so it was the end of the show. All good and bad things end sometime, and I had no regrets, but that wasn't the end of the story. A day later I received a call from Frank that a truckload of frozen large halibut had arrived from B.C. Packers and it was billed to his company directly by Seaport Fish Company in Seattle. This company was owned by B.C. Packers. Frank said, "I bought the fish from you, Norman, but now it looks like they intend to go around you. You tell the powers to be at B.C. Packers that I am going to pay you for the fish or they can send a truck down to get it."

Half an hour later I confronted Eric Turnel in his office and demanded an answer from him. "Eric, what are trying to pull off?" His face turned beet red while he denied he knew anything about the shipment. "Well, Eric, Frank says he bought the fish from me and he is going to pay me for it. You can send a truck down to his plant and take it away if that doesn't suit you."

"Wait here a minute," he said. "I'll come back to let you know what we are going to do." Five minutes later he came back to let me know that the fish had been shipped from their Seattle plant. He told me the fish would be billed to us as usual and we were to rebill it and collect the money as usual and then pay the bill. He claimed it was all a misunderstanding by their Seattle branch. I had no reason to believe that Eric was telling me the truth because of his consistent unethical behaviour. It turned out that B.C. Packers had seven hundred and fifty thousand pounds of halibut in the Seaport Seattle plant that they wanted to dispose of. By shipping under the Seaport billing, they were trying to do us out of our six-thousand-dollar commission. I'm sure Eric had no idea that Frosty Frank was a decent businessman who honoured his commitments and lived by his word — something that was largely foreign to the B.C. Packers corporate ethos as practiced by Eric Turnel.

In due course a commission cheque for three thousand dollars arrived from B.C. Packers. A few months passed and it was obvious there was no second cheque for the additional amount of commission owing. I walked over to see Eric and asked him if he forgot to mail out the balance that was owed to us. "Norman, I've been waiting for you," he said. "We've decided to give you product instead of cash," he offered with a weak smile. "That's your stuff stacked up by the door. You can take it any time you want."

I thought to myself that this was a strange way to pay off a debt as I walked over to inspect the pile. There were two forty-eight-can cases of canned salmon, two cartons of smoked oysters, a couple of small cartons of some other canned product and a case of rye whisky. Rapid calculations of the value of the offer came to approximately a sum just short of three hundred dollars. I turned to Eric and said, "I would rather have a cheque for the thirty-five hundred dollars you owe."

He turned his back on me and offered, "Take it or leave it, Norman, because we figure you've received enough commission payments for the fish you sold for us."

"Come on, Eric," I said. "That's no way to do business." I walked to the front of his desk to confront him. "I can buy ten times as much as that with what you owe. I want the money."

He took some papers out of his desk and pretended to be busy and averted his eyes as he repeated, "Take it or leave it."

I left it. I believed Eric's little power trip was his pathetic attempt to get back at me for whatever slights he imagined. The fact is, I had done him a big favour by selling fish he paid too much for and helping extricate himself from a heap of trouble. I looked at him and said, "Eric, you weasel, I can easily go and see Ken Fraser to get our money. I'm sure he wouldn't see it your way because, unlike you, he's a straight shooter. I'll tell you another thing, Eric, you're pretty near the end of the line in your company, because people who pull off stunts like yours are not good enough to get to the top."

In any case, Eric Turnel had never been a favourite of mine. He saw himself in a much higher class and looked the other way whenever he could unless there was something that could benefit his position. One way or the other, we still did a lot of business with B.C. Packers and I had many good friends in that establishment. But I made it a point to never speak to Eric Turnel again. I went out of my way to snub him. I never did go to see Ken Fraser about Eric's dishonesty. It's not wise to continually bother the head man of such a huge corporation about minor disputes with his flunkies. It's better to hold one's fire for more important matters. True to my prediction, Eric never made it to the big time in B.C. Packers. He ended his days in the publicity and promotions department making speeches and having tea with little old ladies.

MAC AND BOB

Mac Brock, who attended Franklin school in the East End with me in the early 1920s, was a square shooter who worked for years in executive positions at B.C. Packers. Mac was forced to spend a few years in purgatory, working in inventory, because of a slight misjudgement in his behaviour — something a department head in a large company should not do at any time if he wishes to be promoted.

The story as I heard it was that Bob Widdis enticed Mac into a drinking spree that continued on for some months. Booze was Mac's weakness and once he got going, it took a spectacular event or a great deal of persuading to get him to clean up his act. Mac was a gentleman and no fool. He knew his own weakness well, so it was a mystery to everyone why he chose to go on such a frightful bender. Mac could usually handle the stuff, but with Bob pushing he got carried away further than he normally went. One evening when both of them were loaded they left the B.C. Packers' plant after midnight without locking the doors.

The night watchman making his rounds noticed the doors were left wide open. He phoned the police and Ken Fraser, president of B.C. Packers, who decided to check on the plant. Fraser arrived before the police and as he entered the darkened facility he had an unfortunate accident caused by stepping on an empty whisky bottle that was lying on the cement floor. In the ensuing fall he broke one of his legs. Later the police arrived and found Fraser writhing on the floor. The result was Ken Fraser ended up in hospital. When he returned to the fish plant a few days later on crutches and in a cast, the inquisition began. The night watchman kept a record of the shenanigans that went on in the plant at night and he passed it all on to Fraser. Both Mac and Bob were in serious trouble. When he finally had the opportunity to confront Mac and Bob about the incident, Fraser was as angry as a grizzly bear. Bob survived the event by a whisker and Mac was demoted to being in charge of inventory for a number of years.

That was the spectacular event that made a teetotaller out of Mac. Bob was beyond any help. For what it's worth, Mac and Bob never associated again after the debacle of Old Man Fraser's broken leg. In any case, Bob Widdis was never in the same class as Mac Brock. How Mac got mixed up with Bob will remain a mystery to me. In the end I believe Mac realized that hanging around with Bob could only bring more trouble. So he chose to give up Bob and the bottle and suffer in silence until he had another opportunity in business.

Large organizations are often unpredictable when it comes to managing the executive suite. Generally, when somebody fell out of favour with B.C. Packers there was little chance of promotion. But for the fact that he was a really valuable employee who had paid his dues for several years in the large B.C. Packers plant in Gander, Newfoundland, Mac might have suffered worse than a demotion. Ken Fraser, who we called Little Big Man (five foot seven with an exaggerated pot belly), although a hard man, had a heart when it came to most employee matters, but he had little patience for the kind of partying that was consuming Mac. Fraser decided to keep Mac close at hand in paperwork purgatory. Mac, a consummate wheeler and dealer, thoroughly hated the inventory job, which meant keeping track of product and producing figures for various department heads. None of the department heads were even remotely in his class. This was a bean counter's job, a bitter fate for a man who hated bookkeeping. Mac had plenty of time between being summoned to produce figures, which must have led him to pondering his dull work. Mac became a reformed man, a booze fighter who had seen the light. He was a very able man in the company and he was surely on his way to the top. All he had to do was keep away from firewater and bad company. He had plenty of time to regret his actions and he built up a hatred for the party animal who had led him astray. Now he avoided Bob like the plague and if they had occasion to pass on the wharf he never paused to talk.

Bob Widdis was a playboy who seldom came to work before noon. He had been set up to run Seaport Crown Fisheries by his father who, for business reasons, put Bob in bed with B.C. Packers. Seaport Crown was in financial difficulty, so to survive, the elder Widdis made an agreement with B.C. Packers to remain operating under their sponsorship. Bob largely became a figurehead while his cousin Bertha (Bea) ran his plant under B.C. Packers' guidance. Eventually, Bob became excess baggage as far as the business went because of his drinking and outrageous behaviour in life and in business. Several times he was within an ace of being tossed out of the cozy agreement his father had set up for him. B.C. Packers absorbed almost all the profit that this slick arrangement was engineered to produce. Unfortunately Bob Widdis's wild lifestyle took him down early in mid-life.

When employees neglect to mind the store and are impatient to be away enjoying themselves, it can spell trouble for the company that employs them. One day, Bob Widdis, Joe Van Snellenburg and a foreman from B.C. Packers were dispatched by B.C. Packers to go to B.C. Ice and Cold Storage to inspect a forty-thousand-pound parcel of Bella Coola red-meated, semi-bright chum salmon. If the fish passed inspection by the trio it was to be shipped to the Packers' Imperial plant in Steveston for processing. The fish were a good grade of semi-bright chums that passed inspection and they were purchased for B.C. Packers.

Now this is where the trouble began. At that time it cost three-quarters of a cent per pound to ship the fish by ordinary transport or one-and-one-quarter cents per pound by reefer truck. Bob had engineered the purchase of the fish from Jack Elsie through the agent, John Nichols. Bob was getting a fat commission on the deal and the money was already burning a hole in his pocket before he received it. With Joe in tow he left the cold storage in a hurry to celebrate. They left the details of transport in the hands of a clerk back at the office. The result was that someone ordered a truck for the cheapest cost to pick the fish up at B.C. Ice and Cold Storage and transport it to the plant in Steveston. On a hot day in July, forty thousand pounds of frozen salmon went on a thirty-five-mile trip through heavy traffic in a non-refrigerated truck. The truck arrived at the Imperial plant at a quarter to twelve noon and was left out in the sun until the one p.m. whistle blew and B.C. Packers' employees were available to unload the truck.

Joe had been in the fish business a long time before he was employed by B.C. Packers. He knew better than to see the fish shipped in hot weather in this manner. Had he paused to take care of the details in transporting the product, there would have been no problem. However, Bob was in a hurry to enjoy the rest of the afternoon and he and his new buddy set off for some action. Mac Brock was summoned by company personnel at the Imperial plant to come and inspect the half-thawed salmon. When he arrived the fish tails were already drooping over the sides of the wooden tubs. Thawing and refreezing fish causes some discolouration and also devalues the quality to a minor extent. Like anyone else who was looking after company interests, Mac refused the fish and sent it back in the same truck to B.C. Ice and Cold Storage. By the time it arrived back at B.C. Ice, it was considerably more thawed and John Nichols, Jack Elsie's agent, refused to accept it and dispatched it back to the Imperial plant in Steveston. By this time the fish was almost completely thawed out. To save the fish, B.C. Packers had no alternative but to put the one-thousand-pound totes of semi-thawed salmon into their cold storage where the fish froze in clusters. That was not exactly how it should have been refrozen but, in the end, one word led to another, so it was a come and get your damn fish affair.

By this time the problem was out of Mac Brock's department,

so he divorced himself from the dispute. Jack Elsie was in financial difficulties and he wanted his money in the worst way. Because Jack Elsie with his salmon cannery up on the north coast was a pain in the butt for B.C. Packers' fishing interests in those parts, they dug in their heels and refused to pay. It was to their benefit to drag their feet on the issue to keep Jack as hard up as possible, to prevent him from paying his obligations to fishermen.

The controversy went on for more than two months with no sign of a settlement in sight. Obviously, Jack Elsie had no option but to launch a suit against B.C. Packers for payment. Jack asked me to witness for him but I refused his request, so he had a legal document sent to me requiring me to appear in court on his behalf. I believe it is contempt of court if one fails to show up on one of those invitations. It looked as if I was going to have to testify whether I liked it or not.

I promptly went to see Ken Fraser and asked him if they were out of their minds to fight the case in court. I advised him, "Your people inspected the fish and bought it for your account. Arrangements were made by your staff to have it delivered to your Imperial plant. Your representatives are responsible for shipping it improperly, without refrigeration, on a hot day so that the fish arrived at your plant in a semi-thawed condition. You accepted it and have it in your possession. Mr. Fraser, I'm betting that you'll have to pay for it."

Fraser looked at me with sparks flying from his bright blue eyes and he warned me to keep out of it.

I told him that I was going to appear in court against my will but that I would be telling the truth about the deal as I saw it. Once again I said, "You can use the fish, so my advice is to make a settlement with Elsie the best way you can, otherwise it will cost you more in the end."

Fraser got out of his chair in an abrupt manner to end the conversation and snapped at me, "Keep out of it."

"Have it your way," I snapped back. "Just remember that I will not be lying for anybody!" This whole affair erupted at a time when I was enjoying a good relationship with B.C. Packers. Suddenly I realized that if I testified, no matter what the outcome, one of the parties involved was going to be mad at me.

I arrived at the courthouse at one-thirty p.m. It was standing room only with company officials, lawyers, witnesses and spectators completely filling the room. Bob and Joe arrived late and had to squeeze their way into the courthouse and stand with their backs against the doors. From the look of them it was obvious that they had stopped on the way for a few martinis. One witness after another was sworn in and various testimonies referred to silver brights, semi brights, near brights, all brights, red-meated bright chums, red-meated dark chums, black chums, quallas, dog salmon and a few more terms that I had never heard before. The judge sat tapping his pencil in wonderment as he attempted to make some sense of the situation. It was obvious as the case proceeded that he was becoming even more confused.

After I was called to the witness stand on Jack Elsie's behalf and sworn in, one of the B.C. Packers officials sprang to his feet and declared that I was an unqualified witness. He claimed that I was a small operator who knew nothing about the quality of fish. Though I was unhappy being called to testify, I became uneasy at his attack on my credibility. I turned to the judge and politely asked him if he understood what the previous witnesses were saying when they attempted to inform him about the case.

"No, I don't understand any of it," he replied. "I wish someone would enlighten me on these terms they are bantering about."

"Do you mind if I explain the variety of terms used by the previous witnesses?" I asked.

"Not at all," he replied. "Please go ahead and tell me about it." He turned and leaned towards me as I began to explain that they were referring to grades of chum salmon with some slang terms included. Dog salmon was a low-grade term used for late-run chums, because those fish had large fangs in both of their upper and lower jaws. Silver brights were the top-grade ocean-caught fish. They were silver all over and red meated. Semi brights were second grade with a slight dark cast to their skin but were still quite silvery and red meated. Near brights and all brights were just slang names for those two grades. Chums were either dark skinned with red meat or dark skinned with pale meat with some dark or reddish stripes on them. Quallas were very dark skinned with large stripes on their sides with pale meat and they were canned. The label on the canned qualla chum salmon was keta salmon, a trade name for all canned chum salmon regardless of grade. "What we are referring to in this case is a red-meated semi-bright salmon. All the rest of the terms do not apply."

"Thank you very much," he answered. "At least now I know what you're all talking about." The B.C. Packers' lawyer was still attempting to discredit me as a witness but the judge cut him off and advised him that I was very knowledgeable on the subject before the court. "How long have you been in the fish business?" he asked.

"About twenty-five years," I answered.

Then he turned to the lawyer and asked if he had anything new to add. He advised him that if not, he should sit down. There were one or two witnesses to be heard from, but I knew that the judge had already decided on the case.

Suddenly there was a scuffling sound in the back of the crowded courtroom. Bob Widdis (six foot three, two hundred ten pounds) punched John Nichols (five foot seven, one hundred twenty pounds) in the stomach and drove him to the floor with the wind knocked out of him. A couple of people quickly grabbed John under each arm and held him up as he attempted to regain his breath.

"What's going on back there?" the judge demanded in a loud voice while banging his gavel. There was not a sound. The judge glared at the room trying to figure out what the ruckus was about. I'm sure that Bob would have ended up in the slammer for at least thirty days had the judge been aware of what had taken place in the back of his courtroom. However, John kept quiet and the incident passed.

"How much was the fish sold for?" the judge asked. He was informed it was sold for fifty-five cents per pound. The judge then ordered B.C. Packers to pay Jack Elsie fifty cents per pound plus all the costs. Then he banged down his gavel and ended the proceedings. There were loud words spoken in the back of the room as the crowd exited the courtroom, but by then the judge had already departed the scene. There was shouting and cursing out on the sidewalk in front of the courthouse. Bob and Joe were doing their thing, but by now the crowd was dispersing with loud laughter fading away down the street. Bob and Joe warned me that B.C. Packers were going to get even with me and some of the other witnesses.

Later, when I ran into Mac Brock, I noticed the bemused look on his face. When he rejected that load of fish, Mac had carefully played his cards. He knew that Bob and Joe were eventually going to get themselves into trouble, and when he had the chance he set them up for the big fall. It was a signal that Mac was hell-bent on getting back to the top of the management heap. A couple of weeks later I encountered Ken Fraser on the wharf. He seemed friendly enough, so I knew there were no hard feelings. We stood by the ice house and talked in general about the fish business. While he made no direct mention of the court case, Fraser shook his head and indicated that he had to do something about some of the losers in his organization.

Mac Brock waited patiently for a long time before he regained his status in the B.C. Packers' management structure. It wasn't until Malcolm McCallum was killed while on holiday in the Canary Islands that Mac was restored to a rank that suited his considerable business skills. McCallum Sales was owned by B.C. Packers, and Mac Brock was the most knowledgeable and practical candidate they had in the organization to take charge of this subsidiary company. Mac made the most of his second chance. He remained in charge of this plant until he retired. Now may his soul rest in peace.

CANNERY ROW

In the salad days of the fishing industry, after the First World War, there were a great many reduction plants and saltries in British Columbia. Pilchards were coveted for reduction purposes because they yielded more gallons of oil per ton of fish than could be recovered from any other fish taken on large scale by seine boats.

Herring were also taken for reduction and into saltries to be dry-salted for export to China. Oil recovery from pilchards far exceeded the oil recovery from herring, so reduction plants preferred pilchards. The oil was the most valuable item recovered from these fish, used for food and other select purposes in Canada, the United States, and in Europe. The meal was used to fortify animal feed with protein. As well as salted herring, fish meal was also shipped in quantity to China, where it was used as a protein that was added to cereals and legumes for human consumption. It was really cheap food that could be produced in great quantities.

In the late 1930s, the pilchard runs vanished for some reason and they never returned to B.C. waters again until about 1995, when a limited food fishery of a couple of hundred tons was allowed. I believe the pilchards died out in B.C. from overfishing of juvenile fish for canning and reduction plants. A similar fate wiped out the sardine and pilchard in California. When the fishery collapsed in California, dozens of canneries along Cannery Row closed forever. A large number of sardine seine vessels stayed idle for years before winding up in Alaska. Fishing vessels that were not built in British Columbia were not allowed in our fishery, but a few of these California vessels managed it somehow.

The pilchard fishery is only now beginning to recover in California, sixty years later. Now approximately a thousand tons are allowed to be taken each year for the fresh-fish market, salting and canning. We shall see if they allow the resource to recover to its historic level or if they will overfish and kill it like we did our silver smelt fishery off the Point Grey banks. In California, pilchards averaged five to eight fish per pound, while in B.C. we had them all sizes from four ounces to a little over a pound. By 1936, most of the reduction plants in British Columbia had been closed for at least two years and most of them were going to remain permanently shut down. Only the large reduction plants that were more efficient and were closer to cheap labour and transportation facilities, like the ones situated along the Fraser River, survived because of the herring resource. There were two or three others left in the struggle, like the co-op plant in Prince Rupert, but these were marginal players.

The larger plants were combination canneries and reduction companies. Besides herring, they were able to use the salmon and offal from their cannery operations to augment their reduction facilities, and because of their prime locations it was convenient for them to ship their product by truck, rail or by deep-sea ship to any port in the world. In addition, these big reduction facilities could obtain a steady supply of salmon trim and offal from the dozens of small independent canneries that operated around the Burrard Inlet harbour and the Lower Fraser River. These companies were eager to get rid of the offal and sometimes paid to have it removed to the reduction plants, because it was against the law to dump it in the ocean and in the summer months it created an unbearable stink. A towboat with a couple of large barges serviced all the independent canneries. There were always a few independent reduction plants opening, which caused financial problems for the large reduction plants. At that time they paid the fishermen three or four dollars or less per ton for herring for reduction. That doesn't seem like very much money, but there was a raging depression on at the time and a good many people were working for ten to thirty dollars per month.

In those days, no seine vessel would set on a school of herring unless they could take at least two hundred tons in a set. Six- or seven-hundred-ton sets were a common catch when herring were plentiful. The record catch of herring by a seine vessel in the Gulf of Georgia in those days was thirteen hundred and fifty tons in one set. Compare that to the ten to one hundred tons they take today when the herring are spawning. If the herring were not schooled up in bays and inlets at spawning time, the seine vessels would be lucky to catch a couple of hundred pounds per week. The Department of Fisheries and Oceans still claims there is just as much herring now as there ever was — what a load of rot.

The skipper-owner, boat and net would probably get half the take, minus fuel and groceries that was taken from the top, while the rest was divided among the crew members. The skipper-owner also sometimes received a bonus of twenty to thirty cents per ton on the sly that was not available to the crew. In any case, nine hundred dollars split between a five-man crew each week was not a bad take, bringing six or seven times more than schoolteachers were making at that time.

The independent reduction plants that opened up for business from time to time had only one or two seiners fishing for them. They had to depend on taking fishermen away from the larger companies. They would jack up the price to get the independent fishermen to make deliveries to their plants. The company vessels still had to deliver to the major reduction plants, but the skippers and crews complained bitterly when independents got two dollars per ton more from the small operators than these company men could get from the larger companies. These independent fishermen were playing a dangerous game. They tried to deliver to the smaller reduction plants on the sly because they did not want the big operators to learn about their activities. They were worried that if the small plants closed, the major operators would not buy their fish.

Eventually, there were enough small reduction plants in business that they began to take a significant amount of herring and completely upset the relationship between the large reduction plants and their customers. This problem became a huge concern to the big companies because the small ones were undercutting the market with cheaper meal. The major reduction plant operators were caught in a double bind. They had to pay the fishermen more money to keep them happy, and they had to sell for less to compete with a small independent who was happy to upset the apple cart. It was an intolerable situation for the big reduction plants and they vowed to eliminate the problem at any cost. This attitude began to cloud their way of doing business.

Norman and Allan fishing in Seymour Creek.

Norman in his father's arms and his brother Ed with their mother, 1919.

The Safarik Family, 1934: Emilie, Norman, Ed, Johnny, and John.

Fishing boats docked, circa 1930.

A view of the dock shortly after the Vancouver Harbour Commission Wharf was built, circa 1926.

A salmon gillnetter spills over with its catch, circa 1943.

Fishing boats in berths at Campbell Avenue fish dock.

The *Victor F* at dock in front of the Canadian Fishing Company building at the foot of Gore Avenue, 1940.

Piers and docks on the Vancouver waterfront in 1920. Vancouver Ice and Cold Storage and New England Fish Company are visible in the background.

A bounty of crab at the Safariks' Vancouver Shellfish and Fish Company, 1944.

John Safarik (left) unloads crabs, 1944. >

A brail full of sockeye salmon goes into the hold of a seiner, circa 1943.

A view down into the hold of a fishing boat, 1937.

A salmon seiner lifts its catch, and the workers haul in the net, circa 1943.

A haul of fish,
1937.

Unloading
fish on the
Vancouver Harbour
Commission
fish dock, 1937.

Repairing the net, 1937.

A fisherman looks down at a catch of sockeye salmon, circa 1943.

Inside a plant, processing salmon, 1941.

A mechanized butchering device removes the head of salmon in a cannery, circa 1943.

The *Ocean Tor* tied up at the Vancouver Harbour Commission Wharf.

On a break from processing fish, workers sit on the dock, 1937.

Workers at Van Shell wash gutted and headed salmon.

Norman (right) and his boyhood friend, Fred Tsuchia, a gillnet fisherman.

Salmon cover the floor of the Semiahmoo Cannery.

The Van Shell plant in Tofino.

Norman Safarik, in his late
teens, fishing Seymour Creek.

Norman Safarik at Campbell
Avenue fish dock.

Allan and Norman Safarik,
2012.

SHOOT UP AT CAMPBELL AVENUE

Jimmy Fidler was one of the small operators in the 1950s, with a small salmon cannery on the Campbell Avenue fish dock and a small reconditioned reduction plant — about a ten-ton-per-hour outfit — located at Shingle Bay. Jimmy had one large seine boat of his own, *Miss Jean*, that seined for salmon in the summer and went after herring in the winter and spring months.

Jimmy came from a well-established fishing family. Both he and his younger brother, Norman, fished with their father in their own boats when they were students at the University of British Columbia. They were hard workers and good fishermen and they accumulated a substantial amount of capital and owned their own vessels by the time they completed their educations.

Norman was an intellectual who dabbled in many ventures. He discovered a way to clear brush in the Peace River area and he cleared a lot of land in a short time and planted grain in a big way. The only trouble was that a crop could only be harvested once in three or four years. It was either rained out or snowed under, so after losing a bundle he threw in the sponge. After that he made and repaired a variety of batteries in a plant on Terminal Avenue in Vancouver. He was a good hook-and-line fisherman but not too good with a seine net. In 1965, he lost a brand new salmon seine worth at least sixty thousand dollars the first day he was out with it. That was a significant amount of money and it ended his seine-fishing days. Norman continued to fish for tuna and salmon, but I believe the pollution from his days in the battery factory impaired his health and he died of cancer before he was fifty years of age.

Jimmy Fidler carried on in the fishing business, operating the National Salmon Cannery on Campbell Avenue and expanding into the herring reduction business. Jimmy was the opposite of Norman, who was an egghead and aloof from his fellow fishermen. Jimmy was happy-go-lucky, as friendly a person as one could find. When he wasn't hard at work he took time to socialize with the other fishermen, which meant wine, women and song. He was immensely popular around the coast. I can also vouch for the fact that he was one of the most honest people in the fishing industry. However, there were a number of issues that plagued Jimmy as he expanded his holdings. While he was a very successful fisherman and a tremendous personality people loved to hang around with, Jimmy was not necessarily the world's greatest businessman. Expanding too quickly into a risky business and enjoying the high roller's life while employees took care of the day-to-day business was a recipe for disaster. Add to that the fact that bankers were not very friendly towards small fishing companies, especially when the large companies were leaning on the banks to cut down on loans to competitors who were annoying them. Many a company has gone down the tube when a bank has suddenly pulled the plug in mid-season. I know all about it because I have gone through the experience myself, and that was when our company was making enormous profits.

Friday nights were happy times in the National Cannery. Jimmy's accountant, Elsie, would put away the books for the evening and take out the accordion. Her husband was the cannery operator, in charge of keeping the machinery running. Both he and Elsie enjoyed a wee dram now and then, as did most of the men and women who worked in the cannery. Elsie was a tall blonde with the longest pair of fancy legs I ever saw. And she knew it. She wore white shorts or very short skirts to show them off. She was quite a sight to behold as she made her way down the plank wharf in her high heels. The closest I came to getting slugged by a woman was one day when Elsie passed our place and stopped to pick something up off the dock. I couldn't resist the temptation to spray her sexy rear end with cold water from the hose I was using to wash down the dock. Elsie pulled her punch at the last moment as I stood in total embarrassment at what I had done. To this day I don't know what possessed me to carry out such an idiotic act but it was done and I had to accept the consequences.

"Damn you, Norman," she said in mock seriousness before exploding in laughter and continuing on her way.

On many occasions Jimmy sat by himself in his upstairs office brooding over his business. At the end of the day he would invite me over to join him for a drink and to swap information. There he would sit with his glass in his hand and a .22 rifle across his knees. He would pass the ice and the open bottle as he invited me to sit down. He had the door open to the cannery loft, waiting for a rat to appear so he could knock it off with the rifle. We'd sit there for an hour or more shooting the breeze between phone calls and shots. Jimmy was a crack shot who seldom missed.

One night I was locking our big sliding door in the early evening when I heard someone running down the dock. I looked up the wharf and saw Ken Fraser, president of B.C. Packers, running towards me as fast as a short fat man could run. "What's your hurry, Ken?" I asked as he steamed on by.

He paused for a second and declared, "That mad man tried to shoot me!"

"What the hell are you talking about?" I asked as he sped on his way.

He shouted, "That crazy Jimmy tried to shoot me!" I watch him as he ran completely around the horseshoe to the other side of the wharf and entered the B.C. Packers' plant.

I ventured along the dock until I got the National door. It was still open after Ken's hasty departure, and Jimmy was sitting there with a glass in his hand and the rifle across his knees. The usual glass and ice bucket were on the table but one chair was spilled on its side. Jimmy looked at me with a grin and invited me to sit down and have a drink.

Before I poured a drink, Jimmy up and fired, killing another long-tailed victim.

"Jimmy," I said. "I just saw Ken Fraser running down the wharf and he mentioned that a crazy man tried to shoot him. You didn't take a shot at Ken, did you?"

He pointed to the window sill and said, "There's the bullet hole."

"What happened?" I asked.

Jimmy looked at me and said, "We were discussing the price of herring for reduction and Fraser demanded that I reduce my price to the fishermen or there'd be hell to pay. We all know that small independent companies always have to pay more for fish. The big companies control the fleets, so why would the fishermen sell to me for the same price as the large companies pay to them and risk getting on the blacklist? I can't get enough fish from my own seine boat to operate my plant, so I pay a couple of dollars per ton more to get some fish on the sly from independent vessels. All the fishermen find out that we're paying more so they agitate their companies for more money. I suppose it costs them more money, but what the hell, I have to stay in business so I have no choice. I always have to pay a bit more to get enough fish.

"Old Ken comes over here and starts throwing his weight around. We got into an argument, and in the heat of our discussion he threatens to put me out of business. I got mad and decided to teach him a lesson. I was not going to submit to his demands, regardless of his threats. I fired a shot over his head to impress upon him my resolve to remain in the reduction business. He jumped out of that chair and took off in a hurry as I jacked another round into the chamber. That's about it, Norman, I didn't intend to shoot at him but merely shot over his head."

Booze and business seldom make a good partnership. Adding a gun to the mix creates a deadly combination. Both Ken Fraser and Jimmy Fidler had had too much to drink. Ken would never have threatened Jimmy if he had been sober, and Jimmy wouldn't have done such a foolish thing if he hadn't been loaded.

"You better get rid of the gun," I advised, "before the cops show up."

"Oh, hell," Jimmy answered. "Ken knows I wasn't trying to shoot him. How could I miss him at a range of less than five feet? By now he knows he shouldn't have threatened me and that I purposely fired over his head. He won't phone the police." Jimmy's intuition was right on. Ken didn't call the police nor do I think he ever told anybody. There certainly were never any rumours about the incident. Both Jimmy and Ken have been dead for years, so I suppose there's no harm in telling the story.

Jimmy's troubles were just beginning. His banker was causing a lot of trouble, constantly threatening foreclosure, but somehow Jimmy kept on operating. It was a pretty safe bet that the big companies were pressing the bank, trying to put an end to Jimmy once and for all. One Friday afternoon Jimmy's banker phoned and told him that the end was nigh and he wanted to see Jimmy in his office first thing on Monday morning. Jimmy decided to fight back with a vengeance. On Saturday evening he rounded up the crews from his two large packers (ex navy mine sweepers converted to pack fish), the *Miss Jean* (his seiner), and the *Joan F* (his troller) and instructed them to proceed out into the Gulf of Georgia towards the U.S. border and stand by for further orders.

Monday morning he went to the bank to confront the manager. He advised the bank manager to make up his mind about the call on his loan. He informed this gent that if he called the loan, the boats he had put up for security would cross the border and head for Seattle. He promised a vicious battle that would prevent those vessels from returning to Canada for many years. Jimmy demanded a written guarantee that the bank would not foreclose on him for a specified period of time to give himself time to manoeuvre. The banker was quite taken aback by Jimmy's determination and resourcefulness. Jimmy further went on to suggest that if the bank co-operated with him, sooner or later they would get their money back with interest. If not, he would do everything in his power to see the bank got nothing.

The banker withdrew to palaver with some of his associates and finally came back and agreed to Jimmy's conditions. Jimmy arrived back at Campbell Avenue waving the new agreement he had with the bank. That evening his vessels arrived one after the other to tie up at Campbell Avenue.

That morning, before he left for the showdown with the bank, Jimmy had come over to my office and handed me the National warehouse receipts signed over to Van Shell for more than enough fish to cover the twenty thousand dollars he owed us for fish we sold to him for canning purposes. He advised me to transfer the fish to another cold storage and put it in our name in case the bank attempted to seize the fish. He said, "Norman, I don't want you to get harmed because of my banking problems, so move that fish immediately!" I agreed to follow Jimmy's instructions and moved the fish while Jimmy was meeting with the banker.

Now the heat was off and Jimmy went about his business with the cannery on Campbell Avenue and the reduction plant at Shingle Bay. He dedicated himself to winning his right to remain in the herring reduction business, and it seemed like he was doing it. He stopped drinking as much and he began to pay closer attention to his day-to-day business affairs. The two large packers would arrive at our dock, each with a couple of hundred tons of fish meal on them. He would supervise the unloading to prevent the heavy paper bags of meal from being damaged and he made sure that weights were in order. I often saw him with sweat running down his nose as he manhandled the bags. Jimmy was seldom without a smile on his face and he was fine man who always took a few minutes to pass the time with me.

Jimmy was a soft touch and his history with booze meant that he had a regular crowd of freeloaders who kept coming around. Pretty soon I heard rumours that there was serious drinking going on when Jimmy's crews were unloading herring meal on Sunday afternoons. One Monday morning I came to work to be greeted with the sad news that Jimmy had died of a heart attack. Jimmy had been imbibing on

Sunday afternoon while he and the crew worked up a considerable sweat stacking bags of meal onto skids. Suddenly Jimmy felt ill and he dropped dead on Campbell Avenue fish dock. I was devastated. Jimmy was a good friend and a wonderful character. I knew right then and there that an era had come to an end.

The cannery and reduction plant closed up and Jimmy's holdings were largely grabbed by his creditors. Jimmy's younger brother Norman took over the *Miss Jean* and went out fishing. A few years later, when Norman died, the *Miss Jean* was sold to Sandy Petersen. Tragically, Sandy and his crew perished when the *Miss Jean* turned over when she ran into a cable stretched between a deep-sea tug and a loaded barge.

BIG FISH AND BIG BUSINESS

After the Second World War ended, the major fish packers were having difficult times. The old dynasties that amassed fortunes before 1900 and after the turn of the century buying salmon for a few cents each in their private fiefdoms where nobody could trespass had lost their power.

The days when fishermen were paid with private script or wooden money that could only be spent in company stores were gone. Independent operators entered the fishing industry and they paid real money for fish. Fishermen were free to spend their money anywhere in the land. The old system was being replaced by the marketplace. These independent buyers drove the cost of canned and processed frozen fish to new highs each season, causing sales to lag and warehouses to fill up with product. When the situation became desperate for the major players in the industry, the federal government stepped in and bailed them out by buying the surplus to give away or sell cheaply to some needy country. While the product was discounted to about twenty-five cents on the dollar, it was a godsend to the shareholders, who were largely close friends of government. It wasn't long before the big boys were buying the surplus inventory that the independents were stuck with at bottom-basement prices and moving that out with their own goods for additional profits.

However, the decades after the war were particularly difficult and unpredictable for the giants because of the basic changes that were taking place, as a new era of economic order developed. The major companies had a large, highly unionized workforce that demanded decent wages and benefits. In addition, the companies had to cope with a highly paid management pool that was not well equipped to operate in a free market. The independents, who had a personal handle on day-to-day operations, fared better. Lower costs allowed them to move inventories at lower prices through independent brokers. The brokers were experts in sales and they sold the goods quickly at whatever level it was necessary to move product. They developed new markets and accelerated the pace of sales within the industry.

The old-line companies were in serious trouble in the market place. They were in a no-win situation and they were slowly wearing down. Government assistance and generous handouts helped them overcome some obstacles, but the giants were losing ground. They began to abandon the fishery wherever returns were risky or unpredictable. Their boards became more concerned with developing extensive real estate assets that they had accumulated for the better part of a century. Several fish packing companies that sold out their interest in the fishing industry and entered into the real estate business made more profits there than they ever made in any of their various ventures in the fishing industry. Those who chose to hang on slowly dried up and blew away. Today, out of a score of old-line companies who could be considered giants in the fishery, only one survivor remains in business.

One of the first large fishing companies to bow out of the industry was Todd and Sons. They owned canneries, a substantial ground fish processing plant with cold storage facilities in Klemtu, B.C. Ice and Cold Storage in Vancouver and a substantial fleet of fishing vessels. To prevent American processors from buying out Todd and Sons, B.C. Packers and the Canadian Fishing Company bought Todd and Sons jointly. Canadian Fish Company took all the fishing vessels while B.C. Packers took B.C. Ice and Cold Storage, the big plant in Klemtu and some other shore installations. Todd and Sons built B.C. Ice and Cold Storage with a hefty government handout on the pretense that it would be operated as a public cold storage. It was generally not known by the independents, who froze their fish at B.C. Ice, that this cold storage was a B.C. Packers' property. Owning B.C. Ice gave B.C. Packers invaluable information about frozen fish inventories. It was essentially a window into the inventories and business practices of the many independent companies that stored their fish in B.C. Ice. The cold storage was built with public money, and it should have operated completely in that capacity. This was the type of arrangement that big companies in the fishing industry were able to make with the federal government.

Whenever a large corporation takes over or amalgamates with another, some heads are bound to roll. It doesn't take as many administrators to run one super company as it does to run two companies. Some executives on either side are likely to get their walking papers. Whenever there is such a union, the infighting begins in earnest for survival, so directors and management of each company are wary of each other's potential in the new organization. Sometimes both management groups will go out of their way not to co-operate with their opposites in the new organization. Individuals within each group see their opposite number as a competitor for their respective position in the new corporation. These opposites refuse to communicate with one another and take a hostile position about the benefits of reorganization. When it becomes a certainty that two jobs will soon become one, the two employees can easily become combatants who will generally avoid any contact with each other. Cliques of executives dedicated to survival form on either side. Information such as sales contacts and inventories that could be valuable to the opponent group are suppressed. The shakedowns in management always take some time before the pecking order in the new organization is established. Then the knives come out and the redundant executives are selected out of the team. Management cliques prevail or they evaporate, and no quarter is given to the losers. The dog-eat-dog nature of the scenario can play out in several ways. Certain individuals always thrive in chaotic environments and others deteriorate until they become paralyzed in indecision or apathy. Still others who survive being fired but receive demotions that reduce their power and their creativity become embittered executives who loathe the new organization and have an almost pathological desire to see it fail or at least see it ridiculed or shown up whenever the situation might arise. I saw this scenario play out many times over the decades under various economic climates.

The classic case for me was when British Columbia Packers bought out Canadian Fish and Cold Storage in Prince Rupert and dumped John Nichols Sr., the head honcho. Nichols quickly formed a new company and became a powerful competitor. That wrong move cost B.C. Packers many millions until this extremely able man died and his company went out of business.

The following true story that happened long ago illustrates the upheaval that can take place when large organizations in the same business are united into one larger company. One can sympathize with the worries and disappointments that boil up when huge companies merge and long-term personnel are let go.

One morning, forty years ago, a gentleman named Forsythe who I had known from school days arrived at my office with a proposition. I had not seen this fellow for many years and had not known that he was in charge of the fresh frozen fish sales in the Todd and Sons organization. He was angry and came right to the point. "Norman," he said. "We have a substantial quantity of frozen number-one seined silver bright salmon, some large white springs, and some large red springs that the sales department at B.C. Packers will not help us sell. I won't go into the reasons, but I'm sure you can use your imagination. In any case, I'm in a hurry to unload my inventory while I'm still in charge."

Immediately I sat back and gave him my full attention. He went on to ask if I could sell a couple million pounds of silver brights and about one hundred thousand pounds of plus-fourteen-pound large red springs and forty thousand pounds of large white springs. He went on to explain that the B.C. Packers sales department completely ignored his problem even though they now owned his company and his inventory. He quoted me thirty-eight cents per pound across the board for all sizes of the silver brights and offered a two-cents-a-pound discount if I could sell them all. He wanted forty cents per pound for the large whites and sixty-five cents for the large reds. At those prices I knew I could sell all the fish but I had to tie down his offer to make sure there was no runaround.

It so happened that during my daily rounds through B.C. Packers' plant on Campbell Avenue wharf the previous morning, I observed them cutting red-meated dark-skinned chums into steaks. They were packaging these steaks from number-two salmon into their fancy Rupert brand cartons and they were not even good number-two quality chums (third-grade silver brights). My friend Dick Lamb walked through their plant with me, and I asked why they were packing poor-quality chum steaks in their flagship brand. He answered that B.C. Packers had no more silver brights left in inventory and in fact had no chums left at all. He went on to say they were buying the chums from Canadian Fishing Company, and that they were being ripped off on the price. Can Fish knew they were out of steaking fish so charged them forty-two cents per pound for poor-quality fish.

Now I quickly departed for B.C. Ice and Cold Storage with Mr. Forsythe to inspect his salmon inventory. As he had told me previously, all his salmon were beautiful number-one bright fish. His fish was all top grade. In fact, his silver brights looked like big bright sockeyes. The red and white springs were also the best prime fish. I said to Mr. Forsythe that I could ship out a forty-two-thousand-pound load immediately and would move three or four truckloads out per week, providing I had an option on his inventory of salmon for one hundred and twenty days because I did not want to make sales that I could not deliver. His company was owned by B.C. Packers, and surely they would discover the fact that they were buying high-priced number-two chums from Canadian Fishing Company while they had more than two million pounds of the finest fish in their own cold storage — the cold storage that came their way in the split-up of Todd and Sons assets. B.C. Packers actually owned these silver brights that Mr. Forsythe wanted me to sell but alas the merger between the two companies was in some internal turmoil. Meaningful communications between the principals in each company was minimal.

Mr. Forsythe was jubilant about the turn of events. He had sold all the salmon he could and was stuck with the balance. For his own reasons he was anxious to sell off his inventory. He promised me the one-hundred-and-twenty-day option as soon as it could be drawn up, and we shook hands on the deal before I departed. I was in a hurry to get into action. As soon as I got back to my office, I phoned Frosty Frank Metalgin in Bellingham to tell him I was shipping a truckload of prime silver brights to his plant. I told him they were as good as the best I had ever seen.

"Okay Norman," he replied. "But they better be good or I will ship them back to you."

I answered, "I'm not worried about that, Frank, but after you look at them, let me know how many you want, because I am going to move them out in a hurry." I knew Frosty Frank in Bellingham could use a truckload every other day with his ten big Butcher Boy saws cutting salmon steaks two shifts per day.

Frosty said he never saw such beautiful northern red-meated silver brights. He jumped at the opportunity to get a hold of a supply of such prime fish. His California market was a huge pit that he couldn't fill. He was always looking for good fish.

True to his word, just before noon the next day, Forsythe arrived at our office with the one-hundred-and-twenty-day option. The documents were promptly signed and witnessed to make them legal and he left with my assurance that his fish would all be sold long before the option expired. I already had an order for a couple of truckloads from Brad Hall of Booth Fisheries, who were one of B.C. Packers' toughest competitors. Brad advised he could move more fish if they were as good as I claimed them to be.

I felt good about my transactions with Mr. Forsythe but I wondered how long our deal would last before it blew up. So often, I had observed might was right regardless of options or contracts. At least that's the way it was most often in the history of the Pacific fisheries in Canada. Father told me that B.C. Packers was going to be very angry when they found out about my deal with Forsythe. However, I figured their own internal problems caused by their sloppy division of Todd and Sons and their own corporate turgidity were responsible for their own stupidity.

Frosty Frank was burning up my phone line. He was so cordial and complimentary! "Norman, old pal, where did you get that fish! Wow, I'm impressed. I want them all! How many have you got available, my friend?" Then with the next breath his voice changed and he warned that if I sold even one fish to anybody else he'd cut off my bazooka. "I need all those fish for my California steaking orders. When they see the quality they'll all double their orders. Norman, you keep those fish for me. Do you hear me? I want at least three truckloads per week and probably more when the steaks hit the stores."

I knew that lady luck was fickle. I decided to move as many of those salmon as was possible in a short time frame to minimize the chance that B.C. Packers would catch on. Two million pounds is a lot of fish to move out, but I was going to give it my best shot. We were making about twenty-five hundred dollars per truckload net and two cents per pound kickback on two million or more pounds of fish. That was twenty thousand dollars, a lot of money in those days. For quite a few days I mulled over in my mind whether I should be so bold as to sell some of the fish directly to B.C. Packers. After all, they were still paying a premium price to Canadian Fishing Company for low-quality steaking fish.

I went over to see Dick Lamb and planted the seed. I told him that I had some silver brights in my inventory that I could sell to his company for the same price that they were paying to Can Fish for poor-grade fish. I advised, "You really shouldn't be putting those number-two salmon steaks into your Rupert brand boxes." He showed some interest and my pulse quickened when he asked how many we had. "Oh," I answered, "about two hundred and fifty thousand pounds, more or less."

Later that afternoon, he showed up at my office and asked me to deliver five thousand pounds of our fish to their plant so they could inspect them.

We immediately ordered the silver brights out of storage for delivery to B.C. Packers. Shortly after the fish arrived, I got a call from Don Russell to come over to his office right away. I had a good idea that he wanted to buy some fish so I hustled over to the B.C. Packers head office. Russell welcomed me with a big smile as he pointed to a chair. This was unusual because Don did not smile much. In fact, he earned the nickname "Jug Head" because he had a perpetual frown on his face any time we saw him strolling along the dock. Also, he was as stubborn as an army mule, so the moniker really stuck. "How many silver brights have you in storage?" he asked.

"A couple of hundred thousand pounds, more or less," I offered in response.

"They're nice fish and we'd like to buy them from you. How much do you want for them?"

I told him I knew he was paying forty-two cents for dark skinned so I asked for one penny per pound more.

He agreed to my terms and a few seconds later gave me a purchase order for three hundred thousand pounds of silver bright salmon at forty-three cents per pound. "If you have any fish left after the purchase order is filled, I will make up another purchase order for the balance of your fish," were the last words I heard before I left his office walking on air.

B.C. Packers wanted the fish delivered in ten-thousand-pound lots each day. So every morning our truck was at B.C. Ice and Cold Storage at seven a.m. to get the fish out of storage and deliver it to the B.C. Packers plant. Occasionally they took two ten-thousand-pound deliveries in the same day. Father was shaking his head and warning me that all hell would ensue when the cat got out of the bag. Willy Steiner wore a perpetual frown on his face. I didn't really know why they were fretting about my deal. After all, I was buying the fish from them, so what if they wanted to buy it back and we made a profit on the transactions. It was called free enterprise. We were selling almost two hundred thousand pounds of this beautiful salmon per week and everybody was happy. My project moved along smoothly with greater sales than I anticipated. However, I did remain a little nervous about potential complications. Probably all hell would break loose, but it was a legal transaction that was completely above board.

Forsythe came to visit every two or three days and to pick up cheques for our purchases. He would then press me to move out the large red and large white springs that remained in his inventory. Steiner had long-time connections to Jewish businessmen on the East Coast who owned some of the biggest smokers in the United States. For years we did business with many of these companies. Steiner approached one of these companies that had offices both in Bellingham and Seattle to move out the large spring salmon. In due course a representative from the smoker showed up to inspect the springs and he immediately bought both parcels of large spring salmon. He was a tough hombre to deal with, and we only netted ten cents per pound on those two lots.

Forsythe was delighted to see the last of his springs and brought over a good bottle of Scotch whisky to drink a toast to his departing inventory. Everybody was happy until one morning Frosty Frank phoned and screamed in my ear that the chums he was now getting were not the same fish and he was not accepting the most recent truckload. "Norm, those fish are not the same fish. They have McCallum stickers all over them and I don't want them! I hate that bastard and I don't want any of his fish in my plant! You better find another home for them because I want those fish out of here." After he calmed down a bit and I was able to talk with him further, he went into detail about the chums being number-two dark-skinned fish with McCallum Sales stickers on the occasional fish. The last thing Frank uttered was "Someone is pulling a fast one on you."

I immediately rushed over to B.C. Ice and Cold Storage to find out what was going on. I talked to the packing crew in the storage, but they weren't talking. I went to the office to enquire about the switched fish. For a moment they pleaded ignorance but when I got very nasty, management threw in the sponge. "Go home and we'll pick you up in three-quarters of an hour, and then we'll go to Bellingham to see Frosty about those chums and fix up the problem." By the time I changed my clothes, Chris Hendrickson and Bruce Robinson from B.C. Ice were out front honking their horn. Before I could get out the door, Chris was ringing the doorbell and urging me to hurry up. As we walked to the car he flashed a roll of bills that would choke an ox and assured me everything would be squared up so I was not to worry about it.

When we got to Bellingham, I insisted that I would talk with Frank while the boys waited outside. It didn't take much to convince them, since it was Frank who was being burned by the switch, that they had better let me calm him down before they offered apologies. Frank had a legendary temper and a short fuse, and he didn't like being trifled with. Frank went out of control when I informed him that Chris and Bruce were waiting outside, but I urged him to calm down and listen to me for a moment.

"I don't want the fish under any circumstances, and you tell those crooked bastards to vamoose before I lose my temper. Get them out of my plant now!" Frank snarled.

"Please listen to me," I reasoned. "Obviously the fish was switched and now we have B.C. Ice by the testicles. The fish are dark skinned but they are red meated so you should be able to steak them. You can put the screws to B.C. Ice and make a bundle if you play your cards properly."

Finally, Frank quit yelling but still he had an angry look about him. He was a Slav, but now his Scotch blood was taking a hold because suddenly he smelled a good profit in the offing. He said, "Norman, these two scumbags have interfered in our mutual affairs by substituting crap for the good stuff you were supplying. You're right, we have to teach them a lesson." By now he was completely calm and he sat with a crafty look in his eyes. "Tell those two pricks to come in and I'll kick the living piss out of them."

Bruce and Chris were led into Frank's office by the smiling dark-haired beauty who guarded the outer office. Things were a bit close until Bruce struggled through his piece of fiction. Frank was there like a hawk about to swoop down on a wounded rabbit. We all knew Bruce's speech was a pack of lies, but at least he had Frank's ear. "A mistake has been made." Bruce went on and on in a soothing tone. "There is nothing between us that can't be fixed." Bruce was pretty slick, but I knew it was going to be a hard sell. He went on, "Norman sold you the fish for forty-five cents but we will pick up the tab for nine cents per pound and pay the freight so you have thirty-five cents per pound as a delivered cost. That's a good deal for you. We're willing to pay for our mistake."

Frank said, "You don't get it, I don't want those fish!"

Bruce tried another tack. He mumbled something about his offer being a starting point. Frank sat there and shook his head at every reduction in price. I left the office and went for a walk when it got down below thirty cents per pound. I don't know what the exact reduction was but when I got back a deal was done. I suspect that Frank settled for under twenty-five cents per pound. I never discovered the details about how the salmon was switched but I had a pretty good idea who was the culprit behind the scene.

About forty fish had McCallum Sales stickers pasted on them. Frank said to Bruce and Chris, "I don't want any of the fish that have stickers on them at any price. Get them out of my plant! Take them away or you can have all the fish back." It was a good thing the B.C. Ice car had a large trunk, because at Frank's insistence the trunk was opened and the forty salmon were stacked in the bottom and the lid was forced down until it snapped shut.

We drove the rest of the day and most of the night from club to club. Chris knew them all. Money was no object. It flowed like water at each oasis. Nothing was too good for Norman. We arrived in front of my home at about five a.m. In my front yard, Chris opened a new bottle and insisted on more drinks all around. Kathleen was awakened by the loud commotion going on outside on our lawn. She came out took a look around and suggested I come in the house. After a while she came back out with a broom and put the bum's rush on Chris and Bruce. Later in the day I found Bruce's hat on the lawn.

I sent B.C. Ice a bill for the commission I lost on the fish switch. The bill was duly paid. Not a word was said about the matter. McCallum was conveniently out of town or was unavailable until the storm had blown over. He would never admit that he had a hand in the fish switch, but I know darn well that he instigated it. He was the only one who could profit by it. A silver bright is not a dark chum — and besides, the old hands who worked at B.C. Ice would never had made that kind of mistake unless there was something in it for them.

A couple of months after Forsythe's springs had been shipped out of B.C. Ice, Steiner began to fret about the springs we had sold to the smoker. We decided I would phone them and ask what was the holdup in them sending us a cheque. Their excuse was feeble and it looked like we were going to get the runaround. I told Willy that I was going to the United States the next day.

The next afternoon I walked into their office. The three brothers who ran the business were sitting there. They seemed a little surprised to see me. "Boys, I've come for the cheque for the red and white springs we sold you, and I don't want to hear any excuses why you can't pay." They started to argue but I cut them off. "You inspected all the fish and you knew it was top-grade stuff. You bought it so pay up," I implored. I backed up against the door to bar their escape. They knew I was determined to collect one way or another.

There was a silence for a moment and then one of the trio spoke up. "I guess we better pay now," he said as he leaned back in his chair to look at his brothers. They nodded as he began filling out a cheque to our company while whining about some fish that were not so good. I noticed the amount of the cheque was for ten cents per pound less than we billed them but at least we were going to break even.

I took their cheque. I told them, "I don't believe that some of the fish were not so good! You know damn well it was all first-class stuff or you would have argued about it before you accepted our price in Vancouver. You're just deduct artists. You know it and I know it. One of these days we'll meet again, and if I get the chance, you boys are going to get an education. Right now I promise you I'll double the ante when my turn comes around." I knew the cheque would be good. Americans don't write bum cheques as is the custom in Canada, because in the United States it is classed as a much worse offence than it is in Canada. Americans may not pay up but they will not write an NSF cheque because they know they will be in trouble if they do.

When I got back to our plant they were overjoyed to get the cheque despite the deductions. Father muttered a few curses under his breath and let it go at that. Bill Steiner remarked that he always heard they were very good people and he was upset that they had ripped us off. Normally the people who ran the smokers, largely a specialty trade dominated by Jewish merchants, were good payers. We decided to chalk it up to experience, never dreaming we'd get a chance to settle up with these gents within the year.

They had a truck in Vancouver twice a week to buy any good salmon they could find for their smoking operation. In June, when the prime Fraser River springs were in the river, Napoleon Stradiotti was buying fish there for us. One morning he arrived with about four thousand pounds of large red springs and six hundred pounds of large whites all in the sixteen- to fifty-pound range. They were gorgeous fish, a pleasure to handle and easy to sell. We dressed out these fish and had them laid out on a layer of ice.

Boyd Shannon was unloading his packer that had just arrived from

Bute Inlet with a load of fish for his National Cannery. He had taken off about twenty-five thousand pounds of large white springs that were far from prime because their skin and meat was a grey colour. His cannery was jammed, and on that day he was completely disorganized. He had the white springs iced in thousand-pound bins and he begged me to help him out by taking the fish out of the sun into our plant. We took Boyd's white springs out of the sun and top-iced each bin to keep them cold. Because we were putting up a lot of shipping orders and we were running out of space, we threw all of the nice Fraser River springs on top of Boyd's white springs to get them out of our way. The American smoker's truck was parked on the wharf, and Moe, their buyer, with half a cigar clamped into his teeth, was leading the parade. He was followed by his apprentice, a nice young lad named Ed Perry who was a university student. Later, Ed established his own company, San Juan Packers. He was quite successful, eventually selling out to Trident, one of the largest fishing companies in America. He rose in the ranks and became one of Trident's most influential directors before he retired.

Moe strode into our plant like a general taking in everything around him. "Are all those salmon in those bins the same as those springs showing on top?" he asked as he opened bellies with a fat finger to inspect them for quality.

"Yes, they are," I lied. Suddenly I could smell an opportunity to settle the score. "But I'm not interested in selling any fish to you after your bosses made a deduction from our last transaction that prevented us from making any profit. We don't have any trouble selling our fish and we get paid promptly for everything we sell with no deductions. It beats the way your bosses do business." I kind of snubbed Moe as I was setting him up for the kill. He was taking the bait and I did not want to scare him off.

"I'll pay you cash for any fish I buy," he insisted.

"Okay," I said. "But the fish doesn't move until we are assured your cheque has cleared the bank. And cash is even better. And you will have to wait until I tally up the weights before I can bill you."

"That's okay," he replied, his big smile clamped around the stubby cigar. "I'm going over to B.C. Packers for an hour or so, then I will come back and write you out a cheque for the fish. I have no room left on the truck today, so Eddie will be up in the morning to pick up our fish. That should give you a chance to put the cheque into your bank." That arrangement was made to order and I smiled with joy as he went on his way over to the B.C. Packers' plant.

As soon as he was out of sight I rushed over to see Boyd Shannon. I asked him if he wanted to sell those Bute Inlet white springs. "You can really help me out if you take them off my hands," he acknowledged, as if I already didn't know that. "I have twenty-six cents a pound in them — can you pay me that much?" he asked.

"No, I can't," I replied, "but I can manage twenty cents per pound if you want to get rid of them."

"All right, take them," he replied as he walked away towards his office to make out a bill for the salmon he had just sold to me. The Bute Inlet springs were fresh enough but they were a poor grade that were really only fit for canning. They would produce a low-quality product that would end up getting sold to a banana republic or to a poor nation in Asia. Sometimes it took forever to get paid for low-quality canned salmon that was shipped offshore. Boyd felt he was better off taking the loss now and putting the money he received for the fish to better use. He hadn't wanted the white springs to begin with, but there was a big run of these fish in Bute Inlet and his buyer stuck him with the load.

I went to our office and made out an invoice for fifty cents per pound for all the white springs and eighty-five cents per pound for all the red springs we had in our plant. That included the mint ones brought in by Stradiotti. Then I waited for Moe to finish his business with B.C. Packers and return to our plant to write me a substantial cheque for the Fraser River and Bute Inlet springs. I kept my fingers crossed because there still was a remote chance that Moe would inspect the fish. If he did, the ball game was over when he detected the setup.

Moe returned with Ed in tow and without any hesitation wrote us out a cheque for almost thirty-five thousand dollars.

The next morning Ed Perry arrived with the large truck and we quickly loaded the iced fish onto it. I bought Eddie breakfast at the dock cafe while we gossiped about the fishing business. The scam was no skin off Eddie's back because Moe had bought the fish, but just the same my conscience bothered me a little bit as I walked the lamb to his truck and bid him farewell. But I resolved to do this when I thought about my previous dealings with the same company who took us to the cleaners without batting an eye. Eddie waved to me with a smile as he pulled out, and I thought to myself, this is a part of his education that he will never forget. I am sure in the future he will never ever pay for fish without fully inspecting the goods.

We waited for the explosion from down south of the border but we never heard a word from the smokehouse trio. I wondered if they remembered my promise to double the ante when we got even with them. It must have been a bitter pill for those high rollers to swallow, but they took their misery in silence.

Bill Steiner thought maybe we were being too tough and he wanted to soften our revenge by mediating the issue. "After all," he said, "now we have made more than twice their deduction back in profit." However, in the end it was decided to let the matter drop.

The amazing part of it is that forty years later we were still doing business with the same company, and to that day they never made another deduction. We did a lot of business by phone and fax with them and never had a bit of trouble. Two of the trio of brothers were deceased but the cheque writer who made the deductions was still there. He always asked my son Howard, "How is your father? Is he still active in the business?" His employees told my son the surviving brother only came in to sign papers and clip coupons.

The last time we met Ed Perry he was ready to retire. He bought Howard and me lunch at the golf club in Bellingham and he smiled broadly when he was reminded about his first trip to our plant with

Moe. The only rebuke we received for that scam was when Moe arrived the following week to buy fish and took his cigar out of his mouth long enough to call me a big prick and advise that in the future he would inspect every lot. We never had another problem with those boys, so our medicine had lots of power.

Now that we had disposed of Mr. Forsythe's spring salmon, we were anxious to sell the rest of his silver brights as quickly as possible to finish the whole deal. Maybe we would be lucky enough to run out the Todd and Sons fish before B.C. Packers caught on. I kept thinking, my God how is it possible that the largest fishing company in Canada has not found out by now that for two months we have been selling them their own fish? It seems a fairy tale, but I assure you it is a true story, every word of it. We were working under our third purchase order for silver brights received from Don Russell at B.C. Packers. After I had already delivered six hundred thousand pounds of fish, I told Don that perhaps we had a further two hundred thousand pounds in storage.

As I was walking along the wharf with yet another purchase order sticking up in my shirt pocket, I thought this is unbelievable, but who am I to question the greater plan? Maybe we were being paid back for all the slights we suffered through the years from the big companies. God does his work in many ways and he was on our side this time.

The skipper of a halibut boat that was tied up on the Van Shell side of the Campbell Avenue basin was waiting for me when I arrived at our plant. He said to me, "I missed the exchange this morning and I wonder if you will pay this morning's exchange price and take my fish."

"Is that not a B.C. Packer's vessel?" I asked. "They might get upset if you sell me your fish off the exchange seeing that they own the boat."

The skipper answered, "I've been away fourteen days and I want to get the boat unloaded so the crew and I can go home for a couple of days. B.C. Packers wants me to go on to their Steveston plant to get unloaded, but they will not take the fish off until tomorrow and then I will be another day getting back to Vancouver. It's difficult to get home from there and I don't want to sleep on the boat tonight when I could be at home with my family. If I give them the fish, I will lose two days more than I should, and with the short halibut season I will have to go right out again with only one day off at home."

"How much fish do you have?" I inquired.

"The tides were bad and we had a lot of screwups with our long lines, so we have only twenty-five thousand pounds. I don't want to travel all the way to Steveston with that small a load, and the crew does not want to go there either. How about it, Norman? Take my fish so we can get at least three clear days at home."

"Okay," I said. "We will take your fish. If you don't give a damn about B.C. Packers' goodwill, why should I worry about it? After all, they'll get their boat and gear share anyway."

No matter where fish is sold, the cheques for the fish are always sent to the settlement board where the shares are properly allocated after expenses have been deducted for the boat, gear, skipper and crew shares. It does not matter where the fish is sold; the skipper and crew have the right to sell anywhere they want regardless of what the owner of the vessel has to say about it, providing the price is better or at least the same. If the owner wants the fish, his alternative is to kick that crew off and get one that will deliver only to him. Skippers who take good care of the vessel and the gear and who bring in large catches don't grow on trees, so I knew this captain would not have any trouble. B.C. Packers had their chance to get the fish and if they were not willing to co-operate with the skipper and crew to get the fish, it was their loss and our gain. "Get the boat under our crane and we will have you unloaded in a couple of hours," I advised.

I told the foreman we were taking the halibut and to get the grading tables ready and start weighing empty tubs to make sure of their weights. Each tub held approximately one thousand pounds of fish. There was a thirty- to forty-pound difference between a wooden tub that has dried in the sun and one that just had iced fish in it. It was better to weigh the tubs each time to avoid any misunderstandings about the weight. The halibut were lifted from the hold in cargo nets that held approximately one thousand pounds per lift. The gutted head-on fish were dumped on the grading table, where two crew members stood with machetes and long hooks. The head of each fish was lifted by the long, shafted hook and chopped off with the machete. A large fish of one hundred to four hundred pounds might take two or three swipes to manage it, but the heads were cut off as fast as the fish came ashore. After the decapitations, the fish were graded for weight and quality. Halibut grow very large. The largest I saw in my time weighed approximately six hundred pounds. On unloading, often more ice has to be removed in five-hundred-pound bucket-loads than the total weight of the fish. Pen boards and the hold have to be scrubbed and disinfected and everything must be left ready for the next trip. This all takes time to do properly. The cleanup takes longer than loading the vessel. Then the skipper comes into the office to get paid for his fish. The cheque in total is made out to the settlement board, where the money is allocated to all the beneficiaries.

We had about two sling-loads of halibut out of the hold of the vessel when I saw Don Russell coming towards us with the usual dour expression on his face. He went up to the skipper and there was a flareup for selling us the fish. Finally, the argument exploded to the point where the skipper grabbed a ten-pound halibut by the tail and took a swipe at Russell with it. That did not make Russell very happy, so there were more loud exchanges between them.

Russell turned to me and took his jacket off. "You are a goddamned crook," he railed at me. "You not only are selling us our own salmon but now you are taking halibut we need from our own vessel." He put up his fists as he strode towards me and declared, "I am going to knock the hell out of you for that."

At this, the fisherman, Father and our unloading crew all stood with their mouths open as I backed away from this very angry fellow to avoid his well-telegraphed wild swings. I had my fists up and I was using my arms to deflect the blows. Russell was a stocky man who was well put together with an unknown potential. I was in the same category but I was tough as nails from years of handling a lot of fish and shellfish on a daily basis. I had also done quite a bit of boxing for sport with my neighbourhood pals in my high-school days. Long ago I had learned how to avoid getting punched out. Now I put my early experiences to good use as I ducked and smothered Russell's inefficient swings. Don had a mean look in his eyes as he flailed away at me, and it looked like he was not going to run out of gas. I didn't want to hit him, but it quickly appeared as if there was no option but to do so to survive the encounter without being bloodied. I was beginning to wonder what would happen if I waded in and planted a solid blow on his jaw or nose. Blocking his blows only served to increase his fury, and I began to measure him for a counterattack. I decided to wait a little longer until he was all used up and then I'd unleash a furious counterattack and try to finish the matter. All these things were flying through my head as I warded off his mistimed blows.

I had decided it was time to save myself when I caught a glimpse of Ken Fraser running down the wharf. Fraser was waving his arms and yelling at full volume. Don Russell was enraged by now and so determined to finish the job that he heard nothing until Ken grabbed him by one arm and was yelling, "Stop, stop, stop," into his ear. Even then Don threw punches with one arm and tried to tear himself away from Ken, who was attempting to get between us. "I told you to stop," Ken yelled into Don's face from about a foot and a half away as Don continued his assault. Then Ken yelled, "If you don't stop immediately I am going to fire you!" Don kept it up, so Fraser yelled his threat in an even louder voice. Russell finally backed away while threatening to get even. He retrieved his jacket and with a last glowering stare, turned on his heels and walked back to his office.

Fraser took hold of my arm and ordered, "I want to see you in my office as soon as you can get there." Then he turned and paused to glare at the gathering crowd before following Russell down the wharf. His teeth were clamped onto the stub of a cigar that somehow had remained in his mouth throughout the melee.

I went back to work. Father came over and asked, "Are you going over to see Ken?"

"No," I replied, "Why should I? I don't work for B.C. Packers and I do not take orders from him."

Father answered, "He's the president of a large corporation and he's old enough to be your father. It will be an insult to him if you don't do as he requests."

I thought about things for a while and then decided perhaps I should go. Fraser had always treated me with respect whenever we encountered a problem, but still I was apprehensive about the situation that had suddenly boiled over. I removed my rubber boots and slipped into oxfords before making the pilgrimage over to the big chief's office. Willy was nodding in agreement at my decision and reminding me to remain respectful to Fraser. I didn't need that advice because I had enough grey matter between my ears to figure that one out. I still had the latest purchase order in my shirt pocket for the balance of the silver brights. I fully expected that they would want that returned now that they had discovered they were buying their own fish. I walked between the long rows of office girls with their typewriters and adding machines clacking away. Instantly they all ceased work and escorted me with their eyes to the main complex of offices that housed Ken Fraser, president; Mortimer Ferguson, controller; Ross Nicholson, boss of their large salmon seine fleet; Dr. Elsie, chief of quality control; and Mac Brock, who was doing penance under their watchful scrutiny. As usual Mac gave me a big smile of confidence to ease my entry into this hallowed space.

Fraser turned around and ushered me to a chair in his office. He then appraised me with a steely look followed by a thin smile and asked me abruptly, "What are you doing to my boys, Norman? I hear you are selling us our own fish. And damn it, if that doesn't beat it all! For Christ's sake, what are you trying to do to us?"

I lied. "How was I supposed to know that you owned those silver brights in Todd's inventory?"

Ken's sly smile indicated that he did not believe me. "You knew damned well that we owned those goddamned salmon," he shot back at me.

I got bold and said, "Well, Ken, your outfit was buying second-class crappy chums from Canadian Fishing Company for steaking into your fancy Rupert brand cartons and I was only trying to help you out."

"Help us out," he snorted. I had to wait while he composed himself. "Help us right into the poorhouse!" he snapped back angrily.

Ken picked up the phone and a short time later an employee appeared with a tray, ice, water, and a bottle of Scotch and four glasses. By this gesture I knew the worst was over. Mort Ferguson and Ross Nicholson slid into chairs beside me with expressions of mirth on their faces. "What do you make of this guy who is selling us our own fish?" Fraser asked them. They knew all about it before I got there, so loud laughter followed as they gave me their attention.

Ken poured all around and then went into a tirade about the useless hired help in the company. He pulled a box of cigars out of his desk drawer and passed them around. I declined the offer, telling Fraser that I didn't smoke cigars. "Well, you're smoking one now," he declared as he shoved the end of a Havana into my mouth and held up a light for me. I felt a bit foolish but decided it would do me more good if I puffed on it, so I contributed to the cloud of smoke twirling towards the high ceiling.

Fraser was pretty mad about the silver bright caper but he was not really taking it out on me. I was astounded when he summoned in his department heads and laid into them with a sarcastic tirade. He ended the meeting with a savage outburst, telling them he would trade the whole damn lot of them for a couple of guys like me. My friends like Mac Brock, Dick Lamb and one or two others smiled as they departed. But the majority of them were angry, leaving with sullen looks, and two or three had daggers in their eyes. Ken Fraser's outburst at the hired help did not make me many friends in his organization. After that session, very few of them spoke to me again unless it was about business. When I encountered them, business transactions were made in a sombre atmosphere. From then on most of them avoided me like the plague. Throughout Ken's outburst at his lieutenants, Mort and Ross sat there with wide smiles on their faces as they sipped their drinks.

When they had all left his office, Fraser turned towards me with a friendly smile and asked me to come to work for B.C. Packers. "I'll make it worth your while," he confided as Mort and Ross scrutinized me intently for my reaction.

I thought his offer over for a long minute as he leaned towards me waiting for my reply. "If I leave our company, Father and Steiner might go broke. I don't know if I can do that."

Fraser growled, "I know damn well they'll go broke if you leave and then I can go over there and personally nail a two-by-six across the doorway.

"You're a goddamned nuisance to us. You're always picking our bones at every opportunity and I want you on our side picking someone else's bones for a change," he confided as he refilled our glasses. After another round of drinks, Fraser looked me in the eye and asked me if I had made up my mind about going to work for him. I told him I'd have to think about it a little longer. As he rose to end the meeting, he offered me a fifty-thousand-dollar cash bonus to go work for B.C. Packers and he gave me thirty days to decide.

As I was leaving I took the purchase order that I had received from Russell earlier that morning and handed it to Fraser. "What's the matter with it?" he asked. "Is there something wrong with it?"

"For heaven sakes, I don't want to sell you your own fish when you know about it, Ken," I blurted out.

"How much more fish is left?" he demanded.

"Oh, about one hundred thousand pounds more after your last purchased order is filled," I answered.

"Stop in to see Russell on your way out and he'll give you another order for the balance that's left."

"Okay, Ken," I replied. "You'll get the rest of the fish." I still had thirty days left on my option from Mr. Forsythe of Todd and Sons and I had the right to sell the fish anywhere I pleased. That may have been why I received another purchase order for the balance of the fish. Fraser didn't want any more of the silver brights getting into his competitor's hands.

Don Russell was as meek as a lamb when I walked into his office for that final purchase order to clean out the Todd and Sons' silver bright inventory. In a quiet voice he asked if an additional order for another one hundred thousand pounds would do it. "I better make the order out for one hundred and fifty thousand pounds," he said, "just to make sure." Nothing was mentioned about our previous encounter on the wharf. Russell was very polite to me, and we remained on a friendly basis for as long as he remained in the company.

Ken Fraser's offer came as a complete surprise and gave my system quite a jolt. I quickly calculated that I could buy two three-bedroom houses with a standard car thrown in with that amount of money and still have change left over. I mulled his offer over on my way back to the Van Shell office. Father and Steiner were waiting to hear about my walk into the lion's den. Willy said, "I told you there would be hell to pay if we sold them their own fish." Father chose to remain quiet until I said my piece. I offered them a detailed account of the meeting as I slipped back into my rubber boots. Neither of them said a word for some time.

Father went to the window and looked out at the basin in silence. He finally turned and said that I should consider all the angles, because that fabulous employment offer would have some drawbacks and there would be strings attached that I might not like. "It certainly is a heck of a offer," he mused. Steiner said nothing but just sat still in his chair letting his cigar go out.

I had already made up my mind to refuse the offer. I could not see myself surrounded by that gang that Ken had ridiculed and reprimanded. They wouldn't be going out of their way to co-operate with me. I was used to making snap decisions and moving quickly into action when the opportunity was there. I could not see myself going to a meeting and then waiting for a week or two for the go-ahead. By then the barn would be empty. That kind of atmosphere was too stifling for a person like me. Besides, I had determined that all the B.C. Packers department heads despised me for being an upstart. I could expect no quarter from these characters who were attempting to work their way up to the top in head office. I was an outsider they would always see as a competitor. I figured I would be better off with Father and Bill Steiner, doing my own thing. I would be lying if I said I didn't seriously consider Ken Fraser's offer. It troubled me some to think about the size of the salary I was turning down. I stood staring at the Inlet and the mountains a few times wondering if I was making a mistake.

Thirty days passed quickly. One morning while I was sitting in the Van Shell office with Father and Steiner, in through the door walked Ken Fraser. "Norman, the thirty days are up today. What's it going to be? Have you made up your mind about my offer?"

I looked at Father, who seemed transfixed, and at Steiner, who seemed to have shrunk in his chair. I blurted out to Ken, "I'm sorry, but I've decided to do my own thing."

Fraser took the cigar from his mouth as he turned to leave and said, "I thought you were a smart young fellow but now I think you're a fool, Norman." Then the door clicked shut behind him and he was going down the stairs back to his office.

I took a deep breath and said, "Life would be hell over there with them all trying to shoot me down." I decided to stay with Father and Willy. At least they gave me the freedom to make my own deals and I felt at peace with myself.

By now, so many years later, I know that in the end I came out far ahead of the game by staying with Van Shell. Eventually, I bought Father out and Steiner gave me his shares for nothing but the stipulation that he could remain for as long as he wished. He died about three years later.

Bill said that he gave me his shares because without me the company would have gone bankrupt a long time in the past. He told me that at seven o'clock in the evening when I went to visit him in the hospital, and he died at midnight. Now, Father and Steiner are just memories. We had some tough times, but I wouldn't trade in any of the thirty-odd years I worked for them. The good times far outnumbered the bad. In the years after, I took over the company and with the help of my sons built a fish plant in Tofino, on the West Coast of Vancouver Island, and we never looked back.

True to his word, Mr. Forsythe gave me a two-cent-per-pound rebate when all the silver brights were out of his inventory. He also brought over a half a case of Scotch whisky to celebrate the event. We opened one bottle right away to toast the successful completion of our business. "Norman," he said, "that should get some people thinking about sales." He was an honourable fellow who seemed to know what he was doing. By his demeanour, I sensed that Forsythe would soon be leaving the industry. After that meeting, I never saw him again.

MALCOLM MCCALLUM

After the war ended, B.C. Packers had a large war chest obtained through a cost-plus-profits arrangement for their production with the government. With money to burn, the company continued to expand. They took over the Gregory Fish Company, Canadian Fish and Cold Storage in Prince Rupert, Blaine Myers' two operations in Tofino and Johnston Straights, one half of J.H. Todd and Sons Fishing Company and Cold Storage, which included a cannery and fish plant in Klemtu, B.C. Ice and Cold Storage in Vancouver and a cannery on the Fraser River.

J.H. Todd and Sons were an early family in the history of fishing in British Columbia. They once had a grant from Queen Victoria to operate fish traps on the West Coast of Vancouver Island. For decades they caught large volumes of all species of salmon in their traps and made the family fortune. The fish traps were a gold mine and Todd and Sons became an immense company of diverse interests. After the war, Crown grants were cancelled, fish traps were removed, and the sun began to set on the Todd empire. Basically, it was split up between the Canadian Fishing Company and B.C. Packers.

B.C. Packers also took over Nelson Brothers Fishing Company, including their canneries, and McCallum Sales in Vancouver. With their fingers in so many pieces of the action, B.C. Packers easily dominated the fishing industry in British Columbia.

Canadian Fishing Company, the other big player, was a subsidiary of the New England Fishing Company, at that time the biggest fish company in North America. This gave Can Fish a connection to cheap Alaskan fish through their parent company. The Canadian Fishing Company stayed aloof from the smaller independent companies. In my opinion, they had a gentlemen's agreement with B.C. Packers to stay out of each other's territory.

There were a few smiles when it was revealed that McCallum Sales was owned by Nelson Brothers, and Nelson Brothers were owned by B.C. Packers. Malcolm McCallum was a bitter competitor of B.C. Packers. Malcolm had nothing good to say about B.C. Packers. He hated them with such a passion, he muttered curses whenever they came up in conversation. Malcolm found out the hard way that his company had been sold to B.C. Packers. Old Ritchie Nelson, with tongue in cheek, swore that he had nothing to do with B.C. Packers. When Malcolm found out he was owned by B.C. Packers, he was livid. He claimed he would never have sold out to Nelson Brothers if he had known they were owned by B.C. Packers. It was a bitter disappointment.

Malcolm was as shrewd a businessman as you would ever encounter. He was completely devoid of compassion for any fish company down on their luck. He was a tough opponent in any business transaction and certainly a thorn in the mighty B.C. Packers' side. Malcolm used any means he had at his disposal to gain an advantage over a competitor. He was widely connected and had an uncanny ability to know everything about everybody. He was as fine a fellow as one could find for a night out on the town but a dangerous one to do business with. He had a sharp mind and a sharp pencil and an unlimited tolerance for alcohol. No quantities of that stuff would dull him. He was also a great character with enormous passion for life. I believe this gave him a great advantage in his business dealings with the producers and with his customers.

In my lifetime, I saw only two people who could down a large beer glass filled to the brim with overproof vodka or gin. Stuff that came from the duty-free store at the American border or from deep-sea ships in our harbour, not the diluted stuff from our liquor stores.

He accomplished this feat in two pulls and sat with a big smile on his face declaring how good it was. One of my uncles also had the ability to drink like Malcolm.

One of the deals Malcolm tried to pull on me backfired in a big way. The beauty of it was, he could do nothing about it but take his medicine. However, once Malcolm was boxed in a corner, he took it with a smile, put on his coat, and invited his opponent out for a night on the town. I never took Mac up on one of these invitations because they lasted three or four days or longer. But I did spend a lot of time with him and I value the memories. He had imagination and flair and he never let business get in the way of friendship.

One year the net salmon season closed early. The large companies shut down because of the extra costs of handling the dwindling runs at the end of the season. My brother John was on a charter to Todd and Sons with his *Tor II* during the peak of the season. There was a lot of fish that year, so several independent operators were chartered on a weekly basis to help service net fishermen, both gillnet and seine boats, for the large companies. About the tenth of November, Todds laid John off so he was at a loose end. He could go back out bottom trawling but, in late fall, bad weather made that a tough business. He approached me with a proposition to go up into the northern part of Georgia Straight to buy salmon from fishermen still remaining on the grounds. It was a sheltered place with small islands providing relief from storms and good fishing grounds containing prime bright salmon. By this time of the year, the big companies were curtailing their efforts. They pooled their resources and ran only a couple of packers, picking up fish for one another. They only took fish from independent fishermen if they had space on their packers. This left some fishermen in a bind, as they would have to take a three-day trip to Vancouver to deliver their fish to a buyer. Sometimes the packers refused a fisherman in order to force a contract for the next season.

John's proposition was a gamble. He wanted me to put up fifty thousand dollars cash for buying money to pay the independents for their fish. He claimed he could still pick up sixty to seventy thousand pounds at a fair price because there were no cash buyers left on the grounds. The deal was that I would pay for twenty tons of ice (eight hundred dollars), pay for the fuel (twelve hundred dollars) and buy three hundred dollars worth of groceries. There was an additional couple of hundred dollars for odds and ends that rounded off the amount to twenty-five hundred dollars. If he got no fish he would work with his crew for nothing. He would get seven cents per pound commission for any fish that he could deliver.

I wasn't really enthusiastic about the deal. The weather had turned worse and I doubted that enough fishermen remained on the grounds. I didn't think he could get that much fish, so I wanted to give him just thirty thousand dollars so he didn't have to carry money he wouldn't need. A compromise was made to provide forty thousand dollars of buying money and make an arrangement with a bank in Port Hardy to provide additional funds should they be required.

John fueled up the vessel, took on ice and grub and departed for the fishing grounds. Four days later he phoned from his boat to say that he already had sixty thousand pounds of fish aboard. He thought he would be short of buying money because quite a few fishermen were still to deliver. I sent him to Port Hardy, where he received an additional fifteen thousand dollars from the bank. John was in a bad mood because it was a six-hour round trip and he claimed I had not provided enough funds in the first place. He picked up the money, but the salmon run had petered out suddenly, so he used up less then half of it. Some of J.H. Todd's fishermen were still on the grounds with no packer to take their fish. John took their fish for Todd and Sons, intending to charge Todd's for packing the fish to B.C. Ice and Cold Storage, which they owned. John advised me that he had about seventy-five thousand pounds of fish and carried nine thousand pounds of Todd's fish. Todd would pay the packing charges and pay their own fishermen on the delivery slips he provided them. He said he was leaving the grounds and would be in Vancouver tied up in front of our plant on Friday morning at five am.

On Friday morning, just before five a.m., John phoned me at home and told me the *Tor II* was already tied up, ready for unloading. He also informed me that the salmon were all in prime condition and that they had dressed out all the springs as they came aboard to prevent them from burning. (Feed destroys the lining in the body cavity of salmon.) A few early deliveries of cohos were also dressed for the same reason. Springs and cohos do not keep as well as chums because they are always feeding, so it is advisable to remove the viscera. John also suggested that because they had dressed the expensive fish, and I had a winner, perhaps I could up the ante by two cents per pound on their commission to nine cents per pound. I agreed that there could be an adjustment if the fish was sold at a good profit.

I arrived at our plant at six a.m. The crew were waiting in gumboots with aprons on ready to begin unloading and dressing out the salmon. However, the *Tor II* was not tied up in front of our plant. "Where's the packer?" I asked the foreman.

"I don't know," he replied. But Malcolm McCallum was here and he informed me it was his fish and he ordered the crew on the packer to deliver the fish to him at B.C. Ice and Cold Storage. I phoned my brother John at his home, and he got out of bed to tell me he left the *Tor II* tied up in front of our plant and he didn't know why it was not still there.

I had advised Todd and Sons that there were nine thousand pounds of their salmon on the *Tor II* and told them that I would like to buy it from them. However, obviously, someone in that organization sold the nine thousand pounds of booked fish to McCallum Sales. When I phoned Todds about the matter, they claimed my brother John was still on charter to their company and that all the fish in the *Tor II* belonged to them and they had sold it to McCallum.

I had approximately fifty-two thousand dollars invested in that load of salmon, while Todd's nine thousand pounds amounted to about six thousand dollars. At this point, I didn't know how I was going to get my money back out of a deal that was beginning to smell like a rotten fish. I figured I would get my money back, more or less, but probably less the packing charges that had to be paid to my brother. When someone else gets a hold of your money, it is my experience that the transaction seldom proves profitable.

John swore up and down and produced documents that said Todd and Sons had cancelled his charter to them. It appeared that in the Todd organization, either one hand did not know what the other was doing or somebody was creating trouble. I drove to McCallum Sales office at B.C. Ice and Cold Storage to confront Malcolm about him ordering the *Tor II* away from our plant when he was not authorized to do so. He claimed he was informed the vessel was on charter to Todd and Sons and they sold him the fish, so my problem was with Todd and Sons, not with him. Malcolm sat there like a cat that had just swallowed a mouse, and I was beginning to feel that I was going to get screwed.

I advised Malcolm that someone was going to have a hell of a problem when they began unloading my fish and I left his office for a hurried trip to our lawyers' office. I poured out the story to him as I knew the facts. He typed out a letter and suggested I hand-deliver it to Malcolm McCallum. When I arrived back at McCallum Sales, Malcolm had vanished and left his right-hand man, Pat Todd (no relation to Todd and Sons), to deal with the matter. Pat poured me a drink while he unsealed the letter and read the contents. By then I was angry and in no mood to be sociable with anyone in McCallum Sales, so I left the drink untouched.

Pat got up from behind his desk and said to follow him. We went out of the building and onto the dock where the *Tor II* was still tied up with hatches off. However, the cargo remained untouched. He called for the man who was in charge of the vessel. He told him to put the hatch covers back on and deliver the fish to the Van Shell plant, which was done in short order.

By now it was noon, and I knew it was going to be a costly overtime proposition to get the boat unloaded and the fish dressed and prepared for a fresh fish sale in the United States. I phoned Todd and Sons to come pick up their nine thousand pounds of fish and to bring fifteen hundred dollars for the packing charges. I figured by now it was my turn to start screwing them and McCallum, because I now had some of their fish. Pat Todd, Malcolm's associate, was a good person, and I knew that he had nothing to do with Malcolm's attempt to pick up a cheap load of fish. Pat advised me of the facts. "You know Malcolm," he said. "He's a troublemaker, always attempting to gain an advantage. I didn't think he could get away with it and I told him so. But you know, he's my boss."

Todd and Sons informed me by phone that they had sold the salmon to McCallum Sales so not to bother them with my problems. When I finally located Malcolm, he said the fish belonged to Todd and Sons. I phoned each party back in turn and told them to figure out who owned the fish. I stated that I wasn't about to unload their fish. I suggested they bring the fifteen hundred dollars to pay my brother's packing charges and pick up the fish. I advised them that by quitting time the fish would likely be left out on the wharf.

By seven p.m. nobody had showed up to pick up the fish. By now, my conscience told me there was no way I was going to leave it rot, no matter how greedy Malcolm was, or how high and mighty Todd and Sons acted. We were loading the dressed salmon into two trailer trucks for delivery to Seattle at six a.m. Saturday morning. One truck was going to Booth fisheries and the other truck was going to Whiz fish. There was about eight thousand pounds more than the freight trucks could load. My oldest son, Jim, and I decided to take a load down to Seattle in one of our company trucks. Since nobody showed for the Todd and Sons/McCallum fish, we dressed it out and loaded it for sale in Seattle.

After completing our business in Seattle with Brad Hall, we decided to go for lunch. While we were eating, Solly from the Pike Market fish store showed up and gasped, "I've been looking all over for you guys. Where have you been?"

"I'm sorry," I advised him. "Your price was too low and now you're too late. We got a lot more for the fish from Booth than you offered."

"I would have paid fifteen cents per pound more," he cried. "If only you had come back to me."

"Now you'll have to go to Booth and pay fifty cents more," I said. While he stood there with a long face, I reminded him he had chased us away with his take-it-or-leave-it proposition.

On the way back to Vancouver, Jim and I discussed the situation. We wondered how they were going to go about recovering the money Todd and Sons would have to pay out to their fishermen for the booked fish that came down on John's packer. Neither company claimed to own the fish. And now the fish was gone, sold in another country. We wondered who was going to bill us for the fish. I figured, in the end, when McCallum declined to pay them, it would be Todd and Sons.

At the end of three months, we had heard nothing more about the matter. Our accountant, Edith Schmitt, laughed in glee. She said, "We have no bill, they have no proof we kept the fish after you told them to come and get it. Who knows what happened to their fish? Serves the buggers right for the trouble they caused us."

In the middle of May, about seven months later, Malcolm's accountant showed up and asked for a cheque for money we owed to McCallum Sales.

"Do we owe them any money?" I asked Edith.

"I don't think so," Edith replied with a wink and one of her brightest smiles. "I have no bills from your company," she said. "You must be mistaken."

"Malcolm insists you owe us money and he ordered me to pick up the cheque today."

Edith asked, "How much do we owe you? And do you have an invoice?"

He answered, "No, I don't have an invoice and I don't rightly know the amount. Malcolm said you'd know about this matter."

"Sorry," I said. "We don't pay unless we have an invoice and backup slips to verify the transaction."

"Okay," he said, "but Malcolm is going to be mad when I come back without the cheque."

When he departed, we all shook with laughter. Edith wondered what they would do next. "How do you hope to recover money from a company you attempted to cheat?" she mused. Somebody thought they'd look kind of odd explaining this matter to a judge.

A month later Malcolm's accountant showed up again with a bottle of Scotch and begged me to give him a cheque. He whined, "Mac said he'd fire me if I come back without a cheque."

I told the accountant to go back and tell Malcolm to come in person if he felt we owed him money. He hung around our office for two hours getting potted before he had the courage to go back and face Malcolm. When he got completely hammered his face turned sour and he left muttering a prayer.

Malcolm showed up several weeks later. He had his forty ounces of overproof vodka in a brown paper bag. As soon as I saw him I figured he had to come to lay on the charm. He was all smiles as he joked with the two women in the office. Mac was a stocky, ruddy-faced man with light rust-coloured hair. He was always well dressed, wrapped in a four-hundred-dollar gabardine overcoat that suited his complexion. Malcolm was a chartered accountant who could squeeze a dollar out of a twenty-five-cent piece. He was already wealthy and hungry as hell. He regarded business as a kind of sport, a gentlemen's game that had few rules and no sacred cows. As a glorified bookkeeper, he was no slouch. He was about forty years of age and hard as a rock. I'm sure Mac could have handled himself favourably in any kind of a brawl. I was certainly not planning on tempting him in that direction.

He filled two eight-ounce beer glasses to the brim straight from the large bottle.

"Jeezuz, I can't drink that," I said to him and got two glasses out from the cupboard and split the liquor in the glass into three parts. I handed two of them out to the office staff. They couldn't drink it straight, so one of them went out for mixer.

Malcolm was in a joking mood. I could tell he was expecting to get his money. "Where is my cheque?" he asked, turning to look at Edith with a big toothy smile. Mac was halfway through his second glass of vodka.

"But we don't owe you any money," she replied with her strong Danish accent. "We have no bill from you, so how can we pay you?"

The smile vanished from Mac's face and a savage look appeared in his eyes as he turned to me and said, "I hate you, you syphilitic prick!" He then grabbed his bottle and thrust it into the paper bag and turned to go. At the door he turned to face us with a look that almost set fire to our office.

"I'm going to collect that money from you if it's the last thing I do," he declared with a snarl.

The sales clerk Dorothy, in shock, said, "That was quite a performance. He's liable to explode if he doesn't watch himself."

Edith sat in silence. Finally she said, "This isn't fun anymore. We'll have to pay him what you feel we owe him before he turns violent."

By then I felt the same way. It was time to settle the matter. I told Edith to figure out the overhead for the eight girls and two men who waited six hours for the *Tor II* to return to our plant. I told her to figure out the overtime costs that were racked up getting the salmon processed for sale because we were delayed by Mac's caper. "Add the packing charges to it, Edith, and then double the amount and let me know what we owe our friend."

"Why should I double the costs, Norman?" she asked.

I replied that when somebody screws me, I double screw them back at the next opportunity afforded to me. Since I had the additional cost of a lawyer's bill, I was in no mood for compromise.

"I don't want to be here when you give him the cheque," Edith said. "He'll be so mad he's liable to have a heart attack or worse," she warned.

"Edith," I said, "don't worry about it. By now he will settle for exactly what he would do to us if the situation was reversed. He knows he opened a can of worms and he wants to put it all behind him as soon as possible. If we don't make the deductions for the inconvenience, he'll figure we're stupid. It'll also be a message to him to reconsider before he pulls another stunt on us."

A few days later I asked Edith to phone Mac to come for the cheque personally. He said he would and later that afternoon he arrived with a smile and another forty-ounce bottle. He noticed the envelope on Edith's desk with McCallum Sales typed across it. He opened the big bottle and filled the glasses to their brims. He downed a half a glass as his eyes strayed over to the envelope, but he didn't reach over to pick it up until he had completely drained the glass.

Mac opened the envelope and his eyelids fluttered once or twice as he noticed the amount of the cheque. Immediately he opened the statement and growled to himself as he studied it. Edith had moved her chair into a corner and she snuck a glance to see if I was getting ready to defend myself. Mac turned towards me after digesting the statement and leaned over until his nose was only six inches from mine. "I hate you. I hate you," he repeated several times in a low tone, but with a smile on his face. He put the cheque back into the envelope and slipped it into the inside pocket of his jacket. Mac accepted a cheque for less than half of what it should have been. He poured my glass full to the brim and, putting his arm around my shoulder, he said, "Let's drink up, my friend." The more we drank, the more he beamed. For a while he alternated by saying he hated me and then saying he loved me. I knew the feud had ended.

Mac threw me my jacket and grabbed me by the arm. He informed me that he and Ritchie Nelson were having a party with a few of the boys at the Hotel Vancouver and he was personally inviting me to attend. I knew I had to get out of it, because these affairs lasted three or four days or a week and were real debauches that were way over my head. Mac was insistent that I go with him. Finally, I pointed at his suit and said I'd have to go home and get my suit. He thought that was a good idea and made arrangements to meet me later at the hotel. "We'll be expecting you at seven o'clock," he reminded me as he drove his car away. That evening I received several phone calls from the hotel, but I resisted the temptation by letting Mac talk with my wife. She laughed at him and told him my suit was at the dry cleaners.

A few days later Mac showed up at the halibut exchange with a pained expression on his face. It was obvious he was suffering from the bout of partying. He bought a load of fish and came over to me and asked if I had a bottle in the office because his head was killing him. I told him there was no booze in the office, but that I had some at home if he could stand the car ride. "What are you waiting for!" he ordered. It was early in the morning and the bars and liquor stores weren't open and the big bean-counter was desperate for relief. "You drive my car and hurry up," he begged. I made a couple of rough stops in traffic because I was not used to driving such a big car. He grumbled, "Are you trying to make me sick?" At home I could only find a bottle of rye, which Malcolm detested. He was a purist who drank only the finest Scotch whisky, spelled off by the overproof vodka. He frowned as he drank a full glass of rye. It calmed him down and his irascible nature mellowed as he chased with a second glass.

Everything seemed back to normal on the waterfront for a couple of months but then something else triggered another big row. Malcolm was usually at the centre of events. When he was owned by Nelson Brothers, Mac was a smart operator with a great sales ability. When suddenly he was owned by B.C. Packers, his worst enemy, the writing was on the wall.

McCallum Sales was disturbing the fishing industry and becoming a real problem for B.C. Packers. Sooner or later, Mac had to be controlled or destroyed because he was seriously damaging the parent company. Soon after Ritchie Nelson spelled out the facts for Mac, he was summoned to appear before the B.C. Packers board of directors. Mac was stunned by the invitation. He knew he had to swallow his pride and take orders from sworn enemies who knew much less about the fish industry than he did. I sure would have liked to have been a fly on the wall in that first meeting. After that, Mac was required to attend directors' meetings each and every week. I use to chuckle and say, "Mac, I can see you, the black chicken in with the flock of white ones." I knew they wanted to have him around so that they could keep a close watch over his behaviour and let him know how vulnerable he had become. He was never the same classy operator after B.C. Packers put the halter on him. He was used to selling carloads and containers of fish on a moment's notice at any time to anyone in the world. At B.C. Packers there had to be a board meeting to decide when to have lunch. Poor old Mac was trapped in meetings and paperwork. It was like watching a general being demoted to captain.

The new scenario meant that Malcolm had more time to party. Or perhaps it just seemed like it. It always amazed me at how quickly Mac recovered. He remained as tough as ever, with a cast-iron constitution and a razor-sharp wit. But I noticed that some of his favourite partying friends were getting a little rundown around the edges.

Malcolm was a complex individual. One of his favourite business strategies was to agree to a deal and then just do the opposite if it suited him. He had a way of stroking a deal after the fact and sometimes it worked out to his great advantage or to the advantage of both parties. If there was a wrinkle in a deal, Malcolm would find it. I enjoyed doing business with him because he was a bold, incisive man who lived to fight another day if a deal went bad. Over the long haul, we dealt a lot with Malcolm and I believe both of our companies made money from the association.

Mac was a well-educated gentleman who could be as smooth as silk whenever the situation required him to be. He was a thinker, a promoter and a salesman all thrown into one package. Nothing seemed to faze him. He was really a very clever businessman. People either really liked him or loathed him, and he was similar in his own judgements.

Mac and I remained good friends until his tragic demise in 1971, at the age of fifty-six, under the wheels of a taxi at Las Palmas in the Canary Islands, while on holidays with Dulcie, his wife. Unfortunately, he made the mistake of trying to stare down a speeding Portuguese taxi driver. Obviously, the look that made competitors and fishermen cringe had no effect on the miserable cab driver. Malcolm McCallum was one of the most interesting and illustrious characters in the long history of the fishing industry in British Columbia. He took an untimely early departure.

DR. BALLARD

The Ballard Pet Food Company started up another reduction plant on the North Arm of the Fraser River in the mid-fifties. Ballard's plant processed one hundred thousand one-pound cans of pet food per shift. It was the most sophisticated pet food plant in North America. Ballard bought tin plate and made their own cans. The cans were automatically labelled and packed into forty-eight-can cases. In fact, most of the Ballard operation was completely automated, which meant that they employed only a handful of people. I suppose the empty can was worth more than the food in it, so the operation had to be efficient.

Ballard used a large quantity of freshwater smelts from the Great Lakes region in Ontario. These fish were readily available for two or three cents per pound. I believe these smelts were so cheap that they were shipped frozen in thirty-pound blocks by reefer truck to the Vancouver area plant. I don't know why Ballard built a plant in the Lower Mainland. Perhaps they were hedging their bets in case the freshwater smelt fishery collapsed. There was also a good supply of cheap seined herring available in British Columbia. Ballard preferred the freshwater smelts because there was a mild smell to the canned product, where canned herring has a powerful odour. People buy pet food only if it looks nice and has a mild aroma. The pets have nothing to say on the matter.

Eventually, the supply of freshwater smelts failed and Ballard were in a sweat to acquire cheap fish for their cannery. They came to see us at Campbell Avenue and inquired about buying cheap herring. Pet food could be made from herring meal, and Ballard were aware of this fact because they were building their own reduction plant. The large companies who were providing meal to pet food manufacturers did not want to see another reduction plant in business. These companies refused to sell meal to Ballard when they were building a plant to go into competition with them.

For some unknown reason, Ballard wanted the herring frozen in thirty-pound cartons. The seined herring were worth about thirty bucks per ton; at the time it cost an additional thirty bucks to freeze it into thirty-pound blocks in cartons. Ballard offered seventy dollars per ton for six hundred tons of frozen herring delivered to their plant. This meant that after our costs we would be making about five bucks per ton. Father decided it wasn't worth bothering to get into this kind of a business because the returns were too meagre.

Also, the Department of Fisheries and Oceans told us we had no business getting into seined herring and they refused to grant us a licence or a quota. I investigated further because I realized that herring could be taken by trawl for food purposes and pet food was classified as a food product. I made arrangements to take herring from trawlers for fifty dollars per ton and decided to let them fight it out with Department of Fisheries and Oceans. The DFO was forced to back down on their order to us not to take herring for pet food, so if I could get Ballard to pay about eighty-eight dollars per ton we'd be in business. Father still didn't want anything to with it.

I persisted with negotiations with Ballard and the fishermen, and squeezed out about twelve bucks per ton gross for the frozen herring to be delivered to the Ballard plant. This included about six bucks per ton for trucking and did not leave a very large profit. I went to see Ballard's cannery manager and asked him why the herring had to be frozen in cartons. I asked him why it couldn't be delivered fresh in twelve-hundred-pound totes.

"I'll take it fresh in bulk," he said. "I prefer it that way. Who the heck wants to tear eighteen hundred cardboard boxes off blocks of frozen herring each day?"

I pointed out that the contract specified frozen herring. He answered that the Ballard efficiency experts in their office didn't know which end was up. He guessed that their requirements were left over from the days when they shipped smelts from Ontario. He told me to ignore their specifications and he would do the same. "Bring the herring fresh in totes," he said. "They'll never know the difference. In fact, it will be much easier for our operation if you deliver it that way."

This was a new ball game. The herring would cost fifty bucks per ton, trucking would cost six dollars per ton, and we would still receive eighty-eight dollars per ton. This would leave us with thirty-two dollars per ton net profit. Under these terms, we were going into business with Ballard for sure. The trawlers complained about their price so much that I raised the ante to them by four bucks to fifty-five dollars per ton. I also gave the cannery manager five hundred bucks cash to grease the way, and we were all set to go.

I drove to the Dr. Ballard plant and obtained a purchase requisition for sixteen hundred tons of herring at eighty-eight dollars per ton delivered in twenty-ton lots as they required it. The arrangement with the fishermen went like clockwork as deliveries of fresh herring came in right on schedule seven days a week. Father wanted nothing to do with the herring deal because he claimed it was going to be a lot of work and there were bound to be big problems that would eat up the profits. He told me to put the deal through with all costs, overhead, payments to fishermen and money received separately from our other business to prove there would be very little money in it for all the extra trouble it was going to cause.

I went to the Bank of Nova Scotia in Vancouver Heights, Burnaby, to make arrangements to pay for the herring because the fishermen insisted on being paid daily for their deliveries. I had put through thousands of dollars worth of mink food transactions that had been satisfactory, so the bank agreed to the deal without any questions.

Well, to cut to the chase, the herring came in and the money went out. I had left the Ballard purchase requisition at home. The bank manager didn't require any security and I neglected to offer any. I was confident my transactions with Ballard would be satisfactory and that within three weeks there would be a cheque to cover the initial deliveries. However, it took about a month to complete the contract with Ballard, and by then I owed the bank more than seventy thousand dollars.

My wife, Kathleen, urged me to take the purchase requisition to the banks. She said, "My God, when the bank discovers that you owe them so much money, that manager is liable to have a heart attack." I never gave it much thought because I had a paper guaranteeing payments, but I realized the bank didn't know this, so I took the requisition to the Bank of Nova Scotia and asked to see the manager.

The bank manager was sitting in his office smoking a cigar as he studied the stock market page in the newspaper. He shook my hand and asked me to sit down. I wasn't too worried about the matter because this manager had dealt with me for some time without asking for security. I thought quite highly of him because, unlike other bankers I had done business with, he wasn't all obsessed with guarantees and never hassled me about anything. "How much do you owe?" he asked.

"Oh, I don't know exactly but I imagine a little over seventy thousand," I answered.

I think he bit off the end of his cigar as his chair snapped forward and the colour drained from his face.

"Jeezuz, don't have a stroke," I advised him. "Here is a guarantee of payment by a very reputable company for a lot more than I owe you." He studied the document and relaxed as he looked at me with a sickly smile. "I'm sorry for the shock I gave you," I said, "but I thought you'd be monitoring the situation and that you'd have called me in for information long before now if you were uncomfortable."

After a lull in the conversation he pulled himself together and offered me a cigar and a cup of coffee. I refused the cigar but took the coffee. I continued to do business with this bank manager for many years to our mutual satisfaction and never once did he require me to put up a guarantee.

We continued to provide Ballard with scrap fish that was a by-product of our filleting operation, and we sold them some trawled herring each year. However, McMillan Fisheries found out about the order and decided that they wanted in on it, so they cut prices to obtain a piece of the action. This played right into Ballard's hands, and soon the price began to drop until there was only about a five bucks per ton margin to play with. We could make more money selling to mink food operators who came and picked up rather than make deliveries to Ballard. We remained on good terms with Dr. Ballard's pet food organization but we let McMillan supply them with product while we sold elsewhere for more money.

By the time Ballard was dealing with McMillan, they had lost a lot of money in their reduction business. How could they compete with the major reduction plants that were paying only ten bucks per ton when it was costing them about fifty-five dollars per ton from trawlers? I believe Ballard bought herring from Jack McMillan for only one season before somebody in New York head office pulled the plug and that was the end of it.

For all its modern efficiency, the Ballard reduction plant could only handle about ten tons of herring per hour so it was not in the same class as the large operators. However, it sat there on the North Arm of the Fraser like a sore thumb waiting for someone else to take a stab at the reduction business. I also knew there were elements in the Ballard management who felt they should take another shot at the reduction business by getting into the seine boat business.

In my opinion, the only thing to do was to get rid of the plant to one of the established old-line reduction companies. I advised Ballard to do just that. They badly wanted out of the reduction business, so they listened to my free advice. They would realize only about thirty cents on each dollar they invested in their plant, but that was better than selling the plant for scrap or losing more money trying to operate it. I offered to float the proposition of selling the plant to the consortium to find out if anybody was interested in making a deal.

When I talked with Ken Fraser at B.C. Packers about taking over the Ballard plant, he practically threw me out of his office. "We can wait for them to go tits up, so why should we buy their plant?" he offered.

I replied, "They're a huge international company with lots of money. How much will it cost you if they continue to meddle in the reduction business or find out how to run their reduction business at a profit by dramatically changing the way they acquire fish? Wouldn't it be better to put that plant right out of production so there are no surprises in the future?"

After some thought, Ken agreed maybe I had a point about shutting it down for good. "I'll get back to you," he said, "after I've discussed the matter with a few other parties." Three days later he called me over to find out how much money it would take to buy out Ballard's reduction operation. I mentioned that one million dollars should do it. Ken laughed so hard tears ran down his cheeks. "I thought you had an interesting proposition," he said. "But now I know you're a crazy man. You know they want to get out of it. About a quarter of a million is all we're willing to pay."

"Ken," I argued, "you know that's a brand-new plant that cost well over two million dollars to build. It has half a million dollars of electrical equipment, not to mention the driers, presses, grinders, baggers, pumps, cranes, fork lifts and God knows what else. You could use all that equipment in your own plants. A lot of it could provide spare parts. For seven hundred and fifty thousand bucks, it's a bargain so you better grab it."

"I'll let you know," he said as he ushered me from his office.

I went back to Ballard and put the proposition to them, including my fee for putting the deal together. After most of an afternoon was burned up weighing their options and attempting to sweeten the deal, they finally listened to my protestations and agreed that under the circumstances seven hundred and fifty thousand dollars was a fair deal. Time after time I advised them that any attempts to get a higher amount would be futile. Their ass was over the barrel and they had few other options. I did not intend to face the consortium with a half-baked deal that might rise in price at the whim of some incompetent executive who made too many errors of judgement in the first place. I knew the consortium would be only be interested in a take-it-or-leave-it deal.

I had to accept a one-percent fee for my efforts because Ballard whined so much about the money they were losing on the plant. My trips back and forth between both sides were starting to wear on my psyche. The Ballard executives were vacillating and Ken Fraser was a hardass who knew he was in the driver's seat. I had planned on getting a fee from both parties, but the glamour of getting a big fee was quickly fading and nothing could be done about it.

Then came the day when the consortium called me over to the B.C. Packers office to go with them to the Ballard office to finalize the sale of the plant. We arrived and were ushered into the boardroom. Coffee was served, and cigars were lit and silence fell over the room as they waited for me to outline the terms of the deal. I made my pitch and sat down to hear Ballard confirm the sale of the plant for seven hundred thousand dollars.

There was a silence while a couple of officials from Ballard management discussed the deal in low voices. The head honcho stepped forward and agreed that they wanted to sell the plant but indicated that they had decided the price was too low and they could not let the plant for go for less than a million dollars. The cigar smokers removed their cigars and all turned to stare at me with the kind of cold look that makes your stomach churn. I knew instantly that my fee had flown out the window. I forgot which one, but one of the consortium executives spoke up in a growl, saying that they had only come to this meeting because they understood the sale was a done deal at seven hundred thousand dollars. He said, "You've wasted our time. Obviously you have refused our offer, so there's nothing more to say." One by one they filed out of the room without even a glance in my direction. They did not offer me a ride back to Vancouver.

Now I was left alone in the boardroom with the Ballard men. "Why did you not advise me you wouldn't accept their offer?" I asked.

Their answer was a confused one. They mumbled something about me not telling them there wasn't room for movement. I was stunned. I informed them that after three long weeks of going back and forth, it was obvious to even a well-trained Alsatian dog that there was no room for movement. Not only was the whole exercise a waste of time, but my reputation had suffered a terrible blow. I knew the cigar smokers would be vindictive towards me. I shrugged my shoulders and asked someone to call me a cab.

After that I had very little to do with Ballard. I completely rejected their suggestions that perhaps they might reconsider, and I should try to pull the deal together again. I knew a dead horse when I saw it. Occasionally I sold them a little scrap when it suited me, but mostly I avoided having anything to do with them. The Ballard reduction plant remained idle for several years after that, and then it was sold for scrap for less than one hundred thousand dollars.

OFF WITH THEIR HEADS

For many years, salmon heads were stuffed into one-hundred-pound burlap bags and frozen for bait. These hundred-pound bags of frozen salmon heads were shipped in refrigeration to Australia, where they were used as bait in traps for catching Pacific lobster.

The labour and high cost of freezing the salmon heads and shipping them a great distance under refrigeration plus the cost of keeping them frozen Down Under in cold storage until they were used was extremely high and quite impractical. I observed this messy operation at B.C. Ice and Cold Storage when McCallum Sales were putting up the bait. Burlap bags were filled with bloody heads and then stacked on racks that were pushed into the blast freezers. Until they were frozen, blood would ooze out of the bags and cover the floor. I suppose when the bags were thawed out at the other end to get the heads, the same bloody mess was repeated. The heads made good bait so the messy work continued at B.C. Ice during the fishing season.

As I watched this dirty work, I thought to myself, there must be a better way of doing this job more efficiently. We were already buying reject cans of salmon and clams from a couple of canneries for ten cents per can and selling all we could get to local crab fishermen for twenty cents per can. These fishermen punched a small hole into each can before inserting them into the bait holder in each trap. This canned product made excellent bait as the juice oozed out of the cans. Raw fish would go rotten in a couple of days, and the stinky bait had to be discarded, but the cans, which were clean and easy to handle, lasted more than a week.

I got the idea of canning the heads and shipping them Down Under in the category of general stowage rather than refrigerated. The canned product would take less space and be cheaper to ship and would keep indefinitely without being kept frozen in costly refrigeration facilities. It seemed such a good idea to me that I approached Ballard's pet food plant to see if it was a feasible project. They said they could put the heads through their cutters and can them for three dollars and eighty-five cents for forty-eight one-pound cans. To make it pay, they wanted the heads in thirty-thousand-pound lots. They also offered to put me up ten or fifteen cases for a sample. I immediately delivered one thousand pounds of heads to Ballard and a day later picked up my fifteen-carton sample.

When I opened a couple of cans to inspect the bait I was absolutely amazed by what a wonderful product was obtained from the mixed variety of salmon heads I had sent to them. The ground meat in the cans was in solid lumps and a creamy red colour in a bath of pinkish salmon oil. The canned salmon heads looked and smelled as good or better than a lot of the canned salmon I had seen in the past. I broke off a tiny piece of the meat to see how it tasted. I found that it tasted as good as it looked. For a while, I offered around small samples of the product to see how people liked it. Nobody would believe me when I told them the product was made from salmon heads.

I shipped the sample to Australia as quickly as I could get it away. A month later I received a phone call advising me the product made super lobster bait and that a purchase order was in the mail that would pay fifteen dollars per forty-eight-pound case for all the canned salmon heads I could supply.

I was jubilant with this response to my experiment and began making arrangements at once to accumulate large quantities of heads. I approached B.C. Ice on the cost of freezing salmon heads in bulk one-thousand-pound totes, which was the cheapest and quickest way to handle the heads. Ballard would dump whole tote-lots into their silent cutters. The heads were chopped up to the consistency of fine peanut butter before ingredients were added to colour and gel the product in the can while it was being cooked. They called the process a hot pack. The finished product looked and smelled as good as the best canned salmon.

Ballard's pet food plant was a fully automated modern plant. They even made their own cans from sheets of tin plate that was shipped to them in boxcar loads. The product being canned was dumped into the silent cutter and from then on nobody touched it. The product was cooked, cans were then filled, sealed and labelled (our bait was not labelled), and cases were automatically filled and conveyed into boxcars ready for shipping. Most people do not realize it, but all pet food manufactured has to be approved for human consumption because about twenty percent of it is consumed by poor human beings in various parts of the western hemisphere.

In short order, I accumulated a substantial quantity of heads at B.C. Ice. I sent heads from our own facility at Campbell Avenue and I obtained heads from B.C. Ice where, during the fishing season, approximately one hundred and fifty thousand pounds of salmon were headed on a daily basis. Eight percent of that production was heads that I paid them to freeze to our account. The sockeye fishery was in full swing. Eddie Woods was picking up salmon heads from various canneries for reduction. These heads included the collars, which had a substantial quantity of red meat on them. Eddie was paid to haul these loads of heads to Steveston, which was about thirty miles away. It was only a half-mile haul to B.C. Ice, so he was happy to give me the heads for the same price he was receiving for them. The day arrived when I was advised by Ballard to deliver fifteen tons of heads, which we promptly did. A day later I was told that our canned bait was ready for pickup. Ballard had a large warehouse and they agreed to store the bait until we were ready to ship it out.

Now came the most difficult part of the deal. That was to get a permit to export the canned bait. This was one time that I got carried away and put the wagon in front of the horse. I was so sure our product would pass inspection for export, I had proceeded without informing the Department of Fisheries and Oceans' Inspection Department to get the product approved. They were a very uncaring and difficult department for small companies to deal with. These were the same people who cost our company six million dollars in lost profits in less than ten years by enforcing an illegal law. In subsequent years, the World Court overruled the law and the Canadian government was forced to wipe it from the books. Years of unreasonable treatment by this department led to many disputes with our company. However, because of the nature of the product, I was pretty sure they would pass the product for export.

Ballards wanted their custom canning money, so it was time to make a move. I phoned the Inspection Department and told them I had forty-six hundred cartons of canned salmon to ship to Australia for bait. They ordered ten cartons for inspection. One afternoon, ten days later — they were never in a hurry — a half a dozen inspectors showed up. They drew three or four cans from each case and began opening them and dumping them out on clean sheets of parchment paper. It was beautiful-looking stuff. It looked much better than some A grade sockeyes I had seen in the past. They stuck their noses almost into the stuff and inhaled deeply. They took forks from their jacket pockets and proceeded to taste it. Soon they were eating forkfulls of the stuff. The ignored me completely while conferring among themselves as they ate their fill. I thought they would never stop eating as they kept opening more cans.

Finally, they stopped inspecting and surrounded me with smiles on their faces. "This stuff is far too good for bait," they insisted as they tried to read my reaction. "What kind of salmon is in these cans?"

"What difference does it make?" I countered. "Pacific lobsters won't care what kind of salmon it is."

"Come on now, Norman," they insisted. "What kind of fish is in these cans?"

We sparred around for almost an hour while they kept tasting more of the fish and demanding to know what species of salmon was in our cans. They also asked if they could take a few cans away with them.

"Help yourselves," I insisted, in a last-ditch attempt to persuade them to issue me an export permit. By now we had almost twenty-five thousand dollars tied up in the deal, which was not a lot of money where canned salmon was concerned but still it wasn't chicken feed.

They took as many cans as they could handle and swept out the door with loud laughter, advising me that as soon as they knew what species of salmon was in the cans we could have our permit. This posed a difficult problem. If I told them the canned fish was made from salmon heads I figured there was better than a fifty percent chance they would turn me down. Besides, I was going to experience my usual difficulty with them no matter what the issue. A big company would have no trouble getting the permit, but as we were a small company, we were in the usual dilemma. Not enough pull.

In desperation I called the Inspection Department a second time and prepared to put my head on the block by telling them the canned bait was made from salmon heads. The same lot arrived on an afternoon again to inspect my bait. I again attempted to get my permit without telling them what was in the cans, but it was a no-go. Finally, they promised that if I told them what kind of fish was in the cans, they would issue the export permit. It was now or never, so I gave in and told them it was made from salmon heads.

"We don't believe you," one of them remarked as the whole lot of them suddenly stopped eating the bait. It took some doing to convince them it was all made from heads. They just looked at the product and shook their heads in denial. When I got exasperated and made them understand the truth, they stood in silence, not knowing what to make of the information.

"Did you take the eyes out of the heads?" one of them asked. "Did you cut out the teeth?" another inquired.

"No, I did not take the eyes out, and sockeye salmon have no teeth," I replied. "And besides, fish eyes are a delicacy to a lot of people and I don't suppose Pacific lobsters will have a preference!"

Now the leader fixed me with a grim look and blurted out, "That stuff is made from offal and you will never get an export permit!" The others began emptying cans from their coat pockets, throwing them back on the table. Now they were angry with me, so there was no point in pursuing my request for a permit. I knew their word was no good and that I would never get a permit. It was typical of their behaviour.

On the way home from work that evening I decided that the situation called for drastic action. I figured I had better find a way to get an export permit for our bait before Father and Steiner found out that we had one hundred tons of canned product that couldn't be sold. I wondered who might be able to help me out. No matter how hard I pondered the problem, I kept coming back to one name. Much as I hated the thought of it, I knew that Malcolm McCallum would find a way to get me an export permit. Malcolm could charm the birds out of the trees, and besides that, his company was owned by the mighty B.C. Packers and they carried a lot of weight, enough weight to persuade the fisheries inspectors to rethink their decision on the canned bait issue. How ironic it was that Malcolm, my competitor, with his bloody burlap bags full of heads, might turn out to be my saviour. The big question now was, how much of the profit was Malcolm going to demand and how big a share would Packers take? I felt certain that once they took over, it would be out of my hands and they would help themselves on a take-it-or-leave-it basis. However, at that point, I figured it might be a good idea to try to recover our costs and forget about the bait business.

The following morning I arrived at McCallum Sales with half a dozen cans for a sample. "What brings you here so early in the day?" Malcolm asked as he leaned back in his chair with a smile on his face. I laid out the proposition to him as carefully as I could. I knew I was going to get royally screwed but I still hoped for some kind of profit if I played my cards right. He asked one of his office staff to bring a can opener and some parchment paper to cover his desk and he proceeded to open one of the cans. As soon as the can was cracked, the lush aroma permeated his whole office and his staff crowded around to view the contents. Malcolm dumped out the can and exclaimed, "Jeezuz, Norman, do you call that bait? What kind of fish it, anyway?" he asked.

"The contents of that can are made from salmon heads," I repeated to him.

"I don't believe you!" he replied. "It's not possible. What kind of fish is it?" he asked again.

"Malcolm, I told you it was made from fish heads."

By then he had a fork out of his drawer and he was flaking off a small piece of the fish, smelling it and then gingerly tasting it. He then broke off a larger piece and rolled it about in his mouth to get the full flavour from it. "This stuff is good!" he finally declared as he reached for a third forkfull, "better than a lot of canned salmon I have tasted." More cans were opened and his staff were all tasting the contents.

I said, "The head and the collars of the salmon are the fattest part of the fish, where most of the fat and oil are stored. This is what gives it such a wonderful bouquet and good taste." By now they were all eating their fill and proclaiming it was very good indeed.

"You say you put this up for bait," Malcolm asked me again with a quizzical look on his face. "You must be kidding!" he declared with a sly smile. "This is far too good for bait, and you damn well know it. This is a great product!" I decided to tell Malcolm most of the scenario that had already taken place concerning the canned bait. "How much have they offered you for this stuff?" he suddenly asked.

"Fifteen dollars for a forty-eight one-pound can case," I answered.

"Why did the inspection people turn down your request for an export permit?"

"For the same reason you initially thought," I replied. "They think it's too good for bait. They claim that salmon heads are offal and should not be put up for human consumption, so they turned me down. They can't imagine I am really putting up such a good product for bait. I didn't plan it that way — it just happened."

Malcolm said, "I've seen minced salmon and salmon paste that couldn't touch your stuff. There must be some other reason why they won't pass it. Is it all the same quality?" he asked.

"Yes it is," I replied.

"Deliver a couple of cartons of your stuff to the Imperial plant with your bait purchase order, and I assure you we will get it passed for export."

Reassured by Malcolm that my canned bait would be shipped out, I was cheered up some, but now I was in the hands of that son of a bitch. I knew that Malcolm regarded me in the same light as I viewed him. This was one son of a bitch versus the other son of a bitch. I wondered how badly Malcolm was going to rip me off. Malcolm's services did not come cheaply. Beside him, the Sheriff of Nottingham was a saint.

We delivered a couple of cases of the canned bait to the Imperial plant with our purchase order from the Australian company and silently prayed for the export permit. Art Woodland, the manager of that plant, phoned and advised me that the canned product was more than good enough for human consumption. He laughed when he told me that the Inspection Department was hung up on those eyes in the canned heads. "Because it was such a nice pack, they were sure it was destined to be sold for human consumption instead of bait, and they class heads as offal. Don't worry, Norman," he said, "we have been advised that a permit will be issued when all the cans are stamped with a bait label. I don't know just how we will do that, but we'll figure it out." A few days later we were told to have all the cases trucked to the Imperial plant in Steveston so they could get on with it. We sent the whole lot to that plant and kept our fingers crossed that no hangups would occur. I was still worried about the zealots in the Inspection Department. A week passed and a call came from Imperial to tell me that our bait was aboard ship on its way to Australia.

"How did you manage to get a bait label on every can?" I asked.

"Oh, we made a stamp and stamped the top layer of cans in the top cartons on a few of the skids. When the usual dumb shit of an inspector arrived, we showed him the stamped cans in the top layer of cartons on a couple of skid loads and he okayed the shipment," Woodland told me with a chuckle. I was stunned. It seemed to me that the whole business was just an exercise in kowtowing to the Inspection Department authority. Just the same, I knew we would have never been successful in getting the export permit no matter what steps we had taken.

I knew that payment was made when the canned bait was aboard ship and documents were signed by an agent on that ship. However, it was three weeks later when Malcolm dropped by our office late in the day. I was there by myself. He pulled a forty-ounce bottle of vodka out of a paper bag and removed the cap. He poured himself a beer glass full right to the brim, then he pushed the bottle with an empty glass towards me. Four ounces at a time was my limit, with two ounces at a time being my limit when dealing with Malcolm. After he downed the first glass, he dropped a cheque down before me as payment for our canned bait. Rapid calculating while I was on my second drink told me that we got our money back plus two bucks per case profit. Approximately ten dollars per carton was kept by the B.C. Packers/McCallum Sales consortium. How the two companies split the ten dollars is anybody's guess, but I would wager Malcolm got more of it than B.C. Packers. I received the cheque graciously and said nothing to Malcolm about it. He knew that I knew that one son of a bitch had gotten even with another son of a bitch with the aid of the Inspection Department, so there was no point in pursuing the matter.

It was as final as the head bouncing off the block when the guillotine blade dropped to end a matter. Malcolm expected a furious protest on my part, but I would not give him the satisfaction. He smiled as he finished the second glass, capping the bottle and placing it back in the brown bag. He then got up and departed from our office in a good-humoured manner. I breathed a sigh of relief to get out of the mess as well as we did but I still muttered to myself that the son of a bitch owed me one and I was already planning on getting even.

REDS BEARING LOBSTERS

On a bright sunny morning in the sixties, three gentlemen from Cuba climbed the steep wooden stairs to our office above the fish plant on Campbell Avenue. They represented the export sales agency of their government for fishery products. They offered us the sales agency in Western Canada for lobster tails produced in the Caribbean area in the vicinity of Cuba. They had other products to offer, but we were mostly interested in obtaining the rights to selling their lobster tails, which were a super product. They were fresh frozen and packed with four ten-pound boxes per case. A steady supply of these tasty crustaceans would definitely give us a great opportunity to increase our business.

The strangers had first tried to interest B.C. Packers in marketing their lobster tails in Canada, but they were not interested. I assumed that was because B.C. Packers had substantial business interest in the United States and dealing with communist Cuba would not be to their advantage. The Packers steered the Cubans to McCallum Sales, but that failed to pan out, so the Cubans climbed our stairs in search of a business deal.

It was a good day for us when the Cubans made their pitch. These well-educated salespeople were enthusiastic young fellows who made a good impression on me both with their knowledge and the high quality of their product. I was surprised that the Packers and McCallum Sales had brushed them off. Their lobsters were the Atlantic warm-water lobster from the Caribbean area — not at all like our northern cold-water lobster. The Caribbean variety have miniature claws that contain no meat but they have a larger tail than our Atlantic lobster. Our cold-water maritime lobsters have large, meaty claws with a smaller, tougher tail than the Caribbean lobster.

Warm-water lobsters come from Mexico, Brazil, the Caribbean areas, Japan, New Zealand, Australia, the Mediterranean, the Arabian Sea, the Indian Ocean and other South Pacific locations. They have very little meat except in their tails, which are the only parts that are packed for the market. I have sampled most of the varieties of warm-water lobsters and I consider the Cuban ones to be among the most succulent and flavourful.

The Cubans had finally found someone who would listen to their business proposal. They became quite animated in their presentation. They promised to provide the best lobster tails available at very competitive prices. They asserted that if we could sell one hundred forty-pound cases per month I would be invited to visit Cuba and have dinner with Fidel Castro. While I found the last premise to be a bit much, I was impressed with their sincere attitude. We immediately ordered one hundred cases of Cuban lobster tails and offered to do our best in establishing a market for them. The Cuban tails were priced about twenty-five percent below the cost of the tails the market preferred that came from Down Under.

At first the Cuban lobster tails were a hard sell. Much to my surprise, we encountered a hostile attitude from the trade about "the damn communists!" Some customers didn't really wish to discuss the issue. However, I persisted and gradually broke down the thorny issue that threatened to sink the whole enterprise. The Cubans co-operated with us by giving us credit for samples we provided to the skeptics. Once these customers had the opportunity to view and sample the Cuban lobster tails, there was no longer a problem because they had to admit the stuff was top of the line. This strategy worked and sales took off to the point where we were selling more than five hundred cases per month all over Western Canada. Sales increased every hour of the work week despite our competition's efforts at beating the drums about doing business with damn communists!

The Cubans were strange people to deal with. While they were honest and always provided the goods when we advanced the money, they had a peculiar way of doing business. It was not our usual practice to pay for the product before it was even cleared by inspection after it had arrived in Canada. Some of the shipments were in the one-hundred-and-fifty-thousand-dollar bracket, so it was a worrying situation. We dreaded the thought that we were being set up. In addition, the price was gradually creeping up from a dollar seventy-five per pound to two dollars and seventy-five cents per pound. They insisted the money had to be paid up front before the shipment. I began to realize that my Cuban friends were afraid of the consequences if they shipped to us and we reneged on payment. They weren't taking any chances.

Each time we advanced the money and waited for the tails to arrive. Almost always the Cubans came back and claimed that because of storms the price had to go up by five or ten cents per pound. This was baloney, but so long as we were making a healthy profit and were always short on product, who could argue with their demands? Business was booming and the shipments always arrived in good condition as described, so we carried on.

In our trio of Cuban contacts, Hector, the most demonstrative, was their closer. He was eager to help us deal with difficult customers. In one particular case we were having no luck selling the Cuban tails to an extremely high-end steak house that was one of the most popular swank establishments in the City of Vancouver. Hector provided a forty-pound case of Cuban tails as a sample to this most stubborn of customers. Hector and I went to the restaurant for lunch. In spite of providing one hundred and sixty dollars' worth of choice lobster tails, we were given a bill. When the waiter came back and presented us with it, Hector blew up, taking the matter as a direct slap in the face. While red-faced Hector muttered what sounded like curses in Spanish, I paid the bill.

Just before we left the establishment their sleazy purchasing agent arrived to declare that the restaurant found the tails were an excellent product that was up their standards. He ushered us into his office and indicated he would order twenty-five cases right away; however, he advised that he did not want to deal with our company and that the tails would have to be provided by Seaport Crown Fish Company.

I can still see the veins in Hector's neck swell as he pulled out a hefty black automatic pistol from a shoulder holster beneath his jacket and placed it with a clatter on the table. "We shoot sons of a bitches like you in Cuba," he snarled at the purchaser, who took off in a flash, falling down twice in his hurry before he disappeared through doors into the back of the place.

I was absolutely shocked and speechless at the transformation that had taken place in Hector, from being an extremely presentable well-dressed gentleman to becoming little more than a threatening bully. The dapper Cuban diplomat had made an astonishingly quick change to uncouth thug. It took Hector quite a long time to calm down and he did not make the transition back to his usual role in a very convincing fashion. After this incredible luncheon, I sat in my office where I expected to be arrested along with Hector for not only intimidating somebody with a weapon but for even possessing a handgun. Though I had no part in his actions, I felt our association would be enough. I heard nothing more about the incident.

Imagine my surprise when we received an order from the restaurant to supply lobster tails. Of course, it came with the usual problems associated with a purchaser who, for some reason, does not wish to deal with a supplier. We had no complaints for a month, then suddenly, according to the purchasing agent, one of our cases was bad. This was an old story that I had encountered several times in the past. We gave the purchasing agent credit for the case and waited to see what would happen next. Two weeks later we received another complaint, this time stating that two cases of lobster tails supplied by us were found to be discoloured after thawing out. It was becoming pretty obvious that this gent was either attempting to discourage us or forcing us to give him a kickback. I was not about to submit to either of his tactics, so I drove to the restaurant to investigate. The purchaser showed me the lobster tails, and there was no doubt about it, they were discoloured. However, by this time we had sold over two thousand cases of Cuban lobster tails and never had a complaint, other than from this establishment. I knew something was wrong, but I couldn't quite put my finger on it. Before leaving I questioned the cooks and the kitchen staff but they all shrugged their shoulders and I learned nothing.

On my way out through the back I encountered the dishwasher, a Slovak fellow I had known for some years. He sidled over and indicated that he had the information I wanted. He told me that two cases of lobster tails were placed under the sink for two days where they completely thawed out. When frozen tails thaw out, after a reasonable time they darken up considerably if they are refrozen. They also have a tendency to look mushy when they thaw out a second time. Now I realized how diabolical the purchasing agent was going to be in achieving his way. I thanked my friend and returned to confront the purchasing agent. By now I was clear on how to deal with the issue. I told the purchasing agent that he would authorize payment for the two cases of tails or I would go to the restaurant management for satisfaction. We received payment for the two cases of tails and we never had another complaint from this auspicious eating establishment. I knew that by then the purchasing agent had realized that there would be no handout from our company nor would we submit to his sleazy tactics.

Three years of business as usual passed by with the Cubans without any major problems. We still advanced money for each shipment and the price to us increased by a few cents on occasion because of the stormy weather. They never changed that story. The Cubans were my friends by now and were often included in activities with some of my other friends. However, I did not go out of my way to highly publicize my relationship with the Cubans. Cuba was disturbing American interests in the Caribbean and in South America by organizing people to revolt against their masters. Cuba was also involving itself in African politics and spreading its influence in other regions. The Americans had become obsessed about their losses in Cuba as well as the role Cuba was playing in the Soviet orbit. We did a lot of business in the United States, so we felt it was better to keep a low profile with our Cuban connections.

So often in business, good things suddenly come to an end for no apparent reason. Our first indication that something was going wrong with our Cuban venture came when they began withholding substantial quantities of the favoured sizes of lobster tails that were easiest to sell. We were immediately suspicious when we began receiving more than our share of bastard sizes that were difficult to move. The four- to twelve-ounce tails were the favoured item. The sixteen-ounce sizes also sold reasonably well because they could be split in half and served as eight-ounce portions. Minus-four-ounce and plus-sixteen-ounce sizes were sold at lower prices to get rid of them. Anything over twenty ounces could only be used in salads or in soup or some other limited ways, and they moved with great difficulty even at much lower prices. The Cubans didn't cut us off completely but continued to increase shipments of unfavourable sizes to our company that were swelling our inventory. When we further investigated the situation, we discovered that some of our customers were receiving medium-sized Cuban lobster tails from another Vancouver source — a Chinese company that nobody had previously heard of.

We realized the Cubans were two-timing us and that for whatever reason they had decided to deal with a new partner without coming clean to us. We decided it was time to look for a new source for spiny lobsters. In our investigation we discovered that we could buy Cuban lobster tails for twenty-five cents per pound cheaper than the Cubans would sell to us from a French broker. Not only was the price right, but we could get all the favoured sizes we desired. We quickly placed large orders through our new source in France and quietly went into competition with our Cuban friends.

We reduced our orders with the Cubans to only the favoured sizes. This did not sit well with them, so we only received about fifty cases per month (which we could sell in one day) instead of our usual five hundred plus cases. We supplied the market at our usual rate from our new inventory of lobster tails shipped in from France. It took the Cubans several months to stumble onto the fact of our competition. All along, they were assuming that the lobster tails we were selling were the built-up accumulation of our old stock. We knew that the Cubans would wake up sooner or later and that there would be a confrontation, even though the Cubans had no leg to stand on. Three or four months passed, during which we were pumping out cases of the favoured-sized tails to the trade, before the Cubans finally understood that we had a new source of supply.

Late in the afternoon in the spring, four of the Cubans turned up at our office. Hector pulled up a chair and sat down beside me. Jesus, the ever-smooth diplomat, stood nearby with a smile on his handsome face. Hector's assistant, who probably also packed an automatic 45 calibre in a shoulder holster, stood about five feet to the left with a grim look on his face. An elderly grandfather type remained near the office door. I took him out to be the commissar who kept the boys in line. For some reason, I like to think that Jesus and the grandfather were not armed since they exuded class, but perhaps they were even more dangerous than Hector, who was angry, highly agitated and barely able to control himself.

Hector leaned over and demanded in a low venomous voice where I was getting the Cuban lobster tails.

"That's none of your business," I replied.

"You must tell us," he insisted as he reached into his jacket and hauled out the automatic, which he proceeded to wave under my nose.

"Put it away," I said, "or you won't be going back to Cuba for a long time."

Hector pounded the pistol's butt on my desk and continued to insist with curses that I give him the information he wanted. The confrontation lasted about eight or nine minutes and galvanized the attention of everyone in the room, including my office staff who were frozen at attention as Hector's hissing voice demanded an answer. The broad smile stayed on Jesus's lips during the whole confrontation.

When I recovered from the situation, I got up from my chair and walked over to the office door. I opened the door and ordered Hector to put his gun away while I invited him and his friends to leave the premises. I reminded Hector that if he continued to behave in this manner he would soon find himself in one of our prisons. The foursome left our office without further incident. The smiling Jesus stopped at the door and made a gesture with his hands as if to say it wasn't his idea. After they left, the office staff were buzzing about the encounter when the old man came back through the door. He took off his hat and began, "I wish to apologize for Hector's bad behaviour. I am very sorry for the way he insulted you and your staff. Hector will return to Cuba where he will be instructed to improve his manners."

It seemed that this was the end of the Cuban affair, but it was not yet over. A month or two later we received a call from a Mr. Humphrey, who was the manager of Straits Seafood Company, located in Singapore. This Englishman informed me that his company was owned by British interests. One of their specialties was scampi. He told me they serviced the Russian fishing fleet in that area for scampi. They bought the scampi from the Russians and individually quick-froze the scampi tails. Each scampi tail was placed in a plastic bag and they were packed in five pound cartons according to size (one to two, two to three, or three to four ounces) and then placed in forty-pound cases. Samples were sent to us by air freight. I must say they had a wonderful product; it was the best I had ever seen. Mr. Humphrey offered us the agency for all of Canada. He also informed us they had to receive payment for their goods as soon as they passed the Canadian inspection division of DFO. That suited us. Already he was easier to deal with than the Cubans who demanded payment before shipping.

How lucky can you get? Lightning seldom strikes twice in the same place. I got in touch with Morris Waldman of Waldman Fish in Montreal and he immediately booked half of our shipments. We knew all the bad accounts in Ontario and Quebec. One character in Quebec laughed at us when he would not pay his bill. "Anglais never win in our French courts," he boasted. Later, when that character begged us for scampi, we collected the old bill and shipped our products COD to him ever after. There were one or two more delinquent accounts in Quebec that paid up to get cheaper scampi. It is amazing how quickly con men change their tune. We were thankful for Morris Waldman for his business, and his advice and information he passed along to us. Morris Waldman had warned me that doing business with the Cubans would have an unsatisfactory ending because of his own experience, which had proved the Cubans were often unreasonable in their business practices and expectations.

Our first order from the Straits Seafood Company was for a twenty-thousand-pound container of scampi as a trial run. After that, we brought in two or three twenty-thousand-pound containers on a regular basis, every six weeks. In fact, we could have sold more than that, but that was our allotted quota. We had no trouble collecting accounts because there was never enough product to fill the pipeline. The scampi cost us three bucks a pound, which was a substantial amount thirty-five years ago.

Our connection with Straits Seafood remained a profitable enterprise for both companies without any trouble for over three years. Mr. Humphrey was a fine gentleman who was as good as his word in every way. Late one evening I received a call at my home from Singapore. Mr. Humphrey advised me he could no longer ship us scampi tails. "What did you do to the Cubans?" he asked. He said that the Straits had sold out to a Russian-Cuban consortium, and he had been instructed not to provide us with any products from his plant.

I explained the Cuban story to him from the beginning. However, I could not tell why the Cubans broke up our business relationship because I didn't know the reason. Mr. Humphrey had agreed to stay on with Straits Fish for a few months and then he intended to return to England. He said he was going home via Canada and he wanted to stop in Vancouver and visit with us for a few days and so he did.

About six months after he left Singapore, I received a call from the Chinese gentleman who had replaced Humphrey. He asked if I wished to regain the agency for their scampi tails in Canada. He indicated that they would be willing to do business with us again. I was a bit taken aback by their offer. It was obvious to me by the way he was talking that business in Canada was not going so well. I declined his offer because I am not one to look to the past to find the future. I informed him that we had always dealt in good faith with the Cubans and treated them with dignity. Since I no longer trusted them to give us a square deal, I was forced to reject his offer. That was the end of the Cuban experience.

A BLUE SUIT AND A RED ROSE

During the early sixties, we made an agreement with B.C. Packers department head Joe Van Snellenburg to custom cut large sole for thirty cents per pound, on the finished fillet weight, for B.C. Packers. We did this to keep our filleters working on days when we had no fish of our own to cut.

At the same time we helped B.C. Packers by cutting twenty-five-thousand-pound lots of sole when their filleting plant was plugged with fish. After we had cut over one hundred thousand pounds of whole fish, I walked over to B.C. Packers to pick up a cheque for our labour costs. I was handed a cheque by this smiling gent with a statement that had arbitrarily cut our cutting returns to twenty cents per pound without so much as a discussion.

I said to Joe, "This is not payment according to our agreement so you owe me ten cents per pound more. Why didn't you pay the amount we agreed upon?"

This smart gent replied, "Bygate Fish are cutting sole for us for twenty cents per pound, on finished fillet weights, so that's all we're going to pay you."

Well, there are more ways than one to skin a cat. I rushed back to our plant where we were cutting another twenty-five thousand pounds of B.C. Packer's sole fillets. I figured that by keeping twenty-five hundred pounds of fillets, we would be even with B.C. Packers. Then I called the Steveston plant to inform them that we would not be cutting any more lots of soles for them.

The Packers' Steveston manager was upset when informed that we would not cut fish for them any longer. After learning the facts about our disagreement with Joe, he agreed that Joe was out of line because nobody could cut sole fillets for twenty cents per pound and remain in business for long. "See if you can resolve the matter with Joe's boss," he pleaded, "because we sure need your help."

I answered that there was no way I intended to beg for money owed to us. I would keep the twenty-five hundred pounds of finished fillets and sell them to recover our money. In addition, I informed the Steveston manager that we were no longer inclined to do further work for B.C. Packers.

The next afternoon right after lunch I got a phone call from Ken Fraser, president of B.C. Packers. He wanted to see me at once. I had a good idea what he wanted to see me about, but the air needed clearing so I walked over to sort the matter out with him. I was ushered into his office by a nice young secretary who acted like she was about to witness someone going to the gallows. Ken Fraser was a stern, imposing character who put up with very little in the way of shenanigans. As I walked down the aisle between rows of desks, there was hush as the score of office girls punching adding machines stopped their work to gaze silently as I passed by on my way to God's office to learn my fate.

When I entered the office, Ken Fraser fixed me with a cold stare as he pointed to a chair. "Safarik, I hear you are stealing our fish," he snapped. "What have you got to say for yourself?"

"I'm not stealing your fish," I answered. "I'm only keeping what is owed to our company. Your Joe made a deal with me to cut your sole for thirty cents per pound on finished fillet weight. You've been around long enough to know that sole cannot be cut for less than that with union labour. When I came over to pick up a cheque for our labour costs, your Joe arbitrarily deducted ten cents per pound. We were only paid twenty cents per pound because he claims Bygate is cutting for twenty cents per pound so that's all we're going to be paid. Our deal was thirty cents per pound. We kept enough fillets to make up for the shortfall, so what are you going to do about it?"

With a surprised look, he remarked, "Did Joe agree to thirty cents per pound cutting fee and then make a deduction?"

"He did," I replied, "and I made sure we understood each other so there would not be a hangup like we have now. I'm keeping the fillets and we are not cutting fish for you any longer, and Ken, that is my final word on this matter."

He turned to the secretary, who had stayed to witness my downfall, and ordered her to get Joe up to his office at once. He then called Mort Ferguson, the comptroller, and Ross Nicholson, who was in charge of the seine fleet, to come in and sit in on the dispute.

In a minute, Joe entered the office dressed immaculately in his trademark blue suit with a red rose in his lapel. His big smile anticipating my downfall reminded me of a dog about to demolish his dinner.

"Did you offer to pay Safarik thirty cents per pound on filleted weight for cutting our sole?" Fraser asked.

Joe answered, "Bygate is cutting our sole for twenty cents, and I feel that's all we should pay Van Shell."

"I didn't ask you that," Fraser growled at Joe, whose smile was rapidly fading as wrinkles appeared on his brow.

Joe went on. "We can't pay Van Shell thirty cents per pound if Bygate is willing to do it for twenty."

"Joe," Fraser snarled. "I didn't ask you for your opinion. Did you or didn't you agree to pay Safarik thirty cents per pound?"

"Yes, I did," Joe said, "but we cannot."

Before Joe finished his sentence, he was cut off by Fraser's loud, angry voice. Shaking his head, Fraser ordered Joe out of his office to fetch a cheque immediately to pay Van Shell what was owed.

Fraser then turned to me and requested that I send over the sole fillets and said that if we would continue to cut sole for B.C. Packers, he would make sure we were paid thirty cents as agreed upon by Joe. Then he turned to the secretary and asked her to bring in a bottle of Scotch, ice, water and glasses right away and he passed cigars all around. I was not fussy about the cigar, but thought that I better keep quiet and smoke it. "I'm sorry about the misunderstanding," he said as he poured drinks for all of us. "It's so hard to get good help nowadays. Please accept my sincerest apology for the misunderstanding and the best of health to you." He smiled as he lifted his glass.

We had a couple of additional drinks as Mort Ferguson and Ross Nicholson assessed my knowledge of the fishing industry. They were both pretty shrewd businessmen and were invited in to appraise the situation and for another reason that I didn't know about at the time. The women in the office pool smiled their approval as I departed puffing away on the cigar. Mac Brock, my old school pal, gave me the thumbs-up as I passed his office window.

Joe was waiting for me at his office door with a cheque for the balance owing to our company. He grabbed my arm and pulled me in to vent his anger at me for an event engineered by his desire to gain attention from Fraser while depicting me as a crook. "You got me in trouble," he snapped, his red face quivering with anger, "and I am not going to forget it!"

"Give me the cheque, Joe," I replied. "Don't blame me for you getting yourself in trouble. You asked for it." After my parting remark, I left his office.

Joe was a rude man, and nothing he did ever changed that fact. He was always bucking for a promotion, so he passed on trivial information to head office as often as he could dredge it up or manufacture it to suit his purpose. I don't think he realized that he was actually hurting his own cause. The top men in the big fish companies were not impressed by a person in management who consistently required them to settle minor problems. Bosses had bigger fish to fry, like making a profit for shareholders. They got to the top by learning the business better than anyone else and by being honest in all their dealings with both fishermen and other companies. Joe, a petty man, didn't fit into that category and in my estimation was not going anywhere in the B.C. Packers hierarchy.

Another time we had a problem with Joe was when my brother Ed was peeling shrimp in an adjacent plant that belonged to B.C. Packers. Our company was short on space, and because Ed could use the extra work, we moved our crab operation into that plant and made arrangements for him to peel our shrimp production. We were Seaport Crown's biggest competitors in Vancouver, and they were operating under an arrangement with B.C. Packers. This created a lot of friction between us and Seaport, so Bob Widdis wore out a path into Ken Fraser's office complaining about this competition. Brother Ed was leasing the plant from B.C. Packers and he was also peeling some shrimps for the Packers that came out of their Port Alberni plant. Word came down from Packers that none of the shrimp meat peeled in that plant was to go to our company or Ed would be evicted.

This caused us a severe problem, because our shrimp was also being peeled in that plant, and the shellfish business was always in our domain. One way or another we got our shrimp meat out, but it caused a delicate situation. This tricky state of affairs between us and B.C. Packers was right up Joe's alley. He brought a pair of binoculars to his office and scanned our plant for hours each day in an attempt to discover how we got our shrimp meat. Still he could not discover our secret. Time and time again he would walk through both plants in attempts to discover our pipeline, but to no avail. We were not completely at war, yet things were sure heating up. I was always thankful that I had the good sense not to grab Joe by the collar and seat of his pants and run him out of our plant. He was a tall, skinny guy who only weighed about one hundred and thirty pounds, so he wouldn't have presented much of a problem. This state of undeclared war went on all spring while we waited it out.

I will never know how we managed to keep the secret of our shrimp meat pipeline. Packers could not process their shrimp economically because they had a strong union. Brother Ed's shrimp peelers all worked on piecework for so much a pound on finished shrimp meat. So long as they made more than the union wage, the union could not get a foothold in Ed's operation. Any pickers who could not make more than the union rate were not kept on the payroll long enough to cause a problem, so the operation carried on day after day.

The status quo drove Bob and Joe up the wall, because in spite of their campaign to do us in, it was business as usual. Joe had been staring through those binoculars of his so long that the strain was putting dark rims around his eyes that were beginning to make him look like a raccoon. The whole exercise was a joke to everyone except us. Each time that Joe, using his binoculars, observed a metal buggy exiting the adjoining building, he dispatched an employee to inspect the contents. There never was any shrimp meat in any of the buggies, so it was always a dry run for the embarrassed person.

To avoid detection by a B.C. Packers stoolie, we had taken a chainsaw and cut a three-foot-by-two-foot hole in the common wall between the two plants. We installed a sliding plywood panel and repainted the whole wall white to make our work relatively invisible. To further camouflage the opening, some smocks were hung in front of it on both sides of the wall to hide the entrance from prying eyes when it wasn't in use. Every day until the war between us ended our shrimp meat was passed through this hole in the wall in our thirty-pound pans without being detected. We were also processing our crab in one end of that adjoining building, so metal buggies with pans of crab meat and tubs of cooked crabs were being pushed out of that building continuously. We processed shellfish there with more than fifteen workers. So a lot of action took place in a small plant. On one memorable day, we sold eighteen hundred pounds of fresh crab meat just in local sales.

The cat and mouse game continued on day after day without a letup. We always posted a lookout when pans of our shrimp meat were being passed through the opening in the wall to avoid a showdown. Why the scheme was never detected will remain a mystery to us. Perhaps the powers that be didn't want to know about it. In any case, we had a lease arrangement in part of that building, so legally I believe

B.C. Packers were completely out of line with their demand for all the shrimp meat produced in their building.

Joe's attempts to frame us did not end at this point. This was 1962, the year of the World's Fair in Seattle, and we were shipping five- to ten-thousand-pound lots of whole cooked crabs and all of our surplus crab meat at least twice a week to B.C. Packers' competitors in that city. Often we could not get enough crabs to supply that market. B.C. Packers owned Seaport Fish in Seattle and they wanted some of our crab meat and crabs to be shipped to that company. However, the shrimp war had cooled our relationship with them, so when they sent Joe over to get product we ignored him no matter how hard he pleaded for forgiveness.

Finally my friend Dick Lamb came over one morning and advised that it would promote a better relationship between our companies and give us an ace in the hole in the future if we provided B.C. Packers with some of our products. We decided it would be wise to take Dick's advice so we agreed to pack crab meat in five-pound sealed cans for Packers. However, the sticking point was that B.C. Packers had no lithographed crab meat cans in stock and American Can, who provided them, was on strike. They had a large surplus of lithographed shrimp meat cans but we could not pack crab meat into a can with a shrimp meat label and pass U.S. food regulations. We had our own lithographed paper labels that could be glued to the outside of cans. Joe suggested to B.C. Packers that we use their shrimp meat cans with our glued crab meat labels around them to get by U.S. food regulations, and so this practice was mutually agreed upon. Our labels covered the cans completely so their pink labels did not show at all. We shipped about twenty-five percent of our crab production to Seaport Fish in Seattle during that World's Fair without any problems. Joe was on his best behaviour, with his arm around my shoulder at every opportunity as he pretended to be my friend. I knew that this was only a temporary change on his part until another opportunity came his way to stick it to us. "You're making it look bad for me," he would sputter when we wouldn't stand for his nonsense.

The World's Fair in Seattle ended and life returned to a normal pace on Campbell Avenue fish dock. Joe was still peering at us through his binoculars from time to time to keep his nose in it but he had enough matter between his ears to ignore Bob Widdis and stay out of the shrimp business. We were able to carry on with our business out in the open without using the hole in the wall to get our supply of fresh shrimp meat. One morning a year after the World's Fair, I arrived at our plant to find brother Ed waiting there for me. "Have you been stealing cans from B.C. Packers?" he asked.

I replied, "What the hell are you talking about? How could I steal cans from them?"

"Well," he said, "Fraser phoned me and accused you of stealing their shrimp meat cans. You had better go over there right away because he is going to turn it over to the police."

I headed over to Ken Fraser's office to find out about the accusation. When I arrived in Ken's office, he motioned me to a chair with a glint in his eyes and said that Joe was saying we were stealing their cans. Then Joe arrived on the scene — blue suit, red rose in his lapel and a sneering smile on his face — holding a five-pound can of crab meat with our label on it. He took his pen and lifted up a bit of the torn label and, lo and behold, there was a B.C. Packers lithographed shrimp meat can under it.

At once I recognized the situation for what is was worth. "That can came from your Seaport plant in Seattle, did it not?" I asked.

"Yes, it did," Joe answered. It seemed they had too much crab meat and returned ten cases for B.C. packers to sell elsewhere.

"You damned nitwit. You were the one who suggested we put our crab meat label over your shrimp meat can so we could ship product to your Seattle plant during the World's Fair. You have got a lot of gall accusing me of stealing B.C. Packers' cans, you stupid bastard." I strode over to confront him with Fraser holding on to my shirt, but Joe was already making an exit from the danger zone. "Ken," I shouted. "Why do you keep this dumbbell on your payroll?"

Ken said, "Sit down and stop yelling at me. Norman, I'm sorry this happened, so please accept my apology. I know there are duds in this outfit but they are the best we can find. If it will make you feel better, I haven't finished with Joe." I kind of figured the sun was setting for Joe, but there was yet a final event to come that took him out of his blue suit and put him to work in a pair of white coveralls.

Joe and Bob Widdis were fighting a vendetta with one of our salesmen. Larry Magee was a super salesman who was taking customers away from Seaport Crown at such an alarming rate that Bob was in complete panic. Magee came from an illustrious family in Stettler, Alberta. His father was a wealthy rancher who owned a lot of real estate in that province. Two of his brothers and a sister were doctors, and one of his uncles was a senator. Larry was a bit of an oddball but there was no grass growing under the Irishman's feet. Bob and Joe referred to Larry as a damn Jew and a queer. Larry was neither Jewish nor gay, but these racial and sexual innuendoes drove Larry into fits of anger.

Larry was a well-educated man who absolutely detested any form of hatred or intolerance. He decided to give Seaport Crown a run for its money. A slick operator with endless charm and bizarre rushes of energy, Larry was a bad enemy. Those two nitwits were about to pay a heavy price for their ridiculous behaviour. Everybody in the business but Bob and Joe knew that you could not get customers or win friends by using ethnic, racial or gender insults. Larry, who made friends easily, was becoming very popular around town. He was not only taking over business, he was doing it in style. Larry's family connections held him in good stead. It seemed he was on a personal basis with somebody high up in every organization, usually the top dog, be it university, church or hotel chain. It got to the point where Bob and Joe got so desperate in their anger over lost customers that they ridiculed and antagonized Larry on a daily basis. It happened that on this day Joe parked his new car behind Larry's car in our parking stall and he refused to move it. Larry had an appointment with a buyer and was in a hurry, but when Joe was asked to move his vehicle, he merely ignored Larry and continued to wipe his car with a cloth.

"I'll move your damned car," Larry snarled in exasperation and he jumped into his beatup Chevy and backed up against Joe's new car with a bang. It took about four bangs to move Joe's car far enough so Larry could get out.

Joe stood there with his mouth open at this turn of events. When Joe got his wits together, he let out an anguished scream and began yelling unprintable curses at Larry while standing in front of Larry's old Chevy.

"Get out of the way, you idiot," Larry screamed as he tramped down on the gas pedal. Joe jumped out of the way, because by now he had received the message that Larry wasn't fooling around. Eventually, Larry got his car out from the parking stall and he departed the scene with screeching tires.

Joe saw his chance to settle the score so he pressed people to witness for him that Larry had tried to kill him. He then laid some serious charges against Magee that could have put him in jail for quite a spell, if the charges had stuck. Joe could not get anybody to witness for him so he cooked up a scheme with Bob and an employee of the Vancouver Port Corporation Police.

I made a trip over to see Ken Fraser to try to get him to have Joe drop the charges, because everybody knew that the charges were fictitious. Ken turned away and said it was out of his hands. I could see that I was not going to get anywhere with him so I left with the parting words that Magee was going to make fools out of Bob and Joe. "You're going to be sorry," I advised him as he escorted me out of his office with a grin on his face.

As was expected, Joe could not find a witness except for Bob. The Port Corporation Police sergeant was smart enough to remain at arm's length, but a constable was pressured into witnessing against Magee. Joe and Bob were schooling this witness every day in the ice house office on exactly what to say on the day of the trial. These sessions went on for some time, and somehow all this information was passed on to Larry, who was passing it on to his lawyer. I was worried and upset about the charges against Larry, and I advised him that he should get his act together. The Irishman just kept smiling and told me confidently to just wait and see what happens when the smell hit the fan. He went about his business as if nothing had happened and would tell me no more about his plans. This was the biggest event to hit Campbell Avenue fish dock since Pete Ambrose's deckhand from his trawler *Tordo* found his common-law wife in bed with another man and cut her throat. And he was sentenced to hang.

The trial was a big event and everybody was buzzing about it when the big day arrived. When Joe's Port Corporation constable witness hit the stand and began giving his testimony, it was obvious that he was contradicting himself as well as Bob. This did not go over well with the judge, who became agitated with a witness he accused of having little regard for the truth. When Larry's lawyer accused the constable of being involved in a conspiracy and informed him of the potential sentence he could receive for this act the constable stood up and dropped dead in the witness box. This caused quite a stir and created an enormous measure of confusion. Everyone in the courtroom was now aware that there was a conspiracy hatched to get Magee. The judge recessed the trial, and when he reconvened the court, the charges were dropped and the trial ended. The writeup in the press did not enhance B.C. Packers' reputation, and both Joe and Bob were in the doghouse. I made a point of reminding Ken Fraser, but I was rebuffed by the angry little fat man. He was in no mood to discuss the matter when I advised him that Larry was contemplating a lawsuit to teach Joe and Bob a more substantial lesson.

This attempt to railroad Larry was almost the last straw for Joe. The sun was now setting for him, but the pompous ass did not yet know it. He went about his business with airs as if nothing had happened. At this point he was my friend again, while Bob was on the back burner for the time being. Joe was like a chameleon, changing his colours to suit every situation. One morning at about ten a.m., sometime after the big trial, I met Joe on the dock. He as all dressed up in as usual in his best blue suit with a fine red rosebud in his lapel, and his shoes shone so that you could see his reflection in them. "Guess what, Norman?" he asked me.

"Joe, what's the big deal?"

"I'm getting a promotion today," he replied with a haughty swagger. "I'm going to run the big new plant B.C. Packers is building in Steveston," he confided as he puffed himself up again. "I've got orders to be there at eleven thirty a.m., so I have to get going now. I'll tell you all about it later."

At one p.m., I ran into Joe again in the parking lot. His face was white as snow. He looked at me and blurted out, "Norman, I just got fired. What do you think about that? I worked for them like a slave for more than fifteen years and now I'm looking for a job. You give the best years of your life and they toss you out the door. Just like that."

About a month later I got a phone call from Joe. He was working for B.C. Packers again at the new plant in Steveston but, instead of wearing a blue suit and a red rose in his lapel, he had on white coveralls, gumboots and a well-worn hat jammed on his head. He had the tally man's job there and kept it until he retired.

OF SEA LICE AND LIEUTENANT-GOVERNORS

I first encountered the Neish family in the late 1920s. Their large house was located at the edge of the forest fronting the grassy flats that spread out from the east side of the beautiful Seymour River in North Vancouver. They built their own substantial house in stages over a number of years while they occupied it. For many years, the only access to the house was at the back door because there were no front stairs. They were a very earthy family who lived with the bare essentials and served plain but wholesome fare.

Angus Neish told me a story when we were sitting in my office enjoying a wee drop of malted brew. It seems a woman living near the Neish residence was in the habit of dropping in from time to time to while away an afternoon. She was also partial to highland brew and often brought a bottle with her to repay her genial hosts. Money was hard to come by in those days, but one afternoon she arrived with a couple of bottles of whisky. When it came time for her to depart for home, she forgot the Neish residence did not have a set of front stairs. She stepped out and nose-dived into the high grass that was growing where the stairs should have been located. It was a unfortunate incident, but because she was completely relaxed from her libations she suffered no serious injuries. However, the shock of the fall through the air and the subsequent landing in the weeds scared the hell out of her. While she picked burrs out of her hair and wiped the dirt from her nose and forehead she screamed out choice remarks about people who did not have enough sense to provide a set of stairs on the front of their house. Insults flew as she left in a huff on unsteady legs to weave an erratic path through the woods towards her own home. She paused in a clearing to vow that she was going to sue as soon as her aching back allowed her to get to town to see a lawyer.

For a few days after the incident, the Neish family wondered if the woman was really going to make good on her threats. Four days passed and a message was sent to the estranged woman to invite her to a party and let bygones be bygones. She readily accepted the invitation, and by a happy reunion the air was cleared. A couple of pieces of shiplap were nailed over the front entrance to prevent a repeat performance when the happy neighbour again departed for home. Angus acknowledged that it was careless of them to have left an abrupt dropoff from their front door. His family had been quite upset at the thought of facing a lawsuit. However, the facts were, the woman had come visiting regularly for many years and she had always previously arrived and departed via the back stairs. The whole Neish family had been shocked when she got up and abruptly stepped out the unused doorway. Fortunately the woman was not badly hurt and only suffered a temporary loss of dignity.

I never met the whole Neish clan. I was only slightly acquainted with the family patriarch, who was a tall man of enormous girth. I never met Roderick, the eldest son. He vanished from his fishing boat while commercially fishing for crabs at the Sand Heads outside the mouth of the Fraser River. His body was never recovered, so nobody knew what happened to him. Angus swore he was murdered by somebody from one of the trawlers that dragged the same ground for bottom fish. There was bad blood between Rod and another man who worked the same area. Rod's crab traps tangled in a dragger's net and caused a good of trouble before they could be removed. Threats were made but nobody paid much attention to them. Angus swore to his dying day that somebody murdered Rod and that he would not rest until he found the killer. Several boats worked that area, so he figured it was only a matter of time until the truth would come out. Angus felt that such a dark deed could not be contained. There was never a time when Angus had a bit of highland cheer under his belt that he did not declare that he knew who did it but could not prove it. The police gave up on the case from the very beginning. There was really nothing to go on, and it became the tragic story of another lost fisherman.

Angus, who died in 2000, searched for the answer to his brother's disappearance all his days without solving the mystery. It does seem strange that a sturdy young man in his late teens would just vanish from his vessel without a trace. The boat remained anchored on the fishing gear. The engine was still in idle when the search party arrived. The weather was clear and ideal for the work he was engaged in. If there was a confrontation, all evidence of any violence was completely erased. By now it is a certainty that nobody will ever know what happened on the fateful day when Roderick Neish vanished.

I knew Angus and Elgin (Scotty) Neish, the two remaining brothers, very well. For many years I bought the trolled salmon Angus caught with the *Seymour Lass*. His troller was a sturdy vessel, forty feet in length, that he built himself on a grid adjacent to the mouth of the Seymour River. He fished by himself. He would arrive on a regular basis with eight to ten thousand pounds of mixed trolled salmon during the five-month season. He always sold his fish without asking the price, and we never had a complaint with his settlement in all the years he delivered his catch to us.

The two Neish brothers were absolute opposites. Angus was a dark, well-built fellow just under six feet. He was quiet, soft spoken and a deep thinker who seemed able to solve any problem. Scotty, on the other hand, was a blond giant with bright blue eyes. His great size made him appear shorter than his six feet plus height. He was gregarious and vocal in his opinions about government, the Department of Fisheries and the political agenda. Scotty was a staunch socialist. Nobody ever won an argument with him or a political debate. He was strongly opinionated and firm in his determination to establish his point of view. He was also at the top of the hierarchy that controlled the fishermen's union. I think it is safe to say he was one of the more radical members of that left-wing organization. In his early years, Scotty fished for salmon in season on company boats. In winter he fished for Dungeness crabs with his own boat out of Victoria, B.C. He lived in Victoria in a home that was next door to the lieutenant-governor's mansion in Oak Bay. The approximate location of his house to the lieutenant governor's official residence resulted in some conflict. Scotty parked his beat-up truck that smelled of old crab bait with two or three traps in need of repair right in front of his house. Scotty was completely out of step with the decorum that had been established in Oak Bay by his snobby fellow residents, which led to some offers to purchase his home.

The irony in the situation was not lost on Scotty, who revelled in the opportunity to tell about his adventures. He laughed uncontrollably telling me about the sunny summer afternoon the lieutenant-governor was holding a garden party on his beautiful estate. Scotty decided it was time to replace the shake roof on his own home. The garden party was in full swing with an elegantly dressed crowd strolling about the grounds when Scotty began shovelling the worn-out shakes from his roof. A startled lieutenant-governor observed Scotty at work in his grey Stanfields underwear, heavy wool fisherman's pants and hip waders folded down below his knees. He quickly held a conference with his aides and then dispatched a courier with a request that Scotty postpone his roof repairs and get off the roof until the garden party was over. In order to keep the peace, Scotty complied with the lieutenant-governor's wishes.

Scotty loved to tell stories about his august neighbour. Each year on New Year's Day there was open house at the lieutenant-governor's estate. The idea was that citizens could come and pay their respects by having a drink, circulate with the hoi polloi and depart with dignity. Scotty and a few of his fishermen friends would spruce up to attend the affair. He would roar with laughter while telling how he and his friends quickly monopolized the drinks and trays of finger food while dignified guests looked on in horror. The bar would quickly close until the unwelcome revellers departed the scene so that more refined citizenry could be served. Scotty was particularly amused by the fact that Premier W.A.C. Bennett never failed to offer him a broad smile and a tip of the homburg whenever their paths crossed. He was never certain whether Bennett's salute was to ridicule him or to wish him a good day. Scotty deferred to no man. He was not impressed by the elite who basked in social affairs and he scorned official protocol. Although he was offered much more for his home than it was worth, Scotty would not sell and remained there until he died.

Angus was also a socialist, but he had a much different personality. He was a thoughtful man who measured his words carefully and he claimed, while his brother Scotty had a good heart, which everyone knew, his mouth often got him into trouble. In his later years, because of his strong opinions, Scotty found it difficult to get a berth on a commercial fishing vessel. He joined Angus fishing on the *Seymour Lass* and began a long working relationship with Angus fishing crabs and prawns.

The Neish brothers were the only fishermen that I knew who fished successfully for these two shellfish for such a long time. Except for repairs and a couple of weeks off around Christmas each year, they arrived on schedule every second week from Knight Inlet with eight to twelve thousand pounds of crabs and four to six thousand pounds of prawns. This was no easy task. They had to haul their fishing gear up island to Kelsey Bay and load it on the *Seymour Lass* and transport it to their fishing grounds at the head of Knight Inlet. They remained on the grounds there in the *Seymour Lass* fishing for crabs and prawns on a daily basis. The catch was kept alive in the sea until there was enough product to be carried via the *Seymour Lass* to Kelsey Bay, where it was loaded into their large truck and transported more than one hundred miles in the cool of the night to Nanaimo. Then it took a ferry ride to Horseshoe Bay and the last twenty-five miles to our plant in Vancouver. This was an arduous schedule and a difficult way to make a living. The Neish brothers had the area at the head of Knight Inlet all to themselves for many years. It was hard work and long hours without sleep to bring their catch to Vancouver and then return to the fishing grounds for a repeat performance. I wonder how many fishermen would have stayed with it for one trip, never mind for twenty years.

Twice each month they arrived at Campbell Avenue with a full load of shellfish. The crabs had to be alive when the truck arrived at the wharf. During those years, the crabs and prawns were very large. The crabs averaged better than thirty pounds to the dozen — a two-and-one-half-pound average. It is a strange fact that the prawns were the largest size just before the New Year, averaging at nine to ten per pound. After the New Year the prawns vanished for a couple of months only to reappear at the much smaller size of fourteen to sixteen per pound. They would get larger each trip after that until again at the end of the year, when some were as large as four to five per pound.

I remember well the day Angus and Scotty arrived with their prawns and about twelve hundred pounds of large crabs. My brother Ed was kibitzing with the Neishes when Angus remarked that these were the largest crabs they had ever caught. He figured that some of them would weigh over four pounds. Ed turned to scoff at Angus and declare he never saw a crab that weighed more than three and a half pounds. He went on to add that he would produce a bottle of Scotch for every crab that weighed over four pounds.

"I'll take you up on that," Angus remarked dryly with a grin on his face.

"Scotty, give that one over there to Norman for weighing."

I weighed in the crab at four and a quarter pounds. I advised Ed that he was stuck for a bottle of Scotch whisky. By then Angus had two more crabs picked out for me to weigh. One of them weighed in at four pounds nine ounces, and the other one weighed in at four pounds eleven ounces.

By then Ed had enough and said, "Never mind weighing anymore, because you're only going to get two bottles no matter how many crabs you have that are over four pounds." There were laughs all around. It takes a very large crab to weigh in at four pounds but five pounders have been taken in B.C. and were common in Alaska when the Dungeness crab fishery opened there in the 1950s. Ed made good on his promise and he arrived shortly with two bottles of the best he could buy.

We went upstairs to my office and in the course of the afternoon the two bottles were drained. The Neish brothers appeared to be in fair shape when they left to go home. Angus looked no worse for wear; Scotty was a bit noisy but seemed steady on his hefty legs — he weighed about two hundred and seventy-five pounds. Suddenly there were large thumping noise and a tremendous crash at the foot of the stairs. "My God," my wife, Kathleen, shouted. "Call the ambulance. Scotty has fallen down the stairs."

From the bottom of the steep wooden staircase, a faint voice called out, "Don't call the ambulance. Don't call the ambulance. I'm okay."

When we arrived at the foot of the stairs to inspect the situation, Scotty was standing as steady as a rock. He claimed he had no injuries. It is hard to believe that almost three hundred pounds of meat and bone could tumble down twenty steep stairs without getting damaged. The two brothers departed for North Vancouver where they stayed until their next trip. Scotty only went home to Victoria every other trip for about three days. Fourteen days later, the boys arrived with another big load of shellfish and Scotty's big laugh.

Angus spoke in great detail about the problems they encountered while attempting to keep their product alive until they had a large enough catch to make the trip to the marketplace. The sand fleas, sea lice and dogfish were the biggest problem. Sand fleas and sea lice act like ants do on land. Dogfish, with their razor-sharp teeth, continually slashed holes into the large net pounds that held the live prawns. To avoid the sand fleas, lice and dogfish, the net pounds were suspended midway between the surface and the sea bottom. This kept away the sand fleas but not all of the sea lice. By continually mending holes in the net, they kept the dogfish at bay. The crabs were kept in wire bags that held about two hundred and twenty-five pounds of live creatures. There were no problems with the dogfish, because they could not penetrate the galvanized iron wire. However, the crabs had to be suspended at least fifteen feet from the sea bottom to avoid the sand fleas and most of the sea lice. The crabs were tightly packed into the wire bags to keep them immobile and prevent them from eating each other. Because they could not move, the sea lice and sand fleas penetrated their vitals through any body opening to eat them alive. On the sea bottom they could destroy a two-hundred-twenty-five-pound bag of live crabs in less than thirty-six hours, leaving nothing but empty shells. The Neish brothers kept busy avoiding these problems, but still lost more than ten percent of their catch to these pests. Any time spent away from working their traps saw them on the jump inspecting and mending the large net pounds containing prawns and inspecting bags of crabs for damage. No doubt the Neish boys were ready for their bunks at the end of the day, right after getting the news and weather report on their radio.

Long-line fishermen, hook-and-line fishing for halibut, cod, block cod, and more, all have the same problem with those sea pests. As soon as the fish are hooked and become immobile, they are attacked through any opening into their bodies. The sand fleas and sea lice enter the body cavities to feast on their prey. Some of the fish die before the lines are pulled up. About ten percent of these fish are discarded because they are not fit for human consumption. Dogfish will also attack these immobile fish and bite chunks out of them. Some shark-damaged fish can be salvaged and sold at a discount. Sick and immobile fish are soon disposed of by these scavengers so that the ocean is continually cleansed.

Scotty's outlook on the fishing business was that all fish buyers were taking advantage of the fishermen. In my opinion, it worked just as often the other way, so it was a sawoff. Sometimes I found Scotty hard to put up with because of his cynical remarks about all buyers. Angus would repeatedly caution him to tone down his remarks, but mostly Scotty carried on with his degrading chatter. He always had a smile on his face but that did not dull the needle. I was fond of both brothers and did business with them for many years. We had similar backgrounds, growing up around the harbour and waterfront, and starting out in the fishing industry at very young ages.

Occasionally, Scotty's remarks got to me, and I took them personally. One morning after he cautioned me three or four times not to cheat them on the weights, I got fed up and told Scotty to weigh their own damn crabs and stalked away in a huff. Scotty took over the weighing in of their catch with a startled look on his face. Soon he was chattering away with every fisherman who passed by. He knew them all and enjoyed talking with them. The trouble was, he wasn't paying attention to the weights on the crabs as they passed over the scale. When they had unloaded and washed down their truck, Scotty handed Angus the tally and they departed for North Vancouver. Angus had decided to clear the air and depart with Scotty to return in the morning for their settlement. The next morning Angus arrived without Scotty to settle up for their delivery. For a long time he sat quietly without saying a word. Then finally he spoke up to inform me that the weights on his crabs were way out of line.

"Don't complain to me about the weights, Angus, your brother did all the weighing in."

Angus turned red and answered, "I figure we had twelve thousand pounds of crabs, but Scotty only shows about eight thousand pounds on our tally." A sickly smile on his face, he said, "I guess if you insist, we will have to bite the bullet and take our medicine. Damn that Scotty and his big mouth!"

I liked Angus and Scotty in spite of the fact that he pissed me off with his disparaging comments. I said to Angus, "Give me the tally and I'll go down to see Nancy about your weights. Maybe she can figure it out." Nancy Spears was our forewoman in charge of the shellfish department. I told Nancy about the screwup with the weights and asked her opinion on the matter. Without hesitation she replied there were twenty tubs of crabs and they averaged around six hundred pounds each. She pointed out that when she noticed that Scotty was gabbing with every fisherman who passed by, she had figured that he'd mess up his tally sheet. So she kept close watch on the tubs of crabs as they entered the processing area.

I walked back upstairs to the office and told Angus the good news but I also informed him I was not taking chances on a loss, so I could only pay him for eleven thousand five hundred pounds of crabs.

He thanked me very much, saying I was more than fair about the matter. He also advised me that in future Scotty would not be weighing in any of their catch. A couple of drinks and a handshake later Angus departed with a smile on his face. Before he left he asked me not to be too hard on Scotty because, although he was an agitator, he meant well. "Don't pay much attention to him, Norman, he's a bit hard to take at times, but just let it pass because he isn't going to change."

In mid-March one year, the Neish brothers failed to show up with a delivery. I wondered what could have delayed them. The boys could generally cope with minor problems on the grounds with their gear, and there had never been a problem with the old engine in the *Seymour Lass*. We heard nothing, and by noon when they failed to show we figured they must have broken down somewhere along their journey. The women in our crab department were waiting to process the expected six tons of crabs. The Chinese merchants who were waiting for fresh prawns were beginning to return to their stores, resigned to the fact there would be no fresh prawns for sale out of our plant on that day.

Crabs that were delivered to us were butchered alive and cooked as quickly as their caprice (back shell) was torn off and the guts were removed. We had six steam cookers that each held one hundred and twenty-five pounds of cleaned crab sections for each fifteen-minute cooking time. When cooked, the sections had to be chilled in ice water and them dumped onto tables to finish cooking. No ice was put on them until they were completely cold. If the newly cooked sections were covered with ice, it would hold the heat in and cause them to sour. After they were completely cold, the clean sections were covered with ice to keep them fresh for further processing. Crabs that are butchered alive and cooked immediately produce twenty- to twenty-five-percent recovery in meat. Crabs that die in warm conditions but are not spoiled have a poor recovery of fifteen to eighteen percent and the meat is mushy. We iced crabs overnight if they were too lively because they were dangerous for our workers to handle. A frisky four-pound crab can latch on to a finger or a hand and do some real damage. Experienced workers who knew how to handle crabs were seldom bitten. The wisdom is, it is always the crab under the crab you are picking up that will get you. Crabs that are real lively can be heavily iced down until they become dormant. These can be held for up to a week. When they warm up, they are still too slowed down to be dangerous. The meat from these crabs comes out of the shell in first-class condition.

It takes an experienced crew to produce quality crab meat. On our best days we produced and sold more than fifteen hundred pounds of fresh crab meat. It is a very touchy product that can spoil in no time. Once we kept twenty-five pounds on ice for twenty days. When it was tested by the Department of Fisheries and Oceans, it proved to be in perfect condition. On the other hand, if crab meat is handled under unsanitary conditions or is wrapped in a package where it can heat up, it will spoil in less than four hours.

Most of the stores in Vancouver that sold fresh crab meat to the public bought their crab meat from our plant. They could always depend on the fact that our fresh crab meat, if properly kept, would last more than a week. Some stores could sell one hundred and fifty pounds on a Friday and Saturday. At three dollars and fifty cents per pound, they had a big investment to protect. They required crab meat that was absolutely in the best condition possible. I personally never ate any crab meat that did not come out of our plant. If it wasn't ours, I declined to eat it under any circumstance. I knew what the other companies were selling. So did the trade.

By one thirty in the afternoon, the Neish brothers had not shown up, so I went to tell the crew to go home because they had already finished processing all of the crabs that were left in our plant. Our crab workers, who were all women, belonged to the fishermen's union. At that time we had the only unionized crab workers in Vancouver. We could not afford to keep our workers standing around doing nothing. As I walked out on the dock outside our shellfish plant, I saw the Neish truck come around the corner by the ice house. I rushed back in to tell the workers to get ready as quickly as they could to handle the crabs that now waited to be unloaded in front of our plant.

When I walked out to talk with Angus about the details of his late arrival, he seemed depressed.

"I guess we're screwed" were the first words that came out of his mouth. He went on to add that the crabs were dying off and that they would have to get rid of them in a hurry. "Norman, help us out. We'll take whatever price you can manage." Scotty never said a word and was avoiding eye contact with me. I knew by their odd behaviour that they had intended to deliver their crabs elsewhere and for some reason were turned down so they had returned to our plant.

Finally Angus came clean and blurted out, "We were heading for Seattle because Scotty made a deal to get twenty-two cents per pound U.S. down there because they are so short of crabs. This would have given us about one thousand dollars more on this load than you pay us, so I decided to go for it. To cut the story short, because of Scotty's affiliation with the Communist Party, we were denied entry to the United States. You can imagine the rest of the story, Norman. We were detained for a long time and by the time we got back on the highway to Vancouver, the crabs were beginning to die off. We'll take whatever you'll you pay us for the survivors and chalk it up to experience. One thing more. In the future, I won't be taking anymore advice from Scotty. You can bank on that." For once Scotty had nothing to say.

"It's mid-afternoon, the weather is warm and those crabs have to be processed immediately even if it means overtime for our workers."

"I know, I know," he muttered. "So give us what you can, because if we hold them overnight, half of them will be worthless by morning."

"How about seventeen cents per pound?" I offered. "Anything dead has to go in the garbage bin."

Angus looked at me, "You mean to say you will give us seventeen cents per pound?"

"Yes, Angus," I answered. "I hate to kick a man when he's down." The crabs were quickly unloaded and the women worked furiously to run them through the cookers. Most of the load were still alive but they were getting sleepy. If a crab dies under ice where it is really kept cold, the meat will still come out in good condition. If a crab dies under warm conditions — a hot day with no ice — the meat turns into mush. It is still edible but is a low-grade product that is sold at a reduced price to a lower-grade customer.

After the crabs were unloaded, the rig was scrubbed out and the Neish brothers departed without their usual banter. The women worked until eight p.m. to get all the crabs processed and then we selected fifteen hundred pounds of whole cooks to speed up the work. We could always sell that many large whole cooked crabs in a day without any trouble. A couple of us had to wait around until nine thirty to make sure the crabs had cooled enough to be iced down.

The next day Angus showed up around two p.m. with a bag under his arm that contained three bottles of Scotch. "Take down two bottles to the girls," he directed. "I sure appreciate what they did for me yesterday." After the third bottle had been uncorked and we had a couple of shots, Angus thanked me for not taking advantage of him. He confided that they had been prepared to accept eight or nine cents per pound. After the third drink, he told me I was a straight shooter. After the fourth glass of Scotch, he told me that he had not known I was such a nice guy.

"Where's Scotty?" I asked.

"I thought it would be better if he went home to Victoria for three or four days," he said with a laugh.

I thought Angus should have phoned me to let me know they were going to sell to the Americans so I didn't have to keep the crab crew waiting. I had to pay the crew a minimum of four hours whenever they were called in whether they worked or not. However, I let it go. There was no point in stirring the pot.

Generally, Angus was a down-to-earth person with a good head who could be depended on to do the right thing. He never got excited and he was a completely honest man. I enjoyed my relationship with him and now that he's gone I miss him a great deal. He and his brother were never dull.

Our salesman Larry Magee hailed from Alberta. He was always bragging how everything in Alberta was bigger and better. How the average Albertan could down a bottle of rye whisky in one pull without batting an eye. Someone on the dock offered to bet Larry that he could not down a bottle of rye in one pull.

"Why sure I can," Larry bragged.

That person called his bluff by producing a bottle of rye and setting it on the desk in front of him. Larry was a big Irish lug, over six feet tall and weighed about two hundred and thirty pounds. He took hold of the bottle and sure enough he pulled it down without pausing for a moment. He won the bet in front of an astonished audience. He collected his money and made it back to our office on his own power. He then flopped into a chair and sat gasping for air with his mouth opening and closing like a fish just pulled from the water. Someone on the dock told me about the situation, so I rushed into the office to see if he was still alive. Larry looked pale and he was gasping for breath. The office staff thought he was having a heart attack as they fluttered about him uncertain about his condition.

Just then Angus and Scotty arrived and came in to look Larry over. Scotty remarked, "By God, I think he's having a heart attack. Maybe we should call an ambulance."

Angus stood there with a smile on his face and said, "I believe this man is dead drunk." When informed that Larry had drained the bottle in one pull, Angus said in his slow drawl, "That was a pretty big order, Norman. Perhaps you better send someone for a quart of milk. We'll make him drink it, and that will bring him around."

We got the quart of milk in short order and Scotty produced a large cardboard box. Then the ordeal began. Angus forced Larry to down a portion of the milk and just as quickly like a whale he spouted it up into the box. The process went on until Larry had been forced to drink and throw up the whole quart of milk. I believe a good portion of the rye came up with the milk and Larry slowly began to recover. He still sat there as pale as a ghost, the sweat still beading on his forehead, but at least he no longer gasped for air. After the milk was gone the process began all over again with cups of black coffee. Larry protested the cure but to no avail as Angus poured cup after cup of the black liquid into him. It all ended up in the cardboard box.

By about the fifth cup that was poured into him, Larry was able to keep the coffee down and to hold his head up. He still looked pretty green but it appeared he was going to make it. "I'm okay," he offered weakly.

Angus declared, "He's going to be all right now. He didn't shit himself so he's out of danger. A man is never in trouble until he has shit himself," he stated with that dry grin on his face. That was vintage Angus.

Angus continued to deliver us his catch for several more years until he decided to retire. He came in one day and declared he would retire in the coming fall. He was giving his boat, truck and gear to Scotty for nothing. Scotty was going to continue on fishing because he couldn't afford to retire. Angus owned property in North Vancouver, and with lots there going for two hundred thousand bucks a piece he was set.

Scotty took on a new partner who was even more of a radical socialist than Scotty. In my opinion, the new partner was stupid, greedy and a no-good SOB. I didn't believe that partnership would last. After Angus handed over everything to Scotty, that was the end of deliveries to our plant. I was surprised by the fact that two staunch union supporters preferred to sell their fish to a non-union plant. Once or twice Scotty's new partner came over and offered to deliver his fish to us if we paid five cents per pound more than they were getting from the non-union company. We were not that hard up, so I declined the offer. Eventually I lost contact with Scotty. I was sure that Scotty would be on the short end of the stick with his new partner, but it was no concern of mine so I ignored the situation. Angus declined to discuss the matter and I respected his wishes.

Scotty was about five years younger than Angus but he died about five years ahead of Angus. He had a bad leg with a wound that would never heal. The story I heard was that in his youth Scotty had fallen on a steel rod sticking out of a boom stick, and the hole in his leg would never heal properly. This was a terrible sore that Scotty suffered with all of his life. Once he showed it to me, and it was a terrible sight, with the bone being exposed. Scotty was a good friend, though I didn't see much of him in later years. I believe his new partner, another big union man, turned Scotty against us. I always felt bad for him because of the way he suffered through life with his bad leg. Like his brother, he was a good man who worked hard and had great compassion for his fellow man. So the best of luck to you, Scotty Neish, wherever you are.

I always considered Angus to be a close friend and I would like to believe he thought of me in the same way. He and his wife visited us at our home from time to time. Sometimes Angus arrived with Scotty in tow. Angus and his wife were both quite reserved, but when they showed up with Scotty it was a free-for-all as old times were rehashed as glasses were refilled. After he retired, Angus came to the dock a few times each year to see me and we spent whole afternoons discussing old times and the fishing industry, or at least what was left of it. He would shake his head and declare, "Just imagine, Norman, in less than fifty years it has all gone to hell. There is nothing left of it. I often wondered what all those educated guys in the Department of Fisheries were doing measuring the fish all the time, taking samples to tell their ages and counting scales. What a waste of time and money. It was all for nothing. Do you think the resource will ever recover? Oh, well, it doesn't matter to me because I'm not going to be around to find out."

Angus failed to show up at all during the year 2000, so I phoned his home several times but nobody answered my call. He was about three years older than me so by then he was about eighty-five years of age. One morning I read in the paper that Angus had died. When I phoned his number, I was told that Angus had been in and out of the hospital most of the year because of heart problems. I was invited to the private service but did not attend because I preferred to keep my own memories.

CHARLIE WALCOTT AND THE ANNIE TUCK

Charlie Walcott was a personality unlike any other I encountered in my sixty-plus years of working in the fishing industry. Witty, charming and profane, he possessed a loud rasping voice that could wipe barnacles off a rocky ledge. He had a terrible temper when he was angered, but I only saw it displayed once or twice in the years I knew him. His short-term circumstances never interfered with his zest for life. He was the same man, whether he was flush at the end of the fishing season or broke after blowing all his money by Christmas of each year. He had a grin on his face and a razor-edged wit that he used wickedly on any wisecracker who got in his way.

Charlie should have been a politician because of his sharp wit and generous share of shrewdness. Charlie was a well-read man who had a twinkle in his eye and a hearty laugh that always seemed close to erupting. He was an old pro in the fishing business and he felt qualified to address novices if he noticed something amiss on their vessel. He took great delight in explaining to greenhorns the correct way of setting up gear, how lures and spoons should be fished, and the boat speed necessary to maximize the working action of each piece of gear. His advice was offered sincerely with an abundance of humour and goodwill. The result was that he was immensely popular and a well-known character up and down the coast.

If anyone had a right to carry a chip on his shoulder or regard life with a miserable disposition, it was Charlie. Charlie's legs were completely withered from a childhood bout with polio. He compensated some with a well-developed upper body. In spite of his terrible handicap and the excruciating pain that often accompanied it, Charlie had no time to be bitter. He moved over the docks and onto decks of various vessels to visit and chat with his friends, propelling himself on crutches. In spite of his handicap, Charlie would run a fish packer for one of the companies or take a West Coast troller on a share basis and go fishing for the season.

A few days after New Year's, 1962, Charlie arrived at Campbell Avenue and clumped on up the stairs into my office. As soon as I saw him I figured he had come to promote a winter fish-buying proposition. He came into the office, propped his crutches against my desk and sized up my mood with a devilish smile. Seeing I was in a good humour he opened up with a proposal to take the *Annie Tuck* up north for a trip after ling cod, red snapper and rock fish. It was a hell of a time of year to go up north to persuade the Indian fishermen there to go out fishing. However, Charlie was broke and he had to raise some cash just to keep going. The unemployment insurance plan that had just been implemented by the government had put an end to a fishing season in the winter months. It was hard to motivate crews to fish or pack during cold weather when they could stay home and collect pogey.

"Where are you going to get a crew to go out with you at this time of year?" I asked.

"Oh," he answered, "I have some Indians lined up to go. All I need is some fish buying money and a stake for ice, fuel and grub."

I was still a bit skeptical and said, "How do you know they'll fish in this cold weather?"

Grinning at me he replied, "Trust me, I know they'll fish because they're anxious like me to get some spending money."

I thought about it for a while and then said, "Would seven thousand dollars put the show on the road?" I figured hard expenses would include five hundred dollars for fuel, five hundred dollars for groceries and two hundred dollars for ice. At six cents a pound for snappers and twelve cents a pound for ling cod, the fifty-eight hundred dollars left for fish buying should leave enough to put forty thousand pounds of fish aboard the *Annie Tuck*.

"Make it eight thousand or a little more to be on the safe side," he countered. I had no intention of paying for Charlie's debts in town, but I begrudgingly increased the amount to seventy-five hundred dollars. "Okay," he said, "I'll be iced up and ready to leave by tomorrow night."

I knew a part of the buying money would go on Charlie's immediate debts. Though he was always good for his debts, he was in the habit of squaring up whenever he was flush with a new deal. I also knew that Charlie was a resourceful man who had a good relationship with the fishermen in various First Nations communities. Charlie's father had been a missionary at Cooper Island, and although Charlie spent much of his youth being raised by his aunt in Victoria, he spent his summers in Indian country. When he was fishing or packing, his crew members all came from Cooper Island. Charlie was in the habit of making three or four trips packing in the winter to carry him over before he got ready for a season of trolling for salmon. He could pay off his debts quickly and live it up for a couple of days between trips, provided he kept away from the crowd of partying friends he had accumulated around his headquarters in Victoria. They helped him burn up his money. Charlie was a big spender because wine, women and song were costly recreation.

This annual arrangement over many winters was satisfactory for both of us. Charlie made money and we got fresh fish to sell at a time of year when there wasn't much of it around. Charlie was a good fisherman with a lot of experience in handling fish. The ling cod, snappers and rock fish he delivered always looked like they had just come out of the water, and the weights were always right on, so the fish was easy to sell. There were a few times when Charlie blew some of the money before he left port. He never bothered telling me until he phoned from Port Hardy to beg me to transfer him a further three or four thousand dollars of buying money. At times I got pretty mad about it and gave him plenty of hell, but what other option did I have?

Charlie was at home on both coasts of Vancouver Island and in many small ports throughout the Gulf Islands. When he wasn't visiting by boat, he drove around the territory in his car. His partying escapades were legendary among fishermen. He would enter our office with a cheery smile and begin to beguile us with tales of his adventures between loud outbursts of laughter. Once after leaving Sooke after an all-night wingding on his way back to Victoria, he was stopped on the highway by a Mountie in the early morning hours. It seems the officer detected his car weaving in the lane and so he asked Charlie to get out and walk the yellow line. "I complied with the order and walked up the yellow line and back to my car with the use of my crutches," he said. "By then the young officer was a bit chagrined. When I finished, I handed my crutches to the cop and said, 'Now if you think that's easy, you try it.' He made no attempt to duplicate my walk. What the heck would he do with a man with useless legs in any case?" he said with a laugh. "I'm a damned nuisance to them and a lot of trouble they don't want to take on. After a lecture of sorts, he let me go but followed me for about five miles before he turned off." He chuckled. "I know damn well he couldn't have walked that yellow line with my crutches." Knowing Charlie as well as I did, I'm sure the horseman was just as eager to get away from Charlie as Charlie was relieved to get off the hook.

He told me of a visit he made to a friend's place on a private island in the Gulf. "I tied up at his dock and when he came down to the boat for a visit we proceeded to drink to our friendship, our health, to the women in our lives and for many other reasons. Some tourists pulled up and tied their boat alongside but they ignored our offer to be sociable, so we carried on without them. I must admit our partying was wild to say the least. We spent a couple of days commuting between my friend's house and my boat with loud singing long into the night. I suppose the tourists got fed up with us and got in touch with the Mounties. The next morning, the Mounties appeared in their patrol boat and arrived at the house while we were still partying. They arrested us for disturbing the peace. They confiscated the rest of the liquor and bustled us down to their boat and took us to Victoria where we were booked into jail. Just like that, if you please, without listening to anything we said. They advised, 'Tell it to the judge in the morning.' What annoyed us the most is that the officers helped themselves to our booze but wouldn't give us a drop. By the time we came up in front of the judge we were still hung over and had burning throats. When the judge heard that the island and dock were both private property, he turned on the cops and asked them what was their purpose of arresting us on private property. He got his back up and ordered them to promptly return us back to the place they had arrested us. I asked the judge, 'What about all the good liquor they seized from us?' The judge wrote down the amount of refreshment that was confiscated and handed the officer in charge a slip with an order to replace it. We enjoyed the return trip because the officers had to stop at a liquor store and replenish our stock. On the trip back in the patrol boat we poured ourselves drinks liberally without so much as giving them a smell." Charlie ended that story laughing like a hyena. He was a man with dozens of stories to tell when he was in the mood and in good company.

The following winter, Charlie was back at Campbell Avenue with the usual proposition. I noticed he was smoking his own since he hauled out a package of tobacco and some papers. That was a signal that Charlie was broke since he smoked tailor-mades when he was flush. He struck a match to his fly and took a long pull on his cigarette before he spoke. "Joe Babcock said I can take the *Annie Tuck* out for a couple of months for the usual charter price of nine hundred dollars a month. I have an Indian crew lined up and I can ice her up and be ready to go in a couple of days."

I knew it was going to be impossible to say no, so I said, "Okay, Charlie we'll put up the money, but you promise you won't stop in Victoria for another big party before you leave for the fishing grounds."

Charlie agreed to curb the partying and gave me the usual spiel about minding the business end. He planned on fishing some and buying fish at various spots on the coast. Fourteen days later he was back at Campbell Avenue with more than forty thousand pounds of prime fish. Charlie's crew was loyal to him and he had the gift of the gab to motivate them to fish for him in the dead of winter. Just about the time when everyone in town was despairing of no fresh fish, Charlie would come in with his usual rasping laugh, with a full load in the *Annie Tuck*.

For some reason Charlie refused to take advantage of unemployment insurance. We thought he was too proud to do so. At that time, many fat cat fisherman, who made two or three hundred thousand dollars per year, applied for and received unemployment insurance in the winter months. Charlie, who I doubt ever made more than thirty thousand (mostly because he had no boat of his own, so had to split his share with the owner), went out fishing in the bleakest months. The fact that he was badly impaired with his useless legs and still managed to go out in freezing winter to do his job gained him a lot of respect from people in the fishing industry. Charlie also carried an extra crewman because he was restricted to dragging himself about the deck with his arms, so an extra share had to be paid out. Charlie steered the boat, navigated, looked after the engine, did the cooking and supervised the work with the fishing gear. On deck he was at a disadvantage with his handicap, although some said he crawled about giving orders like Captain Bligh when conditions were not to his liking. And with his booming voice and satirical wit, he could reach the crew with a tongue lashing when they were not pulling their weight. However, Charlie had a heart of gold and the same crew remained with him for many years.

Charlie was a hard-driving man on the fishing grounds, from four a.m. until dark. The crew took turns eating and mugging up, but most days they were still dressing and icing fish under lights before washing for supper. They were ready to hit their bunks by the time supper was over and the dishes were washed and put away. This was the last job of the day for the greenhorn on the crew. Charlie seldom ran into a harbour for the night but chose to let out a sea anchor and drift all night so he could be in position to fish the next day at first light. If a storm blew up, they battened down the hatches, threw out the sea anchor and drifted with the wind until the storm blew itself out. Drifting at night was a somewhat dangerous manoeuvre because many large freighters passed through the fishing grounds. A drifting troller was not always recognized on early radar sets. There were a few trollers that disappeared without a trace, their crews never to be heard from again. Others were damaged in near-sinking incidents. Fishermen could hear the engines of a passing freighter as their vessel was touched by the larger ship's wake. No freighter ever reported a collision, because they would have been held in port for weeks pending an investigation and settling insurance claims. Being tied up inactive in port was a costly business. The few freighters that were caught paid claims quickly but most kept on travelling on into the night without stopping.

A troller can seldom work salmon gear in winds that blow harder than thirty miles per hour. In summer on the West Coast of Vancouver Island there is a lot of calm, foggy weather and winds are not usually a problem. However, squalls blew in on the fishing fleet at any time of the season, forcing fishermen to seek shelter behind islands or in some safe harbour. Vessels caught too far offshore were forced to throw out their sea anchors and drift with the wind until they rode out the storm. Trollers were always looking for deck hands because some of the men could not stand the weather or were afraid of the risks, or just became fed up with the hard work or an unreasonable skipper.

Charlie, a good-humoured man, had an edge that sometimes caused him to get crabby with his workers. This temper would show itself if he thought the fish were not being handled correctly. He insisted that the salmon had to be dressed and iced in the hold immediately after being caught. There was no stopping for food and coffee or to rest while there was a round fish on deck. I purchased fifteen-thousand-pound lots of trolled (hook-and-line caught) salmon from Charlie without finding one number-two fish in the entire load. A good fisherman seldom has a bad fish, and Charlie never had any because he drove the crew to handle the fish properly. Since he paid his crew in shares, it was worth their while to put up with his nagging and complaining. Prime fish handled correctly meant extra money in each crewman's pocket.

The *Annie Tuck* was a fishing vessel originally built for sail, with a narrow, square stern. Charlie claimed she was the best sea boat he was ever aboard and he was in love with her. One day he said he would buy her from her owner, Joe Babcock. By this time Joe was well into his seventies and it would not be long before he would have to come ashore for good. Joe and Charlie had an informal relationship that allowed Charlie to charter the *Annie Tuck* for a few months of each year. During these months Charlie mostly packed or fished for Van Shell. Charlie averaged about two weeks per trip to the fishing grounds.

When I got to work in the morning, the *Annie Tuck*, having arrived in the middle of the night, was positioned in front of one of the loading cranes at Campbell Avenue. This was good news because Charlie brought in fresh fish during scarce periods. I'd climb down the steel ladder onto the deck. Usually, the crew was snoring away in the forecastle while Charlie was half awake in his sleeping bag in his bunk in the wheelhouse. His voice boomed out a loud greeting as he struggled out of his bunk. He never took off his wool pants or socks on board a fishing boat because of the effort it took to deal with his withered legs. He came into the galley from the wheelhouse on his crutches and buttoned a wool shirt on over his grey Stanfields underwear. He slipped fleece-lined slippers onto his useless feet and then lit the oil stove. He yelled at his crew to get up and then informed me he had a full load up to the hatch covers.

It was our routine for me to buy Charlie breakfast on the mornings of his arrivals. "You go ahead," he'd say, and I would climb the steel ladder from the vessel's deck until I reached the wharf above. Then it was Charlie's turn. First he heaved the crutches up onto the dock, then he went hand over hand up the ladder with his legs dangling behind until he reached the top. Then he struggled over the ten-by-ten-inch guardrail and reached for the crutches I was holding. I dared not assist him for fear of him getting sarcastic with me. I think his exact words would have been, "What in hell do you think you're doing?" I stood clear and left him to it.

In the Marine View coffee shop one morning, Charlie said that he had a load of nice fish that would be easy to sell. I was anxious to find out how he got back in so quickly with such a fine load. He looked at me with a big smile and answered, "You have to use Indian strategy when dealing with Indians. I'd never get anywhere if I urged them to go fishing in cold weather. They'd merely laugh at me. You have to make a game of it." He told me that when he arrived at the reserve, he handed out pop and chocolate bars to the kids. Then he offered the women prizes to the ones who caught the largest ling cod and the largest snapper. When they started bringing fish in trying to win a prize, he offered them a fair price in cash for the fish. Soon the women were making twenty or thirty dollars each, and it was not long before some of the men asked if they could join in to the game because they saw how much the women had to spend in the band store. It was not long before men, women and kids had joined in fishing. With two hundred people delivering from fifty to four hundred pounds of fish per day, it didn't take long to load the boat.

"We didn't get a chance to fish ourselves, because we were too busy weighing, icing and paying for the fish. At the end of each day, the big excitement was around who caught the largest fish for the daily prizes. Everybody had a good time and the band store was jammed with customers buying pop, chocolate bars, chips, biscuits and other grocery items," Charlie explained. "In the winters there are no other buyers around and there isn't much to do. Make it seem like work in dirty weather and nobody shows up; make it into a game with prizes and fun and everybody turns out."

That winter Charlie's second trip was of similar short duration, and just as he predicted, the Indians were waiting for him to come back to resume the festivities. Everybody got a big laugh when some of the women were found to be stuffing stones into their red snappers to make them heavier. The snappers were delivered in the round so it was an easy trick to pull off. Every day there was a good rivalry between the women and men to see which group the winning fish came from.

After the third trip, Charlie informed me that Joe Babcock wanted the charter money for the boat on that day. He asked me to deliver the money to an address he scribbled on the back of an envelope. When I arrived at the address, I discovered a black hole with no door but a dark staircase leading up in the pitch dark. This was on Main Street, next door to the police station. Halfway up the stairs, feeling my way in the darkness, I thought the hell with this and descended back to the sidewalk as quickly as I could without breaking my neck. I felt a bit uneasy about wandering around with nine hundred dollars in cash in my pocket in this neighbourhood, so I jumped in my car and left.

When I got back to Campbell Avenue, Charlie was waiting for me in the office. "What kind of wild goose chase was that you sent me on?" I asked. "There's nothing at that address but a black hellhole of a staircase going nowhere."

Charlie asked me to wait while he got cleaned up. He smiled at me and said, "I'll go as your bodyguard."

Obviously, Charlie had been there before and knew how to get in. When we arrived at the address, I followed Charlie up the dark staircase. At the landing at the top of the staircase we discovered a door without a handle. Charlie pounded on the door and there was a creak and a clank as someone opened a hatch in the steel door. "We have a parcel for Joe Babcock," Charlie explained. "Just a minute," a voice snapped as the lock on the hatch was shut. A few minutes later, the hatch opened again and the voice asked us to identify ourselves. After we replied, it closed again with a loud creaking sound. A few minutes later, a brilliant white light came on in the ceiling above the landing and we were being observed again through the hatch. Then we heard a series of locks being flipped and the steel door opened and we were allowed to enter into a hallway that led into a brilliantly lit room.

Three doors, one of them steel, led into a larger, well-lit space. The lights in the large room were so bright after the black stairwell that my eyes hurt at first. When they adjusted to the bright conditions, I noticed that we were in a room like a large dance hall packed with tables. Among the large crowd in the room were seven or eight men in police uniforms. I keep my eyes straight ahead and did not bother scrutinizing anyone. I had never seen bunny girls before, nor had I ever heard of them. But here they were with long ears, large half-exposed busts, long legs in high heels, and scanty outfits, each with a bustle that had a large fluffy white tail attached to it. I was in shock, but I kept my cool as we brushed by the girls and were led to a table in an alcove where Joe sat with a glass in front of him. A lady got up and left as we approached and stood appraising us from a distance.

"Hello, Joe," Charlie offered with a big smile.

"Have you got the money?" Joe replied in a curt manner.

"We have the money, Joe. Do you want it now?" Charlie answered.

"Sit down," Joe said. He nodded his head at the peroxide blonde who returned to sit at the table. Joe introduced Josie but he didn't bother introducing Charlie or me. He held out his hand for the money. I handed him the roll and he passed it on to Josie. She quickly tucked it into her voluptuous cleavage and sat smiling at Charlie and me.

"Are you not going to count it, Joe?" I asked.

"I know it's all there," he replied, with a cold smile. "What will you have to drink?" Both Charlie and I ordered Scotch and soda. Joe was sticking to rum. Josie waved to a bunny girl who took our order and delivered our drinks. We finished the drinks quickly and after some meaningless small talk we were on our way.

How Josie managed to operate such a large bootlegging palace right beside the police station wasn't really much of a mystery. The day Charlie and I entered, the premises were full of policemen. The police and prominent citizens in Vancouver obviously profited from the arrangement, because a joint of that ilk could not operate without protection from the establishment. Rumour had it that a tunnel connected the place to the police station.

Charlie knew every fisherman on the coast and stopped to talk with them wherever they congregated. One morning on his way along Campbell Avenue, Charlie stopped to talk with some fishermen who had arrived with a load of sea lion carcasses destined to provide feed for the mink industry. They hunted the animals with high-powered rifles but found the business unprofitable because so many of the wounded sea lions managed to get into the water, where they died and sank, in a very short time, to the bottom. Sea lions killed on shore were difficult to drag off with a heavy rope or wire because they got hung up between the rocks and driftwood when they were being winched in. "How much do you get for that meat?" he asked. The answer was ten cents a pound. Later Charlie came into my office and told me that he thought sea lion hunting could be lucrative because there were thousands of them on various sections of the coastline. "There ought to be a better way of hunting them," he declared.

On his next trip to the West Coast, Charlie questioned the Indians about sea lion hunting. He discovered that they ate sea lion meat when they managed to kill one, and that the carcasses would sink in less than ten minutes after the sea lions were killed in the water. They also told him it only took about five pounds of pull to keep the carcasses afloat. With knowledge gleaned from the Indians, he figured the sea lions would have to be struck with a harpoon before they were shot. The harpoon would be fastened to a large round float called a Scotchman, so the carcasses could be retrieved after the hunt was over.

"How are you going to get near them to place the harpoons?" I asked.

"Easy!" he exclaimed. "By chasing them into the water with the *Annie Tuck*. Once they are frightened off the reefs into the water, they swim away in panic. Sea lions can swim about twelve miles per hour. If you have a dory with an outboard motor that can do fifteen or twenty miles per hour, you can catch up to them. Once the chase begins they will not dive, so you can pull right alongside of them as they swim on the surface." Charlie reasoned that we needed a harpoon gun that had the harpoon fastened to a line and a float. Once they were harpooned, they could be dispatched with a load of buckshot or a rifle bullet in the head. After enough had been killed, it would be easy to pick up the floats and tow the carcasses to the mother ship. With bulls weighing up to two thousand pounds, it would not take long to get a boatload of meat.

I never gave sea lion hunting much of a thought because I figured it was a nutty proposition. However, Charlie showed up one day with a Greener harpoon gun he had borrowed from the federal Department of Fisheries. "With this gun we are going to kill a lot of sea lions for mink feed," he declared. A few days later he arrived and said, "It's a beautiful gun but it only shoots the harpoon about fifteen feet and that's not good enough." A week later he was back with a design for a new harpoon gun. His plan was to use my money to buy half a dozen First World War Lee-Enfield rifles that could be turned into harpoon guns. We bought six rifles for seventy-five bucks, and Charlie took them to a gunsmith friend of his to make the transformation. During the war, a cup was fastened to the muzzle of a Lee-Enfield, a grenade was placed in the cup, and blank shot could fire the grenade four hundred yards. Charlie figured a steel-shafted hunting arrow placed over the muzzle and fired with a blank shot was the answer.

The gunsmith removed the front sights and turned down each barrel in a lathe just enough to make a slight shoulder so the hollow steel shaft could slide smoothly over the barrels. A sharp, three-bladed hunting arrowhead was brazed to each steel shaft and two fins were brazed to the back end of the steel hunting arrow. A loop was brazed on one side between the fins so a line could be fastened to it. Each arrow was less than twenty inches in length. Rods were brazed to the bottom of the magazines that protruded slightly downwards. Wooden cones were drilled and slipped over the rods, and a hundred feet of three-hundred-pound test parachute cord was fastened to each Scotchman that sat in a rack on the gunwale of the dory. The line was wound on the cone, and the other end was fastened to the steel arrow. The line on the cone was held in place with a rubber band. A blank round was placed in the gun's chamber, and it was ready to fire. It seemed workable, provided the blank was not overloaded to blow up the gun and kill the hunter instead of the sea lion.

We purchased a case of a thousand rounds of army steel jacket shells and removed the steel jacket bullets from the cartridges. The cordite in the army shells was removed and replaced a few grains at a time to build up the power of the load without blowing up the gun. Once the correct load was found that would fire the harpoon arrow, it was ready for testing. To our delight, the gun was so accurate with the harpoon in place that a fifty-pound lard can could be hit every time at twenty-five yards. By the time all the Lee-Enfields were converted, we had three hundred shells loaded, a supply of steel arrows, extra wooden cones, plenty of parachute cord, shotgun shells and a number of dories and outboard motors ready for action.

I was still a bit skeptical about the whole program, but Charlie was gung-ho to get on with it. The Federal Department of Fisheries were interested in the scheme and intended to monitor the hunt. They approved the participation of Indians in the hunt. I obtained a contract to provide meat at twelve cents per pound from a reduction plant, and we were in business. Once we were committed, there was no going back, so the hunt was on. Up until this time, the Department of Fisheries was killing sea lions by the hundreds and leaving them to sink to the bottom of the ocean. It was a terrible waste of protein and they were anxious to find a use for the product.

Soon enough, the day arrived when Charlie left Campbell Avenue wharf with a wave of his arm. He headed the *Annie Tuck* towards the north end of the West Coast of Vancouver Island to a remote Indian village, where he intended to take on additional hunters for help in skinning and butchering the sea lions. A day later when he arrived in the village he created quite a bit of excitement.

The trouble was, Charlie only required about ten more men, but all of the men in the village wanted to join the hunt. Picking his hunters from a hundred men was a delicate situation that took some tact on Charlie's part. He finally selected his hunters without hurting too many feelings. He decided to put on an exhibition to show the power of the harpoon guns. A target was put out forty yards away, and Charlie took aim. The whole village had come down to view this spectacle and everybody was buzzing with anticipation. Charlie fired the gun, a puff of smoke left the muzzle and the harpoon sailed twenty feet and fell into the ocean. Two hundred and fifty Indians were roaring with laughter, some so taken with mirth they rolled around on the dock. Charlie stood there with a red face, wondering what had happened. He wound in the line and reloaded a half dozen times with the same result. Now the Indians were beginning to disperse from the dock, taunting Charlie while tears of laughter rolled down their cheeks.

A deflated Charlie phoned me on his radio phone to explain his problem and cursing the gunsmith who reloaded the shells. We found out later that the gunsmith's apprentice reloaded the shells and took it on upon himself to reduce the loads for safety reasons. Charlie said, "I'm going to have to improvise with powder out of shotgun shells to make the harpoon guns work." Charlie decided to add a bit of black powder from the shotgun shells to each load to perk up the results. He told me he would phone back later and let me know how he made out.

"For God's sake, be careful Charlie," I cautioned. "That powder in shotgun shells is much quicker-burning stuff than the cordite in those army shells."

Charlie phoned back in the evening with triumph in his voice. "Boy, are those Indians ever impressed now," he said. "They think we have a hell of a high-powered harpoon gun. I damn near killed myself, but they sure were impressed. When I fired the gun, it blew smoke out the vent and knocked me down on the deck. The hundred feet of parachute line ran out and broke off at the cone without me even feeling it. I was laying on deck with stars shooting out of my eyes. It took me ten minutes to recover and now my face is tattooed black."

When Charlie recovered, the crowd was still looking at the horizon and oohing and ahhing. Some of them wanted to take a turn firing the gun, but Charlie wouldn't allow it for fear somebody would be killed. There was a big fir tree a hundred and fifty feet high, two hundred yards away, and the last time anyone saw the harpoon arrow it was sailing over the top of the tree disappearing into the forest. Charlie now decided it was a matter of working up gradually until a suitable load was arrived at to fire the guns safely. By midnight he had all the shells reloaded to his satisfaction and intended to put on another show for the locals in the morning.

The next day Charlie got the loads right and hit a three-foot target every time at thirty yards. Then he gave several of the Indian hunters a turn at firing the harpoon gun. Now there were arguments about who would shoot sea lions with the harpoon gun and who would kill them with a load of buckshot or a rifle bullet. While the harpoon arrow penetrated right through the great bulk of sea lion, it seldom killed them outright. They had to be finished off with a shot to the head. Charlie got the Indians sorted out and turned them loose to kill sea lions. He offered them twenty dollars for each sea lion delivered, skinned and quartered, to the *Annie Tuck*. The result was the Indians began delivering seven-hundred pound females and ignored the larger bulls. Now Charlie had to inform the hunters that it was five dollars for females and twenty dollars for bulls. They took it all in good humour and soon began bringing in the larger bulls.

The Federal Fisheries Department informed me by phone that Charlie had a successful sea lion hunt, killing seventy-five sea lions in less than one day. By day two of the hunt it was all over, and the *Annie Tuck* left the hunting grounds with the hold fully loaded with additional meat stored on the deck. The sea lion meat smelled all right, resembling horse meat in colour. The Fisheries Department vessel that attended the hunt took cuts of meat for their Newfie crew to eat. Charlie delivered the Indian hunters back to their village and headed towards Vancouver. Charlie was his usual fussy self, wanting to get into port as fast as possible to eliminate any chance of spoilage. When he arrived at Campbell Avenue the carcasses were unloaded and trucked away by Dempsey Neuman to storage, where it was added to the mink feed mix for their own mink and to supply to other mink ranchers.

Charlie brought down one whole sea lion bull that we froze at B.C. Ice on a skid with a two-by-four under its chin to hold its head up level. It was an awesome sight sitting on the skid with its head up looking straight ahead. It took about a week at forty below zero to freeze the critter solid. I intended to ship this creature whole to a pet food plant in Texas to see if they would be interested in buying sea lions from us in the future. Dempsey Neuman reduced his price to nine cents per pound, so we made very little money on the trip because of all the expenses we spent in experimenting for the hunt. We had seventy-five hides salted down and we were counting on selling them to make a profit. Charlie was British to the core, and he wanted to ship them to England to someone he knew there. The skin was about a half-inch thick, so it should have been worth something because it could be split at least three times. It was Charlie's project, so I let him go to it.

In due course, I shipped the whole sea lion carcass to the Texas pet food plant. We had a little trouble getting it through U.S. customs because it was not dyed to prevent it from being used for human consumption. We sent a man out to the U.S. border and had him spray-paint the frozen bull with purple food colouring and the customs officials let it through. When it arrived in Texas, the people in the plant phoned and told me it was very high-quality meat that was about ten percent better than horse meat. They advised me that they dumped the whole animal hide and hair into their meat grinder and said they would ship me back a couple of cases of food for my dog. They said it was good-tasting, healthy meat and they suggested I try it myself.

I said, "You put it through with the hide, hair, penis and testicles and you expect me to eat it!"

They laughed and said it was all good protein. When the cases of dog food arrived, I fed the four-pound cans to my dog, who gobbled it with gusto. My friends all had the same result with their dogs. Every time I opened a can, I smelled the meat but I never had the courage to try it. The Texas company wanted us to ship them more sea lions but the price they offered was so low that we declined the offer.

The market for mink feed and pet food was so up and down, it seemed a futile business to keep up the hunt. I made some effort to find a market for the meat in Japan, but it soon became obvious that the hoops we would have had to jump through to satisfy the government would take years to navigate.

Charlie's attempt to market the hides in England met with some success. However, the payment we received of five dollars per hide was ridiculously low. How could a hide nearly ten feet square and half an inch thick be worth that little? A few months later, the tannery requested more sea lion hides. I wrote to them to say that it wasn't worth the effort. They raised the price to one hundred dollars per hide. The sea lion hides were perfect material for making blacksmith aprons. A few months later they contacted us again, raising the price to two hundred dollars per hide. I wrote back telling that we had gone out of the seal lion hunting business. I couldn't help but tell them that if they hadn't acted like the Hudson Bay Company buying furs from the Indians two hundred years ago and paid us a fair price to begin with, we still might be in a position to supply them with hides.

Today anybody thinking about hunting sea lions would be stopped instantly by the hordes of do-gooders who think of sea lions as cute little animals they'd like to cuddle with. Charlie went back to packing fish and trolling for salmon, and I concentrated on processing fish and shellfish more efficiently and looking for new markets.

During most of his fishing career, Charlie was tied to B.C. Packers because they owned many fishing vessels outright that could be taken out on a share basis. When a fisherman entered into a deal with B.C. Packers, he was obligated to deliver his fish to them. B.C. Packers was a very large company with a layered hierarchy and a pretty strict procedure for doing business. A creative thinker like Charlie was bound to break the rules and do his own thing from time to time. Though he was committed to B.C. Packers, Charlie sold us the odd trip to keep his hand in with us because he knew that we would finance his cod-buying trips in the winter off-season. It was good for us and good for him. B.C. Packers was aware of these isolated transgressions but closed their eyes to them, because it was better to have Charlie work their idle vessel than to have it tied up to a wharf, racking up expenses. They knew Charlie well and left him alone, up to a point, so long as everyone knew when to back off. They were not interested in winter cod-fishing trips because they had plenty of cheap frozen cod for their customers and were not really interested in handling expensive fresh winter fish.

Charlie liked to make social calls on our office. These sessions lasted for hours, and at times heated arguments ensued that might make a stranger believe we were having a disagreement. In reality we were arguing the merits of one scheme versus another. Charlie was a dreamer with big ideas. While he understood everything about catching and handling fish, he understood practically nothing about the problems of selling it. He often wanted to develop products that were excellent quality but were too costly. He claimed that people would buy top-of-the-line every time, even if they have to pay more. Up to a point that was true, but by the time chain stores entered the scene and added their huge markup, the picture became far less clear. I sold fish to chain stores for a dollar twenty-five that they marked up to four dollars and fifty cents. When I pointed this out to them, they told me in no uncertain terms to mind my own business.

Charlie was unaware of the ins and outs of retail selling and the hard-nosed ethics of chain buyers who moved enormous volumes. Charlie was also touchy about his crippled legs, and if booze was introduced into the long bull sessions at the dock, there was always some joker who managed to put his foot in his mouth and get Charlie in a foul mood. On the frequent occasions he came to my house, I pulled the cork from a bottle of Scotch because I knew he expected it. In any case, I didn't have to drive anywhere. Three-quarters of a bottle of whisky in five hours, along with some food, was to Charlie like spitting in the ocean. He handled it without showing anything, except I noticed that he laughed more often and longer. Charlie's stories were entertaining and side-splitting. Between stories and laughs, he brought up whatever project he had in mind, and in his usual charming, relentless way kept it up until I finally agreed or promised to give his idea careful consideration.

Charlie was in love with the *Annie Tuck*. He told me many times that Joe Babcock would sell her to him once he ready to stay ashore. By the time Joe was in his late seventies, he was staying longer on shore but making no move to sell Charlie the *Annie Tuck*. Selling the boat he fished on all his working days was like cutting off his right arm. Joe Babcock was a tough old bird whose name was synonymous with the early years of the fishing industry in British Columbia. So Joe made an occasional, ceremonial halibut fishing trip with the *Annie Tuck* and his ancient Newfie crew. By this time, it wasn't about money with Joe, but about tradition and his love of the vessel and the life at sea. It was apparent to me that Joe would never be able to part with the *Annie Tuck* in his lifetime. This was not a good thing to say to Charlie when he'd been drinking.

Although Charlie lived with a woman, in many ways the *Annie Tuck* was the love of his life that burned like a fire inside him. He became quite determined to acquire this beautiful vessel until he became rather obsessed. I don't think any woman or other enterprise could have replaced his singular drive to own the *Annie Tuck*. But where was he going to raise the capital to buy her? Who would finance a badly handicapped fisherman? Certainly not the bank managers of the times. Often the arguments we got into involved his scheme to have me finance him buying the *Annie Tuck* from Joe. Whenever I doubted that the boat was for sale, Charlie would get mad as a hornet. Charlie thought I was a money pit, and when I begged off, telling him I couldn't afford it, he'd come back at me telling me I was nothing but a two-bit operator. Then I would lose my temper and tell him he was a stupid ass and ask him why he didn't get his high and mighty friends at B.C. Packers to buy it for him. This put a damper on his rhetoric.

Late one evening at my house when the bottle was empty, my wife wouldn't let me open another. Charlie was all primed for a night of boozing. The arguing was getting too intense and we were going over the same old ground, but Charlie thought the night was young and he protested that we were party poopers. He knew of several locales where partying would be just getting up to speed. Though he was drunk, there was no way we could talk him into a bed. I followed him to the front door as he walked on his crutches. There was a heavy frost that evening so the ten stairs to the sidewalk were pretty well iced up. I was afraid Charlie might slip with his crutches and fall down the cement stairs. I got below him and offered to help him down the stairs, but that was a mistake. He blew up in a fit of anger and began to get very unpleasant. He threw his crutches to the bottom of the stairs and with his powerful arms propelled himself down the wrought-iron banister until he got to the bottom. When he got there he picked up his crutches and said, "Don't you ever offer me pity again, you SOB." I felt bad because I was offering common sense, but Charlie was like an angry bear and left in a foul temper. A few days later he showed up at our office with his usual good humour, and the incident was never mentioned again.

One time, Charlie went out on a cod-buying trip about the end of March. He knew that there was an early run of spring salmon off Esperanza on the West Coast. He informed us that he intended to find out if he could get some fishermen to fish that run. When he arrived, there he found out that quite a few trollers were willing to fish for salmon because cod was only bringing in about fifteen cents a pound while salmon would bring in about one dollar and twenty-five cents a pound. The trollers were having no problem catching two to four hundred pounds of springs for a day of trolling, and that was way better than fishing for cod and snappers. Charlie called down on his radio phone to tell us that he had ten thousand pounds of cod on board, but now he was going to buy salmon. Charlie knew we were interested in getting fresh salmon, and this would be a bonanza for the Easter trade.

Five days later he called and said he had twelve thousand pounds of beautiful springs in the eight- to twelve-pound size with not a white spring in the load. He was on his way to Port Alberni to ship the fish to us by West Coast Freight. Port Alberni was a B.C. Packers' stronghold, as they had a big buying station there run by the Gregory family. The springs and cod had to be boxed before they could be shipped on West Coast Freight, so Charlie helped himself to one hundred and fifty empty Gregory fish boxes. Because Charlie worked for B.C. Packers, a good deal of the time nobody minded. They merely assumed Charlie was sending the fish to B.C. Packers on Campbell Avenue. Charlie phoned to say that the truck had departed from Port Alberni on Sunday night, so it should be at Campbell Avenue by noon Monday. On Monday at ten a.m. the truck arrived and pulled into B.C. Packers' loading dock with our shipment of fish. The driver was so used to delivering fish to B.C. Packers that he took no notice of the bill of lading. I was keeping an eye out for the truck's arrival, and when it pulled in on the other side of the dock behind B.C. Packers, I walked over to see what was going on.

They were already unloading the boxes and grading our fish into their own fish bins. Several management types, curious about the shipment, were checking out the fish. The fish was in beautiful condition, and the boys were delighted with the delivery. "Why are you unloading my fish from that truck?" I asked.

"What do you mean by that?" one of them asked. "This fish was shipped to us by Charlie Walcott; anybody knows he works for us."

Getting a little hot, I asked, "Did you look at the bills of lading? I chartered the *Annie Tuck* and gave Charlie the buying money to purchase that fish. It's our fish and I want it back now. You have no business taking if off the truck or even touching it."

One of the managers answered, "The fish is in our boxes and Charlie works for us, so the fish belongs to us. "The argument raged back and forth for a few minutes while the truck driver stood there with a big smile on his face.

I turned to him and said, "You won't have that smile on your face or even a job when I sue West Coast Freight for delivering fish shipped on a bill of lading for Van Shell to B.C. Packers. Look at the bills of lading and see for yourself, you damn nitwit." Now they began to mill around the truck driver and his bills of lading. I returned to our plant and phoned West Coast Freight and told them they'd have a nasty problem if we didn't get our fish back promptly. About twenty minutes later the West Coast Freight truck backed away from the Packers plant and pulled up in front of our place. The driver was not smiling any longer as we began unloading our fish. I asked him about the fish that had already been unloaded, and he shrugged his shoulders. Ten minutes later, B.C. Packers' forklifts trundled the bins of fish over to our plant.

Soon after, one of the managers from B.C. Packers came over and wanted to buy the fish but I was pretty angry about the affair and refused to sell the fish to him. I told him that if they had acted properly and not created an incident, I would have sold at least half of the fish to them, but now they weren't getting any. Pressure was applied on us to sell B.C. Packers the fish, but I would have none of it, even though Father thought I should split the load. This incident created bad blood between our company and B.C. Packers for quite a while, but eventually they cooled off. I might add that Charlie kept out of town for some time, avoiding his friends at B.C. Packers. Months after the incident, he told me that he really got scorched when he dropped in for a visit looking for a packing job.

We had many disputes with B.C. Packers because we were expanding our company. They had most of the fishermen working for them and most of the customers buying from them. Every time we bought directly from fishermen or sold to a new customer, we were interfering with their business. The large fishing companies always

CHARLIE WALCOTT and the *ANNIE TUCK*   309

thought the fish in the Pacific Ocean belonged exclusively to them. Their attitude was that the smaller fish companies should buy from them and sell to small customers. When smaller companies attempted to expand, it immediately brought on the spectre of retaliation and harassment. The big companies applied pressure through the banks and the Department of Fisheries and Oceans. The directors of the big companies were also influential figures in the financial world, and it was no secret in the industry that the Department of Fisheries and Oceans was almost an adjunct of the big companies.

Eventually Charlie wore the aging Joe down and he was able to put a down payment on the *Annie Tuck* at the end of the salmon season. This sum, which included the money I advanced him for a cod trip, probably amounted to about fifteen thousand dollars. I was upset that he had used our buying money as part of his down payment, but that was the way Charlie operated. I had no doubt he would show up with some fish or pay us back one way or another. Charlie was basically honest, with the best of intentions, and he always paid his debts. For a while I was annoyed but I had to admire him for taking the gamble to finally secure the love of his life. This time Charlie had to find some quick money because it was uncertain how long Joe would wait for full payment for the *Annie Tuck*. Charlie decided to make two or three quick trips to fish for tuna and then make his annual cod trips for us. If the gods were with him and his crew and his luck held out, he could make six or seven thousand dollars per trip and another five on the cod, which would be about half the amount owed for the *Annie Tuck*. After another trolling season for salmon, he would have most of it paid off. Then he'd be able to wrangle the rest of the money from a fish company or a bank. He departed in the early fall with the *Annie Tuck* rigged up with tuna gear and headed south to where it was reported American fishermen were taking good catches of albacore tuna.

Charlie said that he intended to a make payment on his debt to us by delivering Van Shell a trip of tuna on his way home after the season. What more could we do but smile and wish him good luck and a good year. After two months passed and we had heard nothing from Charlie, we began to wonder what had become of him. We knew that he was catching tuna off the lower Oregon or northern California coasts, delivering his catch to buyers in those areas. In a way, no news was good news because Charlie was probably too busy to call. Finally, one blustery day, we received a call from Charlie saying that the *Annie Tuck* was on her way into Vancouver with a full load of albacore. However, the weather was bad and she might have to take shelter for a day or two. The next time I heard from Charlie, he told me he fell on the deck during the storm, broke his arm and had to go ashore for medical aid. He thought he could make it to Vancouver but the pain was killing him so he had to locate a doctor. He had to get permission to land in a U.S. port, which further delayed treatment to his wounded arm. By the time he reached a doctor in a U.S. hospital, gas gangrene had set in and nothing could be done to help him. Charlie Walcott died the day after he reached the hospital. I was in shock at this sudden turn of events. Charlie was a wonderful friend, and I knew I was going to miss him.

I have no idea about what happen to the load of tuna or who brought the *Annie Tuck* back to British Columbia. Charlie's common-law wife had no information to offer except that she was broke, there was no money to properly bury Charlie, and a number of liens had been placed against his assets. I phoned Charlie's friends at B.C. Packers, who donated two hundred bucks, I threw in two hundred, Boyd Shannon threw in one hundred dollars and another fishing company added another hundred. She came over from Victoria to visit me at Campbell Avenue. She left with six hundred dollars to cover the funeral expenses. I didn't hear about the details of the funeral or find out where Charlie was buried. It didn't matter. Charlie was on his own, on the final voyage, the last big trip of all the seasons. I finally got a glimpse of his beloved *Annie Tuck* a few years later, when a new owner was aboard. Now so many years later, when I think of Charlie Walcott, I can't stop chuckling. He was a fine man and marvellous character with the greatest laugh in the universe rumbling through his barrel chest.

THE SHAH'S AGENT

On a sunny spring morning in 1977 a visitor arrived at our plant. He was a dusky-skinned, sparsely built middle-aged gent I took to be of Middle Eastern descent. I was right on with my appraisal. When he introduced himself, he informed me that he was from Iran and that he was an agent for the Shah. He was a straightforward man who came right to the point. The reason for his visit was that the Shah wished to import a large quantity of small freshwater fish. He wanted several million pounds in one- to four-pound sizes. This large shipment of fish was required to arrive in Iran timed for a special religious holiday.

"As you know," he explained, "there is a great deal of unrest in Iran. The Ayatollah Khomeini, at present in exile in France, is stirring up the population with religious fervour against the Shah. There have been frequent religious outbursts aimed at the Shah's close association with the government of the United States of America. The Shah intends to import large quantities of small fish to give away to the people in a show of good will to pacify them and boost his image. I have talked to many fishing companies in your country. I have just come from a meeting with B.C. Packers. All of them have informed me that they could not provide such a large quantity of small freshwater fish. Can you help us?"

I told him that there would be no problem producing such a large shipment of fish providing payment was made up front. This fellow assured me that payment would be made promptly. I was skeptical about his proposition but thought nothing ventured, nothing gained.

It's not every day that somebody shows up with such a large order. I knew where there were fish to be located, but the problem would be to put together a deal that would have no risk for our company. I suggest he come back in a couple of days to give me time to put the deal together. I made sure that he was aware that payment would have to be made up front when federal inspection certificates were obtained. He agreed to that arrangement and we parted with a handshake.

I knew, and thought that everybody in the industry knew, that the Fresh Water Fish Marketing Board in Manitoba was stuck with a huge inventory of freshwater fish. In fact, this marketing board had its cold storage plant filled to the ceiling with fish, and probably additional fish stored in public storages. This was a golden opportunity, perhaps a miracle opportunity, for the Fresh Water Fish Marketing Board (FWFMB) to clean out its dead inventory. Some of it was two or three years old, or even older, and was beating them up with excessive storage charges.

I thought about it for a while and decided that, considering the circumstances, the only way to approach this opportunity was to promote a sale while arranging for a commission to be built into the deal in order to eliminate the chance of exposing our company to any risk. I was aware that we were not on great terms with the FWFMB for reasons of their own stupidity and unethical actions.

In the past our company imported almost all of the freshwater fish from Saskatchewan and Manitoba that was shipped into British Columbia. When the FWFMB was created, all of this fish had to be purchased from that organization. They decided to cut us off and chose B.C. Packers to be their distributor in British Columbia. B.C. Packers did not realize that the one hundred and seventy-five sixty-pound boxes of mixed fish had to be divided up each week among seventy customers. Soon B.C. Packers got tired of the hassle and cut their ties to the FWFMB. The board chose two other companies to do business with before finally coming back and knocking on our door to offer the business that we had built up back to us. By that time we had nothing but contempt for the FWFMB way of doing business, so we took the business back on trial. Shortly after resuming our relationship with the FWFMB, we discovered that they were making prepaid shipments to some of our customers who were ordering two or three boxes of fish while we were bringing in close to two hundred boxes of fish. To make matters worse, these customers were getting the same wholesale price that we got for ordering a huge quantity of their fish. A company or broker that makes a deal with someone and then goes around that party by shipping directly to that party's customers is known in the industry as an unethical guttersnipe. We terminated our relationship with the FWFMB and moved on.

Now I was in a quandary. I had no reason to believe that the FWFMB would honour any arrangement made between us because I doubted their ethics would stand the test. However, the prospect of getting in on such a large deal with a foreign buyer tempted me to pick up the phone and make a call to the FWFMB Winnipeg. I knew the manager. He had previously held a minor executive position in a large B.C. fishing company. He had gone to Manitoba to better himself when the position had been advertised. Already several managers had come and gone, and the jury was still out on this new manager, but I was willing to take a chance that he might be up to the challenge. The new manager hailed me by my first name, which is always a good sign in any business situation. I presented my plan before him, and he was overjoyed at the prospect of making such a monumental sale. We had a very productive conversation and he agreed that he would pay my company a good healthy commission, not only for outlining the deal but for introducing him to the customer. I was assured over and over again that a fair commission on the sale would be sent to our company as soon as the fish was paid for. The longer he went on, promising to live up to his end of the deal, the more wary I became. You never know about such an arrangement until the cheque arrives in the mail. In the meantime, many things could happen. The board officials could renege on the verbal contract, or the manager could somehow blow the whole deal. Especially this manager, who was relatively inexperienced in completing large business transactions. Only time would tell if my plan would work out in our favour.

We were never privy to the information regarding the negotiations or the details of the arrangements the marketing board made with the agent buying freshwater fish on the Shah's behalf. The Shah's agent indicated to us that after inspection, the fish was deemed suitable for the Shah's purposes. Other than that tidbit, we received no more encouraging information and we began to get the uneasy feeling that we had wasted our time on the project. It is never a good sign when information is unavailable from an associate in a business venture. That fact usually spells out a failed deal or the prospect of a double-cross.

I wondered if the FWFMB would have enough on the ball to make sure they received payment up front. If they failed to make that arrangement, I felt there was a good chance they would never receive payment at all. We had plenty of experience with foreign buyers and we were well aware that, given any opportunity, a deduction would be made for some reason or another — or there was always a chance the FWFMB would never receive payment.

I waited two months before making contact with the FWFMB regarding the commission we expected from fish that had been shipped to Iran. Now the manager had a different attitude. He was too busy to return my calls, and when I finally reached him his attitude was smug and evasive. He indicated that they did not need our help to make the sale because the fish was not available anywhere else. The FWFMB was the only party with such a large quantity of product that the customer would have eventually had to come to them without our help. My persistence in the matter only brought laughter and the advice that we should be wiser in future business ventures. His attitude was that since we had nothing in writing, we could go ahead and try and collect our commission. It was a bitter lesson, but we had expected as much from that mismanaged marketing board. We had done millions of dollars worth of business for many decades in that manner with dozens of agents and various companies around the world without any trouble.

I discontinued further dialogue with the board because it was futile to keep trying, until one day I picked up the paper and read that the Shah had fled from Iran and was in the United States getting medical treatment for cancer. The new regime taking over in Iran was headed by the Ayatollah Khomeini, who had just arrived there from France. Another very interesting item that came to my attention was that the new government would not honour any commitments made by the Shah just before he fled the country. Now I began to wonder if that high-priced help running the FWFMB had exhibited enough smarts to get their money up front for the fish they shipped to Iran.

There's nothing like getting the information from the horse's mouth, so I called my ex-friend in Winnipeg. I didn't hear any laughter this time when he answered the phone. I received a very cool reception and in the end I was berated for getting the board involved in such a bad deal.

I never really found out what happened regarding the caper with the Shah's agent. Whether the fish was shipped or not was never divulged to me. Obviously the FWFMB was not happy with the deal, so it probably was an expensive experience.

HOW THE WEST COAST WAS WON AND LOST

We had a reasonable relationship with the old guard at B.C. Packers. However, our company was expanding, so we were taking business away from the satellite companies that B.C. Packers controlled. These small companies, such as Seaport Crown and Reliance Fish, were constantly complaining that our competition was hurting them. I have no doubt it was, since we competed fiercely with them for the carriage trade. Our steady production of top-quality shellfish made us hard to beat.

Ken Fraser frequently called me over to his office for chats. Mostly he shook his head and moaned to me about the problems I was causing for him. His pleas for us to ease up on his associates left me cold. They wanted him to completely cease doing business with us. However, that was out of the question, because he discovered that we were his best customer. "What am I going to do with you?" he would mumble. "You buy more than one hundred thousand dollars worth of fish per month and you pay us on time." This was when fish was worth sixty cents per pound.

B.C. Packers' trolled salmon business, fresh fish sales and the steaking operation were all located on the Campbell Avenue fish dock or on adjoining property west of Campbell Avenue. We did a lot of business with them because their door was probably not more than one hundred yards from ours, which was on the east side of the Campbell Avenue fish dock basin. We bought and sold hundreds of thousands of pounds of number-one trolled salmon that were bastard colour grades (spring salmon that was neither pure red or pure white).

The in-between grades that were difficult to sell were right up our alley. It took B.C. Packers at least ten years to learn how to market this off-grade salmon and then they only learned by observing our sales. I made a tour of their plant every morning to buy cheap fish that their personnel did not know how to sell or could not move for whatever reason. We also bought fish from Nelson Brothers, Todd and Sons, Cassiar Packing, Millerd Great Northern and other companies on both sides of the border.

In the beginning, Vancouver Shellfish and Fish Company was a shellfish producer. Crabs, shrimp, clams and oyster were sixty percent of our sales. As we expanded, fish sales climbed to seventy-five percent and shellfish production in volume dropped to twenty five of sales. We clashed with companies that were essentially selling fish with perhaps a bit of shellfish production to accommodate their customers. We had a steady supply of shellfish throughout the year. Most of the other smaller companies were forced to buy shellfish products from us, especially when there were shortages. Since the demand for shellfish was crucial to many restaurants and retail outlets, we often got their fish order as well. It was convenient for them to get it all from one company.

My attempts to expand and move into different areas of the fish business had the effect of further alienating the big companies. Years before, we had clashed with the Canadian Fishing Company over our business fronted by Mr. Parker in Edmonton. Subsequently, we began competing fiercely with B.C. Packers in Calgary. The gentlemen's agreement we had to buy fish from the big companies when we needed it, rather than compete for it on the fishing grounds, was a dead issue. We had always purchased fish directly from fishermen but we kept it low profile to keep the peace. However, once we started moving thirty thousand pounds of salmon a week and looking for more fish to buy, our relationship with the big companies hit bottom.

We no longer bought fish from B.C. Packers on a daily basis because we had our own supply, getting it directly from the fishermen. We still remained on good terms trading and also buying fish for their account on the sly from some of their competitors. I no longer went to their plant each morning in search of bargains. On a whole, I was not welcome by the lower echelon there after Ken Fraser had dusted them off for their various business lapses. Besides that, there were bones with more meat to pick elsewhere.

One fateful early morning, B.C. Packers called me over to their offices and told me they would no longer sell us any salmon.

I said, "Okay, if that's the way you feel, I'll get my fish elsewhere." When I called the Canadian Fishing Company, I got virtually the same story. Obviously our attempts to do more business meant that in some cases we were competing with the big companies for the same customers. I had attempted to reason with the giants by telling them that we were beneficial to them because we moved a lot of their odd grades and sizes of fish that were difficult to sell on the export market. They wouldn't listen to my point of view. It seemed imperative to us that we had to move quickly if we wished to stay in business.

However, by that time we had already realized there was a much bigger profit to be made by buying our fish directly from the fishermen. Historically, we bought forty percent of our salmon directly from the fishermen but we stayed connected to the large companies because they had a more reliable source of supply. It was always a matter of trying to keep a balance while doing business with them, so that no bridges were ever burned. We anticipated that at some point we would be cut off if we strayed too far into their domains.

My son Jim was already advising me to build a plant somewhere on the West Coast, so I asked him where he would go. Jim answered, "Tofino." He said, "Ray Grumback has a good piece of property in Tofino with waterfront access. He already has the oil and fuel concession to serve fishing boats, so a fish buying camp would be an added bonus to him." Jim had been hauling trucks loads of Dungeness crabs from Tofino so he was familiar with the area. I travelled to Tofino with Jimmy the next time he was due to pick up a load of crabs. This was about five years before the new highway was pushed through to Tofino. A rough logging road along a steep mountainside was the only route into town. It was hairy trip with a lot of steep dropoffs and the potential for bad weather made it even scarier.

We arrived at Ray Grumback's place about three o'clock in the afternoon, and Jim took me right over to introduce me to him. Ray and I hit it off, and before long we had worked out the basics of a business deal. Neither of us had much experience drawing up legal papers, so we decided to let our respective lawyers handle the preparation of appropriate documents.

Jim and I loaded about sixteen thousand pounds of trolled salmon and crabs and set off for Vancouver. Snow had been falling in the mountains, so we had to stop and put on chains. We were climbing the steep mountain at the place of the steepest dropoff when we encountered a tourist in a camper truck coming towards us. Jim said, "I bet he pulls over in our lane, stops and makes us pass him on the outside. They always do." Sure enough, the driver stopped and sat, afraid to proceed. Jim said, "If I stop to make him pass on the outside where he should pass, he'll not move for sure."

The steep mountain road was treacherous. If we stopped at this place, it might be impossible to go forward and there wasn't much room for backing up. Jimmy poured the coal to our engine and we roared straight towards the tourist. I thought Jim was mad to attempt the pass. I noticed the camper driver had not even bothered to hug the bank. I thought for sure we were going to drop into the abyss. At the last second with the throttle wide open, Jim moved over as far as he dared go and we squeezed by. We could hear a nasty ripping sound. I don't know how much damage occurred but it must have been substantial, because when I looked back I could see curtains waving in the breeze from the side of the camper and pieces of insulation. We were in a precarious section of road, so we continued on. We breathed a sigh of relief and decided we might as well keep going. The fact was, the camper had violated the rules of the road by occupying our rightful lane. We decided to file our accident report in Port Alberni, which we did. The fish truck, except for a few scratches, had very little damage. The driver of the camper never filed an accident report, and that was the last we heard of it.

Four months later, our fish plant was nearly built and we were almost ready to start buying fish. Rumours had surfaced in Vancouver that we were building a West Coast buying station, and some executives from the big companies were sneering, "Be our guests, you're welcome to join the party."

Problem was, the legal papers were still going back and forth in an unsatisfactory fashion between lawyers who were busy prying legal fees out of both parties. Finally, I went to Tofino to see Ray. He grumbled to me that my lawyer had drawn up an agreement that would not allow him access to his own property.

I said, "Gee, Ray, your lawyer has drawn up an agreement that lets you put us out of business any time you choose." I asked Ray to wait while I rushed down to the co-op store and bought two scribblers and a couple of pencils. About ten minutes later I was back and said, "Let's sit down and draw up an agreement that suits us regardless of what our lawyers have to say about it."

In less than an hour we had hammered out a deal that was agreeable to both of us. It was a simple agreement that specified payments to Ray based on the poundage of fish passing through our plants. When there was an abundance of fish, we both made money. When landings were down, we both made less money. We each had a copy of the agreement in a scribbler and now we needed two or three people to witness both our signatures. I noticed a couple of men walking on the road in front of Ray's house. I hailed them and they walked over. These guys were friends of Ray. Ray explained the situation and they readily agreed to witness our signatures. After we signed we all stood around shaking hands. The next day our respective lawyers each received a scribbler and were told to draw up an official document according to what was laid down in the handwritten agreement.

The first thing my lawyer asked was who drew up the agreement.

"Why do you ask?"

He replied, "It doesn't give you enough protection."

"Never mind," I told him. "Just draw it up as you see it and send me two copies."

Later Ray told me he got the same response from his lawyer and that he also ordered his lawyer to draw it up as the deal existed in the scribbler. Finally, we had the proper legal documents signed and we were both relieved. By the time all the papers were finished being drawn up, we had already moved half a million pounds of salmon through the new plant. This agreement lasted for twenty years until Ray retired and sold us his property before he moved away from Tofino. There were some adjustments made over the years without the benefit of lawyers. In twenty years, we never had a disagreement or a bad word exchanged between us. Ray Grumback was a reasonable, sensible guy who was easy to get along with.

In Tofino we hired Michael White to buy fish and supervise our new plant. I believe his father's family arrived in the Clayquot district when his father was a schoolboy. They were well-known pioneers in the area who were familiar with most of the fishermen working on the West Coast of Vancouver Island. The choice of Mike White for camp man was a good one. He was a trusted local who had many friends. Mike was able to dispatch a truckload of the finest trolled salmon in the world to us at Campbell Avenue at least three times a week. In our first year, we had instantaneous success at a much higher level than we imagined or ever expected. Mike did a great job buying fish for us and he kept the camp in good order. Fishermen learned we would not buy fish that was not in first-class condition. A few times when Mike rejected some fish, a donnybrook erupted and on one or two occasions harsh words were traded. Mike boxed for sport so he had no trouble keeping the peace. Once when things got a bit out of hand, a dog came to Mike's assistance by clamping onto his opponent's rear end.

In the late fall, some Indian net fishermen were in the habit of fishing chum salmon just for their eggs. They argued that they were eggs from their food fish, but we knew that was not true and wanted no part in that destructive practice. They took the eggs but threw the carcasses back into the ocean. Japanese and Korean buyers were in the habit of buying these eggs for about one dollar per pound. After these eggs were processed into salmon roe caviar, they were exported to Japan for up to eighteen dollars per pound, so the temptation was there to take the eggs. I'm not sure if it was an illegal practice, but people got away with it. I cannot remember any of the buyers getting pinched, so perhaps the DFO looked the other way. We decided not to buy these eggs. Sometimes a party would show up at our camp with a thousand or fifteen hundred pounds of eggs when the regular buyers were not available. They screamed discrimination when we refused their goods, and they got pretty angry. We knew that it was not good for the resource, so under no circumstances would we consider buying the eggs, no matter how loud the uproar.

When I arrived in Tofino on business I invariably ended up icing fish late into the night. One night it was close to three a.m. when I staggered into the Maquinna Hotel, where the company had reserved me a room. The sleepy desk clerk advised me that because I had not shown up before eleven p.m., he had rented my room to someone else.

"I'm sorry, my friend," I advised the clerk, "but my room was previously paid for and I want it."

He finally took me out to the back of the hotel where a sort of shed was built up against the wall of the hotel. He unlocked the door and showed me in. There was a double bed, an electric light and one window in the place. "I'm sorry, but this is the best I can do for you now because I can't kick the other party out."

I understood and flopped onto the bed. I had hardly closed my eyes when the window went up and somebody was attempting to enter the room. I turned on the lightbulb and surprised a woman who had just dropped in. I escorted her to the door and locked it behind her.

Ten minutes later another person was attempting to enter my room. When she dropped to the floor, I snapped on the light and showed her out the door. She was so persistent, I had to show her out twice. I no sooner got back into bed when a guy showed up and started opening the window. I managed to get rid of him and finally got back to sleep. However, by now I couldn't sleep so I sat up most of the night. In the morning I was sleepy and in a pretty bad mood. When I left the shed, I noticed a man sleeping on the ground outside the window. However, the service in the dining room was extremely good, with my coffee cup being filled after nearly every sip and there was no charge for the excellent breakfast.

Later I found out that whenever the hotel was overbooked, guests were shown to the shed. My experience was a common one that many people experienced. Because the shed was normally unused, it was a favorite crashing spot for people stranded in the village late at night after the bar had closed.

On another blustery rainy fall evening, I was careful to turn up early in the evening and I was ushered to my room. I deposited my bag and after supper I left to go visit with friends in Tofino. I returned to the hotel shortly after midnight with a heavy rain beating down in tune with a wind that pushed it sideways. I ran up the stairs and attempted to open the hall door, but it seemed to be jammed so I could not squeeze through. Finally, I leaned into it and it gave way far enough so I could slip in amidst good-natured groans, grunts and loud snoring and protests to shut the door because I was letting in the cold wind. I couldn't find a light switch so I stepped gingerly down the dark hallway. I hadn't gone far when a loud groan startled me and then another as I tried stepping in another direction. I decided to light a match to see what lay before me. When the match flared up, I discovered a solid mass of bodies between me and the door to my room. I thought how the heck am I going to make it to the door? I decided enough is enough and I walked quickly over and between the groaning forms until I made it to the door handle. Nobody got really mad, although I heard a few nasty comments. When I got the door open and the light on, five or six bodies immediately came to life and begged me to let them enter the room and sleep on the floor because the hallway was so crowded.

The fumes in the hallway from all the alcohol consumed would have knocked out a horse. Against my better judgement, I allowed three men who looked respectable to come in to my room. I ordered them to lie down on the carpeted floor and suggested they go to sleep. In about a minute they were all snoring like a chorus of chainsaws. I opened the window to let in fresh air and placed my wallet under the pillow and went to sleep. Early in the morning, I was woken by some shuffling in the hallway. I opened my eyes and looked at the ceiling for a moment, wondering where I was. Soon my brain began to function and I thrust my hand under the pillow to fish out my wallet. Everything was in order. I noticed that the three men who had been sleeping on the floor had departed. Twenty minutes later when I entered the dining room for breakfast, I spotted my roommates at a table with several others finishing up their meal. They glanced over at me several times as they drank their coffee. When they left, they looked at me with wide smiles and each gave me a friendly wave as they passed though the door on their way out of the hotel.

When we arrived on the scene on the West Coast there were only three major buyers in the Tofino-Ucluelet area. They were B.C. Packers, Canadian Fishing Company and the Prince Rupert Co-op. Two other companies, Blaine Myers and McCallum Sales, were subsidiary companies, owned by B.C. Packers. Our company was regarded as a nuisance by the three major parties in the area. They figured we'd soon go broke and vanish from the scene. However, they were wrong and, to their chagrin, our company prospered on the West Coast for more than twenty years until the DFO bought back most of the troll fishing licences and put the West Coast troll fisheries out of business.

We had one large plant with four ice-making machines. We sold hundreds of tons of ice to the big companies because when their thirty-ton-per-day ice machines broke down, they were out of business. We had two ten-ton machines and two five-ton machines, so if one had to be serviced we still had plenty of ice. The big companies had a problem with us sitting there in the middle of the show on the West Coast. We could pay three or four cents per pound more for troll-caught salmon because of our efficient plant, and make double the profit that we made from the salmon we formerly bought from the big companies. They each had several buying stations along the coast, and if they met our price in Tofino they had to pay this higher price in all their camps. With a production of trolled salmon that was three or four times bigger than ours, they were reluctant to rock the boat, so they left us alone. Soon after building our Tofino plant, we no longer bought salmon at all from the larger companies. In fact, it wasn't long before the shoe was on the other foot and they were buying twenty- to one-hundred-thousand-pound lots of salmon from us at various times each year.

This uneasy truce remained for several years, until the Japanese companies invaded the fishery. As they were backed by the Japanese government, their arrival produced an uneven playing field that created havoc in the industry. They raised hell in the fishery until nobody, including themselves, was making any money. They went broke as fast as they appeared on the scene, and they took both Canadian and American companies down with them. The Japanese companies did some strange things. They raised the price of roe herring to six thousand dollars per ton. They cut their own throats and everybody else's to boot. Imagine increasing the price of herring to that level when they were the only ones with a market for it. How stupid can it get! Raising the price on a product to an astronomical height when you are the only customer? As I said, the Japanese did some strange things that nobody on this side of the Pacific could understand.

We had a Japanese buyer arrive at our camp. He wanted herring roe in the worst way, and he carried two suitcases that were full of money. He had close to four hundred thousand dollars in cash and he was not about to let go of that money at any time. We were pumping herring onto a steel barge. Tom Harper warned the buyer that he was in the way and asked him to back off. He backed up so far that he fell right off the scow into the water. Tom claimed that the buyer never let go of those two suitcases of money. He held on to them while some of the boys hooked him with a pike pole and pulled him back up onto the scow.

In its easiest days, the roe herring fishery was like the Klondike gold rush. There is a story about a herring fishermen out on the water who saw a black plastic bag floating in the chuck. Out of curiosity he hooked it with a gaff to look into it and he was astounded to find sixty thousand dollars in cash in that plastic bag. Every day, wild stories poured in from the fishing grounds. One buyer of herring who was well known to us received one hundred thousand dollars from a Japanese company to buy herring. He was given the money without being asked to sign for it. He promptly vanished into the sunset with the money and was gone for more than a year. The Japanese company sent a representative to see me because they wanted our help in locating this gentleman. Imagine giving someone one hundred thousand dollars cash without at least asking for a signature. When this man did surface and appeared in court in Victoria, he claimed he was ill and had lost his memory. He said he did not remember receiving the money, and if he did get it, he didn't know what happened to it. He beat the rap because no judge could ever figure that one out. Later, when it was all over, he claimed it was the easiest money he ever made.

One of Bill Kitsel's crewmen got sick so they took him ashore. They needed a skiff man to help tow out the herring seine net. They picked up an unemployed lad on the dock and asked him if he wanted the job until the sick man returned. He accepted, and that afternoon Kitsel made a one-million-dollar set on roe, and the young man received sixty-five thousand dollars for half a day's work or even less. They caught the mother lode in the first set of the day. Such were the rewards in the roe herring fishery in that wild era. As fast as some people were becoming millionaires, others were going bankrupt when they bought herring with no roe in them.

We finally closed our plant when only one or two vessels remained fishing in our area. No commercial fisherman can make a living fishing on a seven- or eight-day season, nor can a fish camp remain open under those conditions.

Sockeye salmon stocks have been depleted by overfishing by both Canadian and U.S. fishermen. Spring salmon, coho, pink salmon, ling cod and halibut stocks enjoy only a small fraction of their original abundance because of overfishing and a lack of feed to sustain them. In addition, because of the depletion of herring stocks, these larger species of fish eat the smaller fish of their own kind to survive. Overfishing of herring stocks for their eggs to export to Japan has caused the fish stocks on both our coasts, Atlantic and Pacific, to collapse. They will never recover until an abundance of feed is there to sustain them.

There is no quantity of large spring salmon left on our coast. Those that remain are thin fish with no fat reserves. The wild coho salmon that once grew in size to over twenty pounds in some systems are now skinny fish that hardly ever weigh more than five pounds. The Capilano River, which once produced hundreds of thousands of cohos in the five- to fifteen-pound weight category, now probably produces fish that are at less than a three-pound average. These fish are runts because they don't get enough to eat. Poor feed, destruction of habitat, pollution and overfishing and poor management are the reasons for the demise of our fishery resources.

In the days after the Second World War, at least twelve million pounds of trolled salmon was produced each season. More than three-quarters of these fish were exported. Van Shell alone shipped up to seven or eight containers of troll-caught head-on frozen salmon per week to Japan. The troll-caught sockeye salmon were worth one to three dollars per pound more than net-caught sockeye. The troll fishery conflicted with the net-fishing and sports-fishing factions. The large fishing companies, mostly net-fishing concerns, and the sports faction had the politicians in their pockets, so the troll fishery was engineered out of the industry.

At the peak of the season, we received a semi-truck load of trolled salmon each day from Tofino, and on some days, two or three semi-truck loads. A poor fishermen could make thirty thousand dollars per salmon season. Good fishermen made seventy to eight thousand dollars, and some highliners made a hundred and fifty thousand or even more. Deckhands made ten to fifteen thousand dollars clear in four months. I bet that's more than twice what the cowboys who guide sports fishermen make today. In the good times during the fishing season, every village, town and city on the coast boomed. Cold storages freezing fish for export were operating twelve to fifteen hours per day, seven days a week. Fish plant and cold storage workers were exhausted from working long hours, but money flowed into their pockets. The destruction of the fisheries has meant that thousands of jobs have gone. The trickle-down effect of the fishing industry into the general economy has been greatly reduced. Communities all over the coast are mere shadows of what they once were.

The finest method of fishing for salmon, trolling (hook-and-line fishing) has vanished. The government would be doing everybody a big favour if they outlawed the insane fishing for herring roe, abandoned the net fishery, and after a period of restoration reintroduced trolling as the only method for catching most species of salmon. The result would be a viable industry that would provide the consumer with the finest possible product. Alas, the lobbyists see it another way. For the foreseeable future there seems little to indicate that the Pacific salmon is making a comeback in Canadian waters. The fishing industry on the once grand West Coast of Vancouver Island remains a dead issue.

THIEVES AND CASH BUYERS

Over the years we had several break-ins at Campbell Avenue. Perhaps this wasn't surprising, considering the fish dock was on the waterfront. Usually the thieves were connoisseurs who hand-picked the goods. They stole lobster tails, scallops, prawns, shrimp meat, smoked salmon sides, king crab legs and other delicacies while ignoring the lower-priced fare. On at least two occasions, they stole our delivery trucks to cart away the merchandise. After one robbery, I noticed that the thieves had been so knowledgeable that they only took the most expensive brand from three grades of shrimp meat. This led me to believe the crooks had been tipped off as to the quality of the goods by insiders.

Eventually, our plant was fortified like Fort Knox after being upgraded after each break-in. These measures did not stop the thieves for long. Once they bent a steel door out like a tin-can lid and on another occasion they used a heavy-duty vehicle with chains and a grapple to tear out a whole wall when they could not break in through the doors. We had an alarm system in the plant and the police station was not more than a few minutes away, but that did not seem to impress the crooks. The police always seemed to arrive the next day to examine the damage and make out a report. The thieves were well informed and well organized. They worked quickly so that the police were never able to apprehend them in the act. I must say that the crooks in Vancouver are tenacious and expert at their vocation. An enterprising group of them came in through a skylight in the roof and dropped more than twenty feet to our concrete floor. They found they could not break into our freezers from inside the plant. They spent several hours trying while the alarm system blared away. They decided to abort their plan but found themselves trapped inside the plant with no way out. Fortunately for them, a key was left in the ignition of one of our forklifts. They used the machine to batter their way through the wall. After that we stopped leaving keys in ignitions and disabled fork lifts at night so they couldn't repeat the escape.

Thieves failed when they attempted to crack our monster steel safe. It was very old, very large and very strong, with a fireproof box and a double steel bottom that had a two-inch layer of asbestos between the two half-inch sheets of steel. It was an impressive piece that appeared intimidating, at least to me. Willy never kept more than a few hundred dollars in it at any time. It was in the office mainly for the protection of company documents and important papers such as contracts. Willy never locked the safe because he figured it was cheaper for the thieves to get a few dollars rather than have them blow the building up.

One weekend some brilliant safecrackers broke into our plant and attacked that safe with a vengeance. I'm sure they expected it to contain a few hundred thousand dollars of salmon-buying money. They turned the safe on its side and went to work on the bottom steel plate with a chisel and sledgehammer. They cut a four-inch slot only to discover the asbestos pad with another steel plate on the other side of it. That is when they stopped the hard work and decided to blow the monster open. They poured nitroglycerin around the door seams and took cover from the blast behind a pile of office furniture. However, while the ensuing blast blew out the office windows as well as other windows on the fish dock, the safe remained snugly closed. Their handiwork scorched the walls and blew approximately twenty thousand invoices around the office and out the windows. Willy had covered the walls with bundles of invoices, about two hundred in a bundle, hanging beside each other for easy access. The result was quite a mess. Some invoices were in pieces, others were partially burned, some were floating in the basin beyond the dock and the office floor was covered by about an inch of paper.

The steel monster was not impressed by the whole experience. It remained unscathed except for the small cut they managed in the bottom plate. Our crew was drafted to upend the safe and help clean up the mess. While this was going on, Willy chuckled as he turned the safe handle and opened the monster's door. The safe had never been locked, and the few dollars and the papers and the first-aid kit were all intact and in their proper order. I wonder what those brilliant thugs would have thought if they had known that the monster they attempted to break into had been unlocked the whole time. Even if they had been successful, they would have earned very little for their hard work. Willy was right — it was better for them to get a few dollars than to cause several thousand dollars in damages. Alas, our thieves were extraordinary. Perhaps trying the handle to see if the safe would open easily was too small a challenge for thieves who took the risk of working with nitroglycerin.

What was left of the invoices was shovelled into a couple of paper totes to keep the tax department satisfied even though nobody could reconcile them. The windows were promptly replaced and a couple of coats of paint were applied to the scorched wall where Willy was already filing the latest batch of invoices. Willy's first move after the cleanup was to stick a big sign on the safe door to inform safecrackers that the safe was not locked. The cut in the safe's bottom plate was welded shut and the safe, impressive as ever, was almost as good as new. Fifty years later, we still had that safe in our office. The combination dial was a little loose after all the punishment it took from the safecrackers. It took a steady hand to dial up the combination. However, after that experience, the safe, still functional and useful, was never left unlocked.

The other safecracking we experienced was in our Tofino plant. For many years, like most other companies in the fish business, we paid out hundreds of thousands of dollars in cash to fishermen. For a long time we worried that eventually we would be targeted for a robbery. We decided it was safer for our employees if we cut down the cash business and paid fishermen by cheque, whether they liked it or not. We were a reputable company with a clean record for more than fifty years, so the fishermen accepted the new status quo without much of a fuss. We still had to keep four or five thousand dollars in a small safe to provide money for fishermen who wanted cash to buy groceries so they could get back out fishing as quickly as possible. This money was replenished every day from the local bank. The money was kept in a safe that was bolted into a heavy cement slab. We knew that the safe would not be hard for an expert to open, but at least it was a place to keep money and to prevent novices from making an attempt.

One evening, after midnight, when the fish was iced down at the end of a long day, a pickup truck went down the short road to our fish camp. Jim was having a late meal, as was his custom in the fishing season, when he heard the truck go by. It is not unusual for fishermen to move about our camp at night, but still Jim was uneasy. He grabbed his twelve-gauge Winchester pump from the closet and decided to investigate. When he got outside the plant, he saw the door had been forced and the crooks were attempting to chop the safe open with our fire axe. Jim yelled at them to get out of the office with a threat to shoot if they didn't come out. They ignored him and carried on hacking away at the safe. It is one thing to say he'll shoot, and it's another thing to actually do it. The robbers continued to ignore Jim's efforts at getting them out of the building. When they finally cracked open the safe, they scooped up the money and calmly walked out from the office. They bypassed the truck and ran away up the driveway. Jim followed after them and ordered them to stop but they completely ignored him as they ran way. As he later told the insurance company, he had no intention of shooting anybody.

In their haste, the thieves left their truck behind, and it was worth as much as they took. I figured the Mounties would soon round up the culprits. How could they get out of Tofino? There is only one road out of the village to the outside world. Jim called the Mounties, and they soon located the man who owned the truck and his pal in the Legion pub. They were picked up and hustled to the police station for an interrogation. They maintained that someone had stolen the truck while they were drinking in the bar. They stuck with their story and eventually the police had no option but to release them. It was very dark on the wharf and inside the plant. Jim had not had the opportunity to get a good look at the robbers.

The police were sure that the two men had pulled off the robbery, but they had no proof and weren't inclined to pursue the case any further. The insurance company had their own view of the action. They flatly refused to pay out the claim because they said we failed to protect the money. They claimed that when Jim came on the scene, he should have taken further action. I'm not sure what he was supposed to have done. If he had shot one of the robbers, I'm sure he would have got life in prison. I felt that by standing by and ordering the robbers out, he had done the right thing. The controversy raged back and forth for about three years without a settlement. Our laws are so vague that it is impossible to cope with a situation like that. Finally the insurance company was forced to pay up. They then raised our insurance premium from about one thousand dollars to five thousand dollars, so we discontinued the policy. There is no point in paying insurance premiums if you have to hire a lawyer to get a claim paid.

For years there were millions of dollars in cash paid out in fish camps and many more millions carried by independent buyers. It seemed logical that when people were willing to rob gas stations and stores for peanuts, someone might take a shot at robbing a fish camp that had forty or fifty thousand dollars on the premises. I don't think I ever heard of any other camps being held up or robbed other than our plant in Tofino and the failed attempt to rob Napoleon Stradiotti in his camp on the Fraser River. They got nothing from Nap even though they fired a couple of shots at him.

One of the slickest deals ever pulled off in British Columbia was when a lad from Victoria got away with one hundred thousand dollars in advance buying money provided by a Japanese company. We knew the fellow and the Japanese roe herring buying company that he bilked very well and were astounded by his audacious act.

The fishing industry had always been a series of frontiers out on the water. For decades, buyers with signs on their boats plied coastal waters looking for product to buy with cash on the fishing grounds. This necessitated buyers taking out large amounts of cash in order to be competitive and able to load their vessel. My brother John's brother-in-law, Alex Vogrig, took home one hundred and fifty thousand dollars of fish-buying money and put it in his clothes closet. He was planning on going out on the water the next day and took the money home rather than leave it in the safe on his boat. A neighbourhood kid about eight years old, playing with one of Alex's kids, saw Alex stash the money. When nobody was looking, he took the money, removed one hundred dollars and hid the balance about half a mile away under a pile of lumber where a new house was being built. Alex almost suffered a heart attack when he discovered the money was missing. The police were called, and during the investigation it was noticed a big spender was treating all the kids in the neighbourhood to ice cream and other treats. It didn't take the cops long to deduce who the culprit was, but getting the money back was another matter.

The kid denied everything. He clammed up when the cops persisted in the interrogation. Finally, with immunity on the table and the offer of a ride in the police car with the siren blaring and being allowed to keep the balance of the one hundred dollars he had left, he lead the police to the loot. By then Alex had taken at least six aspirins and his wife had an ice pack on his head.

Once during a salmon fishing closure, the boys on a packer decided to deposit forty thousand dollars in a Port Hardy bank for safekeeping while they went off partying. At the end of the season, there was a big row about the shortage in cash. Everybody swore on the Bible that they did not take the money. Things were really heating up when the bank manager in Port Hardy phoned to ask how long they intended to leave their money in his bank. The boys must have really been whooping it up that weekend to leave Port Hardy without picking up their buying money.

Twenty thousand dollars stuffed into a metal lunch pail was left under a chair in the Drake Hotel beer parlor. When the fish buyer got home, his mother told him to be sure and look after his money. Suddenly, the bell went off and the buyer rushed out to his car and sped back to the bar. By this time, a half a dozen longshoremen were sitting at the same table. One of them had kicked the lunch bucket out from under the chair against the wall. The buyer grabbed his lunch bucket and opened it on the pub table. He breathed a huge sigh of relief at the sight of his money while six longshoremen sat there with their mouths agape.

Then there was the small error our new accountant made by overpaying a fisherman by eighteen thousand dollars. B.C. Ice and Cold Storage showed a tally of the salmon as they came out of the man's fishing vessel. Then on the bottom half of the tally sheet, they showed the same fish going into the freezer. Rudy, not being familiar with B.C. Ice tally sheets, added the two figures together and paid the fisherman twice for his fish. Rudy was afraid to tell me about his mistake, and my wife, Kathleen, had advised him not to do so for fear I might throw him into the saltchuck. Once again I think I was saved by a higher power. The fisherman returned like a homing pigeon to us with another load of fish. He figured he had it made by being paid twice for his fish and possibly thought it might happen again. Nothing was said as we unloaded his boat at our plant at Campbell Avenue. We watched his face when he received his cheque, less the money overpaid to him on the previous trip. He looked at the cheque and paused for a moment without saying a word. He left with a slight smile on his face, and we never saw him again.

Two brothers who ran a West Coast troller showed up at the end of the season with nine hundred pounds of large northern cohos. It was the last trip of the season. We weighed up their fish, and because it was such a small trip I wrote out the weight and price on a slip of paper and handed it to one of them. On his way up the stairs to the office to get paid, one of them paused long enough to put a one in front of the nine hundred. Now he had a slip that showed nineteen hundred pounds of cohos. The fraud was not detected until the vessel was leaving Campbell Avenue fish dock basin, headed for their home port of Victoria. We immediately phoned the Royal Bank and put a stop payment on the cheque. A year later, the two fishermen still had not asked for payment for their nine hundred pounds. Finally, eighteen months later, they wrote a letter asking for the money owing to them. We said we would pay them only if they showed up personally to receive their payment. It must have been a bitter pill to swallow, but they swallowed it six months later when they came for the money. Nothing was said. Not a single word. A new cheque was issued, and they took it and left as meekly as they had arrived.

There was a fisherman who said he had lost a cheque he had received from us for a trip of halibut. It was a fairly large cheque of thirty thousand dollars. We advised the Royal Bank to stop payment on the cheque and issued the poor man a replacement one. Well, it seems this gent had not lost the cheque after all but had deposited it in a bank in Steveston after we issued him the replacement. The Royal Bank had to honour this amount to the other bank, so they were out the thirty thousand dollars. It took three years for the bank to get their money back. In the meantime the fisherman was collecting the interest.

One time, a Department of Fisheries and Oceans patrol boat tied up alongside a packer my nephew Edward Jr. was skippering while he was a student going to UBC. Edward and his crew went aboard a fishing vessel tied on the opposite side to have a mug up and shoot the breeze with the crew. When they returned to the fishing grounds in the morning, they discovered about ten thousand dollars missing from the cash box. Months later it was discovered that one of the fisheries officers on the patrol boat had burglarized the packer. He took the money ashore and hid it under a stump. The theft was reported to the insurance company and was paid up under protest by the insurer. The police gave Edward Jr. a hard time, even interrogating him at night at his home after he was back in school.

After the season, the fisheries officer drove up island to retrieve the loot and brought it back to Vancouver. He enrolled at one of the colleges on the lower mainland and stuffed the bills into his locker behind a set of coveralls. After ending the course, he left the money in the locker, intending to come back for it at a later date. In the meantime, the school required the locker, so they broke the lock and removed the contents. When they discovered the large sum of money, they called the police. The numbers on the bills indicated they had come from the money the Royal Bank issued to my nephew as fish-buying money. The police put a watch on the locker and a few days later picked up the fisheries officer, who had returned to the college to fetch the money.

I suppose the fish plants being mostly in out-of-the-way locations around the coast made them obvious targets for thieves. With all the restaurant activity in the city, it was and is probably pretty easy to dispose of quality seafood products at cut-rate prices. In an industry that relied on large amounts of cash, it wouldn't take a genius to figure out that some of it must have resided from time to time in various office safes. Considering the number of buyers who travelled to the fishing grounds and tied up in harbours around the coast on vessels with signs in their rigging that read Cash Buyer in large lettering, it is surprising that there weren't more robberies. Some cash buyers handled enormous sums of money that by any standard could have made life risky if the wrong party found out.

THE VANISHING FISHERY

In the early years of the past century, about one hundred and sixty seine boats participated in the British Columbia fishing industry. Most of the vessels were less than seventy feet in length and many of them were thirty-eight to forty-five feet in length. They used heavy tarred cotton netting in their seine nets with tarred wooden floats that were piled on strong tables that swivelled on rollers as the boat went at full speed in a circle letting out the net. Once the net was closed, the rope drawstring was quickly pulled in to close the purse seine, and the salmon were trapped in the bag along with any unfortunate creatures that happened to be mixing with the school of salmon. The salmon were dipped out of the pursed net with a brailer at about four hundred pounds each time, and then they were dumped in the hold of the vessel.

When the net was empty, the lines were released and the net was pulled back and piled on the seine table again using the winch and human labour. The net was pulled up through a large pulley fastened to the end of the boom. Each time the net measured the length of the boom, it was dropped onto the table. Getting the net back aboard was a tedious job, hauling it in twenty feet at a time and piling it properly on the table so it would run out smoothly the next time a set was made. A twisted net or tangle was deadly because the net routine was aborted and it took half a day to get the net sorted out and back on the table ready to work again.

These boats were small and powered with slow-running combustion engines, and the gear was heavy and slow to get out, and it took more than half a day to get it back in. Skippers made sure there were salmon available in sufficient numbers to make a set pay for the amount of work involved. Seine boats fished from six in the morning to six at night, and gillnetters fished from six at night to six in the morning so they did not interfere with one another. Seine boats normally made two sets each day. A slave driver with a timid crew could make three sets. These men had trouble keeping an experienced crew for long because highballing meant sooner or later somebody was going to be seriously injured. With this old-style equipment sometimes these boats took so many fish they were brailed into scows because their hold would not carry the volume taken.

In the past, every shrimper, dragger of bottom fish, towboat or practically any kind of vessel that was proceeding on the coast at slow speed had a couple of lines rigged for catching salmon out the back of the vessel. Large West Coast trawlers came in with a thousand pounds of springs they caught on a ten-day trip with one line trailing a lure from each stabilizer. Towboat crews came in to port with an abundance of fish for family and friends. Each shrimp boat was good for catching a dozen salmon per day as a sideline.

In the eighties and nineties, one of six hundred or more modern seine vessels, sixty to ninety feet in length, with light synthetic gear and automated equipment could make twenty-five sets in a twenty-four day period. Today when there is an opening, it is usually over a twenty-four-hour period. The result is a dog-eat-dog affair. If a salmon jumps out of the water, the net is run out immediately. Blind sets are the name of the game, with the net going out as much as possible, even when there is no visible sign of salmon on the surface or on the sonar system. Sometimes several blind sets come in with a skunk (empty net) or fewer than a dozen fish in the bag. If enough sets are made, and if three or four sets manage to take fifty to a couple of hundred fish, five thousand pounds or more can be taken in a twenty-four-hour period. If they catch three or four thousand fish in a couple of sets, they could end the day with fifty thousand pounds of salmon. With sockeye salmon bringing a dollar and a half per pound on the grounds, a lot of money can made in a short time. Modern seine boats are capable of taking huge quantities of fish when the stocks are available. It would not be uncommon for one boat to catch one million pounds in a season.

About two thousand gillnet boats, in the thirty-five-foot class, also fished with nets, mostly delivering their fish in the round to canneries. These vessels had financial returns similar to trollers. They made sets in the Fraser River and other areas on openings. Since they delivered net-caught fish in the round, there was less handling of the fish. Gillnet fishermen were traditionally tied to the big companies and organized labour in comparison to the mostly independent trollers.

Approximately twenty-five hundred oceangoing trollers in the thirty-eight- to sixty-five-foot class each caught about one hundred and twenty-five thousand pounds of assorted salmon — springs, coho, sockeye, pinks and chums — each year. These fish were caught with hook and line and cleaned and iced for fresh fish deliveries or were frozen at sea. Fresh deliveries were made every ten to fourteen days. Frozen deliveries were sold three or four times per season in twenty- to forty-thousand-pound lots. The trollers increased their share of fish by learning how to catch substantial quantities of sockeyes on hook and line as easily as they caught coho. Later they also learned how to catch quantities of chums.

Day trollers, in the thirty-five-foot and under category, delivered their catch each evening and were paid on a daily basis. They washed out their boat after unloading and took on a half ton of ice from the fish camp. Free ice was always given to fishermen in order to make sure their fish were kept well chilled. In the morning, they shipped out to sea before daylight and had their lines in the water by first light. Day trollers always had the best fish because when it was delivered it was only ten or twelve hours old. Most of the time, day trollers brought in four hundred pounds per day, but some days they brought in fifteen hundred pounds.

Overfishing by thousands of sports fishing enthusiasts has contributed greatly to the pressure on salmon stocks. For years they fished with rods and light sinkers with some sort of lure or spoon or bait. Their big problem was how to get down deep enough with that kind of gear to catch fish. Under certain conditions, a strong tide or a stiff breeze that carried the boat along would not allow the lure to reach the fish, making it almost impossible to catch a salmon. Old-time handlers in skiffs caught fish because they used one- to one-and-a-half pound lead sinkers, so the line went deep enough under any conditions.

When sports fishing gear included downriggers with fifteen-pound lead cannon balls fastened to a main line that could be wound up mechanically on a drum, they essentially became trollers. Two or three rods could be fished out of each side of the boat with their lines attached to the main line with a release mechanism so that heavy cannon balls could be used to take the line to the desired depth. This gave sportsmen the ability to limit out nearly every time. This led to catching fish for sport and releasing them back into the ocean. A high percentage of released fish die or are taken by predators before they can recover. Imagine running for three or four hundred yards and then being held under water for a few minutes to have a picture taken. I wonder how many of us would survive such an ordeal. Sportsmen took immense quantities of grilse (juvenile salmon) that were easy to catch in the saltchuck, striking almost any lure. Now the sports fishing industry is capable of taking as many or more fish than the commercial trollers.

Once I was approached by a so-called sportsman who knew I was in the fish business. He asked me if wanted to buy some pink salmon — humpbacks. Although I was not interested in his illegal offer, I decided to look at the fish. He caught thirty-five late-run Fraser River pinks that already had humps on their backs and were long past their prime. He had some white springs as well, which he was trying to get rid of since his wife would only eat red-fleshed fish. I asked him why he didn't release the humpies. He said he just couldn't do it because he had to keep all the fish he caught on his weekend fishing trips. He had turned his sport of fishing into a kind of game. The fish were gratuitous creatures that had no value but were taken by a perverse desire that put quantity and macho behaviour ahead of any sense of decency or notion of common sense. A slaughter of fish to brag about.

Forty years ago, when one hundred and fifty vessels with antiquated gear worked the resource, there were too many seine boats. There have been at least three buybacks to date by the Department of Fisheries and Oceans to reduce the fleets. Yet there are in excess of five hundred seine vessels with sophisticated equipment designed to catch more fish than ever before. The advent of high-tech vessels and gear has increased the capability of catching fish to limits that have coincided with the gradual demise of the various fisheries. There is a greater ability and capacity to catch and handle more fish when fewer fish are available to be caught.

The commercial trollers were largely a fiercely independent group of fishermen who were well organized and made large donations to political parties. The organized seine fleet, dominated by the big companies, were also adept at applying oil to the hinges. In recent times the organized sports industry also became a powerful lobbying force. Add in the traditional Aboriginal fisheries, which take a high percentage of fish, and bring their own political controversies to the arguments about overfishing and the declining salmon stocks, and it's a wonder there are any salmon left.

The troller fleet were the big losers, with the government buying back licences and boats to eliminate their numbers and virtually put an end to their industry. This seemed ludicrous since the troller fleet produced the top-of-the-line product that was most favoured in the marketplace all over the world. Net-caught fish, which are drowned and abused by the process, cannot compare with hook-and-line fish, which are killed live and handled in a gentler and more efficient way. Hook-and-line fishing also spares many undersized fish and other species that perish wantonly in nets. The troller fleet was sacrificed for the seine fleet, which is largely owned and controlled by the large fishing companies with government patronage. The trollers were also a direct competitor to and victim of the powerful sports fishing lobby and its allied tourism industry, which entices government with visions of enormous numbers of American sports fishing enthusiasts spending American dollars in British Columbia.

Overfishing by commercial interests has also contributed greatly to the current decline in salmon and other fish stocks. In the middle of the past century, we drove the herring to the brink of existence by overfishing for reduction plants. In the last quarter of that century and in the 2000s the big fish companies are the prime players in the unconscionable herring roe industry, which must be abandoned if we hope to see the salmon runs return in abundance. A moratorium on herring fishing is the only sane path to ensuring that enough feed exists in the ocean for our many species of wild Pacific salmon. Fish are big business. When there aren't enough to go around, jobs and a substantial investment are threatened and so is a coastal way of life.

Appendices

Pinks, Crustaceans and Morning Herring

After the roaring twenties, the fishing industry in British Columbia went into a slump. B.C. Packers were in receivership with all their plants shut down. Many companies slowed down or curtailed production. My father's company did not shut down but we split up from our working relationship with the Johnson's Canning Company on the Fraser River and operated in a very conservative manner. Father bought beautiful number-one frozen cohos from the receiver selling B.C. Packers' inventory for one cent per pound.

In the Depression years, sockeye salmon were fifteen to twenty-five cents per fish to the fishermen. Pinks were five cents each and chums were eight cents each. Pinks could weigh up to eight pounds in the round, while chums could reach up to twenty pounds or more in the round. White springs were one to two cents per pound and red springs were four to eight cents per pound. Prices on springs varied some depending on the size and colour of the meat. All small springs under five pounds were ten cents each.

In the mid-thirties, one hundred dollars bought a lot of fish. Seine boats that were selling their fish to the few canneries still operating would arrive at Campbell Avenue attempting to sell their fish to us for a couple of cents more per fish than they could receive elsewhere. Canneries paid eight cents a piece for chums and three cents a piece for pinks. We paid ten cents for the best chums from the top of the load and five cents for the best pinks from the top of the load. We took five or six thousand pounds of the best fish from the top of each boatload that called in on us. The rest went to be put in cans. We sold this fish on the fresh market wherever we could and froze some for sale in the winter months.

Those chums and pinks we bought from the seine boats were all beautiful silvery fish with red meat — all in their prime. I began buying more and more of them and freezing the surplus that we could not sell fresh. Father said, "I don't think we should be freezing that fish because it will never sell." I argued, "How can we lose money buying such prime fish for eight and ten cents a piece?" Some of those chums were up to fifteen pounds each, and the pinks were beautiful silvery fish averaging five pounds, dressed, head off. Father let me have my way but shook his head more than once at my stubbornness. When we had about one hundred and twenty-five thousand pounds of nice pinks and fifty thousand pounds of sliver bright chums already frozen in cold storage, Father put his foot down and ordered me to stop freezing net salmon. "Just buy what we can sell fresh and no more are to go into the cold storage" were his instructions. I obeyed the old man but figured he was wrong.

I thought we could make a pot of money in the winter and in the springtime when the weather was bad and fresh salmon was scarce. I said to the old man, "People will buy that nice fish when there are no fresh fish on the market." He just looked at me and said, "Don't freeze anymore and that's that." I knew it was time to pull in my horns. I attempted to sell the frozen pinks, but nobody wanted them. The chums were moving slowly. By the first of April we still had almost one hundred thousand pounds of pinks left in storage and fifteen thousand pounds of the silver bright chums.

Finally, the old man said, "Norm, when are you going to sell those pinks?" I sweated it out and sold all the silver bright chums, but it looked as if more than ninety thousand pounds of beautiful pinks would have to be held over until the next winter. Suddenly, Father jumped in and sold all the pinks to Burns reduction plant for five dollars per ton. Fred Haddon with his five-ton dumptruck hauled a load away every afternoon for three weeks until they were gone. Father never said much about it after except to ask me if I'd learned anything from the experience. I certainly did, and I put the brakes on after that for several years. It doesn't pay to speculate with food products in a depressed economy. I thought I was predicting but really it was closer to gambling.

In 1936, there were about fifteen trollers fishing the Lower Gulf twelve months of the year. Each week in the winter and spring, we unloaded four or five boats of one thousand to two thousand pounds of nice trolled springs. Weather conditions had no adverse effect on the supply of fish, which remained in constant supply. These were hook-and-line-caught dressed and iced fish. Several of these vessels, *Night Hawk*, *Owl*, *Ona*, *Sea Prince*, *Nightingale* and *Fina*, to name a few, delivered constantly to our wharf. A good part of our production of fresh salmon came from this flotilla of small trollers. A few gillnetters also delivered directly to us, but most of our gillnet salmon came via Takahashi. Some of the fishermen owed the big companies money, so in order to get some cash they sold part of their catch to us.

There were a substantial number of small trollers fishing for salmon in the Gulf of Georgia on the east coast of Vancouver Island, along the Sunshine Coast, Howe Sound and the various inlets. These were small boats, thirty-four feet to thirty-eight feet in length. Three thousand to four thousand pounds of iced fish was about the capacity of their loads, and they arrived at Campbell Avenue fish dock on a weekly basis. They caught bluebacks and spring salmon from the first of May, until the end of January with pink salmon also taken from mid-August until the end of September. By December and January, the bluebacks were large fish, eight to sixteen pounds with large hooked noses and coloured red in their spawning condition.

Our crabs came from Boundary Bay and areas around the mouth of the Fraser River. The best crab fishing areas are always in eel grass shoals in seven to ten fathoms of water near the mouths of rivers. Crabs can be caught in other areas for a short time. These crabs are travelling to eel grass shallows, and the fishing only lasts until they move through to their feeding grounds. There are no crabs in quantity in water more than twenty-five fathoms deep.

Our shrimp all came from a number of small vessels, thirty-three to thirty-six feet in length, manned by Japanese fishermen who fished Burrard Inlet from an area east of the Second Narrows bridge. Most of the shrimp these fishermen caught were large coon stripes, averaging about sixteen pieces per pound. These coon stripes were the best shrimp to eat. At that time the shrimp were sold whole and then peeled by the purchaser. Each fisherman had a stove on the deck and cooked each batch of shrimp in sea water as soon as they were spilled out from the net. The meat was a red colour and very firm in texture. The coon stripe were prolific in the harbour from the First Narrows to where the harbour split into the north and south arms of Balcarre. A baited trap anywhere in this area would produce ten to fifteen pounds of shrimp every twenty-four hours. There were no coon stripes in the North Arm of the Inlet. The water in the North Arm is much deeper on the average and had a few spot prawns and quite a few side stripes. The side stripes were a bit larger than the coon stripes but the meat was softer and not as tasty. Fishing for shrimp in Vancouver Harbour is ancient history now.

During bad weather with a stiff southwest wind or westerly blowing, the small trollers that fished off the Sunshine Coast, Bowen Island and areas fronting the mouth of the Fraser River could not put their lines out. They also could not fish Howe Sound with a north or northeast wind blowing. These fishermen moved into sheltered waters inside the Point Grey–Point Atkinson entrance to Vancouver Harbour. They put poles out and trolled east past English Bay, West Vancouver and Stanley Park through the First Narrows and into Burrard Inlet. They proceeded up the inlet with lines out and turned just past Victoria Drive and then continued on a westerly course back into the outer harbour and out to Point Grey. Then they turned and retraced their course again back into the inner harbour. They continued to fish that way all day when the weather forced them to do it. They caught a substantial number of salmon. Sometimes the fish taken in Vancouver Harbour were larger than the fish they caught out in the gulf. In those days, there wasn't as much shipping traffic entering and leaving the harbour as there is now. However, the trollers' fleet had to be vigilant, especially for towboats and barges or log booms.

In the 1930s there were about twenty small vessels of thirty-two to thirty-five feet in length that fished for both herring and salmon when in season. Some of them only put on salmon nets for a month to fish the sockeye run on the Fraser River. When that ended, they put their herring gillnets back on their drums. A few of them fished only for herring. In those days, there was no fishery for roe herring. There was an agreement strictly observed by all of them to begin fishing on the fifteenth of April and stop fishing in the middle of January. To my knowledge none of these fishermen ever broke their agreement.

They all fished the Point Grey bank from the middle of April until the end of July. In the beginning they were taking two to three hundred pounds of morning herring per day. By the middle of May, they were taking one thousand to fifteen hundred pounds of morning herring per day. After that they were taking four thousand to eight thousand pounds of morning herring per day. The price the first couple of days was twenty-five cents per pound, then it settled to fifteen cents per pound for a couple of weeks, then the price dropped to five cents for the first three hundred pounds, then two cents for the next five hundred pounds, and finally by one or two cents a pounds for the balance of each fisherman's catch. Some years it dropped down as low as half a cent per pound if there was a tough market. The fishermen were a tight group, and God help anyone who even thought about breaking their pact.

Until the end of July, all the fresh herring were sold fresh to various fish stores in Vancouver and there were more than thirty of them. A substantial share of the catch went to eight smokehouses, five days a week. Each of these establishments used at least one ton of herring each day for kippering. At Van Shell, we shipped fifty to one hundred and fifty fifty-pound boxes of this fresh morning herring to the United States at least twice each week. The halibut fleet took the balance for bait. Fresh Point Grey herring were very fat and, along with salmon, made the best bait. In those days the halibut quota exceeded eighty-five million pounds each season, so there was a big demand for this super-fat herring bait. This herring had such a high oil content, the highest in the world at eighteen percent or more at its peak, that it was too fat to freeze. When frozen it turned an ugly yellow colour.

By the first of September, when the fat content was beginning to diminish, some of this fish was put into cold storage to use for kippering in the off season when herring were spawning. From the fifteenth of January to the fifteenth of April, the local fishermen quit fishing for food herring because the fish, full of roe and milts, were too thin for smoking.

In the fall the local gillnet herring fishermen left the Point Grey bank and split up to fish in Nanoose Bay and Pender Harbour. They could load their small boats there in one morning set and be in Vancouver by the afternoon to sell their catch. Each year we would supply some twenty-five-, fifty-, and seventy-five-pound wooden kits and some one-hundred-pound barrels that we bought from Sweeney's cooperage in False Creek to a few of these fishermen. Each fisherman would take as many as his boat would hold with some one-hundred-and-twenty-pound bags of rock salt to Scotch cure the herring as they were caught. Usually, there were two men in each boat and the herring were gibed (guts and gills pulled out), then dry-salted into wooden containers. Every ten days they would return with all containers filled. They unloaded to us and went home to rest for a couple of days. Then they went out with another load of containers to repeat the process. The kits and barrels were laid out in rows in our plant with plugs removed from bung holes in the lids. Each day some ninety percent brine was added to each container through the bung hole until the level of brine remained constant. Then wooden plugs were driven into the bung holes, the metal hoops were given a final tap down with a special tool to make the barrels absolutely leakproof, and they were triple stacked in our plant to await a sale. This type of fishery lasted to the end of each season as the fresh market petered out. By that time in the season, fish eaters had had their fill of fresh herring and the demand was way down.

Up until the war, our company sold a quantity of fish as well as meat, poultry, vegetables and dairy products to several Scandinavian deep-sea vessels, mostly Norwegian, on their visits to Vancouver. They returned on about a two-and-a-half month schedule. It was always a private deal with the respective captains who paid cash for the merchandise. They snapped up every container of Scotch-cured herring that we had on hand. They probably used some themselves but had to sell the balance somewhere along their route. We sold fifteen hundred containers each season without any complaint from the Department of Fisheries and Oceans. I believe that at that time a salteries licence, which cost five thousand dollars, was levied on the companies that were shipping thousands of tons of salt herring to China. The expensive licence was introduced to accommodate the large companies and exclude the small operators. This always seemed to be the main purpose of the Department of Fisheries and Oceans. There was only one policy regarding the herring fishery. It mattered not that we were Scotch curing herring for an elite trade rather than pressing it solid into five-hundred-pound cakes and boxing it for the poorest trade in the world. This China-bound herring was late run and full of spawn, and almost unfit for human consumption. It was not worth buying a licence for the three or four thousand dollars we made annually on our salt herring.

After the war ended, there was an influx of people entering the Department of Fisheries and Oceans from the armed forces. Some of these were good people with common sense while others were narrow-minded people who enforced rules to the letter and always seemed to be bucking for promotion. They were the ones who would lay a charge against a fisherman for eating fish out of season on their own vessel. I thought it was unreasonable for an inspector to go on a fishing vessel and check the galley fridge in hopes of discovering a bit of halibut or some leftover ling cod that the crew had eaten the night before. They were always looking for a small infraction of one of their sacred rules and conducted their working lives in an adversarial manner. We were advised by some of the more sensible fisheries officers that we should keep the salt herring business small and low key because technically we lacked the licence to produce Scotch-cured salt fish. We still continued to put up a great custom packed product for a small client base that was essentially Scandinavian. However, some of the new Department of Fisheries and Oceans recruits began to posture and threaten prosecution, so we terminated that business permanently.

At the time, a score of reduction plants were turning thousands of tons of herring — small, large, fat or thin herring that was in poor condition — along with thousands of salmon, pollock, shiners, flounders, sole or anything else that could be vacuumed out of the sea into cheap fodder for humans to be shipped to Asia. The result was enormous carnage, and the whole Pacific fishery was nearly destroyed with the approval of the Department of Fisheries and Oceans. The DFO completely closed their eyes to the repulsive policies of the big companies and spent an inordinate amount of time and effort in hounding small companies for two-bit offences.

Before the war and up until the late fifties, there were fifteen or sixteen thirty-four-foot herring boats that gillnetted off Point Grey for prime, mature herring that were three-quarters of a pound to one pound each. Herring do not feed after dark, so by midnight there was no feed in their intestinal tracks to ferment and burn their stomach linings. Herring caught before midnight was called night herring. By ten a.m., the bellies in the night herring would begin bursting, so they were worthless. Nobody would buy night herring.

We always asked the fishermen if they were sure the fish was morning herring. Sometimes one of them tried to pull a fast one and brought in the herring mixed together. Father would rip open bellies of a dozen or more fish to see if there was any feed in them. We shipped herring to Seattle, Portland and into California. In order to arrive at their destination in good shape, they had to be morning herring or the bellies would bust and we wouldn't get paid.

The first boat in got the best price, around three cents per pound. This was sold to peddlers who were waiting for fish so they could get on the road. After that the price dropped to two and a half cents, then to one and a half cents, and then the smokers picked up the balance for kippering for one cent or less. These two-man boats with one thousand to five thousand pounds of fish on them made a profit. The first boat in made the most money, and the whole fleet was strung out as they raced in to Campbell Avenue. Old-style Easthope and Vivian gas engines were revving up wide open when this fleet of primarily Scottish fishermen were attempting to beat each other to the fish dock.

The top fish was in the best shape, not crushed and with no scale loss. It went to local and U.S. fresh fish markets. The lower half of herring in each boat went to smokehouses for kippers or was put aboard vessels for halibut and salmon bait. All the herring was top quality, but fresh fish markets required pristine fish that looked as if they had come out of the water only moments before they were sold. To the smokers who made kippers, bloaters and snacks, scale loss was not a detriment. Halibut or salmon trolling vessels also required bait herring that had no scale loss.

Most of the smokehouses were located on the Campbell Avenue fish dock. The main smokehouses in Vancouver were London Fish Company, Pacific Fish Company, Reliance Fish Company, Ocean Fish Company (a Japanese-owned company, not the present-day Ocean Fish), Burnett's Smokehouse and Canadian Fishing Company, who had their own dock at the foot of Gore. Billingsgate's smokehouse was located on the Campbell Avenue fish dock.

Old Man Burnett's business was located on Alexander Street.

He worked with his two sons, when he was not fighting with them. They ran a primitive smokehouse situated in an old brick building that had been put up at the turn of the century. Their seemingly haywire operation produced the best smoked fish in Vancouver, be it smoked black cod, kippers, snacks, bloaters or smoked cod. It was all done the same each time with the right amount of sawdust smouldering under the fish. In the morning when they opened the doors to the kilns, drops of oil glistened on the skin of cooling fish like diamonds sparkling in the sunlight. My mouth still waters when I think of the delicious fish products smokehouses in Vancouver turned out in the Depression.

Several generations of Canadians have never tasted kippers, snacks or bloaters made from fresh morning herring, or barbecued oolichans made from fresh oolichans, or smoked black cod made from hook-and-line-caught black cod or barbecued salmon made from fresh trolled salmon or even smoked cod fillets made from fresh grey cod.

The Ocean Kings

Jack Eagland, with his *Ocean King*, was one of the best highline fisherman. He filled his boat every trip. He died young, at about the age of forty. Bill Kitsel fished Jim Pope's *Welcome Pass* with Pope to learn the trade. He built the *Sharlene K* and sold it to Dennis Guiden. Dennis changed the name to the *Bon Accord*. Kitsel built a new, much larger steel vessel and also named it the *Sharlene K*. Tom Wilson bought the *Cape Norman* after he left Colonial Cannery. He had been the cannery mechanic. He drowned with his crew when the *Cape Norman* sank with a full load of herring. *Cape Norman* had just been rebuilt by Wilson and was in good shape. It must have hit a deadhead or a large log in the storm that sank it. Vessel skipper Tom Wilson and crew were never found. Don Baker owned *B.C. Girl*. He sold her and built a bigger steel vessel called the *Joe Mark*. Pete Ambrose, an excellent hard-driving fisherman, built and fished the *Tordo*. Tom Scoretz, a hard-working highliner, built his own fishing vessels, first the *Haste* and then *Mr. Wind*.

Jack Shannon Sr. owned the *Shannon J*, sold it to Bill Faulkner and built a new vessel called the *Shannon M*. Jack Shannon Jr. fished with his younger brother. *Shannon J* burned to the waterline while on the fishing grounds. The Shannon brothers — Jack, Herb, Boyd and Bill — were a fighting family, always agreeing to disagree, although they helped each other out when it was necessary. I remember them throwing firewood at one another when they had a fight on their father's boat. This was when wood and coal were burned in the galley. The Shannons were known as "the fighting Irish." Boyd

Shannon owned the *Phyllis Carlyle*. He lost his thumb and part of his right hand under a steel cable when winching in the net. When Boyd bought out National Cannery, a fellow named Wingham took over the vessel. Herb Shannon, Boyd's brother, owned *Phyllis Carlyle II*. It sank one October on the West Coast with a full load of chums from the Nit Nat. She was on her way to Boyd's cannery in Vancouver when she completely vanished at sea. The crew were lost and no trace of the vessel was ever found. Bill Shannon, a calm man who was never in a hurry, owned *Fawn Bluff*.

Jimmy Martin owned the *Curlew M*. He drowned in his net when he was knocked overboard by a cable. His brother Marty fished on the *Curlew M* until he retired and sold her. Jim Pope owned *Willow Point* and *Welcome Pass*. He sold both vessels and became Julian Gordon's boss in the co-operative. Louis Summers, another hard-driving highliner, owned the *Louanna S*.

Gigilo, owned by Safarik and Sons, was fished by Harry Alcovich and Harold Hodginson. Harry saved Harold's life when he pulled him from the engine room when the starter motor, meant to crank the Caterpillar engine, caught fire at Campbell Avenue dock. Harry should have received a medal for the risk he took. Harry, a good fisherman, died young, at about age forty. Bill Cozzie on the *B.C. Producer* was one of the best fishermen on our coast. He sold his boat to Jack MacMillan. The *B.C. Producer* sank while fishing for roe herring, and Norman Sigmund's younger brother drowned as a result of the accident.

Ocean Tide, *Bell Buoy* and the *Yuri* were vessels owned, at one time or another, by my brother John Safarik. The *Bell Buoy*, sold to Joe Brown, burned to the waterline and sank. Fortunately the crew got off. *Yuri* was sold to a couple of Polish fishermen. They hit a reef outside of Tofino and started to sink, but the crew made it ashore and were saved. Not much more than the vessel's bow remained above water.

Neil Botting and my son Jim were able to get a towline on the bow of the *Yuri* and slowly tow it in to our plant in Tofino. They raised the vessel with a crane and pumped it out, put a patch on the hull so it wouldn't sink again and split the salvage money from the insurance company. Eventually, the *Yuri* was rebuilt in the Pioneer Boatworks in Ucluelet.

A Brief History of Salmon

After the tenth of September, all spring salmon caught by gillnets on the Fraser River were classed as white springs, regardless of their flesh colour. When red springs enter a river system to spawn, their red meat begins to fade to a whitish colour. So all the spring salmon, white or red meated, ended up with their flesh white or at least a faint pinkish hue that turns white when the fish is cooked. There is always the exception to the rule and for some unknown reason the odd red spring remained red meated until it died.

As a rule all the salmon species, be they spring, coho, sockeye, pinks, chums or steelhead, generally have red flesh colour, although shades of red might be a better way of looking at it. All the salmonoid species except the white spring, always white throughout its lifespan, are red meated, more or less, when they are prime in the ocean. Some are a bit redder than others.

All salmon die after spawning. Steelhead do not die but they are not a true salmon. They are sea-run rainbow trout and they spawn more than once before they die. Steelheads look like rattle snakes after they spawn. They become extremely thin with discoloured skin covered with scratches and sores suffered from fighting their way upriver. Their flesh is then a poor, greenish-white colour and inedible. After steelhead spawn, they are a sick fish when they return to the ocean. It takes at least a couple of months for them to recover the silver skin and red flesh colour that makes them once again good to eat. Both seiners and gillnetters slaughtered these lethargic sick fish that no buyer really wanted.

Buyers only took them to pacify uncaring fishermen who brought them to market. Hundreds of thousands of these thin spawned-out fish ended up in pet food plants or in reduction. If left alone, in a short time these fish would have recovered to be prime red-meated good eating game fish. I will never understand why the Department of Fisheries and Oceans ever allowed steelhead to be taken for commercial purposes. It is a wonderful fish when prime. However, only about twenty percent of these fish taken by net were prime and the rest were in the in-between stage. In this condition, these fish had no value in the can and they were not worth as much as the cheapest salmon on the market. The steelhead is a tough fish that can stand a substantial amount of abuse. They should have been released by commercial fishermen, even though a percentage of those returned to the sea would have died.

Steelhead seemed to enter rivers continuously. There were large winter and spring runs, a lesser summer run and a fair run of very large steelhead in the fall. I weighed one in the thirty-two-pound range and I knew there must have been larger ones. Because these fish ran continuously into rivers and creeks and to the ocean, their colour varied a great deal. There was a market for select bright red-meated fish in France, Eastern Canada and the United States. However, I doubt that more than three hundred thousand pounds were shipped in any one year. A good many poor grades ended up in reduction or as pet food.

Most juvenile spring salmon (one to one and a half pounds) are pale red or white. When they grow larger, many of them gain a good red meat colour. I believe this comes from a heavy diet of shrimp. Fish that feed largely on herring remain a pink meat colour. Fish that remain white fleshed as adults are a subspecies of spring salmon that stay white no matter what they eat. A pure white spring has very pale eggs with a thin black ring of colour around each egg. A red spring has a red colour right through the yolk sack without any visible black discolouration. I have dressed many thousands of spring salmon in my lifetime, and without exception I have always been able to pick out eggs that were taken from white springs.

Some spring salmon grew to more than one hundred pounds in weight. The largest I personally weighed was a tad above one hundred and five pounds. These large fish easily broke trolling lines and even trolling poles, and the mesh in gillnets was too small to take extra large fish. While hundred-pound fish were rare, it was not uncommon to see many fish in the eighty five- to ninety-pound range. These extra large springs must have been more than three or four years of age. Perhaps they remained in the ocean for up to six or eight years. Is it possible that they returned to the ocean after spawning once they were four years old and returned to spawn a second time when they were six or eight years old? It was hard to believe they were only four years old. How could it be possible for these fish to gain twenty-five pounds per year? There do not seem to be any of these big fish showing up anymore, so I suppose we will never know if they were a subspecies of giants, or fish that had more feed and better conditions to grow.

Every stream has their own subspecies of salmon, be they coho, sockeye, spring, pink, chum or our salmon trout that are called steelhead. The salmon in each stream looked a bit different from each other. For example, the spring salmon from the Fraser River and Columbia River had blunt heads with rounded noses. The spring salmon from the West Coast and northern streams had long, sharp noses. The differences in fish were obvious even when trollers caught them way offshore. Rivers Inlet springs also had blunt heads with rounded noses but not as pronounced as the springs that entered the Fraser or Columbia Rivers. I have seen millions of salmon come across our grading tables on Campbell Avenue fish dock. The variations in appearance indicated to me that they came from different river systems.

Trolled hook-and-line-caught salmon from the West Coast and the North Coast were the finest, fattest fish in the world. All the five species of salmon and steelhead have the same bright rainbow colours on them that remain for days after they die, if they are properly iced down. It is difficult for a novice to tell the difference between the taste of an ocean-caught prime spring, coho, sockeye, pink or steelhead and salmon inshore or even in the Gulf of Georgia. An ocean-caught chum is supremely better than an inshore or river-caught fish. The difference in quality is about the same as the difference between a three-year-old grain-fed steer and a worn-out ten-year-old milk cow. The river fish are in the worst shape. The protein is the same and they are edible, but river fish are not even remotely in the same class as trolled ocean-caught fish. I am not saying that net-caught inshore or river fish are not good to eat, but they are not as prime as ocean-caught fish. Anyone who has never eaten a prime fresh trolled-caught fish or canned salmon made from trolled salmon has never really tasted the best fish.

I once had two owners of canneries in Alaska visit me on business. I asked my wife to open two half-pound cans of troll-caught canned sockeye salmon for making sandwiches. The wonderful aroma and appearance of this canned salmon impressed our visitors enough for them to ask what kind of fish was in those cans. I told them that it was West Coast troll-caught canned sockeye salmon. They wouldn't believe me because they had canned millions of net-caught inshore sockeye salmon in Alaska that were not even vaguely comparable in quality. I finally managed to convince them they were eating ocean troll-caught sockeye salmon. They were astonished by the quality of the product.

It is true that British Columbia sockeye salmon are a better quality sockeye than the ones caught in Alaska. There are many grades and subspecies of all the salmonoid fish that vary in quality. However, our Fraser River sockeye are the best quality with the highest fat content. The Japanese buyers for years have paid from one to four dollars more per pound for ocean troll-caught Fraser River sockeye salmon. Over the years our company sold millions of pounds of these troll-caught sockeye salmon into Japan. One year when the Fraser River run was poor, we sold our ocean-caught trolled sockeyes to the Japanese for nine dollars U.S. per pound, and that was at a time when the best net-caught sockeyes sold into that market for less than four dollars U.S. per pound.

Once I had five Department of Fisheries and Oceans biologists from upper management observe us grading a load of trolled salmon that had just arrived at Campbell Avenue by truck from Tofino. Even experienced graders make mistakes now and then. Troll-caught chum salmon look exactly like troll-caught sockeyes. Even a veteran grader has to look at the flesh colour to tell the difference. The sockeye has redder meat colour. I bet these gentlemen each five bucks that they could not grade out the different species of salmon. They refused my offer. After decades of grading salmon, I have often been fooled, so I can't really fault them for their refusal.

Troll-caught pinks (humps) look a bit like spring salmon to a greenhorn. Pinks have no sign of the hump, which they get later in life, when they are prime. I once weighed a thirteen-pound dressed troll-caught pink that came from the Tofino area. It was probably a Fraser River fish passing by. We had sixty thousand pounds of plus-seven-pound head-off trolled pinks in B.C. Ice and Cold Storage one year and at least four hundred thousand pounds of five- to seven-pound head-off fish. As well as selling a couple of hundred thousand pounds of fresh pinks that year, we had more than a million pounds in cold storage.

One morning an official from the Department of Fisheries and Oceans phoned to inform us we had a million pounds of pinks in storage and that they were not going to issue us a permit to export them. He asked my son Howard what were going to do with them. That was an era when the inspection department of Department of Fisheries and Oceans had the power of death over small operators. After fighting with Department of Fisheries and Oceans for six weeks, we finally received permission to sell all the frozen pinks into England. It was typical of the times.

Today, net-caught fish are a second-class product or worse after being frozen. Farm fish does not smoke well because its mushy flesh falls apart in a smokehouse. It can't be canned either because it turns soupy in the cans. Our wild hook-and-line-caught fish was the best fish in the world when there were enough herring left in the ocean to sustain them. Now the wild fish that are left are skinny and undersized because the food supply has been so severely reduced. Once we could not find enough four- to six-pound trolled coho to fill export orders after the middle of July because the fish were all more than six pounds in weight by that month. Today in September the coho still only weigh in at one and a half to two pounds.

An industry producing a mediocre-quality product, be it farm fish with all of the ancillary worries that brings, or poor-quality net-caught fish, combined with an uninformed, feeble Department of Fisheries and Oceans directed by politicians with vested interests is a formula for disaster. This has been exacerbated for decades by the horrible record of science in its attempts to deal with fisheries. The entire past century is rife with unspeakable policies and actions that have impaired, threatened and destroyed the various fisheries on the Atlantic and Pacific coasts. For the better part of this time, I have been asking questions of the experts about these problems, but instead of getting answers I have been consistently told I was misinformed.

Letter to the Commission on Pacific Fisheries

The following letter, addressed to the attention of Dr. Peter Pearse, was sent to the Commission on Pacific Fisheries Policy on December 9, 1981. Dr. Pearse, a professor at the University of British Columbia, had been appointed by the federal government to chair this body that was empowered to investigate the fisheries and develop policy for future decades. Now, nearly thirty years seems to have passed in no time at all. In 1981, there were very serious problems in the fisheries and we all knew it. In the succeeding thirty years, these problems, which were never seriously dealt with, grew exponentially until the fisheries were largely in a shambles. Many of the issues of the eighties are still relevant after the turn of the millennium.We can only hope and pray that in the coming new decades we will be wise enough and strong enough to make a genuine attempt at restoring the environment and rebuilding the fisheries, once an almost unlimited resource of immense wealth. The tragedy of a barren coast, sterile rivers and a depleted ocean do not bode well for the future of mankind. I am an old man who will never live to see the policy changes and the human effort that will be necessary to make the fisheries even a shadow of its past glory. I offer this letter once again, as a starting point.

British Columbia is one of the largest natural fish hatcheries in the world. Lumber companies, industry and urban development have destroyed the salmonoid habitat for more than a hundred years. Commercial fishermen, sportsmen and predators have take billions of pounds of salmon in that time and still some salmon are entering most of our streams to spawn. Some of the creeks are gone forever —

filled in for industrial sites (e.g., Hooker Chemical plant built over a stream on the North Shore of Burrard Inlet that at one time supported a couple of thousand chum salmon, a few coho and a few steelhead). The Federal Department of Fisheries probably did not even know this unnamed waterway existed, much less that it supported families of salmon.

What is gone we cannot weep over at this time, but now we must take inventory of every stream that remains no matter how small it is and drastically improve what we have left to make up for those creeks that are now lost to us forever. We must see to it that not even one more stream, no matter how small, is ever taken out of salmonoid production again. Most of the spawning grounds, even those away from urban areas, are devastated and are still being devastated by the same people doing business as usual, apparently with provincial government approval. Unless the British Columbia government has a change of heart and co-operates with the Department of Fisheries and Oceans on salmonoid enhancement, it will be impossible to save salmon for even the sports fishermen much less for the commercial fishery. If both governments co-operate, our freshwater systems can be improved to sustain even greater runs of salmon than they normally did at the turn of the century.

Some rivers, like the Zeballos River (a substantial waterway unable to support a maximum salmonoid reproduction), should have obstructions removed to allow more prolific runs of all species of salmon to thrive there. I'm certain there are many other creeks and lakes that cannot support good salmon runs because of obstruction (logging debris, mud slides, cave-ins) that could be removed or by-passed so salmon stocks could be reintroduced into them. There are areas where flows of water seep out in such a way that they form impassable swamps rather than draining through a creek. Spawning channels could be engineered into those places without disturbing the ecological balance, so even swampy areas could support substantial populations of salmon. Swampy areas are not suitable for growing good timber, so there would be a dual benefit to the province from that kind of improvement.

Salmon are a tough species and it seems no matter how hard we try we cannot completely wipe them out. Just imagine what the results would be if we gave these fish half a chance. There is no end to the improvements that could be made to our freshwater systems so that salmon runs could be rebuilt to historic levels. It requires federal and provincial co-operation to provide the muscle, and it requires knowledgeable and enthusiastic DFO personnel with an unswerving determination to succeed with the enhancement program. I am afraid that DFO personnel not only are not supported by the authorities to enforce the remedies to improve salmon stocks, but also they do not seem dedicated to the program or they are not energetic or knowledgeable enough to cope with problems that are contributing to the demise of our salmon. In any case, they do not seem to think on a large enough scale to provide the solutions that will reverse the decline in our salmon populations. No one in the DFO seems to have an idea of the magnitude of our salmon runs at the turn of the century or even before the Second World War. They all think in terms of off seasons and fifty salmon per creek rather than salmon every season and thousands of salmon in every creek.

One thing we are blessed with on the western Pacific slopes is plenty of rain and the prolific growth of trees. This is a perfect setup for production of fish if only people could be persuaded to take care of our environment.

If we do not make a real effort to clean up our act now, then waterways like the Fraser and other streams that are in trouble with pollution, hydro problems and clear-cutting practices will cease producing sufficient salmon to sustain a fishery by the end of the decade.

The provincial government position advocated by Jack Davis and others, with their fish hatcheries and fish farming schemes with fish traps located in rivers, are all wild proposals touted by people who appear to know very little about our salmon.

Their plan is akin to having a beautiful valley containing the very best bottom land for growing super crops and polluting this valuable property out of production by covering it with junk yards — and then introducing a plan to raise the same crops in backyard gardens. The only way their proposals can be summed up is that these gentlemen cannot see the forest for the trees. We are actually destroying a natural resource capable of providing untold millions of dollars of income and food in perpetuity without any expense for people in this country in exchange for industrial development that will not produce even one percent as much in the long run to the detriment of mankind.

There is no salmon in the world that is better than our prime British Columbia products. The Japanese, for instance, will pay more for our troll-caught sockeyes taken offshore than they will pay for the same Alaskan species because ours is a better-quality fish. Troll-caught (hook-and-line caught) salmon from the ocean is the best-quality fish when it is bled and dressed immediately to preserve the rich flavour. This fish can be compared to prime grain-fed beef, and this type of product brings the highest prices on the export market. Net fish taken outside or in the straits, a second-class-quality fish with some bruising, blood clots and incidental net damage, is not as rich in flavour and can be compared to grass-fed beef. Net fish taken in bays, inlets and in rivers is a third-class-quality product comparable to dairy milk cow beef. This latter product is condemned for export by federal inspection so is canned or consumed fresh by the Canadian public. How then can the provincial government entertain a plan to farm fish and catch them in traps located in our rivers? All they would get out of that fishery is poor-quality salmon worse than old bull beef that would not be allowed to be exported by federal inspection because of the poor quality.

Net salmon caught late in the season is not really fit for human consumption and yet the DFO allows a net fishery to take this late-run spent salmon. I suppose the stuff is edible but I imagine old running shoes would taste better. I believe that this spent salmon should not be taken for food, but should be allowed to continue on to the spawning grounds so their progeny could be taken in the ocean at the peak of their prime so Canadians can benefit from the best return on the export market and the Canadian consumer could eat good fish.

Once the salmon encounters water with a lower salt content near any river, the flesh of this fish deteriorates very quickly. The degree of this deterioration (discolouration of skin, covered with a heavy mucus slime, pus spots, worms, unpalatable odour) is a preliminary decomposition setting in and the quality retained in the flesh of the salmon depends on how far the fish is going upriver to spawn. Fish spawning in the interior areas are in better condition than the same fish spawning within a few miles of the river mouth. Salmon fighting their way upriver a hundred and fifty miles or more are a hardier subspecies of salmon that nature has endowed with the system to survive the arduous journey.

If we are to have a good enhancement program and a fair fishery for all the people engaged in the industry, then the Department of Fisheries and Oceans must be completely above board and impartial in their dealings with all the fishermen and companies. I am afraid that this has never been their policy in the past and is not their policy at present. This "do as I say and not as I do" method of administrating the fishery breeds discontent and animosity towards the department by both fishermen and fish companies. For example, the DFO introduces regulations at will, protecting select groups of processors. The excuse for this protection is that it creates more work for Canadians by funneling more fish to the cannery operators. Is it reasonable to curtail the troll fishery that catches the most valuable fish when cannery operators are allowed to freeze net salmon and dump this cheap second-grade salmon on the export market to dilute the demand for high-priced troll salmon? If the canneries require protection and must get cheap fish to stay in business then they should can all the net fish they take and not interfere with the fresh frozen market to the detriment of the trolling fleet that are taking a premium product for the fresh and frozen domestic market and for the fresh frozen export trade.

Perhaps if the cannery operators canned trolled salmon, and the DFO in their wisdom allowed a trolled salmon label on the cans so the consumer had a choice in the supermarket, the canners would receive a premium for the product. There is no doubt in my mind that there would soon be a demand for this high-grade canned product and a better return to the fishermen for this better-quality fish. Federal inspection scrutinizes trolled salmon for export and in their zeal condemn a large volume of this fish, which must be canned or sold on the domestic market at a lower price, and yet a fourteen-day-old trolled salmon properly cleaned and iced is a better-quality product for export than a one-day-old net fish that has been smothered with the guts left in and transported to port floating in chilled brine, regardless of what the government experts have to say about it. Trolled salmon are condemned for export if a few scales are missing from the fish, yet seined fish packed to port in the champagne system (highly recommended by the department and generally installed under subsidy) have virtually no scales left on them but they are allowed to be exported. It seems the department has been brain washed into this position even though the program is obviously absurd and comes full circle to contradict the obvious intent of the regulations. This exercise by the department in effect reduces the return to the Canadian economy from the export market. To the best of my knowledge, the Americans, Japanese, Russians and any other exporters of fresh frozen fish are not confronted with such unrealistic regulations.

The crux of the whole problem is that most personnel in the inspection department do not know anything about inspecting fish for quality. What one inspector passes for export when it is fresh, another inspector will not pass for some reason after the fish has been frozen and vice versa. Salmon that is condemned for export, when fresh, is passed for export after samples are thawed for inspection. No one in the department knows why it was condemned in the first place. A sane, practical inspection program helpful to the processors would be welcomed by the industry. I am afraid this is not to be, so most of us will end up in mental institutions with ulcers. I always thought the inspection branch was a part of the civil service established to assist and benefit the fish processing plants and our country, but I am afraid it is a monster that is going to destroy the independents left in the industry and those who cannot obtain government assistance to stay in business.

The inspection department is in its infancy so far as the fish business is concerned, but it is sure costing the country as a whole a lot of money. What is needed is to bring into the department people with practical experience of management, not just biologists and scientists, so many of its operations will make more sense.

The DFO touts the seine fishery as the only fishery they can control, while anyone with any knowledge at all about the way seiners operate knows that this is not so. A seine boat equipped with a drum, power block and the high-speed machinery in use today can make in excess of twenty sets per day so it becomes too efficient a fishing machine that the government has no control over. The machinery used today purses up and hauls the net in so quickly, the meshes close up diagonally, not allowing even a smelt to escape. Consequently, large numbers of salmon grilse and other small fish are destroyed in this type of fishery. Removing the drum and fishing with only the aid of the power block would help a lot because it would slow up the operations so the meshes would not close up as much, thus allowing small fish to escape the holocaust.

I have seen five to six tons of immature spring salmon under two pounds each in seine boats tied up in front of company plants. In the peak of the reduction business in British Columbia, sometimes half the fish being reduced was salmon. Millions of salmon went through reduction with the herring over the years without comment. We handled over one million pounds of trolled salmon this year, and only one steelhead was included in this volume of trolled fish. In comparison we bought in excess of thirty thousand pounds of steelhead last year from Cassiar's seine boat operation and I wonder how many more steelhead are taken by the seine fleet. The sportsmen are begging for more steelhead in the streams, but the seine fleet are cleaning them up faster than they can reproduce, taking more kelp (spent fish) than good fish, because they are sick from spawning and the fish, being lethargic, are easy to catch.

The volume of rotten salmon delivered by the seine and gillnet fleets ending up in reduction or being dumped back in the ocean is another tragic part of the history of our net fishery. There were terrific losses incurred by the canning industry under the best of conditions from shrinkages in recovery, as it was a common practice to scrape ten to thirty percent and even more of the decomposing flesh from salmon before it went into the can. In this net fishery it is quite normal to process eighty to ninety pounds of pink salmon in order to produce forty-eight pounds of canned salmon. The same problem persists to this day, although improved refrigeration and less salmon production have reduced losses in this fishery to some extent. However, even today this method of taking and processing net salmon is reflected in the lower prices paid to net fishermen. All concerned must agree that the best-quality salmon that brings the best return to our country and fishermen is produced by the troll fleet. Why then is the DFO curtailing fishing time to the troll fleet and at the same time extending fishing time to the seine fleet? Could the reason for more restrictions on the troll fishery be an attempt to give processors that control the seine fleets a stranglehold on the salmon fishery?

In view of this, it is obvious the trollers with hooks and gillnets with specific mesh sizes lend themselves to controls and conservation much more so than seine boats can ever be adapted. You might say the seine boat is just a large floating trap taking everything in its path.

The United States would love to curtail our troll fishery so they could expand their own troll fleet to take advantage of the situation.

Some of the previous buyback vessels were bought by U.S. fishermen and were soon back on the fishing grounds competing with Canadian fishermen for salmon, herring and ground fish.

The First Nations food fishery problem will continue to fester so long as a dollar can be earned by selling fish. There is no doubt that First Nations should be able to profit in some manner from harvesting a percentage of salmon, either for food or to sell as they wish. A quota could be set aside for this purpose. Perhaps the fish could be sold through a native co-operative. Perhaps if the First Nations leaders were included in the scheme to supervise and police it themselves, it would help a great deal to eliminate the hostility evident today between fishery personnel and the natives. Wasteful practices like taking salmon just for roe sold to unscrupulous egg packers or letting fish rot through negligence should be severely dealt with by removing the culprits from the fishery.

The food herring and roe fishery today as a whole is a disgraceful affair. It is a wasteful fishery taking mostly immature stocks from our coast. In the 1930s there was a fleet of about twelve gillnet boats catching food herring on the Point Grey bank for the Vancouver market. Beginning in May, this fishery continued through the season, only stopping about three weeks to let the fishermen take in the peak of the sockeye run on the Fraser River. Herring were so prolific and the catches so bountiful that some of these fishermen did not even bother to fish for salmon. The catch was small in the first days of May, but catches increased daily from one hundred and fifty pounds per boat in the beginning to one thousand and even six thousand pounds for each vessel per day by the end of May and throughout the rest of the season. This was a real food fishery, taking only mature morning herring better than a half pound each in weight, using mostly two-and-a-half-inch mesh nets. This fishery was a going concern with demand for fresh fish sales in Vancouver and for export fresh to the United States via train to Seattle, Portland, Los Angeles and San Francisco and other Pacific locations. The smoking trade (kippers, snacks, bloaters), salting and the bait trade, primarily used by the large halibut fleet, were all in search of good herring. In those days, there were at least eight smokehouses operating in Vancouver. Each of these employed three to eight women and two to three men while turning out product from fresh herring six days per week. This super fresh gillnet morning herring and the fresh smoked kippers were delicacies present and future generations in Vancouver will never have the opportunity to taste. Today, the seine boats are landing immature fish that are not large enough for curing or smoking and are hardly worth eating fresh. The Europeans did not want this jack herring, now taken as food fish (today nobody in Canada knows what a food herring is), but this market would pay us the best price for herring if it was a decent-sized quality fish.

The Japanese do not want this small fish either because they do not eat this product. When they do buy it, they dry it and produce a low-grade product to barter to the poor Asian countries. Consequently they cannot pay a fair price for this type of herring. Today the skinny salty kippers available in our markets would make better shingles for a roof than food for human consumption. The problem today is if a gillnet boat went out to fish on the Point Grey bank with a two-and-a-half-inch net in May it would fish for days to even catch five pounds of herring. It's a tragic situation but I suppose the desire to make money and gain affluence from our dwindling resources is going to bring our house crashing down on our heads sooner than we think.

The purse seine fishermen fight over what is left of our salmon and herring stocks like a bunch of hungry dogs fighting over a bone, and the DFO is making a futile effort to manage the resources around this brawl not really knowing what to do about it. I believe the purse seine fleet was expanded by a higher percentage than any other part of the fishery with aid from power-hungry fish-packing companies and with approval from the DFO (they issued the licences) so that these companies should be in a position to dominate the industry. Now the buyback will be the vehicle used to remove the surplus vessels (at a profit to those concerned, no doubt) at the expense of most of the fishermen who had no part in creating the problem. During this mad rush into the industry, anyone able to pry a licence from the DFO could get financing from banks or credit unions regardless of the consequences to the industry. I say there should be no buyback of these surplus fishing vessels built under clandestine conditions at considerable expense to Canadian taxpayers. Let the principals concerned take their lumps like anyone in business who has made a bad deal.

The excessive price of fuel and the extremely high overhead tied to operating commercial fishing vessels combined with poor catches and low prices (because of poor economic conditions) will contribute to quickly eliminating the mediocre and part time fishermen from the industry. For the same reasons it will also remove substantial numbers of sports fishermen from the fishing grounds. Consequently I feel the fishing effort will be reduced enough so that a buyback of vessels will not be necessary.

The skillful, dedicated fisherman will survive under these conditions, which will be better for the industry in the long run. Any money provided for a buyback should be put to better use — mainly salmonoid enhancement.

There must be some changes implemented in the licensing of fishing vessels and fishermen so that the profit would be taken out of trading in these fishing licences. This will also help to reduce the fleet because it will remove promoters and opportunists who jumped into the fishery and are waiting for a change in the climate which will give them the opportunity to make exorbitant profits from their licences. This change in licensing fishermen will also give the young men in the industry the chance to participate eventually as vessel owners without first acquiring a quarter of a million dollars for a licence to do so.

I believe American fishermen are taking more salmon from our Fraser River system than we are aware of, either through the ignorance of the DFO or by might. I have observed American companies weighing in sockeye from U.S. seine boats at twelve to thirteen hundred pounds per unloading bucket and marking down one hundred fish per bucket in the tally book. I pointed out that sockeye do not average thirteen pounds each and they replied that that was their count for the stupid Canadians.

They also start fishing at Point Roberts and in Boundary Bay, taking Fraser River salmon for six to eight weeks before Canadians are allowed to fish these runs. About three years ago I phoned the Canadian arm of the Salmon Commission about this, wanting to know why American fishermen were fishing and Canadians were not. They told me the American vessels were not catching any fish to speak of, but they could not quote figures to substantiate their point of view. I took the liberty of phoning an American packer who was unloading for several companies at Blaine, Washington, to find out what the landings per boat might be so early in the season. I believe this was in the middle of May. He quoted me landings for approximately twenty vessels that were fishing for a major American packer. The catches per boat were fifteen to twenty springs and seven to fifteen sockeyes per boat for the poor fishermen, one hundred to one hundred and fifteen springs and thirty to thirty-five sockeyes per boat per day for the highliners. From these figures, the catches were substantial. At three dollars per pound straight for springs and one dollar fifty cents per pound for sockeyes, some American vessels were making as much as six thousand dollars per day on springs and up to four hundred dollars per day on sockeyes. I phoned back to the Canadian arm of the Salmon Commission and quoted these catch figures per boat for the weekly fishing days. I received no comment on the situation and heard no more about this matter from the Commission.

In 1981, American trollers were taking Fraser River pinks four or five weeks before Canadian trollers were allowed to keep one pink. I asked the DFO about this one, and their answer was that they were U.S. pinks and Canadians shouldn't be fishing for them. In 1980, there was an enormous body of pinks off the West Coast of Vancouver Island. Again Canadian trollers were not allowed to take these pinks because they were supposedly required as brood stock for some Canadian river systems. These pinks eventually entered river systems in the Seattle area, and American plants were swamped with these fish working twenty-four hours a day, seven days a week, to process this enormous catch. Some of my friends in American packing plants told me they were exhausted and fed up with handling so many fish. Canadian fishermen went without participating in the bonanza. In view of these fiascoes, is it possible the DFO is working for the Americans or could it be because the DFO personnel are interested in seeing Americans take all U.S. salmon and more than their half of our Canadian fish?

If there is to be another buyback of fishing vessels will the proposed tax on salmon apply to the buyback of combination vessels fishing for salmon, herring, ground fish, shrimp, etc.? Will it take in new combination vessels built to fish black cod, abalone, crab and salmon? Will it apply to fisherman who cannot make a go of it? Will it apply to schoolteachers, hotel owners, firemen and others who only derive part of their income from the fishing industry and are really in it to fish the peak of the runs and to speculate on licences? Will it take in old vessels that have not floated since the last buyback or that are in the woods? I would hazard a guess that thirty percent of the fish taken out of the Gulf of Georgia and a substantial percentage of fish taken in other areas of our coast are sold for cash to the public and to various restaurants, retail stores, jobbers, peddlers, and to a lot of brand-new Canadians. The DFO is well aware that no receipts are made out for this fish, no money is contributed to compensation, income tax or to fishery statistics. How is the tax to be collected from this bunch of operators?

It certainly will not be equitable for the bona fide salmon fisherman to pick up the tab for the Johnny-come-lately opportunists in the industry. It surely will not be equitable for bona fide salmon fishermen and legitimate fishing companies to contribute to a buyback or salmon enhancement while the fishermen selling for cash and carpet baggers buying for cash from fishermen without submitting records to the

DFO or providing receipts for tax purposes avoid contributing a penny towards our economy, much less towards a buyback. Scores of transactions take place on government docks daily in the Vancouver area, never mind what cash transactions take place daily in various other fishing areas of British Columbia. The DFO is well aware of what is going on, but I'm sure they feel that legitimate operators are fat capitalists getting too rich so why not let the carpet baggers take advantage of the system to the detriment of these capitalists and to our country. They forget that the capitalists contribute substantially towards the economy of our country and towards paying their wages.

Norman Safarik

Acknowledgements

Making books is an intensive, collaborative activity. The authors wish to thank the team at ECW, especially Emily Schultz for her editorial acumen, Ingrid Paulson for her cover design, Rachel Ironstone for the typography and Crissy Boylan for her skill in guiding this project and her attention to details. Finally, this project came to life and found its way into print because of Jack David, a visionary publisher with a penchant for adventures in all the regions of Canada.

Ayr